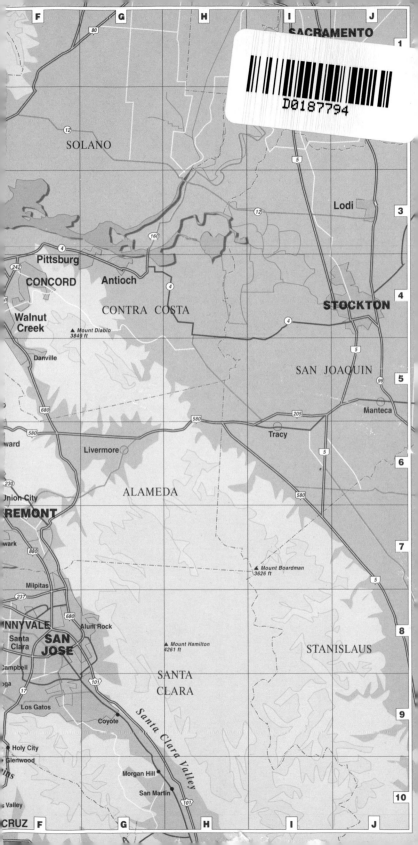

Green Street Wharf, San Francisco, 1849 (photo O.V. Lange).
"But to what can we attribute this multitude of ships arriving
from the four corners of the world to discharge swarms of
wretched people onto the Californian shore? Is Europe
delirious. . . ? It is gold, they say, gold that turns people's
heads, gold that deprives men of their sanity and reason. . . . "
A. Bernard de Russailh

Cable car turntable (photo Max Yavno). "They turn corners almost at right angles, cross other lines, and for all I know, may run up the sides of houses." Rudyard Kipling

Copyright © 1993 Alfred A. Knopf, Inc., New York

All rights reserved under International and Pan-American Copyright Conventions.
Published in the United States by Alfred A. Knopf, Inc., New York, and
simultaneously in Canada by Random House of Canada Limited, Toronto.
Distributed by Random House, Inc., New York.

*Originally published in France by Nouveaux-Loisirs, a subsidiary of
Gallimard, Paris, 1993. Copyright © 1993 by Editions Nouveaux-Loisirs*

San Francisco. English
San Francisco / [Gallimard editions].
p. cm. – (Knopf guides)
Includes bibliographical references and index.
ISBN 0-679-74913-6 : $25.00
1. San Francisco (Calif.) – Guidebooks.
I. Gallimard (firm). II.Series.
F869.S33S23 1993
917.94'610453-dc20
CIP 9325441

First published April 1994
Second edition September 1994
Third edition February 1995
Fourth edition September 1996

NUMEROUS SPECIALISTS AND ACADEMICS HAVE
CONTRIBUTED TO THIS GUIDE.

CO-ORDINATION:
GRAPHICS: Elizabeth Cohat
PHOTOGRAPHY: Éric Guillemot,
Patrick Léger
MAPS: Vincent Brunot
ARCHITECTURE: Bruno Lenormand,
Jean-Philippe Chabot
NATURE: Frédéric Bony, Philippe Dubois

SAN FRANCISCO:
EDITORS: Isabelle de Coulibœuf
Assisted by: Anne-Valérie Cadoret (itineraries),
Marie-Hélène Carpentier (arts and traditions,
practical information), Gérard Dietrich-
Sainsaulieu (architecture), Jean-Pierre Girard
(practical information), Valérie Guidoux
(nature), Julie Wood (architecture)
LAYOUT: Laurent Gourdon (list of addresses),
Natacha Kotlarevsky
PICTURE RESEARCH: Isabelle de Coulibœuf,
Randolph Delehanty, Nathalie Pommier
NATURE: Greg de Nevers, Jacques Dupont, Erik
Gonthier, Zeke Grader, Claire Peaslee,
Rich Stallcup
HISTORY: Malie Montagutelli
ART AND TRADITIONS: Anthony Bliss, Alain
Dister, Malie Montagutelli
ARCHITECTURE: Michael Corbett, Isabelle
Gournay
SAN FRANCISCO AS SEEN BY PAINTERS:
Herma Kevran
SAN FRANCISCO AS SEEN BY WRITERS:
Lucinda Gane

ITINERARIES: Lisa Anderson, Eleonore
Bakhtadze, Gray Brechin, Alain Dister,
Michel Frizot (F 64 Group), Valérie di Givry,
Gladys Hansen, Herma Kervran,
William Kostura, Malie Montagutelli,
Pierre-Yves Pétillon (Jack London),
Ariel Rubissow, Autumn Stephen,
Bonnie Wach, Véronique Wiesinger

ILLUSTRATIONS:
NATURE: Jacqueline Candiard, Jean Chevalier,
Gismonde Curiace, François Desbordes,
Bill Donohue, Claire Felloni, Gilbert Houbre,
Catherine L'héritier, François Place, Pascal
Robin, Jean Torton, John Wilkinson
ARCHITECTURE: Siena Artworks Ltd, London
ITINERARIES: Jean-Philippe Chabot, Donald
Grant, Olivier Hubert, Jean-Michel Kacédan,
Jean-Marc Lanusse, Bruno Lenormand, James
Prunier
PRACTICAL INFORMATION: Maurice Pommier
MAPS: Vincent Brunot, Claire Cormier,
Jean-Marc Lanusse, Bruno Lenormand,
Sylvie Serprix, Harvey Stevenson
COMPUTER GRAPHICS: Sophie Compagne,
Paul Coulbois

LOCAL CORRESPONDENTS: Bellatrix Cochran,
Jennifer Kerr
PHOTOGRAPHY: Andrew McKinney

WE WOULD ALSO LIKE TO THANK:
Anthony Bliss, Les Caves du Monde, Michael
Corbett, Kimberley Harrington, Jennifer Kerr,
Anne-Marie Lopez, Jean Marin (IFREMER),
Claire Peaslee, Steve Sullivan (Acme Bakery),
Ed Ueber

TRANSLATED BY ANTHONY ROBERTS AND SUE ROSE.
EDITED AND TYPESET BY BOOK CREATION SERVICES, LONDON.
PRINTED IN ITALY BY EDITORIALE LIBRARIA.

The three-master *Star of Zeàland* leaving the bay of San Francisco in 1935, during the construction of the Golden Gate Bridge at the Golden Gate (photo Gabriel Moulin).

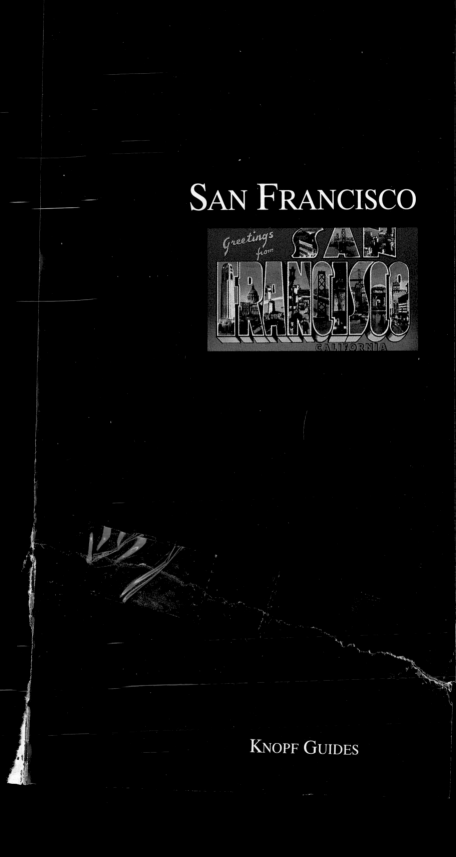

SAN FRANCISCO

KNOPF GUIDES

CONTENTS

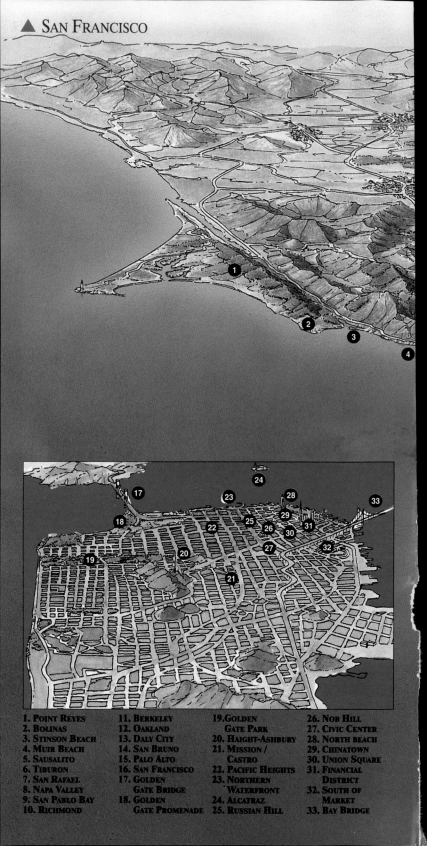

▲ SAN FRANCISCO

HOW TO USE THIS GUIDE
(Sample page shown from the guide to Venice)

The symbols at the top of each page refer to the different parts of the guide.

■ NATURAL ENVIRONMENT

● KEYS TO UNDERSTANDING

▲ ITINERARIES

◆ PRACTICAL INFORMATION

The itinerary map shows the main points of interest along the way and is intended to help you find your bearings.

The mini-map locates the particular itinerary within the wider area covered by the guide.

● ▲ ■ ◆
The symbols alongside a title or within the text itself provide cross-references to a theme or place dealt with elsewhere in the guide.

★ The star symbol signifies that a particular site has been singled out by the publishers for its special beauty, atmosphere or cultural interest.

At the beginning of each itinerary, the suggested means of transport to be used and the time it will take to cover the area are indicated:

🚢 By boat
🚶 On foot
🚲 By bicycle
⏱ Duration

THE GATEWAY TO VENICE ★

PONTE DELLA LIBERTA. Built by the Austrians 50 years after the Treaty of Campo Formio in 1797 ● *34,* to link Venice with Milan. The bridge ended the thousand-year separation from the mainland and shook the city's economy to its roots as Venice, already in the throes of the industrial revolution, saw

🚶 Half a day

BRIDGES TO VENICE

NATURE

■ SAN ANDREAS FAULT

LOCAL ROCKS
1. Ferriferous sandstone
2. Serpentine
3. Biotite granite

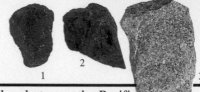

1   2   3

San Francisco sits on the boundary between the Pacific Plate and the North American Plate, which slide horizontally past each other in opposite directions. The San Andreas fault, which is the active frontier between these two shearing plates, runs vertically through California for 634 miles, subjecting the region to earth tremors that can be extremely violent. Huge build-ups of stress have unleashed catastrophes that have left their mark on the city's history: that of April 1906, for example, estimated to have reached 8.25 on the Richter scale, which ravaged 601,400 square miles, or more recently, that of October 1989.

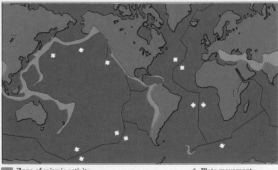

■ San Andreas fault,
▢ Urban area

The San Andreas fault, with its retinue of small lateral faults, is a model example of a transform fault.

■ Zone of seismic activity   ◇ Plate movement

San Andreas was the earliest occurrence of a transform fault to be described. Such faults are found all over the earth. An earthquake takes place when the stress caused by displacement of the plates is released.

It is not the quake itself that causes most deaths, but its secondary effects – burst pipes, collapsing buildings, landslides, fires.

San Francisco, October 1989, the day after the earthquake.

All along the Californian coast and the San Andreas fault, the risk of earthquakes is constant and impossible to predict. Seismologists can never accurately forecast how plates will move after a quake.

This road, which dissected the line of displacement, was split into two.

The fault line marking the boundary between two plates preserves the plate surfaces, in contrast to other types of natural boundary, such as ocean ridges and trenches.

In places the fault has left visible scars on the landscape (opposite).

The San Andreas fault shifts horizontally; thus the opposing drift of two tectonic plates produces a grating effect which unleashes seismic waves without any consequences to the rock formation.

THE WRENTIT
These non-migratory birds
dwell exclusively in the
chaparral, bathed by fog.

San Francisco benefits from a maritime climate that is intimately connected to the oceanographic cycle. In spring the Californian Current enriches the coastal waters with plankton, which is good for wildlife. At the same time the notorious fog comes down: until July it cools the air on a regular basis, demonstrating the smooth functioning of the marine ecosystem. In this Mediterranean climate the warmest months are August and September. The rainy season lasts from November through April.

The winter storms are vital here: snow falls on the Sierras, and then melts to fill the reservoirs with water later in the year.

2. The wind whips up the California Current. The surface waters are deflected toward the open sea.

4. The cold, deeper waters come into contact with the warm air that arrives all year round from the Pacific and a fog forms.

HOW THE FOG FORMS
1. A strong northwesterly wind blows off the coast in spring.

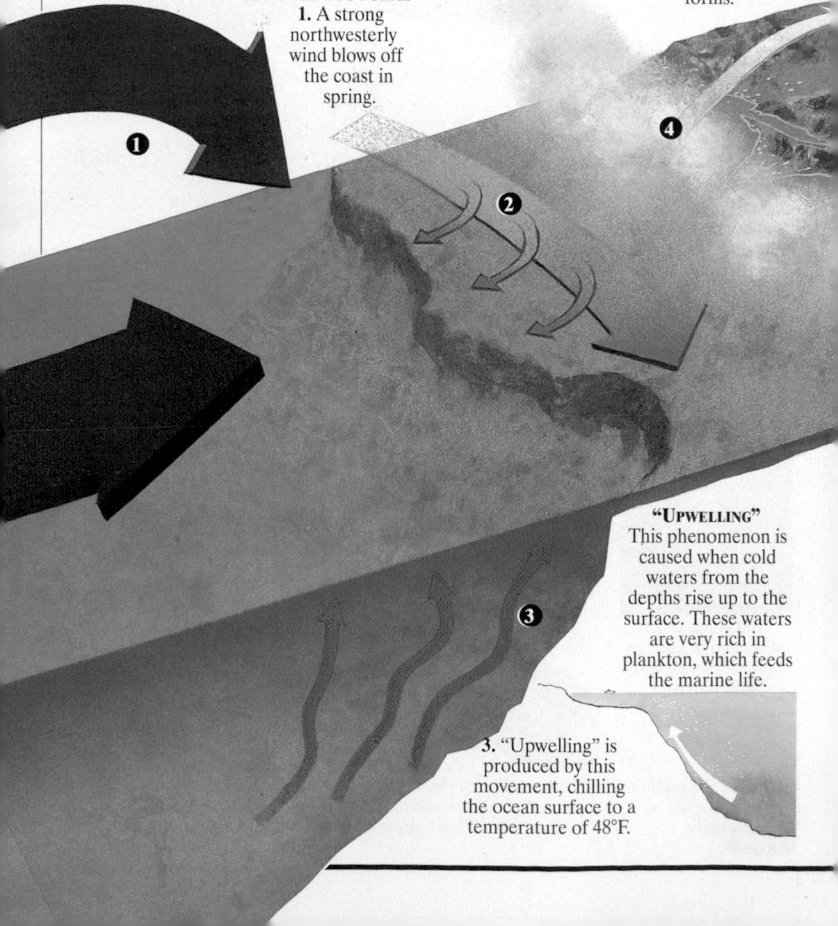

❶

❹

❷

"UPWELLING"
This phenomenon is caused when cold waters from the depths rise up to the surface. These waters are very rich in plankton, which feeds the marine life.

❸

3. "Upwelling" is produced by this movement, chilling the ocean surface to a temperature of 48°F.

5. High inland temperatures draw the fog over the coastal ridges and into the valleys.

6. When the fog has cooled the Central Valley, which in summer enjoys extremely hot temperatures, it retreats as far as the Farallones: so the entire Bay Area has "breathed".

In summer the fog has been known to blanket the shore for several days at a time.

6

5

The fog forms what resembles a floating river when it comes level with the Golden Gate ▲ *142, 244*.

Coastal redwoods derive much of their annual water supply from the fog.

YELLOW BUSH LUPINE   **BISHOP PINE**
These two plants thrive in the fog, but also need heat to scatter their seeds.

PACIFIC BRANT GOOSE
During migration these geese stop off in the estuaries, where they feed mainly on beds of eelgrass.

COMMON LOON. These birds migrate along the Californian Current, feed around the Farallon Islands and rarely come ashore.

BOLINAS SALT MARSH

CASPIAN TERN. After breeding these birds nest along the southern shore of the bay.

Bolinas Lagoon

Areas of marshland
■ Before 1850
■ Today

Fringing San Francisco Bay and little coastal estuaries such as Bolinas Lagoon, muddy tidal flats and salt marshes provide a home for a great many animals and plants whose life follows the rhythm of the tides. The temperate climate and calm waters of these habitats provide an abundant source of food for the invertebrates, fish, and above all the huge flocks of birds that spend the winter on these marshes. The bay area welcomes up to a million shorebirds during the peak migration period in spring.

The waders retreat at high tide when the vegetation has been flooded, and return to feed on the mudflats at low tide.

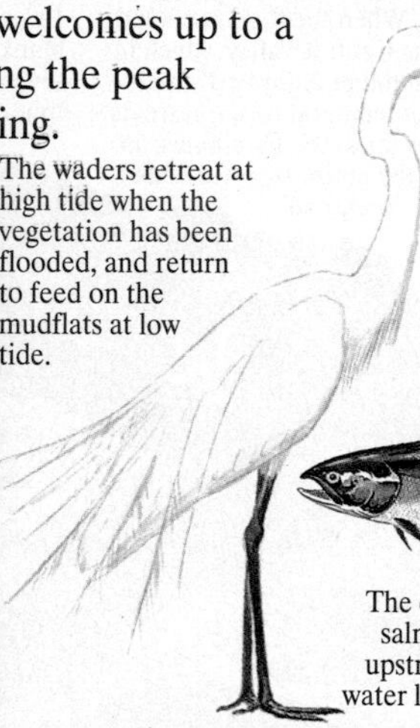

GREAT WHITE EGRET
These birds nest in the treetops of nearby canyons, but come here in summer to find the food they need for their chicks.

COHO SALMON
The estuary enables young salmon, hatched further upstream, to adjust to salt-water life before venturing out into the ocean.

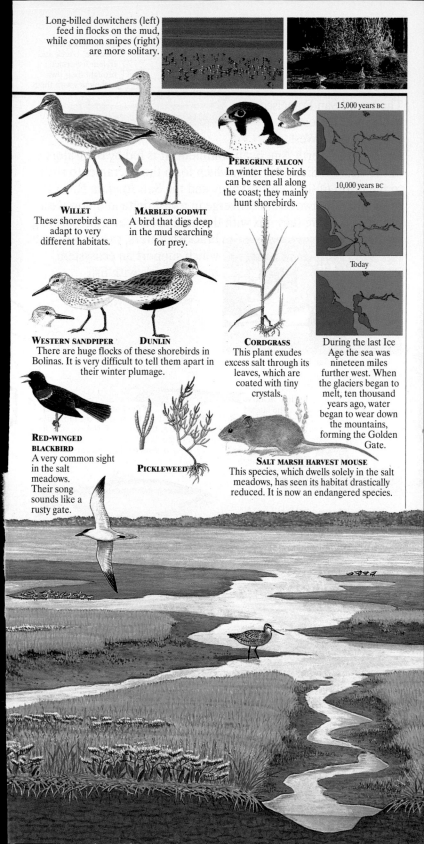

Long-billed dowitchers (left) feed in flocks on the mud, while common snipes (right) are more solitary.

15,000 years BC

10,000 years BC

Today

WILLET
These shorebirds can adapt to very different habitats.

MARBLED GODWIT
A bird that digs deep in the mud searching for prey.

PEREGRINE FALCON
In winter these birds can be seen all along the coast; they mainly hunt shorebirds.

WESTERN SANDPIPER   **DUNLIN**
There are huge flocks of these shorebirds in Bolinas. It is very difficult to tell them apart in their winter plumage.

CORDGRASS
This plant exudes excess salt through its leaves, which are coated with tiny crystals.

During the last Ice Age the sea was nineteen miles further west. When the glaciers began to melt, ten thousand years ago, water began to wear down the mountains, forming the Golden Gate.

RED-WINGED BLACKBIRD
A very common sight in the salt meadows. Their song sounds like a rusty gate.

PICKLEWEED

SALT MARSH HARVEST MOUSE
This species, which dwells solely in the salt meadows, has seen its habitat drastically reduced. It is now an endangered species.

JUNK. Immigrant Chinese, Greek and Italian fishermen brought their own techniques with them.

The bay of San Francisco is the most important estuary on the West Coast of the North American continent. It is fed by the waters of the western Sierra Nevada, which form the Sacramento river to the north of the Central Valley and the San Joaquin River to the south. The two rivers converge in a vast delta and flow west to the bay, where they mix with the tidal ocean currents, forming brackish waters, rich in nutrients, which support an ecosystem once teeming with fish.

The port of San Francisco today.

PACIFIC HERRING. The largest commercial fishery in the bay concentrates on herring, which is caught for its roe.

PURSE SEINE
This type of net has floats at the top and is weighted at the bottom. It closes gradually around schools of fish that have been located by sounder beforehand.

"LAMPARA" BOATS
Used to catch herring and anchovy on the sea bed.

"MONTEREY CLIPPER"

Derived from the felucca-style fishing boat with sails, but larger and furnished with a motor, a modest cabin and a fish hold, this form of boat was built throughout the 1930's.

KING (CHINOOK) SALMON. Commercial fishermen catch this prized species by trolling in the ocean.

Nowadays motors have replaced sails for commercial fishing and sport fishing alike.

DRIFT NET
Spread out in the open sea, this gillnet enables fishermen to be selective in their catch. Permitted for herring, its use is banned for salmon and bass.

LEOPARD SHARK
Line fishermen catch this shark in the bay.

Monterey clippers at Fisherman's Wharf in 1936. This type of boat can still be seen in the port.

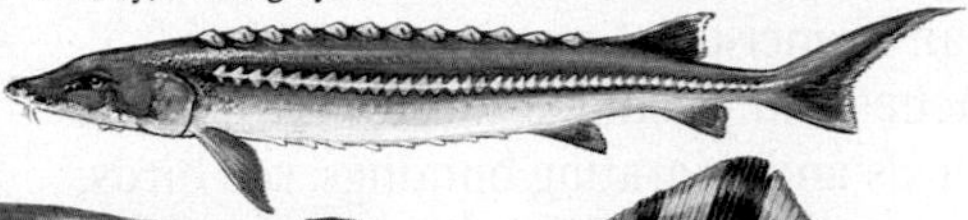

WHITE STURGEON
The largest fish in the bay, and highly valued.

CALIFORNIA HALIBUT
Commercial fishermen use otter trawls ("dragnets") or wire lines to catch halibut.

STARRY FLOUNDER
These fish are caught in the bay and off the Golden Gate.

BAT RAY
The ray has a barb at the end of its tail which can inflict a painful sting.

DUNGENESS CRAB
This crab is caught commercially in nearshore waters, using steel and wire traps (pots). But individual fishermen also catch it using ring nets thrown from piers along the bay.

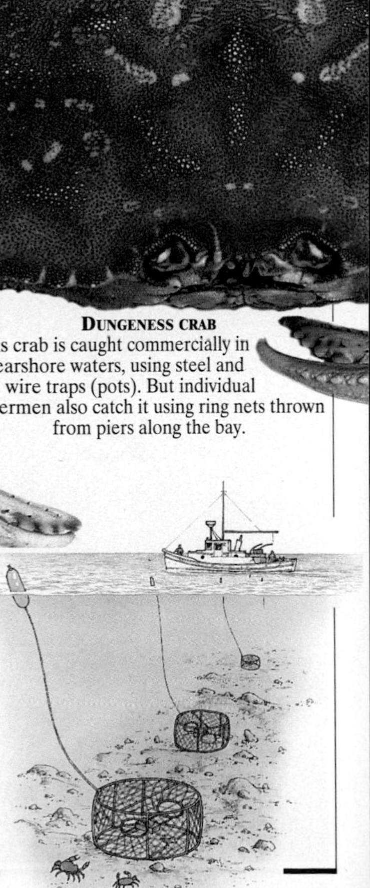

CRAB TRAPS OR POTS
These are dropped from boats onto the sea bed to catch crabs.

OYSTERS
There are two main species found in the bay: the native Pacific oyster and the giant Pacific oyster.

POINT REYES

Clumsy on land, the California sealion hunts its prey under water with speed and agility.

The Point Reyes peninsula, lying west of the San Andreas fault, is a geological "island" which stretches out into the cold waters of the Pacific, north of San Francisco. An extensive rocky shoreline, vast sandy beaches and pristine estuaries form a true wildlife paradise. Shorebirds and migrating buntings, sea birds, invertebrates and marine mammals are all well equipped, in their various ways, to take advantage of this prime habitat. Further inland, a dairy farming tradition is still preserved alongside the natural habitat of this "island in time".

The shoreline of Point Reyes ▲ 328 can be sandy and calm – at the foot of the cliffs on Drakes Beach, for example – or rocky and buffeted by wind and waves.

Pacific harbor seals often float with their heads out of the water, while sealions play together in the waves.

24

The Pacific harbor seals (left), like gray pelicans (right), need a peaceful place to rest.

NORTHERN GUILLEMOT
These birds nest on cliffs and guard each others' eggs.

PIGEON GUILLEMOT
Their eggs are concealed in narrow rock crevices.

BLACK TURNSTONE
They feed on small crustaceans found beneath the algae on the rocks.

BROWN PELICAN
In the fall brown pelicans fish in the hundreds on the schools of anchovy along the coast.

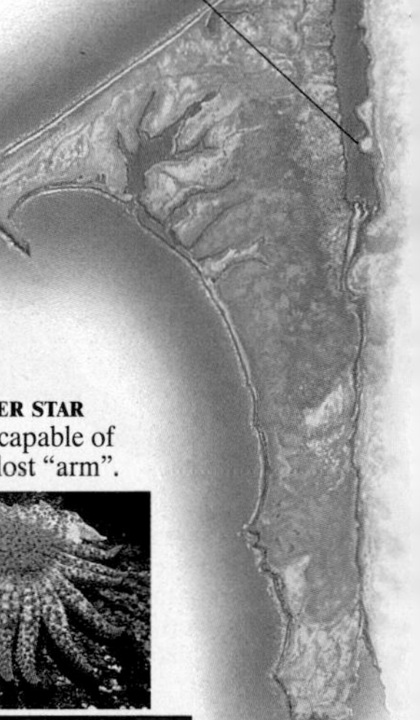

The San Andreas fault runs between the peninsula and the continent.

Point Reyes lighthouse.

WANDERING TATTLER
They nest in Alaska but feed on the shoreline here during migration.

PACIFIC ROCK CRAB
This is both a predator and a scavenger of carrion.

WHIMBREL
The birds feed mainly on sea worms and shrimp.

SUNFLOWER STAR
Starfish are capable of regrowing a lost "arm".

Just 25 miles from San
Francisco, visible on a clear day,
the Farallones are small granitic islands
which are exceptionally important for wildlife.
Sea birds, sealions and seals have established huge
breeding rookeries there. Protected from land-based
predators, great numbers of birds feed in the
nutritious waters of the California
Current. In winter and spring they can
sometimes be seen from Point Reyes.
In fall humpback whales and, less
commonly, blue whales, migrate up or down the coast.

Puffins and northern guillemots nest on the cliffs,
cormorants and pigeon guillemots on the steep
slopes, gulls and auklets on the broad ledges, while
pinnipeds frequent the rocky coves.

TUFTED PUFFIN
Occasionally seen on
these islands, tufted
puffins turn
completely black in
winter.

**DOUBLE-CRESTED
CORMORANT**
This bird fishes in the
shallower waters just
offshore.

**BRANDT'S
CORMORANT**
The most common of
of the three species. Its
gular pouch turns blue
for breeding displays.

PELAGIC CORMORANT
The least gregarious of
cormorants, it requires
food sources very near
to the island to raise
its chicks.

REDWOOD FORESTS
MUIR WOODS

Millions of years ago the northern hemisphere was covered mainly by redwoods, which formed part of the dinosaur's diet. Of the five surviving members of the redwood family (*Taxodiaceae*), two evergreen species can still be found in California. The giant sequoia (*Sequoiadendron giganteum*) grows in isolated stands on the heights of the Sierra Nevada. Around San Francisco there are forests of coastal redwood (*Sequoia sempervirens*), which grow only in the zone of coastal fog influence, at low altitudes. Their shallow but thick roots spread out around the foot of the tree: in this way they can catch the water that drips from the needles when the fog blows over them in the dry season.

Coastal redwood

Giant sequoia

CONES AND NEEDLES
The seeds of the redwood, which come from tiny cones, only germinate on mineral soil stripped bare by a flood or a fire.

MULE DEER
The antlers of the male are renewed annually.

Oak woodland is one of the most widespread habitats covering the hills of California. Oak trees form the basis of an extremely important food chain in the region: 101 species of bird and 37 mammals depend on the acorns, as did the Indians who once lived in the forest. The trees are very resistant to the forest fires which are a regular phenomenon in California. The average return cycle for fires is every fifteen to thirty years but Indian settlements made them even more frequent: the open woodlands of today are partly a result of human activities.

BOBCAT
A nocturnal predator, the bobcat stalks its prey, waits in ambush, then pounces. Its retractable claws immobilize rabbits, squirrels, mice and quail, which are then finished off by a quick bite.

RACCOON
An agile climber, the raccoon takes refuge in the trees when disturbed and is quick to puff out its coat to frighten off an enemy.

F.Desbordes

VALLEY OAK   **BLUE OAK**   **INTERIOR LIVE OAK**   **CALIFORNIA GREEN OAK**   **POISON OAK**

Oak trees are identified by their leaves, acorns and acorn caps. Valley oaks and blue oaks are deciduous.

POISON OAK
A form of poison ivy, this shrubby plant secretes an oil which can cause an itchy rash.

RED TREE VOLE
This tiny rodent never comes down from the trees.

ACORN WOODPECKER
A bird that announces its presence from a distance by its hammering and its rolling, laugh-like call.

WESTERN TOAD
An amphibian well adapted to its habitat.

RED-TAILED HAWK
This bird of prey feeds on rabbits, prairie dogs and snakes. Its high-pitched scream is very distinctive.

MOUNTAIN LION
This big cat can occasionally be seen on the Point Reyes peninsula.

CHAPARRAL

WRENTIT
The wrentit's call resembles the sound of a distant ping-pong ball.

Chaparral

The chaparral is a dense, scrubby brush-land, covered in herbaceous plants and shrubs that can grow as high as 15 feet. It covers dry, south-facing slopes of inland hills and mountains. This habitat is characteristic of the Mediterranean climate and has counterparts in southern Europe. Its name is derived from the thick leather "chaps" worn by Spanish *vaqueros* when riding through the scratchy bushes. The tangled vegetation provides many animals with perfect cover for lairs. The borders of the chaparral are grazed bare for 5 to 10 feet around: jackrabbits and small rodents do not venture far from the bushes to feed and take cover at the slightest sound.

Barren stretches are caused here by deforestation or repeated chaparral fires.

SCRUB JAY
They feed mainly on acorns.

RUFOUS-SIDED TOWHEE
These birds scratch the packed earth in search of seeds.

Chamise chaparral is characteristic of dry, sun-baked hills away from the coast.

TURKEY VULTURE
The bird gets its name because its featherless red head and dark body feathers resemble a turkey.

JACKRABBIT
The favorite prey of the golden eagle, it rarely strays far from protective shelter.

CALIFORNIA (GOLDEN) POPPY
This golden poppy (*Eschscholzia californica*) is the state flower of California.

MANZANITA
This bush, related to the blueberry, is typical of the chaparral.

CREAM BUSH OR OCEAN SPRAY
This plant is named for its flowers, which recall the foam on waves.

The manzanita, "little apple" in Spanish, is named after the shape of its fruit. There are sixty species of this plant, most found only in California.

COFFEE BERRY

TOYON

The toyon is popular with birds in winter for its berries. The bark of the coffee berry has laxative properties.

CALIFORNIA BUCKWHEAT
This flowers in midsummer or fall in inhospitable rocky habitats.

If you touch the tiny white stigma of the orange bush monkeyflower, the plant closes slowly.

CHAMISE
This bush is the second most important source of food for deer, after acorns. Following a fire, it grows strong and is heavily browsed.

CALIFORNIA QUAIL
The official state bird of California. These quail are quite tame, and a female sitting on her eggs will not fly off until the very last moment.

COYOTE
Frequently hunted down, these animals change their breeding activities to reflect available resources: if prey is plentiful, they rear more young.

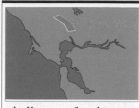

Halted in mid-expansion by Prohibition, the Napa Valley wine business has grown hugely over the past thirty years. But development is again being checked by the insect phylloxera, forcing owners to uproot many vines and replant with varieties that are more resistant to it. Napa's propitious climatic conditions produce wines that are in many respects as good or better than any in the world. Virtually every bit of suitable land on the valley floor and the surrounding gentle slopes is given over to vineyards.

The Napa Valley ◆ 348, with its two neighbors, Sonoma and Carneros, is the most famous wine-producing region in the US.

Phylloxera-resistant varieties are used for replanting vineyards.

PHYLLOXERA
This insect, which battens onto the roots and leaves of the vine, devastated European vineyards in the late 19th century.

GEWÜRZTRAMINER
A highly perfumed white wine grape, now less common.

CHARDONNAY
This grape produces some of California's most highly regarded wines.

SAUVIGNON BLANC
Second only to Chardonnay as a popular white dry table wine grape.

MERLOT
These red wine grapes produce good varietal bottlings or are blended.

PINOT NOIR
The grape of French burgundy proved difficult to grow in California until recently.

CABERNET SAUVIGNON
The classic red wine grape.

ZINFANDEL
The most distinctly Californian of all the grapes, it produces a powerful and substantial wine.

Napa Valley alone has some 200 wineries, including tiny "boutique" producers.

The Napa Valley floor, which varies from three to four miles in width in the south to less than a mile in the north, together with the lower slopes of the Mayacumus Range to the west, is the source of most of the best-known Napa wines.

STERLING VINEYARDS.

ESTATE BOTTLED

1987
Cabernet Sauvignon
Napa Valley
California
Product of U.S.A.

GROWN, PRODUCED AND BOTTLED BY STERLING VINEYARDS CALISTOGA, NAPA VALLEY, CA. BW CA-4388
13% Vol. 75cl ℮

GLEN·ELLEN
1992
Proprietor's Reserve
CHARDONNAY
California

MADE & BOTTLED BY STRATFORD ST. HELENA, CALIFORNIA, USA • ALC. 13.5 % BY VOL. • 750 ML

1991
CALIFORNIA
SAUVIGNON BLANC
STRATFORD

Dry Creek Vineyards

1990 ZINFANDEL
Dry Creek Valley

1988
Napa Valley
PINOT NOIR
ALCOHOL 13% BY VOLUME
PRODUCED AND BOTTLED BY
ROBERT MONDAVI WINERY
OAKVILLE, CALIFORNIA

BENZIGER

1991
SONOMA COUNTY
CHARDONNAY
13
ALCOHOL 13.5% BY VOLUME

39

The brown pelican visits the port between June and November. It nests on the offshore islands of Mexico.

Except for cosmopolitan species such as sparrows, rock pigeons, starlings and cats, wildlife is rather scarce in the center of the city: the only evidence is the sight of reintroduced peregrine falcons hunting pigeons among the skyscrapers, and the clamor of gulls. But on the waterfront you may see brown pelicans fishing a few feet away from passersby, or California sealions basking on a wharf.

In late fall and winter California sealions rest on buoys, wharfs and marinas.

WESTERN GULL
This bird is the only species of gull to visit the city in summer, but in winter six other species of gull or seagull can be seen.

The raccoon is a nocturnal mammal, which will happily rummage through trash cans.

SKUNK
A nocturnal inhabitant of parks, its spray can make even the toughest of dogs turn tail.

CALLISTEMON

CHESTNUT-BACKED CHICKADEE
Common all year round in the city; the name "chickadee" is derived from their call.

ANNA'S HUMMINGBIRD
This bird, which looks like a giant insect in flight, feeds on the nectar in flowers.

MONARCH
Mainly seen in winter, this butterfly migrates as far as Mexico.

EUCALYPTUS
These trees were brought over from Australia in the 19th century and planted around the city to act as windbreaks and for timber. Some trees may reach a height of 150 feet, but they are not particularly attractive to native wildlife.

MONTEREY CYPRESS

Native to the Monterey peninsula, 100 miles to the south, the Monterey cypress is the most common conifer in San Francisco.

HISTORY
OF SAN FRANCISCO

FIRST INHABITANTS

Ohlone Indians
print by L. Chloris.

900–1000
*Viking expedition to
America.*

1492
*Christopher
Columbus' first
voyage.*

1494
*Treaty of
Tordesillas: divides
the New World
between Portugal
and Spain.*

THE INDIANS. The native inhabitants of America were probably descended from Asians who crossed the Bering Strait twenty thousand years ago and populated the continent. The Indians who lived on this part of the Californian coast can be divided into four main ethnic groups, each with its own specific language: the Yokuts, the Wintuns, the Miwoks and the Ohlones, themselves subdivided into forty tribes. The Ohlones settled in the Bay Area of San Francisco about five thousand years ago and, according to anthropologist A. L. Kroeber, around 1770, three thousand Miwoks and ten thousand Ohlones were living along the coast between the Bay Area and Big Sur. The site of the future city, a sandy peninsula buffeted by sea winds, was occupied by some Ohlones, gathered around Lake Merced and Mission Creek and in several villages along the southern and central bay shoreline and Islais Creek. The life of the Ohlones, a peaceable, pantheistic people, was based on simple social structures. As they did not farm, they moved with the seasons, living off what they could hunt and gather.

Although they had a monetary system, the concept of land ownership was alien to them, as it was to other native Americans. The arrival of "Whites" overturned this world, which had scarcely changed since the Stone Age and from which only a few everyday objects and some fine basketwork survive. By 1930 the Ohlones had all but disappeared from the Bay Area.

THE 16TH AND 17TH CENTURIES

1508–15
*Spanish conquest of
Puerto Rico and Cuba.*

1519–21
*Hernán Cortés
conquers the Aztec
empire and founds
Mexico.*

1542–4
*Fourth war between
Charles V and
Francis I.*

Sir Francis Drake

1562
*Outbreak of the wars
of religion in Europe.*

1588
*Defeat of the
"Invincible Armada".*

EXPLORATION OF THE COAST. Around 1530 Spain reigned supreme over a large part of central and southern America, especially Mexico, while the lands north of the Rio Grande remained *terra incognita.* However, even before the conquest of the Philippines, in 1565, two Spanish expeditions were sent to reconnoiter the West Coast of the North American continent. In 1532 Hernán Cortés came across a "peninsula stretching out between the gulf and the ocean", which he called "California", but the discovery of California is officially attributed to Juan Rodriguez Cabrillo, ten years later. In 1579 Sir Francis Drake, who was in the pay of the queen of England, dropped the *Golden Hind*'s anchor north of the bay and claimed that stretch of coast for England, calling it "New Albion". The Spanish, who had established a busy shipping route between Manila and Mexico, wanted to set up a port of necessity on this coast, and the reconnaissance expeditions were resumed. In 1602 Sebastían Vizcaíno discovered the Bay of Monterey. But it took another century before the entrance to the Bay of San Francisco, obscured from navigators by fogs most of the time, was discovered.

The Discovery of the Bay by Portola, by A. Mathews.

1600
English East India Company formed.

1685
Edict of Nantes revoked: exodus of French Protestants.

1713
The Treaty of Utrecht confirms England's maritime supremacy.

1763
The French relinquish their North American land to the English.

1776–83
American War of Independence, concluded by the Treaty of Versailles.

1789
Ratification of the American constitution. George Washington becomes president. Outbreak of the French Revolution.

DISCOVERY OF THE BAY. In the 18th century Spain, whose power was on the wane, focused its attentions on its South American colonies. The presence of Russian trappers from Alaska in northern California worried the Spanish, who sent an expedition, taking an overland route, headed by Gaspar de Portolá. In March 1769 sixty men and about one hundred mules left San Diego, which had been in Spanish hands since July. Their orders were to go back to the Bay of Monterey, establish a Spanish presence in this part of California and help set up some Franciscan missions. In September the expedition reached Monterey but did not recognize the bay that had been so highly praised by Vizcaíno, and they continued on toward the north. In November, by chance, they came across the Bay of San Francisco. On August 5, 1775, Juan Manuel de Ayala became the first explorer to pilot his ship through the Golden Gate straits. He drew up a topographical chart of the bay, and named most of the sites.

SPANISH SETTLERS. On June 27, 1776, thirty-four Spanish families accompanied by the Franciscan monk Father Palou, left Sonora in Mexico under the protection of Juan Bautista de Anza and settled in the Bay Area. They constructed two buildings as a symbol of Spanish might: the Presidio, a fort situated at the entrance of the bay, and a church, further south, dedicated to Saint Francis of Assisi ▲ 292. They christened the bay "San Francisco", after the mission's patron saint, and called the site "Yerba Buena", after the wild mint growing there. This village stood on the site of what is now Chinatown/west Downtown. The Ohlones welcomed them and over the next few years four more missions were built. The one in San Francisco flourished, and by 1802 numbered 814 residents. Many Indian "converts" died here as a result of exposure to European diseases and much of the native culture was destroyed. Numerous Spaniards left the Mexican colonies to settle in Yerba Buena. These "Californios" made their living rearing stock and selling hides to ships.

Map of the Bay Area drawn up in 1777 by Father Pedro Font.

Dance by the Californian inhabitants of the San Francisco mission.

THE 19TH CENTURY

After 1810, foreign ships made the bay a more frequent port of call. The Russians built a fort, later called Fort Ross, and American pioneers settled in the peninsula.

Californios on a bear hunt.

MEXICAN INDEPENDENCE. In 1821, Mexico broke off its relations with Spain after a war that had lasted ten years and, in 1824, became an independent republic. The new state, which did not want to lose Upper California, decided to secularize the missions, installed a governor and encouraged Mexican settlement by giving away extensive parcels of land to settlers. In 1835 Mexico rejected President Jackson's offer of $500,000 for the purchase of California.

THE AMERICAN SETTLERS. In 1835 William Richardson built a wooden house not far from the mission, and laid out a street (the future Grant Avenue ▲ *156*) and a little square, the nerve center of what was to be a *pueblo* for American settlers. In no time at all the Mexican government found that it was unable to check the influx of pioneers who were arriving down the Oregon trail. Nor could it check the ambitions cherished by the government in Washington to gain control of the region, worried by the interest that France and England were showing in it. In 1846 President James Polk decided to annex this area, come what may; the news that California might be surrendered to England in payment for an outstanding debt acted as a catalyst. On May 13, 1846, the United States declared war on Mexico.

GENERAL FREMONT

1846: THE "BEAR FLAG" REVOLT. One month after war was declared, some Yankees, led by Ezekiel Merritt and William B. Ide, forced the Mexican governor, Vallejo, to sign a document in Sonoma surrendering California. Their captain, John Fremont, raised their flag, a white square featuring a grizzly bear, the "Bear Flag", and William B. Ide was named president of the short-lived republic. On July 9 in the same year John Montgomery, captain of the sloop of war *USS Portsmouth*, berthed at Yerba Buena and seized the *pueblo* in the name of the United States. The soldiers of the Presidio surrendered. From then on the Union's flag flew over Yerba Buena, which was rechristened San Francisco on January 30, 1847, thereby linking the name of the city to that of the bay. On February 12, 1848, the Treaty of Guadalupe Hidalgo made California an American territory, and in 1850 it became the Union's thirty-first state.

1848: GOLD! Life in San Francisco, a small town of about three hundred people and the chief port of entry for the West Coast, was turned upside-down by the discovery of gold in American rivers ▲ *48*. The news spread like wildfire and in the space of a few months the town's population soared to over 25,000 inhabitants. The first arrivals lived in tents; these were soon replaced by wooden barracks, which were regularly

destroyed by fire. San Francisco became California's first city. The easy money created a fertile breeding ground for violence and vice: gambling clubs, brothels and opium dens proliferated. Gangs instituted a reign of terror. In June 1851 the people of San Francisco, tired of the law's impotence in the face of this extortion, organized themselves into a militia and created the Vigilance Committee under the aegis of the Mormon Sam Brannan. By 1853 the main lodes of gold were dead. Immigration ground to a halt, money and property values plummeted, and shops went bankrupt. The city, with more debts than it could pay, reeled in the hands of corrupt politicians, whom the press made it their business to denounce. The murder of the editor of the *Evening Bulletin* ● *70*, in May 1856, led to the formation of a second Vigilance Committee, which dealt out an even more summary brand of justice.

Goldminers.

1859. SECOND WIND. Henry Comstock's discovery of a very rich band of silver in Nevada, 105 miles northeast of San Francisco, gave a fresh boost to the city's economy: the mines were a long way off, but San Francisco was the only place within reach that had banks and a stock exchange ▲ *209*. This time the mining of these lodes, embedded deep in the rock, was handled by capitalists, rather than by all-comers. San Francisco welcomed the "Bonanza Kings", wealthy silver-mine owners who ploughed back their profits into the city, creating an economic boom that was to everyone's advantage. Roads were built, accommodation, offices and factories shot up, and banks, shops and hotels were opened. A cultural life began to materialize. However, one problem still remained: San Francisco was cut off from the rest of America. The passing of the Pacific Railroad Act ● *54* in 1862 gave the go-ahead for the construction of an intercontinental railroad, which was to be completed in 1869. Although the train opened up California, it also brought a variety of economic and social problems in its wake and plunged San Francisco into a period of depression. It was time to concentrate on the development of a more varied, stable economy. In 1894 a group of reformers, determined to cure the city of the corruption that was gnawing away at it, persuaded Adolph Sutro to put himself forward for mayor and replace the highly corrupt Christopher Buckley, president of the Democratic Party. But Sutro, at the age of sixty-five, did not feel up to the task and stepped down. In 1897 James Phelan, an upright man, was elected mayor and committed himself to a political and urban clean-up program for the city during his term of office. As the 19th century was

1876
The telephone is invented by A.G. Bell. Universal Exhibition in Philadelphia.

1898
Spanish-American war in Cuba and in the Philippines. Hawaii is annexed.

Hanging of a man by the Vigilance Committee.

1901
Death of Queen Victoria.

1903
The United States is given responsibility for the administration of the Panama Canal, opened in 1914.

HISTORY OF
SAN FRANCISCO

Clay Street Hill
Railway in 1875.

winding to a close, though badly scarred by financial and
political corruption, San Francisco was regaining a semblance
of prosperity and expanding westward. Eight cable car lines
● *68* and numerous trolleys crisscrossed the city, which
boasted some fine Victorian houses and which had a thriving
cultural life. Sea trade and ship traffic through the port were
booming. San Francisco, which had only recently begun to
develop as a port, could now pride itself on being the "capital
of the Pacific".

THE 20TH CENTURY

The beginning of the 20th century ushered in a Golden Age
for San Francisco, which now numbered some 400,000
inhabitants, in other words, about 45 percent of the total
population of the state. But it also saw corruption hit an all-
time high. In 1901, following a series of strikes, the unions
created the Union Labor Party, whose candidate, Eugene
Schmitz, was elected mayor of San Francisco. But the new
mayor, a puppet in the hands of the brilliant lawyer Abe Ruef,
could not curb the abuses perpetrated by the municipal team,
which was infamous throughout the city for its corruption and
nepotism. In 1905 another group of reformers, led by
James Phelan, Fremont Older and Rudolph Spreckels,
decided to overthrow Schmitz and his team. But
their efforts were interrupted by the earthquake.

1906: THE EARTH TREMBLES. On April 18,
1906, the city was woken by violent earth tremors
● *58*. All over the city the earthquake started
fires, which took firemen four days to put out,
with a little help from the rain. The damage was
extensive. Camps were set up in the parks for
victims of the disaster. Reconstruction work began
almost immediately, thanks to financial assistance
from around the world, and proved to be amazingly
speedy: it was virtually finished by 1912. The city took

advantage of this opportunity to remove Schmitz and Ruef.
James Rolph, who became mayor, initiated a period of
political reform and economic restructuring. The completion
of the Civic Center ▲ *224* and the opening of the Panama
Pacific International Exhibition ▲ *236* celebrated this new era
and the reconstruction work.

1917: WORLD WAR ONE. The United States entered the
war in April 1917. The world
conflict resulted in an economic
boom for San Francisco by giving
a new lease of life to farming and
manufacturing industries, specially
ship-building. Bases were set up,
and the local economy found itself
yoked to military activities. The
population grew by 20 percent.
San Francisco also shared in the
prosperity experienced throughout
America in the 1920's: financiers
and industrialists erected the first
skyscrapers ● *100*.

Poster by P.W. Nahl
for the Panama
Pacific Exhibition.

PANAMA PACIFIC
INTERNATIONAL
EXPOSITION
SAN FRANCISCO 1915

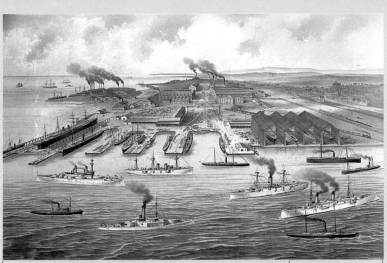

1930: THE DEPRESSION. San Francisco bore the full brunt of a recession that hit its port activities especially hard, and in 1934 one of the most severe strikes in its history broke out. Organized by the International Longshoremen's Association ● *64*, it lasted more than three months and, on Thursday, July 5, degenerated into a violent show-down between police and strikers, known thereafter as "Bloody Thursday". San Francisco nevertheless managed to keep its economy afloat with the implementation of some major new building projects, including the construction of Coit Tower ▲ *170* and, in particular, that of the Bay Bridge and the Golden Gate Bridge ▲ *242*, opened in 1937.

WORLD WAR TWO. After the attack on Pearl Harbor in December 1941, which caused the United States to declare war on Japan, San Francisco became the main military port in the Pacific. Many new shipyards sprang up, the number of factories tripled, and the number of workers doubled. Thousands of African-Americans from the American South came to San Francisco to work in the wartime factories. Apartment blocks were built and houses converted into apartments in order to accommodate the newcomers. During the war, an estimated 1½ million people and 23 million tons of equipment passed through the bay.

SINCE 1950. The post-war years heralded substantial economic and social changes. At the end of the 1950's, San Francisco was a wellspring of iconoclastic, anti-establishment and counter-cultural trends. The Beat generation ▲ *166* was followed by the hippies of the Flower Power generation ▲ *276*. The city philosophically welcomed these alternative movements. The University of California, at Berkeley on the other side of the bay, was the intellectual hub of political activism in the 1960's and a focus for violent opposition to the war in Vietnam. But these days San Francisco has found a status quo somewhere between culture and counter-culture that might be envied by many American cities.

Potrero Hill.

1950–3
Korean War.

1963
Assassination of John F. Kennedy.

1969
Americans walk on the moon.

Strikers in 1934 in the port of San Francisco.

1973
Ceasefire in Vietnam signed in Paris.

1974
Resignation of Nixon following the Watergate scandal.

1991
Gulf War.

1993
Bill Clinton succeeds George Bush as president.

47

The news that gold had been discovered in the Sacramento Valley, in January 1848, leaked out in just a few weeks. In less than a year it had spread worldwide, causing one of the greatest migrations in history. In three months San Francisco shot from 300 inhabitants to 25,000, and it is estimated that during the first three years of the Gold Rush over 200,000 people made the trek to California.

The prospectors spent all their savings on buying the gear

GOLD IN FORT SUTTER
On January 24, 1848, James Marshall, a carpenter, discovered a nugget of gold in the mill race of the sawmill that he was building for Johann Sutter, in Coloma. Sutter, a former Swiss soldier, owned 73 square miles of Central Valley but in February 1948, after California became American, his lands were confiscated and he died in poverty.

needed by a gold miner, including a sturdy pair of boots and occasionally a mule.

THE THREE ROUTES. There were three routes to San Francisco. Most people traveled by boat, either rounding Cape Horn, the cheapest and the longest journey (six to eight months), or via the isthmus of Panama, the shortest route but the most arduous. Crossing the continent overland was just as grueling and fraught with danger.

LA FORTUNE
COMPAGNIE DES MINES D'OR DE LA CALIFORNIE

THE FOREST OF MASTS. In 1849 a whole host of ships converged on San Francisco, the port nearest to the gold lodes. Three-masters, schooners, whaling boats, steamers, frequently in a dreadful state of disrepair, were abandoned by sailors who headed off to prospect in the Sierra Nevada. By the end of 1849 more than six hundred ships rode at anchor in the port of San Francisco.

THE "FLYING CLOUD"
In 1850, shipyards in New York built a new ship known as the clipper, which was capable of making the voyage from the East Coast in 89 days instead of 182 days.

THE "FORTY-NINERS"
The first wave of fortune-seekers who landed in San Francisco in 1849 were called "Forty-Niners". For the most part the men who had come to try their luck were disinherited sons, adventurers or political undesirables.

● THE GOLD RUSH

PANNING FOR GOLD

The first arrivals found a fortune in gold in the riverbeds. They had only to wash the dirt from the alluvial deposits in a batea, or washing pan, with water from the stream: the so-called "frying pan" technique. But this exhausting work soon proved unable to provide a high enough yield, so the prospectors replaced the batea with the "Long Tom" (below).

"LONG TOM"

The earth was poured into the upper, perforated section of the "Long Tom", to be washed. The grains of gold gathered in the slightly sloping lower section where the cross-bars caught the alluvial deposits. The yield was four times higher than when using the more rudimentary batea. The gold miners subsequently increased the size of the upper filter (from 20 to 23 feet long) so that it could receive the stream water directly, using wooden pipes or troughs called "sluices".

GOLD!

The lucky ones found nuggets: others had to be content with gold grains or dust. Offices were set up to measure the gold content of the ore. To prevent excesses, the San Francisco Mint set an official gold rate of 16 dollars per ounce in 1854.

THE "MOTHER LODE"

The Mother Lode, the main gold vein in the Sierra Nevada (between Fort Sutter and Mariposa), was quickly parceled out. To get there from San Francisco, prospectors had to travel up the Sacramento River to Sutter's Fort and then continue on foot or by mule.

EXTRACTION SITES

Sacramento River

Coloma

Sutter's Fort

Sacramento

Stockton

San Francisco

San Joaquin River

THE CAMPS

This painting by C. Nahl, *Sunday Morning at the Mine*, shows life in the mining camps. Undernourished, with no protection from the sun by day or the damp at night, the miners suffered from fevers and dysentery, discovering too late the down-side of the gold digger's dream. Many met their death there.

> "OUR FINGERS ITCHED, WE WERE CONSUMED BY THE GOLD WE HOPED TO FIND; SO, LESS THAN HALF AN HOUR AFTER OUR ARRIVAL [...] WE WERE ALL HARD AT WORK, JUST AS KEEN AS THE OTHERS...."
>
> J. TYRWHITE-BROOKS

OTHER TECHNIQUES

So-called "sluice"-washing consisted in scooping out the earth where the current was so strong that the heavy particles settled at the bottom. Around 1850 the miners invented the "coyotinh", a technique that consisted of digging shafts and galleries in order to reach the rocky bed of a river where they might locate a pocket of gold. All these techniques needed a great deal of water, which was indispensable to any mining activity. In 1849 the goldminers collected the equivalent of 10 million dollars: the figure was 40 million in 1850 and 80 million in 1852, a record year. But by 1854 the manna had already run out!

THE CLAIMS

The state granted stakes of land, or claims, between 18 and 24 square yards. In 1850 the government enacted the Foreign Miners License Tax, a tax of 20 dollars levied on foreigners allowing them to prospect. The mines emptied, and San Francisco filled up with bankrupt foreigners. The law was abolished in 1851.

EMPIRE GOLD MINE

Miners going down into the Grass Valley gold mine, between 1880 and 1890. This mine, which was very rich in ore, was worked by the British and remained in operation until 1950.

In the space of just a few years San Francisco expanded considerably, as can be seen from these prints, from 1873 (below) and 1868 (right). Market Street is clearly visible, with streets running off it diagonally. It splits the city culturally, geographically and meteorologically, as Herbert Gold observed.

● THE TRANSCONTINENTAL RAILROAD

The Gold Rush had highlighted the need for California to be made more accessible by building a transcontinental railroad. Even though the clippers had broken all the records, the route around Cape Horn was still long and dangerous. In 1862 Congress ratified the draft layout drawn up by a young engineer, Theodore Judah. Two companies took charge of the work: Union Pacific, supervised by Congress, was to construct the East–West section, from Omaha, while Central Pacific, founded by the "Big Four", was to build the West–East section, from Oakland. It took six years for this project to be successfully completed, at the cost of many lives. After 1869 the journey from one coast to the other only took six and a half days.

"CROCKER'S PETS"
This was the nickname of the fifteen thousand Chinese "coolies" who were brought over to build the railroad. Although they were paid more or less the same salary as whites, they had to provide their own food. They worked in teams of twelve to twenty, each with a cook, a tea-maker and an extra man as a standby in case of mishap.

THE COOLIES: IMPORTED WORKHANDS
The difficulty of finding a stable and inexpensive work-force prompted Charles Crocker, Central Pacific's director of works, to enter into an agreement with a secret society in Chinatown, whereby they committed to supply him with laborers imported directly from China.

THEODORE JUDAH

This East Coast engineer, who had just completed a 28-mile-long railroad linking Sacramento with the gold mines in the Sierra Nevada, was the true father of the Transcontinental Railroad, but he rapidly lost control of the project. Shocked by the dishonest practices of the "Big Four", Judah sold his shares and tried to find financial backing on the east coast in order to buy back the company. Fate was against him: he died of yellow fever, which he caught on his journey across Panama in 1865.

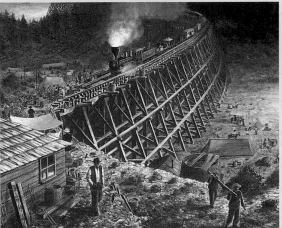

The Pacific Railroad Act granted the two companies large tracts of land and subsidies, the amount of which was in direct proportion to the distance to be covered, which had been fixed for each company. In order to protect their capital outlay, the "Big Four" demanded absolute financial control over the work. Government funds were paid to the Crocker Company, which contrived to have the construction work done at the lowest possible prices (using only basic equipment) and to pay back the surplus to the four partners. To obtain further subsidies, Crocker shamelessly invented mountainous terrain where there were actually plains, by bribing specialists and geologists.

THE "BIG FOUR": THE RAILROAD BARONS. The Transcontinental
Railroad was to cross the Sierra Nevada and the Rocky Mountains, a superhuman undertaking that did not alarm Judah, who was convinced that the project was feasible. Four wealthy businessmen from Sacramento (Collis P. Huntington, Mark Hopkins, Leland Stanford and Charles Crocker), the "Big Four", founded Central Pacific to finance his project. They managed to prevail upon Congress and President Lincoln, who signed the Pacific Railroad Act in July 1862. This law provided for the creation of a second railroad company. Work started on January 8, 1863.

● THE TRANSCONTINENTAL RAILROAD

PROMONTORY POINT. The two lines met at Promontory Point in Utah on May 10, 1869. Central Pacific had laid 683½ miles of railroad track, and Union Pacific had laid 1,081 miles. The Transcontinental Railroad had cost 118 million dollars, had made the "Big Four" very wealthy, and had killed a great many Chinese workmen.

On April 29, 1869, the two companies challenged each other to lay 7 miles of track in one day. The eight hundred coolies working for Central Pacific beat this record in twelve hours.

TWO RIVAL COMPANIES

The work done by Central Pacific progressed more slowly than that of Union Pacific because of the difficult terrain. It took a year to dig Summit Tunnel, to create the underground passages and lay the ramps in the Sierra. The severity of the winter in 1866 did not help matters. By the end of 1867 Union Pacific had laid 311 miles of track while Central Pacific had laid only 87 miles. Crocker therefore decided to boost performance efficiency, and in 1868 he laid 217 miles, setting a record of nearly ¾ mile per day.

THE FINAL NAIL

There was much jubilation as the final section of railroad was laid at Promontory Point. It was fixed to the sleepers with three sleeper nails made of precious metal, presented by the states it crossed (California, Nevada and Arizona).

In view of the progress made by the Chinese workers, Huntington suggested that the law should be amended so that each company was authorized to continue laying the railroad until the tracks met. From that time onwards the companies became rivals instead of associates, each trying to lay as much track as possible.

● THE EARTHQUAKE OF 1906

The town on fire, painted by William Coulter in 1906.

San Francisco had been hit by earthquakes on a regular basis, but the one in 1906 was unusually severe. It caused a widespread conflagration which burned for three days, devastating a large part of the city. It is difficult to assess the level of damage to property and the loss of life caused by the earthquake itself, because the local authorities, anxious not to worry the population or investors about the risk of earthquakes, ascribed the worst damage to the fire and cynically scaled down the figures. Like the phoenix, its symbol since the 19th century, the town rose again from the ashes with remarkable speed. The reconstruction work took barely six years.

FORTY-EIGHT SECONDS

On April 18, 1906, at 5.16 am, an earthquake measuring 8.25 on the Richter scale hit the city. The ground began to undulate, creating waves of earth 6 to 9 feet high, while in other places, yawning fissures split the ground, swallowing everything in sight. In less than a minute much of the area around what is now the Civic Center and South of Market Street was leveled, the county hospital and the City Hall collapsed like houses of cards.

TERRIBLE EARTHQUAKE IN SAN FRANCISCO

THE USE OF DYNAMITE

General Funston (right), commander of the Presidio, at his own initiative and without authorization from the mayor, decided to take control of the fire-fighting operations. He instituted martial law and organized first aid services. He ordered buildings at the edges of the conflagration to be dynamited, to create firebreaks, but the explosions only fed the fire and made it burn twice as fiercely. Thousands of people were trapped by the flames. On April 21 the wind dropped, and a drizzle helped to put out the fire.

THE CITY IN FLAMES

When the electrical cables for the trolleys snapped and the gas pipes exploded, some fifty fires started across the city. The water mains had also burst, so firemen were unable to control the fires, which spread rapidly and formed one huge, unstoppable conflagration. An unbearable heat (2700°F) enveloped the city. Iron and steel sagged, marble melted and sandstone split. The glow could be seen from 50 miles away,

and smoke billowed up in a column five miles high. In a few hours all lines of communication had been lost. The city was cut off from the rest of the world and unable to coordinate its rescue operations.

A HEAVY TOLL

By the time the flames were extinguished, Nob Hill, Chinatown, and the entire northeastern part of the city, from South Pacific Depot to Telegraph Hill, were in ruins. It is now thought that over 3,000 people died, rather than the scaled-down official figure of 700, and that 250,000 people were left homeless. As for damage to property, this was substantial: 514 blocks, 28,000 buildings and an estimated 500 million dollars in material losses went up in smoke.

RESCUE OPERATIONS

From April 18 the army organized rescue measures and evacuated civilians. A naval ship, the *USS Navy*, picked up hundreds of people fleeing toward the sea. Many took the ferry for Oakland, but the majority of San Franciscans took refuge in the city's parks, where tents were erected. People remained calm and even retained their sense of humor. On one of the refuge barracks, in reference to the age-old rivalry that existed between San Francisco and Oakland, were the words: "Eat, drink and be merry, for tomorrow we may have to go to Oakland!"

LOOTING. From the early hours of the disaster there was a problem with looting. The mayor decided to have any looters who were caught red-handed shot, assuming that it would be impossible to arrest them in the prevailing state of panic. General Funston felt that the police would not be able to restore order unaided, and used his troops to assist them. Seven people were executed in this way.

This cover of the magazine *Nick Carter* depicts the problem of looting.

A DIFFICULT AFTERMATH
Nearly one half of the city's population was made homeless. There was no electricity, and drinking water was scarce. For fear of fire, the mayor prohibited cooking indoors, so the survivors set up their stoves in the street. The insanitary conditions in which the refugees were forced to live for several months sparked off another catastrophe: the city was overrun with rats, which spread the plague. Some two hundred people lost their lives.

● RECONSTRUCTION WORK

THE EXPO

SAN FI

Just before the 1906 catastrophe San Francisco was the major financial, industrial and commercial center of the West Coast. As a result the entire region was badly hit by the destruction of its administrative buildings, office blocks, shops and factories. Although nothing but ruins now remained, the town planning project drawn up by architect Daniel Burnham ● *104*, ▲ *224*, and approved by the local council before the earthquake, lay gathering dust. This was because it would have entailed the compulsory purchase of countless private properties, at a time when everyone was clinging to the boundaries of their former property, seeing this as the best way to ensure they received compensation. A committee was set up to organize the work and deal with the most pressing problems. As the banks had been completely destroyed, the funds necessary for the reconstruction work were not forthcoming. But it did not take long for New York banks to agree to make a contribution and for insurance companies to compensate their customers, while several foreign countries, in particular Japan, added their support. Work began rapidly and it was a cleaner, more modern city that rose from the ashes, sporting many steel-frame sky-scrapers. One advantage of this overall reconstruction

PANAMA
PACIFIC
EXPOSITION

NCISCO

program was a greater degree of architectural unity. By 1912 most of the city had been rebuilt, a feat that was celebrated with the exhibition of 1915 ▲ *236*. The success of the reconstruction program was thanks to the sheer solidarity and survival instinct of the city's people. It heralded a phenomenal boom for this "instant city" ● *90*.

● LONGSHOREMAN'S ASSOCIATION

Until the 1950's the work done by longshoremen in the port of San Francisco was as vital to the city as that of bankers and property developers. These men worked long days in hazardous conditions for a pittance of a salary, a large part of which was paid to recruitment agencies that ensured they had jobs to go to. Founded in 1898, the ILA (International Longshoremen's Association), the largest of the unions, endeavored to protect their interests. After the failure of a strike in 1919, however, it was replaced by the Longshoreman's Association, an organization under the control of the shipping companies. It was not until 1933 and Roosevelt's National Recovery Act that the longshoremen again rallied together and resuscitated the ILA.

1934 STRIKE. In May 1934 a strike was called in support of a local closed shop, regulated hiring, better safety conditions and higher pay. For three days the dockers raised barricades against the police. On

Thursday July 5, 1934, known as "Bloody Thursday", the police opened fire, killing two dockers. A general strike expressing solidarity with the dockers brought the city to a standstill for three days. The dockers went back to work on 31 July after the intervention of an arbitration board. In the 1960's the dockers were severely affected by the introduction of containerization, which rendered the old jetties obsolete.

HARRY BRIDGES
This Australian was taken on as a docker in San Francisco in 1932 and played an active role within the ILA. In 1937 he founded a new union, the International Longshoremen's and Warehousemen's Union (ILWU), which he chaired for forty years. By his death in 1990, at the age of eighty, he had worked for sixty years in the port industry of his adoptive city.

LIFESTYLES

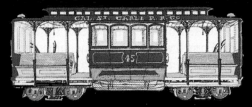

● Levi Strauss & Co.

Levi Strauss was a German immigrant who landed in New York in 1847, aged eighteen. In 1853, he moved to San Francisco and began to build an empire through hard work and business acumen. He is famous for giving America one of its most universal cult symbols: blue jeans.

The name "jeans", which was occasionally used to describe these trousers at the end of the nineteenth century, came from the French word, *Gênes*, (meaning Genoa), as Strauss's thick trousers were reminiscent of the pants once worn by Genoan sailors. "Blue" came from the indigo color of the imported *serge de Nîmes* used in their manufacture after 1860. But it was not until the 1930's that these pairs of tailored breeches came to be definitively known as "jeans" and assumed their current form.

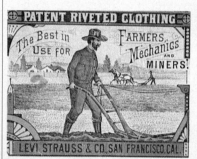

TROUSERS FOR MINERS

When Levi Strauss arrived in San Francisco, the Gold Rush was in full swing. Strauss had the idea of manufacturing work pants, sturdy enough for miners to wear, out of the tan coarse canvas which was used for making tents and wagon covers. Their durability swiftly ensured their reputation as a high-quality product. By 1860 this canvas fabric had run out so Levi Strauss decided to use fabric imported from Nîmes (the label's famous "Denim") which was just as hard-wearing, but blue in color: thus jeans became blue jeans.

RIVETS

In 1872, a tailor from Nevada suggested fixing metal rivets to the points of stress on pocket seams to reinforce them. He subsequently became Levi Strauss's partner.

THE "LEVI" TRADEMARK

The loops on the waistband appeared in 1922 and the red label in 1936. Stitched onto the right-hand pocket, this label, along with the rivets, became Levi's unmistakable hallmark.

LEVI STRAUSS & CO.

The jeans were made in New York by Strauss' brothers and shipped to San Francisco. In 1873, Levi Strauss and his partner opened their first factory in San Francisco. Every product which emerged from the workshops carried a maker's number.

A FASHION PHENOMENON

Cowboys took to wearing jeans daily because they were so durable. By the end of the century the jeans worn by the miners had become the ideal working clothes. The craze for the Wild West, which swept America during the 1940's created fresh demand for this item of clothing at every level of American society. The fashion had caught on.

In the 1950's jeans were sported, along with the leather jacket, by a younger generation of rebels; they hero-worshipped screen idols such as James Dean and Marlon Brando, who also wore them. Jeans shifted from being working clothes to the uniform of the non-conformist. Twenty years later they had become classic wear, unaffected by fashion or social barriers.

A FAMILY BUSINESS

"Levis" have been exported to seventy countries in Europe and Asia since 1980. The Haas family still head the company: in 1984, Levi Strauss's great-great-grand-nephew took it over.

In 1869 the engineer Andrew Hallidie saw five horses die on the slopes of Nob Hill, killed by the very heavy load they were pulling. This prompted the engineer to work on a system of transport that would be better suited to the city's topography. He devised an underground cable, propelled by a powerful motor, capable of drawing a vehicle along a track at a constant speed. The cable car, an unusual rack-tramway, was born in 1873, and by 1889 there were eight lines cutting across the city with 112 miles of track. Only three lines have survived and, although more valuable as a historical curiosity, they continue to provide transport for thousands of travelers every day.

THE CABLE
The cable, made up of 114 strands of twisted steel, runs in a groove between the rails, 27 inches deep. To connect the cable to the car, Hallidie invented a grip device which is operated by the driver with a lever: the car will not move forward unless the grip is clamped to the cable; once the grip has been put into action, it pulls the car at a constant speed of around 9 miles per hour.

A HISTORIC METHOD OF TRANSPORT
Badly damaged in the 1906 earthquake, the cable car was only partially restored.
In 1947, the city government tried to replace it with trolleys and buses, which were more economical. But San Franciscans managed to save three of the eight lines and funded their complete restoration between 1981 and 1984.

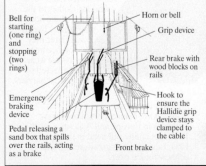

CABLE CAR BARN. This building houses the machinery that operates the three cables of the Mason, Hyde and California Street lines, which are all "continuous loops". At the end of the route the cable winds round a large wheel, which allows the car to be brought back to where it started.

Bell for starting (one ring) and stopping (two rings)

Horn or bell

Grip device

Rear brake with wood blocks on rails

Emergency braking device

Hook to ensure the Hallidie grip device stays clamped to the cable

Pedal releasing a sand box that spills over the rails, acting as a brake

Front brake

> "THE CABLE-CARS HAVE FOR ALL PRACTICAL PURPOSES MADE SAN FRANCISCO A DEAD LEVEL [...] AND, FOR AUGHT I KNOW, MAY RUN UP THE SIDES OF HOUSES."
>
> RUDYARD KIPLING

ANDREW S. HALLIDIE
The son of a London cable manufacturer, Hallidie arrived in California in 1853. Before setting up his North Beach factory, he constructed tramways for the mines in the Sierra Nevada. In 1873 he sank his whole fortune in the construction of the first line, on Clay Street. The following year, the success of this brand new method of transport was guaranteed in San Francisco, when eight lines were built.

TWO MODELS OF CAR. The majority of lines operated a one-way car (right). At the end of the route the driver had to turn the car around on a turntable to go back in the opposite direction ▲ 65. Two-way cars were fitted with a driver's cab at either end. To go back the way it had come, the cable car switched points, and the driver just changed cab.

In 1889 a car with a driver's cab at either end appeared on the California Street line.

The Daily

With the Gold Rush, a host of newspapers were founded in San Francisco, confirming its status as the capital of the West Coast. In 1887 William Randolph Hearst, the son of an extremely wealthy miner, became editor of the *San Francisco Examiner* and initiated a new type of journalism: sensationalism. This was the perfect recipe for success, and Hearst soon found himself at the head of the most extensive press empire in the US. The 20th century saw the dawning of a corporate era in which the media had a powerful, central role. In 1965 the "underground" press, which concentrated on events neglected by the other media, made its appearance in the Bay Area, representing a continuation of the San Franciscan tradition of a free, outspoken brand of journalism.

"ALTA CALIFORNIA"
The first San Franciscan newspaper, the *California Star*, was published by Sam Brannan on January 9, 1847. The same year another weekly newspaper was launched in San Francisco, the *Californian*, which had first appeared in Monterey in 1846. In the summer of 1848 the two newspapers merged to produce *Alta California*, which became daily in January 1850.

"SAN FRANCISCO CHRONICLE"
This theater magazine, founded in 1865 by the brothers Charles and M.H. de Young ▲ *258*, became a daily newspaper similar to the *Examiner* in 1868. In 1880 the son of Mayor Isaac Kalloch, the Labor Party candidate who had become the pet target of the *Chronicle*'s attacks, murdered Charles de Young. By 1965 this daily newspaper was the *Examiner*'s only rival.

Clint Eastwood — The Good, Bad and Ugly/*See Page 83*

San Francisco Chronicle

WEDNESDAY, MARCH 31, 1993

White House Retreat

Bears on Parade

Is Supervisor Maher on the way out? | Th

San Francisco Exami

Oscars!

Israel Seals Off Big Hotel
Territories to To Bargain

"EVENING BULLETIN"
This was founded in 1855 by J. King of William, who was murdered a year later for his views. In 1929 W.R. Hearst bought the *Bulletin*, which folded in 1965.

"S.F. DAILY EXAMINER"
On March 4, 1887, W.R. Hearst bought this newspaper, which was in a state of collapse. He took on a team of high-flyers: Samuel S. Chamberlain (of the *New York Herald*), George E. Pancoast, future inventor of color printing, and the famous writer Ambrose Bierce.

Examiner.

W.R. HEARST (1863–1951). At the age of twenty-four, this pleasure-seeking young man, who had studied as a journalist under Joseph Pulitzer in New York, became the chief editor of the *S.F. Daily Examiner*. He aimed to make this a mass circulation newspaper, attracting readers with sensationalist scoops, color illustrations and wide-ranging, outspoken campaigns, more often than not denouncing abuses of power. He finished by controlling a chain of about forty newspapers.

LITERARY AND SATIRICAL PRESS
In the 19th century authors west of the Mississippi relied on these magazines because there were no local publishing houses. First there was the *Golden Era*, founded in 1852, then from 1868 *Overland Monthly* became the key literary review on the West Coast. *The Wasp*, a late-19th-century satirical magazine, was renowned for its color caricatures.

"SAN FRANCISCO ORACLE"
Run by Allen Cohen from 1966, the *Oracle* claimed to reflect the major spiritual trends doing the rounds of the hippie communities that had settled in Haight-Ashbury ▲ *276*. This newspaper, with its psychedelic colors and innovative graphics, contained articles, poetry, and theater and music reviews.

COMICS AND THE UNDERGROUND PRESS
In 1968 R. Crumb with his "Mr Natural" ▲ *278*, Gilbert Shelton with his "Freak Brothers", and S. Clay Wilson with his "Hell's Angels Cannibals" launched *Zap Comics*, which used comic strip characters to disseminate their ideas. The monthly magazine *Mother Jones* continued the fight led by the anti-establishment press of the 1960's, like the *Berkeley Barb*.

Printing arrived late in California. A press operated in Monterey, at that time the capital of the Mexican province, between 1834 and 1836. But it was not until the arrival of Sam Brennan in 1846 that San Francisco saw its first newspaper. By contrast, it took less than fifty years for a quality art press to be established there: in 1877 Edouard Bosqui published his *Grapes and Grape Vines of California*, the first luxury publication to be produced by a San Franciscan press. Other talented printers were quick to follow suit, settling in the city to give an increasing number of writers the benefit of their services. San Francisco rapidly gained a high reputation in this field, a tradition that continues to this very day.

wrists. It was the magical line. An instant before, Stubb had swiftly caught two additional turns with it round the loggerhead, whence,

Darting harpoon

by reason of its increased rapid circlings, a hempen blue smoke now jetted up and mingled with the steady fumes from his pipe. As the line passed round and round the loggerhead; so also, just before reach-ing that point, it blisteringly passed through and through both of Stubb's hands, from which the hand-cloths, or squares of quilted canvas some-times worn at these times, had acci-dently dropped. It was like holding an enemy's sharp two-edged sword by the blade, and that enemy all the time striving to wrest it out of your clutch.

Thrusting harpoon

"Wet the line! wet the line!" cried Stubb to the tub oarsman (him seated by the tub) who, snatching off his hat, dashed the sea-water into it.* More turns were taken, so that the line began holding its place. The boat

*Partly to show the indispensableness of this act, it may here be stated, that, in the old Dutch fishery, a mop was used to dash the run-ning line with water; in many other ships, a wooden piggin, or bailer, is set apart for that purpose. Your hat, however, is the most convenient.

Traditional printing techniques still survive in San Francisco despite increasing competition from computers. The city is home to Mackenzie and Harris, the largest printworks in the United States, as well as to several clubs for people interested in every aspect of book creation and book binding.

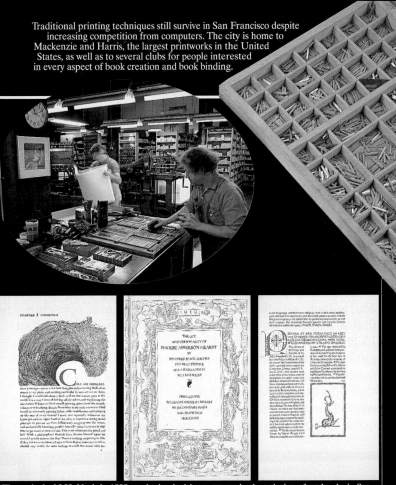

The arrival of J.H. Nash in 1898 marked a decisive moment in the printing of art books in San Francisco. Although he preferred large-format folios with brightly colored, highly stylized borders, he could also display subtlety (see center). The Book Club of California, formed in 1912, encouraged finely produced editions. Through this association Nash endeavored to forge the trademark of San Franciscan publishing. In 1921 the Grabhorn brothers settled in the city. They produced hundreds of books but always tried to ensure perfection in the printing, a good balance between text and illustrations, and high quality paper and binding.

PRINTED FOR

WILLIAM RANDOLPH HEARST

BY JOHN HENRY NASH

SAN FRANCISCO

MCMXXVIII

The 1950's witnessed the arrival of a new generation of printers, such as Adrian Wilson, William Everson and Jack Stauffacher. Andrew Hoyem's Arion Press took over from the Grabhorn brothers in 1969. Their 1982 edition of *Moby Dick*, illustrated by Barry Moser, is regarded as their masterpiece (opposite and above left).

"GRAPES AND GRAPE VINES OF CALIFORNIA" Printed and published by Edouard Bosqui in 1877, this work (right) launched the art printing tradition in San Francisco.

In the 19th century San Francisco's emergence as a metropolis coincided with the "Aesthetic movement", an artistic phase characterized by a taste for virtuosity and elaborate flourishes in the visual arts. At the beginning of the century the Arts and Crafts movement, which had originated in Britain, reached San Francisco. But it was the reconstruction work following the 1906 earthquake that gave Bay Area designers the chance to create a truly Californian style. The world fairs were another decisive step along the way: they were a focus for talent and, as such, gave the designers an unprecedented opportunity to find an audience for their work. The international Golden Gate Exhibition of 1939 exhibited furniture designed for mass production, rather than one-of-a-kind pieces. Nowadays skilled furniture manufacturers have more in common with artists, in their approach to design and production: their pieces are not created for a particular customer but grow out of a personal quest; they are often one-of-a-kind designs or limited editions.

"NATURE FURNITURE" BY GAIL FREDELL
Finished in 1992, this long, narrow table is an abstract depiction of nature, which is the main source for the artist's recent creations. Entitled *Canyon Landscape*, it represents part of a deep gorge. Steel, covered with an iron patina, is designed to evoke the canyon's rocky crags.

HEIRS OF THE ARTS AND CRAFTS MOVEMENT
During post-1906 reconstruction work on the city, many designers were commissioned to make high quality furniture and decorative objects. Arthur and Lucia Mathews used their skill in various media to incorporate painting into their furniture. This drop-leaf writing desk, dating from 1910–15, took its design from a painted panel depicting pre-industrial Arcadia (in Greece).

SLEEP ON WATER THANKS TO CHARLES HALL

While still a design student, Charles Hall invented the water bed in 1968. Members of the counter-cultural movement promoted these plastic mattresses filled with water, with help from rock radio stations, which advertised them over the air. Sleeping on water became a symbol of the hippie lifestyle.

BURDICK GROUP FURNITURE

In the 1970's, the advent of the personal computer altered office layout and working methods. The Burdick group designed a range of versatile "work units", able to cope with all the different types of new office equipment. The desk above, a real "control station", was manufactured by the Herman Miller company. From a central module with several units attached to it, workers can organize their work schedule in line with individual priorities. This gives employees the feeling that they are not merely using the desk, but actually in control of it: the shape it takes reveals their activities, the way they work and, by extension, even their personality.

THE BABY BOOM "BOOMERANGS"

The Bay Area experienced a huge population explosion after World War Two: when they returned to the USA, many soldiers decided to settle there with their families. Luther Conover, a furniture designer and manufacturer in Sausalito, helped to reduce the furniture shortage by creating pieces that were inexpensive and light, as well as sturdy, such as the "Boomerang" coffee table.

BACHELOR BEDSIT

This room by Fritz E. Baldauf is made up of components that he designed for the H. Miller furniture company – a first for this artist who usually makes furniture on commission only.

PHILIP AGEE

Each part of this "Crepe Kingdo" chair, designed by Philip Agee in 1992, is indispensable. Its subtle coloring, which seems to emerge from the grain of the white-leaded oak, highlights the impressive structural details.

STANFORD

Nicknamed "Silicon Valley", the area that stretches between Palo Alto and San José, south of San Francisco, became famous during the 1970's as the site of most of the industries manufacturing integrated circuit boards (microchips) from silicon. It boasts huge research laboratories, where a whole spectrum of revolutionary appliances, from the personal computer to the video cassette recorder, were invented. This boom industry, built around the information technology sector, has considerably altered the economic and social landscape of the region.

THE FIRST COMPUTER
Military needs in World War Two prompted the completion of the fastest calculator in the world. ENIAC (Electronic Numerical Integrator and Calculator), the first electronic computer, was perfected in Philadelphia in 1946.

THE INTEGRATED CIRCUIT

Invented in 1959, the IC replaced the mechanical relays and lamps used in early computers. Its miniature dimensions, which earned it the nickname "microchip", increased the speed of calculations. Silicon, a semiconductor ideally suited to handling the flow of electrons, rapidly became the basic component of the IC, and enabled smaller, more complex and more powerful chips with memory to be produced. By the end of the 1970's, these chips were being used in a wide range of equipment.

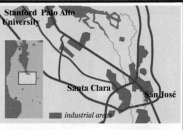

Stanford Palo Alto University

Santa Clara

San José

industrial areas

STANFORD UNIVERSITY

Founded in 1891, this university ◆ *352* has become a leading research center in the fields of medicine, science and technology. Close collaboration between the university and the industrial sector has contributed greatly to Silicon Valley's expansion.

THE PIONEERS

In 1939 William Hewlett and David Packard set up their first electronics firm in Palo Alto. In the 1960's, they were one of the first companies to produce minicomputers and programmable calculators fitted with the revolutionary microchips.

VISIONARY TECHNOLOGY

When Steve Jobs and Steve Wozniak launched their legendary Apple Company in 1975, they introduced a revolutionary new approach to computing: simplicity, user-friendliness and access for ordinary mortals to the resources of information technology.

THE MICROCOMPUTER

Apple II, the first microcomputer, appeared on the market in 1977. IBM replied in 1981 with its own version of the PC.

"BEAU-BRUMMELS"
The first local group to hit national headlines, in 1965, were greatly inspired by British rock music. Their manager, Tom Donahue, was the inventor of FM Radio.

The name of San Francisco is still linked to the "psychedelic" rock of the late 1960's. The trend-setting groups of the period, the Grateful Dead, the Jefferson Airplane, Santana, the Steve Miller Band and Quicksilver Messenger Service, symbolize a Golden Age, which was celebrated in August 1969, paradoxically on the opposite coast of America, at the Woodstock festival. These bands were America's answer to the invasion of British groups, such as the Beatles and the Rolling Stones. In San Francisco the underground press, FM radio and the new style of graphic design used for pop concert posters brought this music into the spotlight as the perfect vehicle for a cultural rebellion led by hippies.

THE "GRATEFUL DEAD"
In 1966 this group started out on its legendary journey in Ken Kesey's magic buses ▲ 276. Running the gamut from the Hell's Angels to Neal Cassady ▲ 166, the Grateful Dead quickly came to embody the ideals held by the inhabitants of Haight-Ashbury ▲ 274, where they settled. The Grateful Dead, who have triumphantly survived the test of time, are still very much a part of the music scene: their traditional New Year concert at the Oakland Coliseum is always packed.

BILL GRAHAM
He played a major role as a promoter and manager of San Francisco's rock

groups in the 1960's. In 1965 he took over a huge concert hall on Geary Boulevard, the Fillmore Auditorium, also known as the Fillmore West, and the Winterland.

"BAY AREA MUSIC"
BAM is a well-known rock magazine. It is a free monthly with one hundred or so pages covering the contemporary music scene: records, concerts, in-depth feature articles, interviews and classified advertisements.

"ROLLING STONE"
This specialist monthly journal was founded in San Francisco in 1967 by Ralph J. Gleason and Jann Wenner. *Rolling Stone* was the first magazine to deal with rock music as a cultural phenomenon as important as the cinema and literature.

"THE JEFFERSON AIRPLANE". In 1965 the Jefferson Airplane, who used to perform at the *Matrix* club, were the foremost exponents on the West Coast of the style of folkrock created by Bob Dylan and the Byrds.

NOSTALGIA
Twenty-five years down the line, there seems to be a resurgence of interest in the period and some old psychedelic recordings are being remastered.

THE OFFS
DEAD KENNEDYS
THE PLUGZ
THE EXTREMES
1839 GEARY
FRI OCT 26
9:00 PM

AFTER THE 1960'S
Other new waves have swept through the city of rock: groups reviving the spirit of the 1960's (Flamin' Groovies), soul enthusiasts (Sly Stone), and politicized punks (Dead Kennedys), among others.

THE "CHARLATANS"
Part-way between a "comedy show" and rock'n'roll, they sport a "fin-de-siècle" look that evokes life in the saloons during the Gold Rush.

JANIS JOPLIN (1943–70)
She grew up in Texas, rubbed shoulders with blues musicians in clubs in Austin, and modeled herself on Bessie Smith, the blues singer who died in 1937. In 1965 she settled in San Francisco, on Lyon Street, and sang with the group Big Brother and the Holding Company.

San Francisco regularly lets its hair down for the celebration of Asiatic, South American and European festivals, which enable the communities living there to get back to their roots. But the inhabitants are also celebrating the history of a city that has been American for less than two hundred years. San Francisco, the seat of tolerance, seems to be exorcising the years of racial segregation, and, proud of its acceptance of all "differences", revels in the wild parade of homosexuals.

EXOTIC-EROTIC-HALLOWEEN BALL
For the traditional festival of Halloween on October 31, when children dress up in disguise and go from house to house collecting candy, San Francisco organizes a huge parade on Market and Castro Streets – for adults only. The most outrageous costumes are the rule in a milling crowd of homosexuals and heterosexuals, who dance the night away later at the Concourse Exhibition Center.

LESBIAN AND GAY FREEDOM DAY PARADE
This event, the largest of its kind in the United States, has been held at the end of June since the early 1970's. It commemorates the riots at *Stonewall,* a bar in New York, in 1969
◆ *302,* which marked the start of the gay liberation movement in the United States.

CHINESE NEW YEAR

The Chinese New Year begins on the day of the new moon, between January 20 and February 1. The festivities, including the election of "Miss Chinatown USA", last for two weeks and finish with the giant dragon parade accompanied by fireworks. This huge march brings many spectators to Chinatown every year ▲ 152.

"CINCO DE MAYO"

May 5 is an opportunity for the Mexican community to live it up, celebrating the victory of Mexico over the French troops in Puebla in 1862 with a parade to the Civic Center. In the Mission district there is folk and Indian dancing, folk songs performed by *mariachis*, exhibitions and tastings of regional products.

MARTIN LUTHER KING CELEBRATIONS

The anniversary of the death of Martin Luther King, Jr, celebrated at the Civic Auditorium ▲ 227, is the occasion for a huge festival on the third Monday in January. San Francisco is the second city after Atlanta to honor his memory in this way.

CABLE CAR BELL-RINGING CONTEST

The drivers of the famous cable cars vie with each other in Union Square to win the prize for the best bell-ringing ● 68.

SHAKESPEARE FESTIVAL

From August to October, free shows are put on for audiences in Golden Gate Park ▲ 254.

CARNAVAL

Held in the Mission, this festival has a parade with bands of costumed dancers from all Latin American countries.

CHERRY BLOSSOM FESTIVAL

In April the Cherry Blossom Festival attracts over two thousand people to Japantown. This festival, when national costume is worn, spans two weekends and is the Japanese community's most important annual event.

ST PATRICK'S DAY PARADE

Since 1850 the Irish have celebrated St Patrick's Day on March 17. Custom dictates that, dressed in green they must "drown the clover", the national emblem of Ireland in alcohol. After the parade mass is said in St Mary's Cathedral.

THE BLESSING OF THE FISHING FLEET.

On the first Sunday in October mass is said at the Church of Saints Peter and Paul ▲ 169 in honor of the patron saint of fishermen. This is followed by a parade down Columbus Avenue to Fisherman's Wharf ▲ 180, where the priest blesses the fishing fleet.

San Francisco offers a wide range of options for people who enjoy watersports. While the bay, with its strong currents and frequent winds, is perfect for yachtsmen and windsurfers, the Pacific Ocean, with its spectacular breakers crashing onto the beaches, gives the many surfers all the excitement they crave. Three of the nation's professional football and baseball teams are based in the San Francisco Bay Area. And last but not least, the city has beautifully laid out parks where its residents can enjoy nature, jog through breathtaking surroundings or put giant kites through their paces.

"BAY-TO-BREAKERS" Since 1912, every third Sunday in May, there has been a race over the 7½ miles from the bay to the ocean. It is the occasion of a large-scale festival in San Francisco, with over 100,000 people taking part.

BASEBALL. The North American championship is made up of twenty-eight teams split into two leagues, the National League (NL) and the American League (AL). The annual season runs from April to October, and the final, the World Series, is a play-off between the winners of the two leagues. The local teams are the Oakland A's (AL) and the San Francisco Giants (NL). One of the best teams in the last two decades, the Oakland A's had three consecutive wins in 1972, 1973 and 1974 and another, more recently, in 1989.

Joe Montana, former quarter-back for the San Francisco Forty-Niners.

Born in San Francisco, Joe DiMaggio, a star baseball player in the 1950's, first started playing in this city and finished his career in New York. He was Marilyn Monroe's second husband.

REGATTAS. In the bay the yachting season begins on the last Sunday in April. Highlights include the Memorial Day Regatta in May, the Pacific Interclub Yachting Association Regatta over the third weekend in July and the St Francis International Masters Regatta which closes the season at the end of October.

KITES
San Franciscans are well versed in the art of flying kites and are fond of making them dance over Ocean Beach and Marina Green. The most popular sport involves making kites controlled with two lines perform precision acrobatics. There is a large kite shop, *Go Fly a Kite*, on Fisherman's Wharf. It was opened in the 1970's by Dinesh Bahadur, who came from Ahmadabad (India), where the largest annual international kite-fighting event (between kites on a single string) is held. Every year, in September, there is a kite festival on Ocean Beach.

The bay and ocean are perfect for surfing and windsurfing. Regular competitions are held.

The Bud Surf Tour, which has taken place for the last six years on Ocean Beach during the second week in October, is the most important event of the year for surfers and bodyboarders.

AMERICAN FOOTBALL

The twenty-eight professional teams in the US are divided between two conferences: the National Football Conference in which the Forty-Niners play (opposite, Roger Craig, one of their players), and the American Football Conference. The season runs from September to December, and there are sixteen games. Play-off games lead to the Super Bowl (at the end of January), set up in 1967.

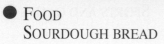

"Sourdough" bread first appeared in California at the time of the Gold Rush. According to some, it originated in the Basque country in France, while others claim that it was imported by a French pastrycook. It was popular with the gold-miners, who would take the precious leaven into the Sierra, ensuring they always had the necessary ingredients for the life-saving bread, which already held pride of place on San Franciscan tables.

THE LEAVEN
¾ cup semi-skimmed milk, 3 tbsp fat-free yoghurt, 1 cup flour.

1. Warm the milk, then remove from the heat and add the yoghurt. Pour the mixture into an insulated container and cover.

2. Leave to stand in a warm place (75° to 100°F/27° to 38°C) for six to eight hours. The mixture is ready when it is frothy and has formed thick milk curds. If a clear liquid has settled on the surface, stir again. If the mixture has turned pinkish it should be discarded.

3. Once the milk curds have formed, blend in the flour to obtain a smooth paste. Leave to stand in a warm place for two to five days until there are bubbles in the mixture and it gives off a distinctly sharp smell.

DOUGH FOR MAKING BREAD
1 cup warm water, ¾ cup leaven, 3 cups plain flour, 1 tbsp salt, 2 tbsp cornflour.

1. Mix the water, the leaven and 1 cup of the flour in a large container to obtain a smooth dough. Cover with food wrap and leave to rise overnight. The dough will thicken and become spongy.

2. Add the salt and remaining flour, and stir until the dough is firm but easy to handle. Lightly flour a pastry board and knead the dough for one or two minutes. Then leave to rest for ten minutes.

5. Put the cornflour on some waxed paper and place the bread on top. Cover with a cloth without pressing the bread. Leave the bread to rise until it has doubled in size. Pre-heat the oven (375°F/190°C/Gas Mark 5).

6. With a razor blade or sharp knife make a cut ½" deep in the top of the bread, then spray the bread with cold water. Place in the oven and leave to cook for ten minutes, then spray again with cold water. Repeat this procedure once more. Cook for a further forty minutes (total cooking time is one hour). Place the bread on a baking sheet and leave to cool.

ACME BREAD

COMPANY EST·1983
2730 9TH ST. AT PARDEE BERKELEY CA 94710

"BOUDIN BAKERY"
Isidore Boudin, a French pastrycook who emigrated to San Francisco at the time of the Gold Rush, was, so the story goes, the first to sell this famous sour-tasting bread, which is an integral part of the San Francisco experience. The firm still produces sourdough bread. The other large company that specializes in baking it is Acme Bread.

3. Again knead the dough for ten minutes, until it becomes elastic in consistency. Add flour as required to prevent it from sticking. Place in a greased container, cover and leave the dough to rise until it has doubled in size.

4. Flatten the dough by slapping with the palm of your hand and knead it. Shape it into a ball.

The bread has a thick, crusty exterior with a soft inside, and has a slightly sharp flavor.

Some Dungeness crab is caught in the bay ◆ *22*, along with shrimp and prawn. Abalone has been scarce for some thirty years and fishing for it is subject to strict regulations. These crustaceans account for some $60 million every year in California.

MARKET-GARDEN PRODUCE

California is the largest fruit and vegetable producer in the United States. Furthermore, the San Francisco Bay Area is the foremost American market for organically grown food. The Californian organic farmers are grouped under the umbrella label CCOF (California Certified Organic Farmers), which guarantees that no pesticides or chemical fertilizers are used on the crops. The farmers produce 2 percent of America's organic fruit and vegetables.

"Molinari" salami and traditional "Vella" cheese are products of Italian influence.

CALIFORNIA WINE ■ *38*, ◆ *341*
California produces about 90 percent of US wine. Half of its eight-hundred vineyards can be found in the Napa and Sonoma valleys.

BEER
The Anchor Brewing Company, which was founded in San Francisco, is one of the largest and oldest American micro breweries.

"GHIRARDELLI" CHOCOLATE ▲ *176*. Son of a famous Italian chocolate maker, Domenico Ghirardelli settled in San Francisco in 1852 and opened his chocolate shop on the waterfront. His classic chocolate is still produced.

"FORTUNE COOKIES" ▲ *263*
Although the Chinese adopted these rice cakes with their lucky message inside, the recipe was perfected in San Francisco in 1894 by a Japanese cook.

ARCHITECTURE

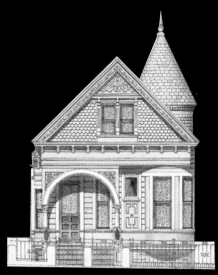

The Spanish, who occupied the San Francisco Bay Area between 1776 and 1821, established various missions there. These were Franciscan communities arranged around a cloister, a "presidio" (military fort), and "pueblos" (villages built by the settlers). In all these cases, the buildings were usually adobe structures with one or two floors. The "provincial" character of these missions, often left derelict after their secularization around 1833 fired the imagination of Californian architects at the end of the 19th century. The Franciscan buildings were the inspiration for the simple forms of the Mission Revival style, which were enhanced by curved, pedimented gables, whitewashed walls with high arches, and low, sloping red tile roofs. This style reached the peak of its popularity between 1905 and 1915, and subsequently spread throughout the United States.

THE LAYOUT OF A MISSION
The missions were active centers where Indians were converted, then baptized and set to work at agricultural tasks. Mission Dolores, like the others, comprised a group of buildings including a church and an adjoining cloister, where the Franciscans lived, a cemetery, and also gardens, fields, farm buildings (stables, cowsheds, barns etc.), many workshops and the Indians' huts.

THE "MISSION REVIVAL" STYLE: BURLINGAME STATION

Built in 1894, the station at Burlingame, a residential area on the bay, is one of the earliest examples of the Mission Revival style. This style, which was part of a more general quest for regional identity, was born out of the State of California's efforts to promote tourism and urbanization. In the early 20th century it was used for public buildings, in particular schools and libraries, as well as hotels and private residences.

ADOBE
This Mexican bricklaying technique, using bricks made of mud mixed with straw and dried in the sun, was brought to California by the Spanish. Once the walls had been built of this material, they were whitewashed.

SECTION OF AN ADOBE BUILDING
During the Mexican period ranches (used for cattle-rearing) could cover up to 50,000 acres. This sectional plan shows the construction and layout of the covered buildings that stood at the center of these vast properties.

"MISION SAN FRANCISCO DE ASIS" MISSION DOLORES (1782–91)
Mission Dolores ▲ *294* is the oldest building in the Bay Area and the only surviving Spanish structure in San Francisco. The monastery and the barn have unfortunately been demolished. The church, with its adobe walls over 3 feet thick, was restored in 1920 by the architect Willis Polk. The façade is topped by a roof with projecting eaves, crowned in turn by a modest cross, and is flanked by two sets of columns. The bells are housed in openings in the gable.

MISSION REVIVAL STYLE CAMPANILE
The campanile at Mills College, inspired by the bell towers of the early missions, was built in 1904 from plans drawn up by Julia Morgan, the first woman to graduate from the Ecole des Beaux-Arts in Paris. It is an early example of the use of reinforced concrete, which was a new material at the time.

THE "INSTANT CITY"

San Francisco took its nickname, the "Instant City", from its swift growth: in the space of just three months, the news that gold had been discovered in California transformed this village of a few hundred people into a city of several thousand. The new built-up area spread over a vast tract of unoccupied land in the checkerboard layout that was then popular in the United States. Although this system facilitated the division, sale and registration of plots of land, it took no account of the topography of the area. The "grid" of blocks was imposed on the hilly terrain, systematically demarcating the boundaries of land for building sites and creating roads with precipitous gradients – one of the attractive features of San Francisco today.

VERDANT HEIGHTS
The hilltop slopes, which were sometimes extremely steep, were initially parceled out for poor families. Because of the modest price of this land, several parks (Lafayette Park, Alamo Square and Pioneer Park) were created on the upper slopes. Once connected up by the cable car, these green and spacious areas became the home of more wealthy families.

ABANDONED SHIPS
In 1849 a number of ships were abandoned in the marshy cove of Yerba Buena by their crews, who had caught the "gold fever". In response to the shortage of building materials and the need to find accommodation for an ever-expanding population, pontoons were built out to these ships, which were refurbished and converted into shops, restaurants and hotels.

> "HERE [IN PRIENNE] THE SITE ... SEEMS ... TO HAVE BEEN DEVELOPED WITHOUT THE LEAST REGARD FOR ITS ORIGINAL CHARACTER, AND A CHECKERBOARD LAYOUT HAS BEEN IMPOSED ON IT EVEN THOUGH THE STEEPNESS OF THE LAND WORKS AGAINST IT."
>
> M. POËTE, 1926

A GRID SYSTEM DIVIDED INTO PLOTS

Each block to the north of Market Street was divided into plots of land approximately 26 feet by 98 feet. This completely abstract grid system took no account of the constraints imposed by the hilly terrain. As a result, the steepest slopes had to be provided with stairways rather than paved streets.

THE CHECKERBOARD LAYOUT OF AMERICAN CITIES.

Comprising no more than a few blocks around the *plaza* (now Portsmouth Square) of the *pueblo* of Yerba Buena, the first plan of San Francisco was drawn up in 1839, at the request of the Mexican authorities, by the Swiss navigator Jean-Jacques Vioget. In 1847 Jasper O'Farrell expanded Vioget's 12-square block platting. Also based on Spanish units of measurement, his plan drew Market Street and provided for fifty residential blocks to the north and laid out some larger blocks to the south to accommodate expected industrial expansion. This inflexible layout of streets intersecting at right angles was based on the typical blueprint for American cities.

BUILT ON RUBBLE

The cove at Yerba Buena was gradually filled with rubble from the hills, where houses were mushrooming. Houses were then built on this landfill, and boats that had run aground on the mud soon found themselves surrounded by buildings. This is how a large part of what is now "Downtown" was reclaimed from the bay.

San Francisco is famous for its wooden houses, dating from between 1860 and 1900, with their brightly colored, highly decorated façades. Inspired by the rows of private terraced houses in London, they were often prefabricated and mass-produced by specialist firms such as the Real Estate Associates, who in 1875 delivered 350 of them in a single year. The houses had every modern convenience then available: electric lighting, central heating, running water and plumbing. In order to build them, the abundant forests of redwoods that once grew in the Bay Area were practically razed to the ground.

DESIGNED FOR PRIVACY
Victorian houses were built overlooking the street on plots of land 26 feet wide by 98 feet long. Each individual room, devoted to a different activity, opened off a side corridor in order to preserve the sacrosanct principle of privacy: on the ground floor were the reception room, music room, dining room and kitchen; the bedrooms, on the first floor up, shared the same layout. The wooden structure made it possible to create a variety of forms and detailing based on a relatively standard plan.

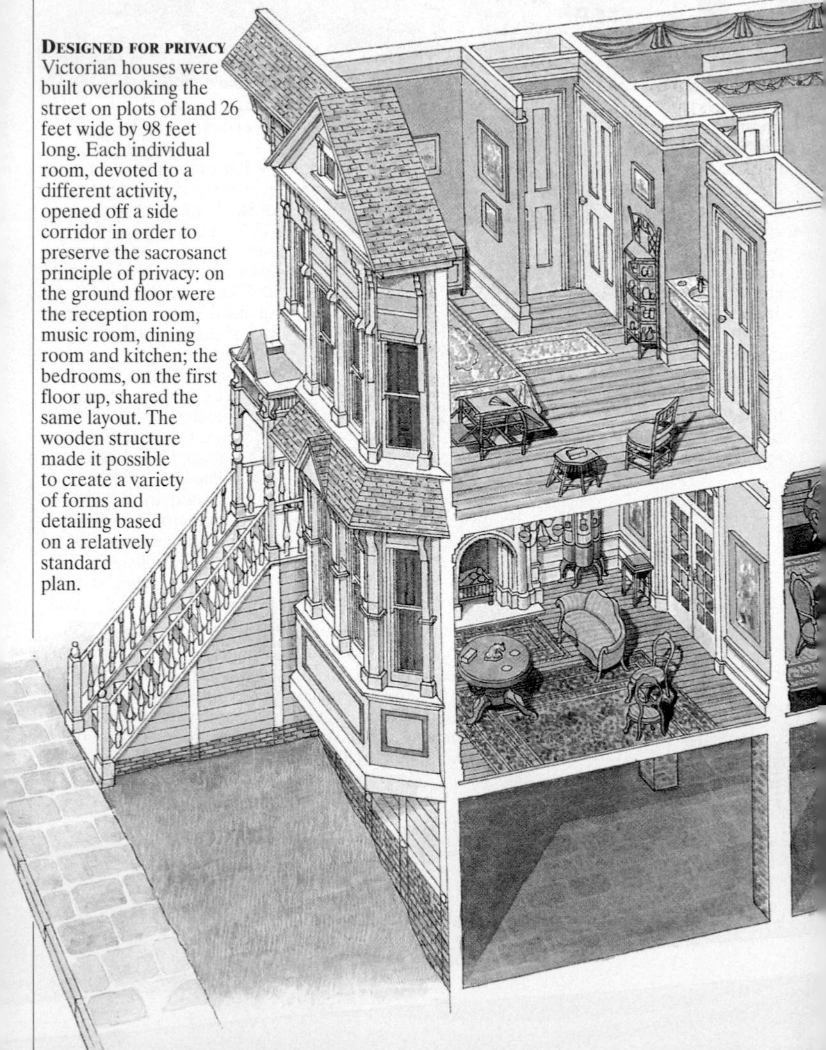

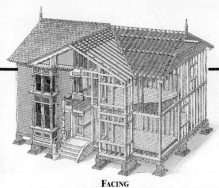

FACING
The planks used to cover the "balloon frame" ensured better protection against the rain.

"BALLOON FRAME"

The development of the "balloon frame" (a derisive nickname given to this light structure by traditional carpenters) coincided with the introduction of the mechanical saw and mass machine production of nails. This flexible frame, invented by G. Washington Snow in the 1830's, was well suited to earthquakes. Only the rigid sections (brick supports) made it vulnerable.

WINDOWS
Leaded-glass, plate-glass, beveled and engraved windows were all factory-produced.

SIGNS OF WEALTH
The quality of reception room furniture and the decoration of the façade were indications of the owner's social status.

PERIOD PATTERNS
Hearths and built-in cupboards in certain rooms often picked up the decorative motifs on the façade.

Although the layout, structure and materials for San Francisco's Victorian houses remained virtually unchanged throughout the 19th century, their decoration underwent several stylistic transformations. San Francisco houses were more elaborately ornamented than elsewhere, the plethora of styles reflecting a thriving society and the wealth of the middle classes, as well as fierce competition within the building industry and the carpenters' expertise. At the beginning of the 20th century styles became more subtle as society stabilized. Despite the havoc wreaked by the fires of the 1906 earthquake, a great number of these houses are still standing today. Visitors can therefore see for themselves that the stylistic diversity is restricted to the façades and that, more often than not, the houses were decorated in a composite style based on a range of standard designs.

"QUEEN ANNE"

The Queen Anne houses of San Francisco, in vogue during the 1890's, have nothing in common with houses built in England during Queen Anne's reign or with the "Queen Anne" style houses built elsewhere. Those in San Francisco displayed as much variety and imagination as the "Eastlake" houses, and their inventiveness was apparent in the overall, asymmetrical use of form as well as the details of ornamentation. These

houses had pointed roofs and, often, towers and turrets. The sumptuous decoration of the façades included "Eastlake" elements, as well as more sober traditional details such as shingles and logs.

DECORATIVE WOODWORK

The new steam-operated woodworking machines resulted in more varied ornamental work. Jigsaws and scroll-saws could cut two-dimensional shapes, while lathes could

fashion three-dimensional elements, for example, the balusters of a spiral staircase. These decorative forms were hand-finished before being attached to the outer walls of houses. They were mass-produced and used in various ways on an array of façades to achieve different effects. Major contractors owned their own factories where these ornamental details could be manufactured as cheaply as possible.

ITALIANATE STYLE

Rows of houses in the style of Italian villas first flourished in the elegant suburbs of eastern America.

They are characterized by the Italian Renaissance detailing of their cornices and of their window and door frames. A certain number of these

houses had bay windows. Many were built in San Francisco between the late 1860's and the early 1880's.

"EASTLAKE" STYLE

This style, peculiar to San Francisco, was very popular in the 1880's. Its distinctive feature is the inventive design and composition of its façades. The name comes from Charles Eastlake, a British furniture designer, and, unlike other styles, it did not claim inspiration from any particular historical trend. The resulting structures were a showcase for the work of various individual designers and some skilled carpenters. The example seen here, with its square bay windows, is a semi-detached house.

GOTHIC REVIVAL

This term may of course be applied to buildings with quite obvious Gothic features, but it can also describe small, very simple houses with only a few elements reminiscent of that style.

In 1893 the International Exhibition in Chicago sanctioned a return to the architectural language of classical antiquity and the Renaissance, in line with the principles propounded by the Ecole des Beaux-Arts in Paris. San Francisco was attracted by the "City Beautiful" movement, whose vision reflected the city's dreams of wealth and power. In the center of town the classical trend made its mark primarily on business and civic premises, reaching its apogee, after the 1906 earthquake, with the Civic Center.

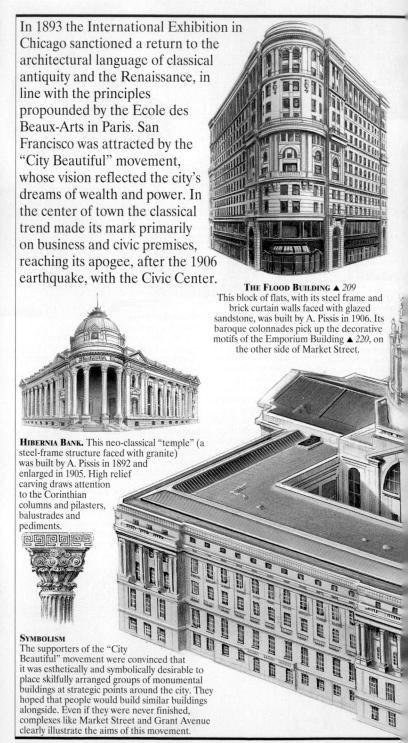

THE FLOOD BUILDING ▲ 209
This block of flats, with its steel frame and brick curtain walls faced with glazed sandstone, was built by A. Pissis in 1906. Its baroque colonnades pick up the decorative motifs of the Emporium Building ▲ 220, on the other side of Market Street.

HIBERNIA BANK. This neo-classical "temple" (a steel-frame structure faced with granite) was built by A. Pissis in 1892 and enlarged in 1905. High relief carving draws attention to the Corinthian columns and pilasters, balustrades and pediments.

SYMBOLISM
The supporters of the "City Beautiful" movement were convinced that it was esthetically and symbolically desirable to place skilfully arranged groups of monumental buildings at strategic points around the city. They hoped that people would build similar buildings alongside. Even if they were never finished, complexes like Market Street and Grant Avenue clearly illustrate the aims of this movement.

PALACE OF FINE ARTS ▲ *238*. Designed for the Panama Pacific Exhibition, this temporary structure was permanently reconstructed in concrete between 1964 and 1975. It is an octagonal rotunda linked to an exhibition hall by a semicircular Corinthian peristyle. Maybeck, who was inspired by Piranesi, intended to create the illusion of a classical building half overgrown with trees and bushes.

FAIRMONT HOTEL ▲ *192*. The interior of the hotel was destroyed in the 1906 fire and had to be completely rebuilt. The refurbishment was handled by Julia Morgan. Its monumental proportions and the overwhelming impression of opulence created by its off-white glazed faïence façades illustrate the notion of the grand hotel as the ideal setting for society.

CITY HALL ▲ *226*. In 1912 the local council commissioned the building of a civic center. The architects J.G. Howard, F. Meyer, and J. Reid Jr put forward the idea of an esplanade lined with monumental buildings and dominated by the City Hall. This white granite building, designed by J. Bakewell Jr and A. Brown Jr, former pupils at the Ecole des Beaux-Arts in Paris, was finished in 1916. The high drum, with its columns, and the dome topped with a lantern were inspired directly by Jules-Hardouin Mansart's chapel at the Hôtel des Invalides. This cupola houses a large lobby decorated in neo-classical style.

Around 1900 young architects adopted the ideals of the East
Coast Shingle style and of the British Arts and Crafts movement.
Freely interpreting their forms to build modestly sized houses,
they created the Bay Area tradition. This style was characterized
by the simple layout of the houses, the use of redwood as the
main building material, the juxtaposition of local
decorative motifs with classical or Gothic
elements, and the deliberate
contrasting of different scales in
ornament, and of external masses
and inner spaces.

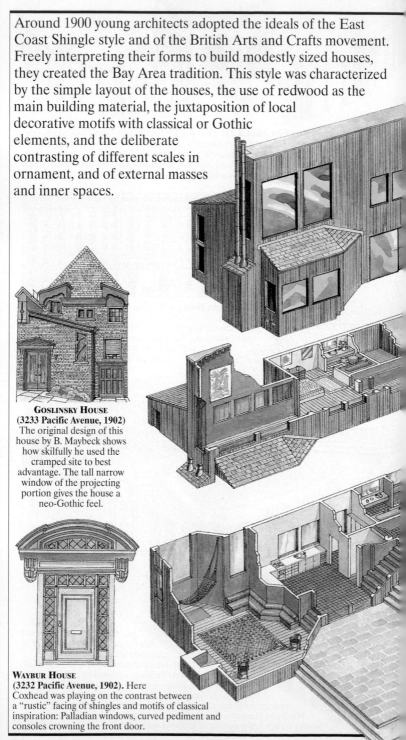

GOSLINSKY HOUSE
(3233 Pacific Avenue, 1902)
The original design of this
house by B. Maybeck shows
how skilfully he used the
cramped site to best
advantage. The tall narrow
window of the projecting
portion gives the house a
neo-Gothic feel.

WAYBUR HOUSE
(3232 Pacific Avenue, 1902). Here
Coxhead was playing on the contrast between
a "rustic" facing of shingles and motifs of classical
inspiration: Palladian windows, curved pediment and
consoles crowning the front door.

Architects inspired by the Bay Area style include
B. Maybeck, W. Polk, E. Coxhead and J. Morgan between
1890 and 1910; W. Wurster, J. Esherick and G.
Dailey between 1930 and 1950; C. Moore,
W. Turnbull and C.W. Callister between
1960 and 1980; and, lastly, D. Solomon,
the Ace group and J. Kotas today.

SEA RANCH
C. Moore designed the houses on this
6,180-acre site in 1964 after a town
planning survey
by Lawrence
Halprin.

It stands on a stretch of
coast north of the city that
was cleared of trees in the
19th century.

The architects had to conform
to extremely rigorous design
constraints in order to preserve
the untamed character of the
site: the predominant use of
redwood, for example. Small
residential blocks were
designed in such a way as to
avoid the monotonous
appearance of traditional
housing estates. Condominium
1 is composed of ten dwellings,
the size and vertical plank
facing of which resemble
those of neighboring
barns.

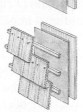

"SHINGLE" STYLE
The "balloon frame"
was covered with
tarred brown paper,
then with rows of
laths onto which
shingles (varying
lengths of redwood)
or weatherboards
were nailed.

GREGORY-INGRAHAM
HOUSE
(140 Laidley Street).
The layout, dimensions
and height of this
house, designed by
Shaffer and Kotas in
1989, are a free
interpretation of the
architectural
conventions of
terraced houses.

AN OPEN SPACE
Steeply sloping roofs
cover the vast areas of
the living rooms. Charles
Moore and his team designed
open spaces, flooded with light
from huge bay windows, that amply
mirror the spirit of the Bay Area
tradition, a style designed to appeal
primarily to the well-off middle classes in
search of a healthy, relaxed lifestyle.

● EARTHQUAKE-RESISTANT TECHNIQUES

The devastating fires and violent earth tremors that hit San Francisco between 1850 and 1860 swiftly prompted legislators and architects to concentrate on safety measures. At that point, however, no-one could have foreseen the enormity of the 1906 catastrophe. The program of reconstruction work that followed was characterized by the use of new materials (reinforced concrete and steel). Despite the institution of rigorous guidelines and the continual improvement of construction techniques throughout the 20th century, the earthquake of 1989 damaged or destroyed many modern buildings, although those conforming to current standards fared best. Further lessons have since been learned about the use of roofing materials and the dangers of some plant materials, such as eucalyptus.

BRICKS AND IRON SHUTTERS
Following the fires that devastated San Francisco at the time of the Gold Rush, a law was passed stipulating that brick was to be used for buildings in the business district. Attaching metal shutters and safety curtains to windows and shopfronts increased the buildings' resistance to fire.

BRICK AND IRON
The seven floors of the Palace Hotel, built in 1873 ▲ *216*, were made of brick reinforced with bond iron. The hotel survived the earthquake, while City Hall, similar in design but built from substandard materials, was devastated. The steel frame of its tall tower collapsed onto the body of the main building, and flames spread through the rubble.

REINFORCED CONCRETE
In 1906 the dramatic powers of resistance demonstrated by structures built of reinforced concrete resulted in a repeal of laws that had previously restricted the use of this new material. For the first time concrete was used on a large scale, but care was taken to cover façades with stucco or terracotta so as not to spoil the appearance of the buildings. Ernest Ransome, an English immigrant, was the first to exploit the potential of this material, in particular using cold-twisted square-cut iron rods.

BERNARD MAYBECK'S EXPERIMENTS
This architect attached great importance to residential safety measures and he tested a whole spectrum of building materials and techniques. The Lawson House (1515 Laloma Street in Berkeley), completed in 1907, was made of beton brut; the First Church of Christ Scientist (1910, Berkeley) was covered with asbestos-cement boards; and the "Sack-house" at 2711 Buena Vista Way (1924), also in Berkeley, was built of air-entrained concrete covered in sackcloth hardened by cement.

City Hall after the great fire of 1906.

METAL FRAMES

It was the more recent office blocks, built using fireproof materials (reinforced concrete, brick and glazed faïence) on a metal frame, that were best able to resist the fires of 1906. Although in general the flames gutted the interior, the framework survived. As a result, plans for several office blocks in the process of being built, such as the Humboldt Bank, were revised, and the structural elements reinforced.

US GEOLOGICAL SURVEY BUILDING

The steel girders that cover the façade of this reinforced concrete building have a decorative function as well as offering protection against earthquakes.

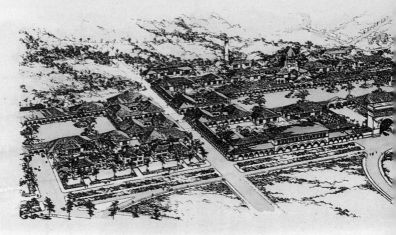

The campus, a specifically American institution, is where university students and professors live and work. The campus may be built in open countryside at some distance from the city, creating a form of academic village; it may sprawl close to the city, surrounded by a residential suburb that has grown with it; or it may be built within the city and contribute to the urban architectural fabric. Stanford University is a complex of impressive buildings in open countryside, while Berkeley is a suburban campus with its own university suburb.

BERKELEY, "NEW ATHENS OF THE WEST" ▲ *320*
In 1895 it was decided to refurbish the campus to make Berkeley the largest university center in the West. The new campus, characterized by monumental buildings lining roads as straight as a die, forms a vast neo-classical composition in the spirit of the "City Beautiful" movement. It is dominated by SATHER TOWER (1914, ▲ *322*), which is modeled on the campanile in the Piazza San Marco in Venice; it houses an observatory and a carillon.

SOUTH HALL ▲ *320*
This red-brick building, in Second Empire style with a Mansart-style roof, was designed by David Farqharson. It is all that survives of the first campus, founded in 1868.

THE 1888 PLAN
Built in the open countryside, Stanford University was reached by a long central walk through a forest of eucalyptus trees. Designed by Frederick Law Olmsted, the landscaped gardens that surround the campus reflect California's very dry natural setting, which is further emphasized by plantations of palm trees.

STANFORD UNIVERSITY, THE "SPIRIT OF CALIFORNIA" ◆ *352*
On the death of his only son, Leland Stanford ▲ *188* decided to devote his huge fortune to building a university. The architectural aim of this project, realized in 1891 by Shepley, Ruan and Coolidge, was to help develop further a truly Californian style: the buildings, made of local sandstone with red-tile roofs, were arranged around arcaded courtyards, after the fashion of the Californian missions. A triumphal arch and a church topped with an impressive bell tower stand on the main thoroughfare of the complex.

A TRIUMPHAL ENTRANCE
The triumphal arch that marks the entrance to the Stanford campus ◆ *352* is decorated with a sculpted frieze entitled *Civilization on the March*, depicting the Aztecs and the Incas, Pizarro and Cortés and, in the center, Leland and Jane Stanford on horseback in the Sierra Nevada, followed by a locomotive.

STANFORD MEMORIAL CHURCH
The church was largely rebuilt after the 1906 earthquake (and restored after the one in 1989). With its decorative mosaics, it remains a stunning example of 1890's architecture.

EARLY SKYSCRAPERS

The elevator doors of the Medical-Dental Office Building (450 Sutter St) have Mayan-style decorations.

The growing need to build office blocks within a confined area led to the advent of the skyscraper: at the end of the 1870's in New York and Chicago, and ten years later in San Francisco. These "giant houses", which astounded European travelers, met the aspirations and new requirements of American business. Their construction was made possible by the invention of the elevator and of a strong metal frame that was lighter than traditional masonry. The high cost of land, which forced the financial districts to expand upwards, went hand in hand with a fiercely competitive spirit that saw skyscrapers as a way of emblazoning the name of a businessman or company against the sky.

THE INFLUENCE OF THE CHICAGO SCHOOL

The Mills Building ▲ *214*, commissioned in 1890 from Daniel Burnham, is now the oldest skyscraper in San Francisco. The shape of this ten-story office block was influenced by the Chicago School. The tripartite composition of its brick-covered façades is borrowed from that of the classical column (base, shaft and capital). The neo-Roman decoration of the central part of the main building and of the entrance reflects the fashion launched on the East Coast by the architect Henry Hobson Richardson.

HUMBOLDT BANK BUILDING
(783–5 Market Street)
This building which was under construction in 1906, was demolished then rebuilt applying the lessons learned from the City Hall disaster. The ground floor is made of sandstone and the rest of the façade is faced with glazed faïence.

PACIFIC TELEPHONE AND TELEGRAPH CO.▲ *286*

Twenty-six stories high (buildings grew markedly taller from the 1920's), the L-shaped tower has a façade of pale gray glazed faïence, imitating granite. The concentration of decorative work on the ground floor and upper stories accentuates the sense of verticality. On the parapets, the embedded colonettes open out into stylized lotus leaves. The carved eagles are replicas of the original ornaments, which were removed around 1950 for fear they might crash to the ground in the event of an earthquake. The block has been recently restored. Its entrance hall (open to the public) is particularly noteworthy with its dark marble décor and its ceiling patterned with motifs of Chinese inspiration.

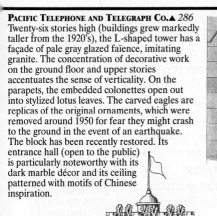

NEO-GOTHIC
The Russ Building is an imposing edifice with a metal frame (1927). Its E-shaped structure allows all the offices to benefit from natural light and adequate ventilation. The Gothic-style ornaments are made of molded, glazed terracotta.

A STEPPED SKYSCRAPER
In San Francisco, as in other American cities, the telephone companies opted for the new fashion of stepped skyscrapers for their head offices. This trend started in New York after regulations passed in 1916 stipulated the use of successive offsets in order to prevent the streets of Manhattan from being plunged into shadow.

After an interval of almost three decades due to economic depression and World War Two, the construction of office blocks was resumed in the 1960's. At the same time ambitious renovation programs were undertaken, and the San Francisco skyline saw the arrival of an escalating number of towers. Skyscrapers were usually placed in the center of wide esplanades, which varied the regularity of the city layout but often created a windy environment and were rather unattractive. In 1985, to curb the anarchic proliferation of such towers, San Francisco approved the Downtown Plan, which restricted the height and size of commercial office blocks in the city center and insisted on an in-depth investigation of all new projects.

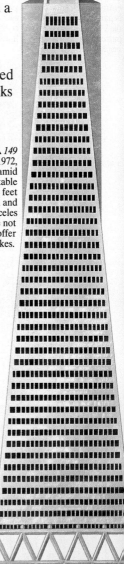

ALCOA BUILDING. Designed in 1964 by Skidmore, Owings and Merrill, this skyscraper was the first to display conspicuous cross-bracing. The steel girders covered in anodized aluminum were superimposed on the curtain wall, crisscrossing the entire façade and providing the only form of decoration.

TRANSAMERICA PYRAMID ▲ 149 Designed by W. Pereira in 1972, this 853-feet-high pyramid contains fifty-three habitable stories capped by a spire, 220 feet tall, housing the ventilation and heating machinery. The isosceles tetrahedrons of the base are not only decorative, but also offer protection against earthquakes.

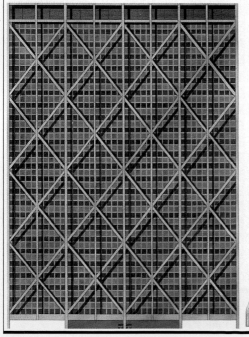

The skyline of San Francisco.

EMBARCADERO CENTER ▲ *207*
This complex, which contains the Hyatt Regency Hotel, was designed by John Portman Jr and Associates (1971–81). Distinctive features include the setback design of its four towers and the successful marriage between office space and commercial outlets (the first three tiers of each tower are occupied by shopping arcades).

345 CALIFORNIA STREET
This post-modern tower ▲ *210*, built in 1986 to plans by Skidmore, Owings and Merrill, is one of the tallest in the city. It was constructed at the center of a block so as not to mar the appearance of the historic buildings nearby. The ground floor and lower stories contain arcades and shops; the middle part of the building houses offices and there is a hotel at the top.

CROWN ZELLERBACH BUILDING ▲ *217*
Instead of being installed in the body of this eighteen-story building (1959), the elevators have been placed in a transverse wing, the dark mosaic facing of which can be seen clearly through the glass walls of the office areas.

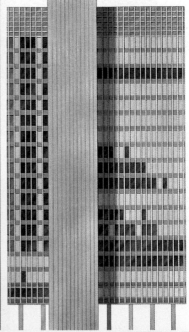

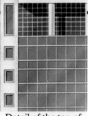

Detail of the top of the American President Lines Building.

Recent building in the Oakland, San Francisco and San Jose areas has been of special interest in terms of town planning. In effect the policy has been to give priority to quality in everything to do with new construction. This concern is evident in the prototype residential projects submitted by Dan Solomon; other examples are the office buildings that have appeared in the city since 1986, the renovation works carried out in many neighborhoods, and the new premises currently under construction for the San Francisco Public Library.

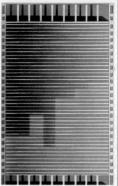

AMERICAN PRESIDENT LINES BUILDING, OAKLAND ▲ *306*
Completed in 1991 by Gensler & Associates in collaboration with Richard Deutsch, it sits between two landscaped areas adorned with sculptures.

SAN FRANCISCO PUBLIC LIBRARY
In the accepted plans for the new Public Library, the building presents its traditional façades to the City Hall and its neighbor, the former library, while on Market Street it sports a modern façade that mirrors its internal layout. The triangular light well is a courtyard one floor deep.

CHILDREN'S MUSEUM, SAN JOSE
Built in 1991, from plans by Ricardo Legoretta, this building is characterized by the bold colors of its stucco walls and the simplicity of its geometric masses. It is situated in landscaped grounds with attractive expanses of water.

SAN FRANCISCO
AS SEEN BY PAINTERS

Most 19th-century Californian painters devoted themselves to illustrating the splendors of nature, which were a favorite subject at the time ▲ *316*. During the 1860's several painters from the East painted the Californian landscape: Albert Bierstadt, Virgil Williams, William Keith and Thomas Hill (1829–1908) (3).

The bay, one of San Francisco's most distinctive features, inspired several painters. Thomas Hill produced a number of views, including *The Golden Gate from Point Lobos* (1872) (2). Influenced by German Romanticism and the French Barbizon School, he used a palette of delicate hues. Though admired by his contemporaries, he was consigned to oblivion after his death when his majestic landscapes ceased to be fashionable. In 1887 Percy Gray (1869–1952), a native San Franciscan, painted *The Golden Gate and Fort Point* (1) in a style that was relatively naïve and sparing of detail. Gray subsequently concentrated on painting watercolors of the green, flowery landscapes of northern California ▲ *327*.

"Far to the westward opened the Golden Gate, a bleak cutting in the sand-hills, through which one caught a glimpse of the open Pacific."

Frank Norris

Sansome Street, one of San Francisco's oldest streets, was teeming with activity when William Hahn (1829-87) painted his *Market Scene on Sansome Street* (1) in 1872. Born and educated in Germany, where he attended the art academies of Düsseldorf and Dresden, William Hahn emigrated to the United States in 1871. This genre painting was very popular with his contemporaries and was praised by critics of the period. The composition, which is full of details about life in San Francisco in 1872, was influenced by German genre scenes. A friend of the painter William Keith, Hahn was one of the first members of the Bohemian Club ▲ *222* and for a short time presided over the San Francisco Art Association (which became the Mark Hopkins Association in 1893, and the San Francisco Art Institute in 1963 ▲ *199*). This work, bought by Judge Crocker for $2,500, is now exhibited at the Crocker Art Gallery in Sacramento. The *View of Howard Street in the Fog* (2), painted around 1860 by the Mexican painter Fortunato Arriola (1827–72), is in marked contrast to the rest of his work: he specialized in tropical scenes. Having gone back to live in Mexico after his first visit to San Francisco, he returned to settle for good in the Bay Area in 1862. Fascinated throughout his life by the play of light the painter here creates an image in which the translucency of the fog is conveyed by a masterly use of back-lighting. Clarkson Dye (1869–1955) painted *View from my Window* (3) in 1905. Born in San Francisco, Dye spent his entire life in California, dividing his time between San Francisco and Santa Barbara, although commissions for decorative murals took him to Mexico and Texas from time to time. This view of the bay is somewhat reminiscent of the panels depicting tourist spots that used to adorn the dining rooms of large hotels at the turn of the century.

1

2	3

The exoticism of Chinatown ▲ *152*, with its "multicolored façades, up-tilted roofs, gilt decoration, greenish animal entrails, baskets of dusty fruit and mysterious spices" (Jules Huret, 1910), was another source of inspiration for San Franciscan painters. Although painted by different artists at different times, these three paintings are curiously similar in technique because of both their Fauvist colors and their Impressionist touch. *Sacks, Bottle and Rags* (2) by Jules Pagès (1867–1946), painted in the 1920's, conjures up a contemporary scene in the early 20th century. The title of this work refers to the shouts of rag-and-bone men, who scoured the streets with their carts salvaging scrap. Born in San Francisco, and a pupil at the School of Design, Jules Pagès left for Paris in 1888 to study at the Académie Julian, where he gained a fair measure of renown. He returned there in 1912 to teach, acting as director for a while. Influenced by French naturalism, he was primarily interested in scenes of everyday life. Henry Nappenbach (1862–1931) painted this alley in *Chinatown* (3) in 1906, a few months before the earthquake that devastated the area. Around the same time Gordon Coutts (1868–1937) painted this very similar street scene in *Chinatown* (1).

1	2
	3

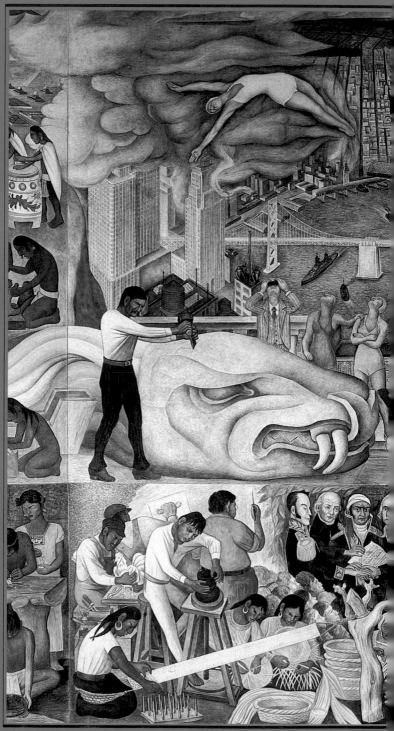

"I HAVE BEEN HAUNTED BY A PRESENCE IN THE AIR, AN AUTUMNAL DUSTING OF GOLD, A SHIMMERING BRIGHTNESS WHICH PIERCED ME TO THE CORE AND THE SADNESS OF COMING TO THE END OF AMERICA."

W. PERCY

Influenced for a while by Cubism, the Mexican painter Diego Rivera (1886–1957) found his true vocation in mural painting, especially after a trip to Italy where he admired the frescos by Giotto and Cimabue. When he returned to Mexico, he became one of the founding fathers, with José Clemente Orozco and David Alfaro Siqueiros, of Mexican muralism, a heroic genre with both a decorative and a didactic function. In 1931 Rivera and his wife, the painter Frida Kahlo, left for San Francisco, where Rivera painted several murals. He then visited Detroit in 1932 and New York in 1933. He did not return to San Francisco until 1940, when he painted, for the International Golden Gate Exhibition ▲ *306*, the huge fresco for City College (22 feet by 80 feet), composed of ten sections, and known as the *Panamerican Mural.* The aim of this fresco was to use the evolution of history to demonstrate artistic unity between the North and South of the continent. The detail shows the Oakland Bay Bridge surrounded by several famous figures and symbols. Rivera had a profound influence on American painters, as much for his fresco technique as for his choice of historical and social subjects, especially during the great Depression of the 1930's ▲ *171*.

B orn in Sacramento, Otis Oldfield (1890–1969) trained as an artist in San Francisco, then left for France in 1911. The painter gained a certain notoriety in Paris, where he lived until 1924. When he returned to California, he joined the colony of artists who revolved around the San Francisco Art Center. This canvas, *Telegraph Hill*, exhibited at the Gallery of Fine Arts in San Francisco in 1927, is a tender and poetic composition which captures the soul of the Italian quarter, known formerly as "Goat Hill" ▲ *169*. Oldfield depicts the activities of its inhabitants using a naïve style. The *San Francisco Daily Examiner* of November 6, 1927, carried an article by Jehanne Bietry Salinger, in which he wrote "This is born of years of observation, of a simple and comprehensive perception of this famous beauty spot in San Francisco, of a real passion for this place and of no less than five months' work. It is the most outstanding canvas Oldfield has painted to date. Many years after Telegraph Hill may have disappeared from the life of San Francisco, this painting will survive as a poetic and historic record." Oldfield (self-portrait above) occasionally joined forces with the muralists, including the leading figure of the movement, Rivera ● *119*, and was one of the thirty or so mural painters who in 1934 decorated Coit Tower ▲ *170*. His fresco took port activities as its theme.

SAN FRANCISCO
AS SEEN BY WRITERS

THE IDEAL BAY

Richard Henry Dana (1815–82), a product of the New England puritanical Protestant élite, broke off his law studies at Harvard in 1834 for health reasons and got a job as a common sailor on a trading ship bound for California. This initiatory voyage was to last two years and took him, among other places, to San Francisco in 1835, where he had his first sight of the magnificent bay. His enthusiastic account contributed to the East Coast's craze for California.

❝We sailed down this magnificent bay with a light wind, the tide, which was running out, carrying us at the rate of four or five knots. It was a fine day; the first of entire sunshine we had had for more than a month. We passed directly under the high cliff on which the presidio is built, and stood into the middle of the bay, from whence we could see small bays making up into the interior, large and beautifully wooded islands, and the mouths of several small rivers. If California ever becomes a prosperous country, this bay will be the centre of its prosperity. The abundance of wood and water; the extreme fertility of its shores; the excellence of its climate, which is as near to being perfect as any in the world; and its facilities for navigation affording the best anchoring-grounds in the whole western coast of America – all fit it for a place of great importance.❞

RICHARD HENRY DANA, *TWO YEARS BEFORE THE MAST*,
FIRST PUBLISHED 1840
DODD, MEAD & CO., NEW YORK 1946

GOLD

Blaise Cendrars (1887–1961), real name Frédéric Sauser, was born in La Chaux-de-Fonds, Switzerland. He arrived in the United States in 1909 and came to San Francisco, where he wrote his biography of General Sutter, the Swiss immigrant who founded an empire in California – Nueva Helvetica – only to see it confiscated in 1848 when gold was discovered. At a time when thousands of men were arriving from all over the world, attracted by the lure of the gold, Sutter died a ruined man.

❝There are Indian legends of an enchanted land – of towns built of gold, of women who have but one breast. Even the trappers who come down from the north with their bundles of pelts have heard tell in their high latitudes of marvelous lands in the West where trees are laden with apples of gold and pears of silver.... He has just come up the estuary in a canoe and has traversed the lake in a little pirogue with a triangular sail. He sets foot on land in front of a miserable mission station. A Franciscan monk, his teeth chattering with ague, opens its gate. ...He is at San Francisco. Fisher huts in baked clay. Bluc-skinned hogs that sprawl luxuriously in the sun. Meager sows suckling litters of a dozen shoats. This is the country Johann August Sutter has crossed a continent and an ocean to conquer. ...A chance blow by a pick, and all this vast mechanism is set in motion. Hordes fighting for the exit west. First, those from New York and the ports along the Atlantic seaboard. Immediately afterward, those from the interior and Middle West. It is a vast human watershed. The decks of steamers bound for Chagres are black with humanity. They cross the Isthmus, on foot, traverse marshes where nine in every ten perish of yellow fever. The remnant who reach the Pacific coast club together and charter sailing-vessels. ... In 1856 more than six hundred vessels enter the bay.❞

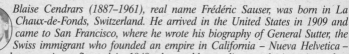

BLAISE CENDRARS, *SUTTER'S GOLD*,
TRANS. HENRY LONGAN STUART,
HARPER & BROTHERS, NEW YORK, 1926

Bayard Taylor (1825–78), born in Pennsylvania, was one of the most talented journalists of his day. Sent to San Francisco by the New York "Herald Tribune" to get to the bottom of the extraordinary stories that were being circulated about California, he was greeted, on his arrival in 1849, by a sight that beggared all description. He depicted the abrupt transformation of San Francisco brought about by the Gold Rush

❝When I landed there, a little more than four months before, I found a scattering town of tents and canvas houses, with a show of frame buildings on one or two streets, and a population of about six thousand. Now, on my last visit, I saw around

me an actual metropolis, displaying street after street of well-built edifices, filled with an active and enterprising people and exhibiting every mark of permanent commercial prosperity. Then, the town was limited to the curve of the Bay fronting the anchorage and bottoms of the hills. Now, it stretched to the topmost heights, followed the shore around point after point, and sending back a long arm through a gap in the hills, took hold of the Golden Gate and was building its warehouses on the open strait and almost fronting the blue horizon of the Pacific. Then the gold-seeking sojourner lodged in muslin rooms and canvas garrets, with a philosophic lack of furniture, and ate his simple though substantial fare from pine boards. Now, lofty hotels, gaudy with verandas and balconies were met with in all quarters, furnished with home luxury, and aristocratic restaurants presented daily their long bills of fare, rich with the choicest technicalities of the Parisian cuisine. Then, vessels were coming in day after day, to lie deserted and useless at their anchorage. Now scarce a day passed, but some cluster of sails, bound outward through the Golden Gate, took their way to all the corners of the Pacific.❞

BAYARD TAYLOR, *EL DORADO OR THE ADVENTURES IN THE PATH OF EMPIRE*, VOL. II, GEORGE P. PUTNAM, NEW YORK, 1850

THE NEW WORLD

The Scottish writer Robert Louis Stevenson (1850–94) is best known for "Treasure Island", which he imagined as being south of Monterey, at Point Lobos. His trip to California in 1879 marked a decisive turning point for Stevenson, allowing him to move away from the style of his past work and offering him new inspiration. On arriving through the Golden Gate, he exclaimed that he had found the "perfect bay", and he was overwhelmed by the landscape and the ethnic diversity of San Francisco.

❝Thus, in the course of a generation only, this city and its suburb have arisen. Men are alive by the score who have hunted all over the foundations in a dreary waste. I have dined, near the 'punctual centre' of San Francisco, with a gentleman (then newly married), who told me of his former pleasures, wading with his fowling-piece in sand and scrub, on the site of the house where we were dining. In this busy, moving generation, we have all known cities to cover our boyish playgrounds, we have all started for a country walk and stumbled on a new suburb; but I wonder what enchantment of the Arabian Nights can equal this evocation of a roaring city, in a few years of a man's life, from the marshes and the blowing sand. Such swiftness of increase, as with an overgrown youth, suggests a corresponding swiftness of destruction. The sandy peninsula of San Francisco, mirroring itself on one side in the bay, beaten on the other by the surge of the Pacific, and shaken to the heart by frequent earthquakes, seems in itself no very durable foundation. According to Indian tales, perhaps older than the name of California, it once rose out of the sea in a moment, and sometime or other shall, in a moment, sink again. No Indian, they say, cares to linger on that doubtful land. 'The earth hath bubbles as the water has, and these are of them.' Here, indeed, all is new, nature as well as towns. The very hills of California have an unfinished look; the rains and streams have not yet carved them to their perfect shape. The forests spring like mushrooms from the unexhausted soil; and they are mown down yearly by the forest fires. We are in early geological epochs, changeful and insecure, and we feel, as with a sculptor's model, that the author may yet grow weary of and shatter the rough sketch. Fancy apart, San Francisco is a city beleaguered with alarms. The lower parts, along the bay side, sit on piles; old wrecks decaying, fish dwelling unsunned, beneath the populous houses; and a trifling subsidence might drown the business quarters in an hour. Earthquakes are not only common, they are sometimes threatening in their violence; the fear of them grows yearly on a resident; he begins with indifference, ends in sheer panic; and no one feels safe in any but a wooden house. Hence it comes that, in that rainless clime, the whole city is built of timber – a woodyard of unusual extent and complication; that fires spring up readily, and served by the unwearying trade-wind, swiftly spread. ... Next, perhaps, in order of strangeness to the rapidity of its appearance, is the mingling of the races that combine to people it. The town is essentially not Anglo-Saxon; still more essentially not American. The Yankee and the Englishman find themselves alike in a strange country. ... The shops along the streets are like the consulates of different nations. The passers-by vary in feature like the slides of a magic-lantern. For we are here in that city of gold to which adventurers congregated out of all the winds of heaven;

> ## "THE EARTH HATH BUBBLES AS THE WATER HAS,
> AND THESE ARE OF THEM."
>
> WILLIAM SHAKESPEARE,
> *MACBETH*, ACT I, SC. III

we are in a land that till the other day was ruled and peopled by the countrymen of Cortes; and the sea that laves the piers of San Francisco is the ocean of the East and of the isles of summer. There goes the Mexican unmistakable; there the blue-clad Chinaman with his white slippers; there the soft-spoken, brown Kanaka, or perhaps a waif from far-away Malay. You hear French, German, Italian, Spanish and English indifferently. You taste the food of all nations in the various restaurants. ... For every man, for every race and nation, that city is a foreign city; humming with foreign tongues and customs; and yet each and all have made themselves at home.

ROBERT-LOUIS STEVENSON,
THE OLD AND NEW PACIFIC CAPITALS,
HEINEMANN, LONDON, 1922

A HARBOR CITY

Mark Twain (1835–1910), born Samuel Langhorne Clemens in Missouri, can be regarded as one of the pioneers of American literature. His liking for the new and unexpected prompted him to try his hand at numerous jobs (miner, gold prospector, publisher, journalist). An indefatigable traveler, he crossed the American West and arrived in San Francisco. With the discovery of silver at the Comstock Lode in 1859, the town experienced a fresh boom and a period of prosperity that are portrayed by Twain in "Roughing It".

I fell in love with the most cordial and sociable city in the Union. After the sage-brush and alkali deserts of Washoe, San Francisco was Paradise to me. I lived at the best hotel, exhibited my clothes in the most conspicuous places, infested the opera, and learned to seem enraptured with music which oftener afflicted my ignorant ear

than enchanted it, if I had had the vulgar honesty to confess it. However, I suppose I was not greatly worse than the most of my countrymen in that. I had longed to be a butterfly, and I was one at last. I attended private parties in sumptuous evening dress, simpered and aired my graces like a born beau, and polkaed and schottisched with a step peculiar to myself – and the kangaroo. In a word, I kept the due state of a man worth a hundred thousand dollars (prospectively), and likely to reach absolute affluence when that silver-mine sale should be ultimately achieved in the East. I spent money with a free hand, and meantime watched the stock sales with an interested eye and looked to see what might happen in Nevada.

MARK TWAIN, *ROUGHING IT*,
FIRST PUBLISHED
UNIVERSITY OF CALIFORNIA PRESS, BERKELEY, 1872

SAN FRANCISCO FROM THE SEA

Bret Harte (1836–1902) was born in Albany, New York. Harte, who is known primarily for his short story "The Luck of Roaring Camp", created a new West Coast version of the moral tale, with its portrayals of the reformed gambler and the prostitute with a heart of gold. In 1864 he and Charles Webb founded "The Californian", a literary magazine that rivaled the renowned "Golden Era" and helped to promote local writers such as Ina Coolbrith, Ambrose Bierce and Mark Twain. In this poem the author describes the city's early beginnings before condemning its moral depravity.

Serene, indifferent of Fate,
Thou sittest at the Western Gate;

Upon thy height, so lately won,
Still slant the banners of the sun;

Thou seest the white seas strike their tents,
O Warder of two Continents!

And, scornful of the peace that flies
Thy angry winds and sullen skies,

Thou drawest all things, small or great,
To thee, beside the Western Gate.

. . . .

O lion's whelp, that hidest fast
In jungle growth of spire and mast!

I know thy cunning and thy greed,
Thy hard high lust and wilful deed,

And all thy glory loves to tell
Of specious gifts material.

Drop down, O Fleecy Fog, and hide
Her sceptic sneer and all her pride!

Wrap her, O Fog, in gown and hood
Of her Franciscan Brotherhood.

Hide me her faults, her sin and blame;
With thy grey mantle cloak her shame:

So shall she, cowlèd, sit and pray
Till morning bears her sins away.

Then rise, O Fleecy Fog, and raise
The glory of her coming days;

Be as the cloud that flecks the seas
Above her smoky argosies;

When forms familiar shall give place
To stranger speech and newer face;

"GREAT ON THE WEST, ERE DARKNESS CRUSH HER DOMES,
WINE-RED THE CITY OF THE SUNSET LIES."

GEORGE STERLING

When all her throes and anxious fears
Lie hushed in the repose of years;

When Art shall raise and Culture lift
The sensual joys and meaner thrift,

And all fulfilled the vision we
Who watch and wait shall never see,

Who, in the morning of her race,
Toiled fair or meanly in our place,

But, yielding to the common lot,
Lie unrecorded and forgot.

BRET HARTE, "SAN FRANCISCO (FROM THE SEA)",
FIRST PUBLISHED 1868,
THE COMPLETE POETICAL WORKS OF BRET HARTE, LONDON, 1903

THE CABLE CAR TAKES THE HILLS BY STORM

Rudyard Kipling (1865–1936) started out as a reporter then devoted himself to writing books, the most famous of which are still "The Jungle Book" and "Puck of Pooks' Hill". He was awarded the Nobel Prize in 1907. In 1889 Kipling visited San Francisco and was struck by the prevailing air of barbarism, and also by the unusual method of transport that was born in San Francisco in 1873: the first tramways or cable cars.

❝O'Grady went to 'Frisco, and he came back with a very bad head and no clothes worth talkin' about. He had been jailed most time, but he had investigated the mechanism of these cars yonder – when he wasn't in the cage. He came back with the liquor for the saloon, and the boys whooped round him for half a day, singing songs of glory. 'Boys,' says O'Grady, when a half of Bow Flume were lying on the floor kissing the cuspidors and singing 'Way Down the Swanee River,' being full of some new stuff O'Grady had got up from 'Frisco – 'boys,' says O'Grady, 'I have the makings of a company in me. You know the road from this saloon to Bow Flume is bad and 'most perpendicular.' That was the exact state of the case. Bow Flume city was three hundred feet above our saloon. The boys used to roll down and get full, and any that happened to be sober rolled them up again when the time came to get. Some dropped into the cañon that way – bad payers mostly. You see, a man held all the hill Bow Flume was built on, and he wanted forty thousand dollars for a forty-five by hundred lot o'ground. So we kept the whisky below and the boys came down for it. The exercises disposed them to thirst. 'Boys,' says O'Grady, 'as you know, I have visited the great metropolis of 'Frisco.' Then they had drinks all round for 'Frisco. 'And I have been jailed a few while enjoying the sights.' Then they had drinks all round for the jail that held O'Grady. 'But,' he says, 'I have a proposal to make.' More drinks on account of the proposal. 'I have got hold of the idea of those 'Frisco cable-cars. Some of the idea I got in 'Frisco. The rest I have invented,' says O'Grady. Then they drank all round for the invention.

I am coming to the point. O'Grady made a company – the drunkest I ever saw – to run a cable-car on the 'Frisco model from 'Wake Up an' Git Saloon' to Bow Flume. The boys put in about four thousand dollars, for Bow Flume was squirting gold then. There's nary shanty there now. O'Grady put in four thousand dollars of his own, and I was roped in for as much. O'Grady desired the concern to represent the resources of Bow Flume. We got a car built in 'Frisco for two thousand dollars, with an elegant bar at one end – nickel-plated fixings and ruby glass. The notion was to

dispense liquor en route. A Bow Flume man could put himself outside two drinks in a minute and a half, the same not being pressed for urgent business.**99**

REPRINTED IN *KIPLING IN CALIFORNIA*,
ED. T. PINNEY, THE FRIENDS OF THE BANCROFT LIBRARY,
UNIVERSITY OF CALIFORNIA, 1989

A TOWN IN PERIL

Jack London (1876–1916) was a native San Franciscan, son of an astrologer father and a spiritualist mother. He earned his living in various ways, working in a canning factory, as a sailor, and also taking part in the 1897 Klondike gold rush, before becoming known as a writer. He was a confirmed socialist, who wrote passionately against capitalism. When the 1906 earthquake struck San Francisco, he was so shocked that at first he refused to write about it. Later he relented and agreed to write the piece that follows, entitled "The Story of an Eyewitness", for "Collier's" magazine, a New York weekly. Some of the scenes he witnessed also inspired the descriptions of a city collapsing in his novel "White Fang", published in 1906.

66An enumeration of the buildings destroyed would be a directory of San Francisco. An enumeration of the buildings undestroyed would be a line and several addresses. An enumeration of the deeds of heroism would stock a library and bankrupt the Carnegie medal fund. An enumeration of the dead will never be made. All vestiges of them will be destroyed by the flames. The number of victims of the earthquake will never be known. South of Market Street, where the loss of life was particularly heavy, was the first to catch fire. Remarkable as it may seem, Wednesday night, while the whole city crashed and roared into ruin, was a quiet night. There were no crowds. There was no shouting and yelling. There was no hysteria, no disorder. I passed Wednesday night in the path of the advancing flames, and in all those terrible hours I saw not one woman who wept, not one man who was excited, not one person who was in the slightest degree panic-stricken.

Before the flames, throughout the night, fled tens of thousands of homeless ones. Some were wrapped in blankets. Others carried bundles of bedding and dear household treasures. Sometimes a whole family was fastened to a

carriage or delivery wagon that was weighted down with their possessions. Baby buggies, toy wagons, and go-carts were used as trucks, while every other person was dragging a trunk. Yet everybody was gracious. The most perfect courtesy obtained. Never, in all San Francisco's history, were her people so kind and courteous as on this night of terror.**

JACK LONDON, *THE STORY OF AN EYE-WITNESS*,
COLLIER'S, MAY 5, 1906

A CHRONICLE OF SAN FRANCISCO

 Frank Norris (1870–1902) was born in Chicago but settled in San Francisco at the age of fourteen. "McTeague", which begins in the manner of an in-depth social chronicle of a street in San Francisco, is actually a study of unbridled human passion. This novel, as prodigious as it was marginal, turned Norris into the father of the "realist novel" in the United States.

**Then one day at San Francisco had come the news of his mother's death; she had left him some money – not much, but enough to set him up in business, so he had cut loose from the charlatan and had opened his "Dental Parlors" on Polk Street, an "accommodation street" of small shops in the residence quarter of the town. Here he had slowly collected a clientèle of butcher boys, shop girls, drug clerks, and car conductors. He made but few acquaintances. ...

The street never failed to interest him. It was one of those cross streets peculiar to Western cities, situated in the heart of the residence quarter, but occupied by small tradespeople who lived in the rooms above their shops. ... At one end of the street McTeague could see the huge power-house of the cable line. Immediately opposite him was a great market; while farther on, over the chimney stacks of the intervening houses, the glass roof of some huge public baths glittered like crystal in the afternoon sun. Underneath him the branch post-office was opening its doors, as was its custom between two and three o'clock on Sunday afternoons. An acrid odor of ink rose upward to him. Occasionally a cable car passed, trundling heavily, with a strident whirring of jostled glass windows.

On week days the street was very lively. It woke to its work about seven o'clock, at the time when the newsboys made their appearance together with the day laborers. The laborers went trudging past in a straggling file. ... This little army of workers, tramping steadily in one direction, met and mingled with other toilers of a different description – conductors and "swing men" of the cable company going on duty; heavy-eyed night clerks from the drug stores on their way home to sleep; roundsmen returning to the precinct police station to make their night report, and Chinese market gardeners teetering past under their heavy baskets. The cable cars began to fill up; all along the street could be seen the shop keepers taking down their shutters.

Between seven and eight the street breakfasted. Now and then a waiter from one of the cheap restaurants crossed from one sidewalk to the other, balancing on one palm a tray covered with a napkin. Everywhere was the smell of coffee and of frying steaks. A little later, following in the path of the day laborers, came the clerks and shop girls, dressed with a certain cheap smartness, always in a hurry, glancing apprehensively at the power-house clock. Their employers followed an hour or so later – on the cable cars for the most part – whiskered gentlemen with huge stomachs, reading the morning papers with great gravity; bank cashiers and insurance clerks with flowers in their buttonholes.

At the same time the school children invaded the street...

Towards eleven o'clock the ladies from the great avenue a block above Polk Street made their appearance, promenading the side-walks leisurely, deliberately. They were at their morning's marketing. They were handsome women, beautifully dressed. They knew by name their butchers and grocers and vegetable sellers. ...They all seemed to know one another, these grand ladies from the fashionable avenue. Meetings took place here and there; a conversation was begun...

From noon to evening the population of the street was of a mixed character. The street was busiest at that time; a vast and prolonged murmur arose – the mingled shuffling of feet, the rattle of wheels, the heavy trundling of cable cars. ...At six the great homeward march commenced; the cars were crowded, the laborers thronged the sidewalks, the newsboys chanted the evening papers. Then all at once the street fell quiet; hardly a soul was in sight; the sidewalks were deserted. It was supper hour. Evening began, and one by one a multitude of lights, from the demonian glare of the druggists' windows to the dazzling blue whiteness of the electric globes, grew thick from street corner to street corner. Once more the street was crowded. Now there was no thought but for amusement.❞

FRANK NORRIS,
McTEAGUE: A STORY OF SAN FRANCISCO,
W. W. NORTON & CO. INC., NEW YORK, 1977

BLACK HUMOR

Ambrose Bierce (1842–?1914), born in Ohio, was a prominent figure on the literary and journalistic scene in San Francisco. Bierce arrived in San Francisco after the American Civil War and divided his time between journalism, writing and escapades. In "The Man out of the Nose", realism takes a back seat to human anguish.

❝At the intersection of two certain streets in that part of San Francisco known by the rather loosely applied name of North Beach, is a vacant lot, which is rather more nearly level than is usually the case with lots, vacant or otherwise, in that region. Immediately at the back of it, to the south, however, the ground slopes steeply upward, the acclivity broken by three terraces cut into the soft rock. It is a place for goats and poor persons, several families of each class having occupied it jointly and amicably 'from the foundation of the city.' One of the humble habitations of the lowest terrace is noticeable for its rude resemblance to the human face, or rather to such a simulacrum of it as a boy might cut out of a hollowed pumpkin... As a face, this house is too large; as a dwelling, too small. The blank, unmeaning stare of its lidless and browless eyes is uncanny.

Sometimes a man steps out of the nose, turns, passes the place where the right ear should be and making his way through the throng of children and goats obstructing the narrow walk between his neighbors' doors and the edge of the terrace gains the street by descending a flight of rickety stairs. **99**

THE COMPLETE SHORT STORIES OF AMBROSE BIERCE,
DOUBLEDAY & CO. INC., NEW YORK, 1970

DEAD CALM

 Dashiell Hammett (1894-1961) was born in Connecticut. From 1921 to 1929 he lived in San Francisco, where he wrote most of his crime novels featuring the detective Sam Spade, on screen frequently played by Humphrey Bogart. "The Maltese Falcon" is one of the best known of his novels.

66. . . the springs creaked again, and a man's voice said:
'Hello. . . . Yes, speaking. . . . Dead?. . . . Yes. . . . Fifteen minutes. Thanks.'
A switch clicked and a white bowl hung on three gilded chains from the ceiling's center filled the room with light. Spade, bare-footed in green and white checked pajamas, sat on the side of his bed. He scowled at the telephone on the table while his hands took from beside it a packet of brown papers and a sack of Bull Durham tobacco.
Cold steamy air blew in through two open windows, bringing with it half a dozen times a minute the Alcatraz foghorn's dull moaning. A tinny alarm-clock, insecurely mounted on a corner of Duke's *Celebrated Criminal Cases of America* – face down on the table – held its hands at five minutes past two. **99**

DASHIELL HAMMETT,
THE MALTESE FALCON,
ALFRED A. KNOPF INC., NEW YORK, 1929

THE CALIFORNIAN LIFESTYLE

Dylan Thomas (1914–53) was born in Wales. He worked as a journalist, broadcaster and film-maker before becoming famous as a poet, and also as a hard-drinking, exuberant personality. He married Caitlin Macnamara in 1937 and in the 1950's he undertook a series of lecture tours in the US. In the following letter he describes his impressions of San Francisco to his wife. He died during his fourth visit to the US.

66But oh, San Francisco! It is and has everything. Here in Canada, five hours away by plane, you wouldn't think that such a place as San Francisco could exist. The wonderful sunlight there, the hills, the great bridges, the Pacific at your shoes. Beautiful Chinatown. Every race in the world. The sardine fleets sailing out. The little cable-cars whizzing down the city hills. The lobsters, clams, & crabs. Oh, Cat, what food for you. Every kind of seafood there is. And all the people are open and friendly. ... Everyone connected with the universities is hard-up. But that doesn't matter. Seafood is cheap. Chinese food is cheaper, & lovely. Californian wine is good. The iced bock beer is good. What more? And the city is built on hills; it dances in the sun for nine months of the year; & the Pacific Ocean never runs dry. Last week I went to Big Sur, a mountainous region by the sea, and stayed the night with Henry Miller. ...He lives about 6,000 feet up in the hills, over the blinding blue Pacific, in a hut of his own making. He has married a pretty young Polish girl, & they have two small children.**99**

DYLAN THOMAS, *LETTER TO CAITLIN, APRIL 7, 1950,*
PUBLISHED IN *THE COLLECTED LETTERS OF DYLAN THOMAS,* ED. PAUL FERRIS,
J. M. DENT & SONS LTD, LONDON, 1985

CRADLE OF THE BEAT GENERATION

Allen Ginsberg was born in New Jersey in 1926. This poet, who described himself as being inspired by bardic and Hebraic traditions as well as by Herman Melville, burst upon the literary scene with the public reading of his poem "Howl", on December 13, 1955.

66I walked on the banks of the tincan banana dock and sat down under the huge shade of a Southern Pacific locomotive to look at the sunset over the box house hills and cry.
Jack Kerouac sat beside me on a busted rusty iron pole, companion, we thought the same thoughts of the soul, bleak and blue and sad-eyed, surrounded by the gnarled steel roots of trees of machinery.
The oily water on the river mirrored the red sky, sun sank on top of final Frisco peaks, no fish in that stream, no hermit in those mounts, just ourselves rheumy-eyed and hung-over like old bums on the riverbank, tired and wily.**99**

ALLEN GINSBERG,
COLLECTED POEMS 1947–1980,
HARPERCOLLINS PUBLISHERS, INC., NEW YORK, 1984.

END OF LAND SADNESS

Jack Kerouac (1922–69), born in Lowell, Massachusetts, symbolizes the legendary figure from "On the Road" (1957), a traveler with divine, grandiose qualities. His spontaneous prose also includes a cycle of poems, "San Francisco Blues" or "The Dharma Bums" which was written at ten sittings and in one continuous outpouring of fifteen thousand words.

66There was a little alley in San Francisco back of the Southern Pacific station at Third and Townsend in redbrick of drowsy lazy afternoons with everybody at work in offices in the air you feel the impending rush of their commuter frenzy as soon they'll be charging en masse from Market and Sansome buildings on foot and in buses and all well-dressed thru workingman Frisco of Walkup??...
But it was that beautiful cut of clouds I could always see above the little S.P. Alley, puffs floating by from Oakland or the Gate of Marin to the north or San Jose south, the clarity of Cal to break your heart. It was the fantastic drowse and drum hum of lum mum afternoon nathin' to do, ole Frisco with end of land sadness – the people – the alley full of trucks and cars of businesses nearabouts and nobody knew

or far from cared who I was all my life three thousand five hundred miles from birth-O opened up and at last belonged to me in Great America.**

JACK KEROUAC,
LONESOME TRAVELER,
ANDRÉ DEUTSCH, LONDON, 1960

LIFE IN THE BAY AREA

The memoirs written by Carolyn Cassady (born 1923), Neal Cassady's wife, tell the story of shared years of wandering, success and neglect. Neal Cassady was Kerouac's traveling companion, his Dean Moriarty in "On the Road". They worked together, making tape recordings, for example, to discover uses of language which were ever more spontaneous.

**I had learned to love the Bay area when training with the Army at Mills College in Oakland,butSanFrancisco held a special charm. I reveled in the openness of the city, the air that smelled washed with soda, the casual, friendly people – far more sophisticated a place than Denver, and a striking contrast to New York. Beset with fears myself, I longed to be more like these defiant, courageous folk, who dared to construct buildings on hills so steep that cars parked sideways and steps, not sidewalks, flanked the pavement. The clear blue of the sky and sea brought exhilarating nostalgia for my beloved Michigan waters, and even the moan of the protective fog horns recalled those on Lake Michigan, reviving memories of my secure roots.

I got a job selling jewelry in a big store, and for a couple of weeks I lived in a quaint house on Telegraph Hill with a wild woman who rented me a cot and a chest in a corner of her glassed-in front porch overhanging the bayside cliff. My landlady was in her 70s, the widow of a famous artist. She wore her platinum-dyed hair in thick bangs and a long page-boy bob, fluttered long claw-curved fingernails enamelled in brilliant red, dressed always in Oriental pajamas, and drank gin all day. By the time I got home after dinner each night, she'd be staggering wildly and frequently just barely avoided catapulting out the front porch windows into the Bay. She would sit in her rocker opposite my cot, flailing away at a ukelele to the accompaniment of a radio, set at a jumble of sound between stations. After learning to sleep through this cacophony, I was often wakened later by her one-sided telephone conversations, carried on at the top of her lungs – in Chinese. Sometimes she'd mistake me for her long-lost daughter and weep over me in bed, clutching me to her bosom; on other nights she'd insist I stay up late into the early hours and drink mug after mug of tannic acid – 'Tea like they make it in India,' she'd say.

I didn't really mind any of this; to me, she was a San Francisco 'character', whose antics I used to relate for the entertainment of the girls at work.**

CAROLYN CASSADY,
OFF THE ROAD,
WILLIAM MORROW & CO., INC.,
NEW YORK, 1990

THE END OF AN ERA

Tom Wolfe was born in Virginia in 1931. He studied at Yale then worked as a journalist on the "New York Herald Tribune" and at "Esquire". Credited with inventing the "new journalism", which mixes reportage and fiction, he is also the author of "The Right Stuff" and "Bonfire of the Vanities". "The Electric Kool-Aid Acid Test" is a factual novel giving an eyewitness account of the hippie revolution in Haight-Ashbury in the late 1960's.

❝So I rented a car and started making the rounds in San Francisco. Somehow my strongest memories of San Francisco are of me in a terrific rented sedan roaring up hills or down hills, sliding on and off the cable-car tracks. Slipping and sliding down to North Beach, the fabled North Beach, the old father-land bohemia of the West Coast, always full of Big Daddy So-and-so and Costee Plusee and long-haired little Wasp and Jewish buds balling spade cats – and now North Beach was dying. North Beach was nothing but tit shows. In the famous Beat Generation HQ, the City Lights bookstore, Shig Murao, the Nipponese panjandrum of the place, sat glowering with his beard hanging down like those strands of furze and fern in an architect's drawing, drooping over the volumes of Kahlil Gibran by the cash register while Professional Budget Finance Dentists here for the convention browsed in search of the beatniks between tit shows. Everything was The Topless on North Beach, strippers with their breasts enlarged with injections of silicone emulsion. The action – meaning the hip cliques that set the original tone – the action was all over in Haight-Ashbury. Pretty soon all the bellwethers of a successful bohemia would be there, too, the cars going through, bumper to bumper, with everybody rubbernecking, the tour-buses going through 'and here ... Home of the Hippies ... there's one there,' and the queers and spade hookers and bookstores and boutiques. Everything was Haight-Ashbury and the acid heads. But it was not just North Beach that was dying. The whole old-style hip life – jazz, coffee houses, civil rights, invite a spade for dinner, Vietnam – it was all suddenly dying, I found out, even among the students at Berkeley, across the bay from San Francisco, which had been the heart of the 'student rebellion' and so

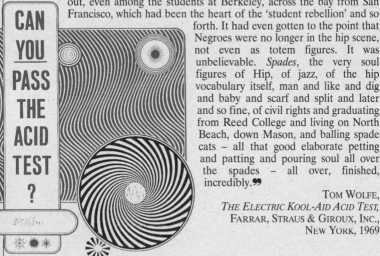

forth. It had even gotten to the point that Negroes were no longer in the hip scene, not even as totem figures. It was unbelievable. *Spades*, the very soul figures of Hip, of jazz, of the hip vocabulary itself, man and like and dig and baby and scarf and split and later and so fine, of civil rights and graduating from Reed College and living on North Beach, down Mason, and balling spade cats – all that good elaborate petting and patting and pouring soul all over the spades – all over, finished, incredibly.**❞**

TOM WOLFE,
THE ELECTRIC KOOL-AID ACID TEST,
FARRAR, STRAUS & GIROUX, INC.,
NEW YORK, 1969

THE END OF AN ERA

Richard Brautigan (1935–84) took the inspiration for his wild and baroque tales from the landscapes and towns of the Pacific coast. Between 1950 and 1970 he was part of the poetry scene araund North Beach, where he was well-known for his gentle sense of humour and the free and easy style of his writings.

> Like most Californians, I come from someplace else and was gathered to the purpose of California like a metal-eating flower gathers the sunshine, the rain, and then to the freeway beckons its petals and lets the cars drive in, millions of cars into but a single flower, the scent choked with congestion and room for millions more. California needs us, so it gathers us from other places. I'll take you, you, you, and I from the Pacific Northwest: a haunted land where nature dances the minuet with people and danced with me in those old bygone days. I brought everything I knew from there to California: years and years of a different life to which I can never return nor want to and seems at times almost to have occurred to another body somehow vaguely in my shape and recognition. It's strange that California likes to get her people from every place else and leave what we knew behind and here to California we are gathered as if energy itself, the shadow of that metal-eating flower, had summoned us away from other lives and now to do the California until the very end like the Taj Mahal in the shape of a parking meter.

RICHARD BRAUTIGAN, "THE GATHERING OF A CALIFORNIAN"
IN *REVENGE OF THE LAWN: STORIES 1962–70*, POCKET BOOKS, NEW YORK, 1972

THE CITY

John Steinbeck (1902–68) was born in California and used the state as the setting for many of his early novels and short stories.

> When I was a child growing up in Salinas we called San Francisco 'the City'. Of course it was the only city we knew, but I still think of it as the City, and so does everyone else who has ever associated with it. A strange and exclusive word is 'city'. Besides San Francisco, only small sections of London and Rome stay in the mind as the City. New Yorkers say they are going to town. Paris has no title but Paris. Mexico City is the Capital. Once I knew the City very well, spent my attic days there, while others were being a lost generation in Paris. I fledged in San Francisco, climbed its hills, slept in its parks, worked on its docks, marched and shouted in its revolts. In a way I felt I owned the City as much as it owned me. San Francisco put on a show for me. I saw her across the bay, from the great road that bypasses Sausalito and enters the Golden Gate Bridge. The afternoon sun painted her white and gold – rising on her hills like a noble city in a happy dream. A city on hills has it over flat-land places ...Over the green higher hills to the south, the evening fog rolled like herds of sheep coming to cote in the golden city. I've never seen her more lovely. When I was a child and we were going to the City, I couldn't sleep for several nights before. She leaves a mark.

JOHN STEINBECK,
TRAVELS WITH CHARLEY,
VIKING, NEW YORK, 1962

ITINERARIES
IN SAN FRANCISCO

▲ View of San Francisco from Marin County.

▼ The Financial District by night.

The Financial District skyline and the Oakland Bay Bridge. ▼

Some of the "Painted Ladies" have been repainted in psychedelic colors (following page).

Golden Gate Bridge. ▶

▲ Details of the bridge's superstructure, in mist (above) and in full sunlight. ▼

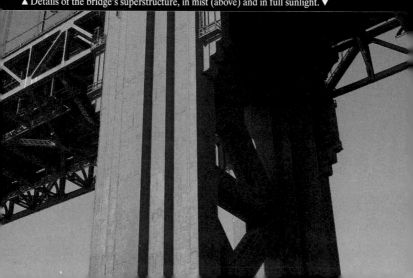

▲ Napa Valley vineyards, north of San Francisco.

▲ Alcatraz looming out of the fog.　　　Sailboats in Belvedere Lagoon, Marin County. ▼

HISTORIC
SAN FRANCISCO

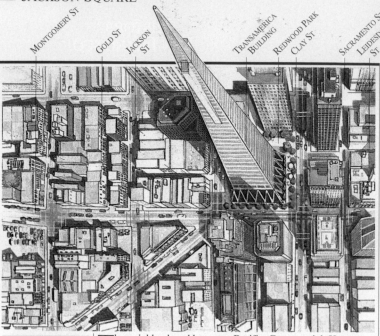

MONTGOMERY ST · GOLD ST · JACKSON ST · TRANSAMERICA BUILDING · REDWOOD PARK · CLAY ST · SACRAMENTO ST · LEIDESDORF ST

🕐 Two hours

This short itinerary can be combined with that of the Financial District ▲ 206.

THE PRISON-HULK
In 1849 San Francisco's only prison was a former school building on the plaza ▲ 158, but the arrest of ten prisoners at once created a problem since the plaza prison was too small to house them. First of all they were locked in the hold of a frigate; then, when the vessel had to put to sea, an abandoned ship was run aground in the bay to make a secure new prison.

The neighborhood between Pacific, Commercial, Kearny and Sansome Streets is the historic heart of San Francisco. Its brick buildings, some of which date from Gold Rush days, are in strong contrast to the skyscrapers of the adjoining Financial District. Previously known as the Barbary Coast, on account of its slums and constantly changing population, this neighborhood was almost totally annihilated in 1906 ● 58, then renamed Jackson Square after one of its streets.

YERBA BUENA COVE

In 1847 the sea met the land along the line of today's Montgomery Street, with the eastern side forming a bay fringed with dunes. In 1849 a few months after the first news of the discovery of gold, the inhabitants of Yerba Buena saw hundreds of ships drop anchor in the bay; their crews simply abandoned everything, cargo and all, and headed for the hills to look for gold ● 48. By 1851 about 775 ships lay deserted in

the bay, and thousands of prospectors were camped in makeshift huts near the village. The vessels had to anchor about 800 yards offshore because at that time the wide curve of the bay was no more than a swamp at low tide. As soon as a ship had found a point of anchorage, her passengers made their way to the shore in rowboats, while their supplies were moved by lighters and barges. The newcomers stepped on to dry land (a spit of black sand) to find an as yet shapeless city. From April to November 1849

port activity intensified at breakneck speed. A total of 549 sailing vessels, 233 of them American, brought in 35,000 passengers, together with 3,000 sailors determined to jump ship. The problem of providing sufficient moorings was solved by the construction of a wooden jetty, the Long Wharf, which stretched 800 yards into the bay. The roadstead was cleared of abandoned ships. To begin with they were used as warehouses, shops and hotels; one was even converted into a prison. Then they were dismantled and used as landfill for streets, or as timber for building houses.

THE CITY THAT ROSE FROM A CESSPOOL. New arrivals were invariably dismayed by the state of San Francisco. Apart from the problem of finding lodgings, it was almost impossible to find food at reasonable prices. The streets were in an awful state; during the rainy season they turned into lakes of filth. Deep quagmires formed, and men and horses were said to have drowned in them. Planks were laid across the thoroughfares for the convenience of pedestrians, and attempts were made to stabilize the main roads with anything that came to hand: branches, coffeebean sacks, pianos, cooking pots. The first two plank streets were Montgomery Street (1850) and the road between San Francisco and Mission Dolores. However, San Franciscans quickly showed astonishing organizational ability. Within months a real town had taken shape where before there had been nothing but tents. Because of the chronic

shortage of level space, before long a decision was taken to build facing the sea on reclaimed land. If the ships could not get to shore, the shore would have to go out to meet them. Wooden houses on pilings, linked by pontoons, quickly appeared above the marshes, and a port began to form. "In front of the town's present site," wrote the French explorer, August Bernard Duhaut-Cilly, "there stretched a broad sandbank above which the water was too shallow to allow ships bearing supplies to pass to land. . . . the Yankees dealt with this difficulty by building their town on the sandbank, which they prolonged by creating a ring of wharves, all of which were easily accessible even to the biggest vessels." The houses gained on the water, eventually encircling the ships that had been turned into hotels or stores: thus the two floors of the *Niantic Hotel* stood on the deck of a ship, the prow of which rose so high above the street that patrons had to climb a ladder to get into it. Duhaut-Cilly also describes the port area at this time: "The result is that this part of San Francisco has a most remarkable aspect; the stranger who goes there has no inkling that he is walking through a city built, like

PACIFIC AVENUE
Along this main road were opium dens, cabarets, squalid bars and "dance halls". Between numbers (mostly ribald songs, French can-cans and obscene routines) the women were expected to serve their customers with drinks, dance with them and eventually

Amsterdam or Venice, on wooden pilings, until he sees water a few feet below him beneath the planks which form the pavement . . . then he will come upon a ship aground in the mud, left behind amid a cluster of houses, and now become a house itself after serving as a floating hotel during the penury of the town's first years."

THE BARBARY COAST

The name of "Barbary Coast" was given to this district shortly after the first gold strikes, for within a few months the oceanfront here had been transformed into a "jungle full of

wild beasts and their prey", complete with the gambling dens, saloons and houses of ill repute that gave San Francisco its longstanding reputation as the most dangerous city in the world. During the 1850's sailors and prospectors flocked to Pacific Avenue ("Terrific Pacific") and Broadway for their pleasures. As the years passed, Broadway expanded to include Chinatown and a part of the present Financial District.

sell them their charms. From dusk until dawn these dives were packed, not only with drunks but also with murderers and thieves, who preyed on prospectors, sailors and farmers out on the town. The neighboring streets quickly acquired

"SHANGHAIED". In the early days many ships from the Far East stopped at San Francisco to recruit crew members. It was not unusual for naïve seamen frequenting the Barbary Coast saloons to be drugged, kidnapped and pressed into service on one of these "hell-ships". The crossing to Shanghai was long and perilous, so when a vessel put to sea for a difficult voyage it was said to be "off to Shanghai", hence the term "Shanghaied" for these San Francisco kidnappings. It is thought that as many as twenty-three kidnap gangs were operating in the city in 1852, making big profits.

sinister names such as Killers' Corner, Death Alley and Devil's Acre.

BARBARY COAST BY NIGHT, SAN FRANCISCO, CAL.

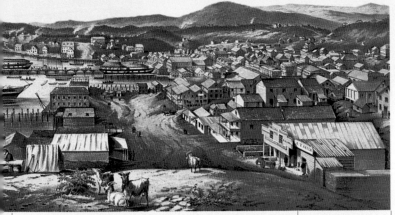

THE END OF THE BARBARY COAST. The Barbary Coast maintained its reputation as a modern Sodom until the close of the nineteenth century. Preachers came and went, but since most of the proprietors enjoyed the protection of corrupt high-ranking officials, any attempt at reform was doomed to failure. The earthquake and fire of 1906 did not spare the Barbary Coast, but life continued as before despite the devastation, and it was not until 1917, when a federal decree forced the closure of brothels, that this chapter in San Francisco's history came to an end.

> "A great city covers the sandhills on the west, a growing town lies along the muddy shallows of the east; steamboats pant continually between them from before sunrise till the small hours of the morning."
> R. L. Stevenson

ALONG MONTGOMERY

Montgomery Street, laid out along the old shoreline, was for many years the busiest thoroughfare in San Francisco. At a very early stage it became a center for the business and financial community, and it was associated with the names of celebrities such as Mark Twain, Bret Harte and Charles Eliot Norton, who lived there for a spell ▲ *158*. Furthermore, it was to Montgomery Street that Sam Brannan brought news of the discovery of gold in January 1848, thus triggering the California Gold Rush. ● *48*.

LEIDESDORFF STREET. On this small street, which runs parallel to Montgomery and links Clay and California Streets, stands one of the oldest groups of small office buildings in the neighborhood. A few red brick constructions with colored façades add a note of gaiety; at the southwest end of the street, on the corner, stands the brick and stucco building that housed San Francisco's first printworks, founded by Britton and Rey in 1852 ● *72*.

IN MEMORIAM. A copper plaque on the corner of Montgomery and Merchant Streets marks the site of the old Pony Express office. This legendary messenger service was founded in April 1860; by October 1861 it had been driven out of business by the telegraph. Its relays of riders succeeded in covering the 1,965 miles between Saint Joseph, Missouri, and San Francisco in just ten days.

TRANSAMERICA PYRAMID ★. This pyramid-shaped skyscraper, which has occupied 600 Montgomery Street since 1972, is the work of William Pereira and Associates. At 853 feet, it is the

WILLIAM LEIDESDORFF
A navy officer from the Virgin Islands, he reached San Francisco in 1841 and decided to settle there. Despite prevalent racism, this black pioneer became one of the most prominent men in the community. He made a fortune in maritime trade and built the first city hall of San Francisco, before becoming municipal treasurer, head of the first college in California and US vice-consul in Yerba Buena.

149

JACKSON SQUARE
The offices, banks, factories and consulates that grew up behind the docks during the 1850's moved further south in the 1890's, making way for printers and traders in tobacco and spirits. Many of them went bankrupt in 1929, at which time the now cheap neighborhood was turned over to artists and writers. These were succeeded in the 1950's by designers, interior decorators and architects, who set about restoring the old Victorian buildings. They renamed the district "Jackson Square" after the many historic buildings on the 400 block of Jackson Street.

tallest office building in the town, occupying the site of the former MONTGOMERY BLOCK (above), which was better known in its time as the "Monkey Block". This was a four-story construction, built by Henry Halleck in 1853, which at the time was famous as the "largest and solidest building west of the Mississippi". It occupied an entire block and housed the offices of several newpapers and various other businesses, along with a number of bars and restaurants. The Monkey Block is famous as the scene of the pistol assassination of James King of William (editor of the *Evening Bulletin*) by James Casey, a killing which led to the founding of the second Vigilance Committee ● 45. The proprietor of a Turkish bathhouse situated in the basement is said to have been the inspiration for Mark Twain to create the character of Tom Sawyer. The Monkey Block survived the 1906 catastrophe, only to fall victim to real-estate promoters, who demolished it in 1959 to build a parking lot. Despite the mockery of San Franciscans who called it "Trans-Am's Teepee", the Transamerica Pyramid is now an accepted feature of the city and serves as a landmark for new arrivals trying to get their bearings. Temporary exhibitions are mounted in the lobby, but the principal attraction here is the panoramic view from the twenty-seventh floor, which is well worth visiting. The intersection of Columbus, Montgomery and Washington Streets marks the frontier between North Beach ▲ *162–71*, the Financial District ▲ *206–17* and Jackson Square ▲ *146–51*. **BLOCK 700.** This part of Montgomery, between Washington and Jackson Streets, boasts a number of handsome buildings dating back to the 1850's. At no. 722 is the BELLI BUILDING, built in 1851 by the engineer Henry W. Halleck. The building was originally a tobacco warehouse, then it became a theater, a Turkish bath (around 1880), and a medical facility, successively. In 1958 the lawyer Melvin Belli bought it, restored it and gave it his name. During the restoration work the original brick was uncovered, and new decoration was added. At an adjoining site, nos. 728–30, is the GENELLA BUILDING;

TRANSAMERICA
REDWOOD PARK
PROVIDED FOR THE ENJOYMENT OF
OUR EMPLOYEES, TENANTS AND FRIENDS

"I HAVE SEEN PURER LIQUOR, STRONGER CIGARS, MORE REAL
GUNS AND PISTOLS, BIGGER KNIVES AND DAGGERS AND PRETTIER
COURTESANS HERE IN SAN FRANCISCO THAN ANYWHERE ELSE."

H.R. HELPER

in 1851 Joseph Genella acquired this site and demolished the
house that stood on it, which had been the scene of the
founding assembly of California's first Masonic lodge
(October 17, 1849). Two years later he replaced it with a
three-story building to house his glass and china factory.
Genella was succeeded by several other tenants before Joe
and Isobel Strong moved in at the turn of
the century with their painting studio.
The Strongs were quickly joined by other
artists, notably Jules Tavernier, Arthur
Mathews, Emil Carlson, Maynard Dixon
and Dorothea Lange ● *46.*

Jackson Street and
Hotaling Place were
restored by antique
dealers, who opened
shops there in the
early 1970's.

JACKSON STREET ★

The block on Jackson Street between
Montgomery and Sansome, heart of the Jackson Square
Historic District, stands on the site of the old *Laguna
Salada,* a small inlet crossed by the first bridge ever
constructed in San Francisco. Miraculously spared both
by the 1906 catastrophe and by the march of progress,
the 1850–60's buildings here were restored during the
1950's, then classified as historic monuments in 1971.
Most are now occupied by antique-dealers. The SOLARI
BUILDING WEST, at no. 472, is the oldest of them; built
between 1850 and 1852, it served as the French consulate
from 1864 to 1876.

**FORTUNY FABRICS,
415–31 JACKSON
STREET**
This building,
constructed in 1853,
was the home of the
Ghirardelli Chocolate
Factory from 1855 to
1894 ▲ *176.* At 407 is
the firm's former
annex.

HOTALING BUILDINGS. The Italianate building at 451 Jackson
is the best-known and best-preserved monument
in the street. It was constructed in 1866 by
A.P. Hotaling, a whiskey merchant who kept
his distillery and offices on the premises. It
survived the 1906 fire unscathed – an irony
that was not lost on San Franciscans, who
wondered why, if the catastrophe was
divine punishment visited on the city for its
frivolity, the Good Lord had nonetheless
spared Hotaling's whiskey establishment. Later,
no. 451 was used as a warehouse by an import-export
firm trading to Alaska and the South Seas. In 1860 Hotaling
built an annex at nos. 463–73, in a similar Italianate style,
before buying the stables of the Tremont Hotel (no. 445),
built in 1860. The small street leading off to the right,
formerly Jones Alley, is now called Hotaling Place. By 1870
Hotaling was a wealthy man; and in that year he constructed
two more buildings behind his distillery, to serve as stables
and warehouse. BALANCE STREET, opposite, San Francisco's
shortest street, was given its name because of a boat that was
discovered there during the excavations. It led to Gold Street,
a narrow artery where the gold prospectors brought their gold
dust and nuggets to be weighed.

❝Jackson Street is
almost entirely made
up of bars which, in
the evening, become
public dancehalls
frequented by young
people. There are
Mexicans, South
Americans and
negresses, all in flashy
costumes. Since there
are hardly any women
of loose morals [in
the town], no one
hesitates to visit the
dancehalls and
display themselves
there.❞

Léon Lemonnier

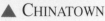

✖ Three hours

This itinerary can be combined with a tour of the Financial District ▲ 206, or North Beach ▲ 162.

ST MARY'S SQUARE
ST MARY'S CHURCH
CHINATOWN GATE
STOCKTON ST
GRANT AVE
SACRAMENTO ST
BUSH ST
KEARNY ST
PINE ST
CALIFORNIA ST

The maze of narrow streets that is Chinatown sprawls beneath the skyscrapers of the financial district, between Broadway, Stockton, Bush and Kearny Streets. One of the oldest districts in the city of San Francisco, Chinatown also has one of the largest Chinese populations outside Asia.

CHINESE IMMIGRATION

There were Chinese in San Francisco well before the discovery of gold. Chung Ming, a Cantonese merchant who arrived at Yerba Buena in 1847, is generally supposed to have spread news of the gold strike among his compatriots. In 1848 China was in dire straits, a prey to flood, famine and lawlessness; moreover the Manchu regime, defeated in the First Opium War (1839–42), was taxing the Chinese people heavily to pay a heavy war indemnity demanded by the British. So when the windfall of gold was announced, large numbers of Chinese took ship for California, which they called *Gum San* or "Golden Mountain", in the hope of striking it rich. Chinese immigration began in earnest in 1848, and in the second half of the 19th century 2.5 million of them left their native country, of whom 320,000 ended up in California. In 1851 4,000 arrived, and 25,000 followed during the next twelve months. Soon the flow of immigration became controlled by rich merchants, who founded the Canton Company or Sam Yup Association in 1851. The Sze Yup Association, also called the Four District Association, was created by a group of impecunious Cantonese peasants determined to escape the exploitation of the powerful Chinese bosses.

A PERILOUS CROSSING
The Pacific crossing took 62 days on average, and conditions aboard ship were appalling. Fights occurred frequently between the immigrants, who were crushed together like cattle.
In 1854, when the *Libertad* arrived in San Francisco from Hong Kong, 100 of her 500 passengers were dead.

OUT OF CHINA, INTO THE MINES. As soon as they disembarked, the Chinese immigrants were moved on to the mines, where they were put to work in teams. Having quickly understood that there was nothing to be gained by competing

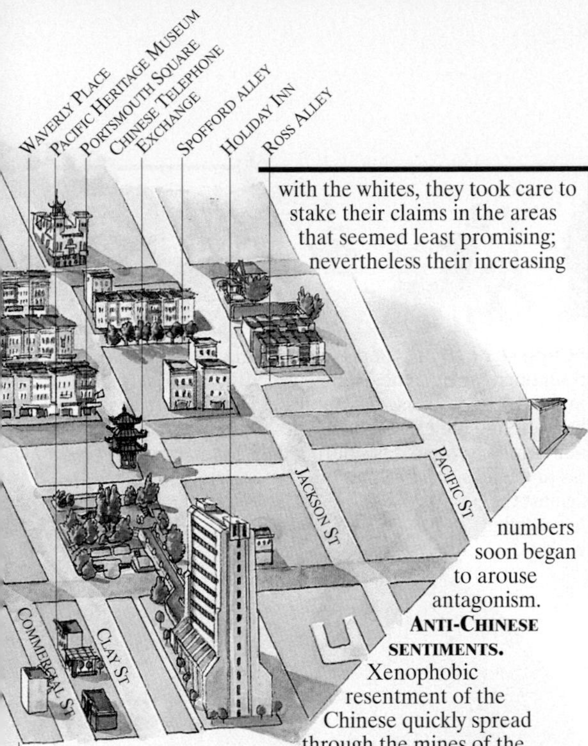
Waverly Place
Pacific Heritage Museum
Portsmouth Square
Chinese Telephone Exchange
Spofford Alley
Holiday Inn
Ross Alley
Pacific St
Jackson St
Clay St
Commercial St

with the whites, they took care to stake their claims in the areas that seemed least promising; nevertheless their increasing numbers soon began to arouse antagonism.

Anti-Chinese sentiments. Xenophobic resentment of the Chinese quickly spread through the mines of the Sierra Nevada. In 1850 the Foreign Miners' Licence Tax had been imposed, levying a charge of 20 dollars per month on all miners of foreign extraction; this measure was originally aimed at Latin Americans, who at the time represented about one-third of the population of California. Prior to 1852 no significant anti-Chinese feeling had emerged, but in that year Governor John Bigler denounced the immigrants from Asia, whom he accused of threatening the stability of the state. Subsequently, the iniquitous Licence Tax was renewed and even increased by 3 dollars per month, with an automatic increase of 2 dollars per year thereafter. The Chinese, not unnaturally, were aggrieved by this law, which was published in Cantonese in 1855. Much more seriously, they began to be victimized by random assaults; hundreds of their number were murdered with impunity by prospectors and tax collectors. These outrages became so common that they gave birth to a new expression in English: to have "not a Chinaman's chance." In the end the Chinese were forced to abandon the gold mines, and San Francisco, which in 1860 contained only 8 percent of California's Chinese population, had by 1880 acquired upwards of 30 percent. The Chinese settled on Kearny Street, the only thoroughfare on which they were permitted to rent rooms. In 1852 the local press dubbed the area "Little Canton."

Telephone booth in the Chinese quarter.

A ticket to exile
Three ways of paying their voyage were open to Chinese. Usually, they bought a credit-ticket, whereby a Chinese company advanced the cash against payment by instalments from an immigrant's wages. In the contract-labor system, a US company paid for the trip and the immigrant then worked for the company, repaying it little by little. To all intents and purposes the coolie trade was simple slavery, by which potential workers were either kidnapped or duped with fake contracts. The Chinese exiles disembarked in the ports of San Francisco or Oakland (below) on the far side of the bay.

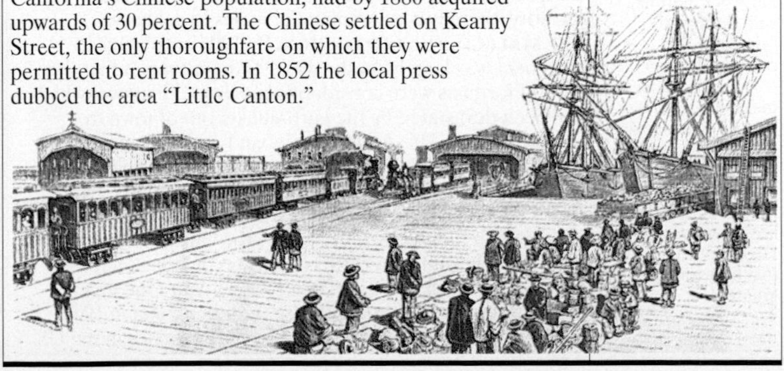

DENNIS KEARNY
An Irish ship's boy who was promoted to officer at twenty-one years old, Kearny arrived in San Francisco in 1868 and took American nationality. Uneducated but self-confident and authoritarian, he was hard hit by the failure of his own business venture, for which he blamed the Chinese. He accused them of driving the whites out of work by accepting slave wages. On July 23, 1877, he made an inflammatory speech with the slogan "Chinese out!" He then started a union, the Workingman's Trade and Labor Union, later known as theWorkingman's Party of California, with the aim of "cleansing the country of cheap Chineses labor by any means to hand." Kearny, who openly invited riots, declared that he longed to be assassinated, so that his movement would be redoubled in force. His opponents prayed that his wish would be granted.

"CHINESE OUT!". Unemployment continued to foster resentment against the Chinese, who were routinely attacked in the streets. Chinese prostitutes were evicted from the brothels and molested, and Chinese laundries ransacked. The authorities continued to churn out discriminatory laws, from a tax on pigtails to a prohibition against the use of yokes for carrying baskets, culminating in a Cubic Air Ordinance limiting the number of occupants permitted for a single lodging. In 1880 the government amended the Burlingame Treaty with a view to regulating Chinese immigration, and two years later Congress voted the Chinese Exclusion Act, halting all immigration from China for a period of ten years. In 1884 the law was strengthened with an article forbidding Chinese women to enter American territory, thereby condemning the males to celibacy.

THE STRUGGLE FOR INTEGRATION. By 1906 anti-Chinese sentiment was largely on the wane, though even at that time the Californians were considering moving Chinatown, which had been devastated by the earthquake, out of town to Hunter's Point. This project was abandoned for financial reasons, because San Francisco needed the tax revenue generated by the hard-working Chinese community. In any event the Chinese profited from the earthquake; all the immigration files were destroyed by the catastrophe, so many were free to claim American citizenship or bring their children across from China. After World War One they benefitted from the anti-Japanese sentiment, and in 1941 many Chinese-Americans volunteered for service in the US

armed forces. In 1943 President Roosevelt asked Congress to repeal the Chinese Exclusion Act, and the right to naturalization was restored. The War Brides Act of 1946, which remained in force for three years, allowed Chinese women the freedom to join their husbands in the USA. But it was not until the 1950's that Chinese residents were authorized for the first time to buy homes outside the Chinatown ghetto. During the 1960's immigration laws were relaxed even further, particularly in 1962 when John F. Kennedy gave permission to opponents of the Mao regime living in Hong Kong to emigrate to the United States. Chinatown had to absorb yet another wave of immigrants, and its population density became ten times greater than that in the rest of the city. Today eighty thousand people live in Chinatown.

CHINESE CRAFTS. In a city with a population that was 92 percent male, the Indian and Spanish laundresses of Washerwoman's Lagoon, the natural washing place at the base of Russian Hill, were unable to cope; San Francisco's dirty laundry was sometimes shipped as far afield as Canton or Honolulu. Aware of the huge demand, the Chinese opened laundries all over the city. Beginning in about 1849, other immigrants started restaurants and quickly acquired an appreciative Western clientèle with their subtly spiced and inexpensive cooking. Still others became barbers or prawn fishermen, using broad nets imported from China. Some succeeded as farmers, and others entered the service of rich white families as butlers, cooks or footmen, where their efficiency, honesty and loyalty became legendary. Others again found jobs in shoe factories, cigar factories and soap factories. Finally, after about 1866, tens of thousands of Chinese were shipped to San Francisco to supply the manpower to construct the transcontinental railroad ● 54, 55, a project that was to cost many of them their lives

THE YELLOW PERIL
A caricature from the *Wasp*, November 1885. Encouraged by the Burlingame treaty in 1868, which guaranteed them fundamental rights, the Chinese came to the US in huge numbers. But the Californians became alarmed at the spectacle of 15,000 Chinese immigrants a year between 1870 and 1880 and began to talk of "The Yellow Peril." Violence became commonplace, in particular on the docks of the Pacific Mail Steamship Co., where the ships from China put in. The immigrants were subjected to a range of discriminatory laws, and in 1868, 40,000 Chinese miners were expelled from the country.

CHINESE LAUNDRIES
Unable to exercise their traditional professions as farmers and shopkeepers, the Chinese turned to the laundry business, which required only a small initial investment. It became their principal occupation for over fifty years. In the 1880's, there were 7,500 Chinese laundries in San Francisco. In 1920, 30 percent of Chinese in the country were in the business, many of them keeping their establishments open round the clock.

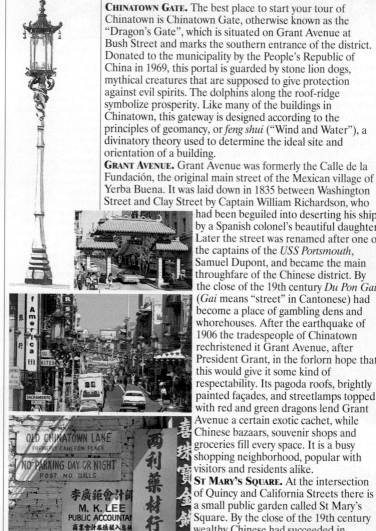

GRANT AVENUE

CHINATOWN GATE. The best place to start your tour of Chinatown is Chinatown Gate, otherwise known as the "Dragon's Gate", which is situated on Grant Avenue at Bush Street and marks the southern entrance of the district. Donated to the municipality by the People's Republic of China in 1969, this portal is guarded by stone lion dogs, mythical creatures that are supposed to give protection against evil spirits. The dolphins along the roof-ridge symbolize prosperity. Like many of the buildings in Chinatown, this gateway is designed according to the principles of geomancy, or *feng shui* ("Wind and Water"), a divinatory theory used to determine the ideal site and orientation of a building.

GRANT AVENUE. Grant Avenue was formerly the Calle de la Fundación, the original main street of the Mexican village of Yerba Buena. It was laid down in 1835 between Washington Street and Clay Street by Captain William Richardson, who had been beguiled into deserting his ship by a Spanish colonel's beautiful daughter. Later the street was renamed after one of the captains of the *USS Portsmouth*, Samuel Dupont, and became the main throughfare of the Chinese district. By the close of the 19th century *Du Pon Gai* (*Gai* means "street" in Cantonese) had become a place of gambling dens and whorehouses. After the earthquake of 1906 the tradespeople of Chinatown rechristened it Grant Avenue, after President Grant, in the forlorn hope that this would give it some kind of respectability. Its pagoda roofs, brightly painted façades, and streetlamps topped with red and green dragons lend Grant Avenue a certain exotic cachet, while Chinese bazaars, souvenir shops and groceries fill every space. It is a busy shopping neighborhood, popular with visitors and residents alike.

ST MARY'S SQUARE. At the intersection of Quincy and California Streets there is a small public garden called St Mary's Square. By the close of the 19th century wealthy Chinese had succeeded in "curbing vice" by concentrating here all the brothels and cheap saloons frequented by sailors on shore leave. These ill-famed establishments disappeared in the great fire of 1906 and were replaced by public gardens during the reconstruction of the district. Today St Mary's Square, frequented in the mornings by practitioners of the martial arts and at lunch hour by office workers, is an oasis of calm and quiet.

ST MARY'S CHURCH. In 1852 the Paulist Brothers built this church at the corner of California Street and Grant Avenue. Granite for the foundations was imported from China, while the bricks and the steel frame for the superstructure were transported by ship from New England. On the clocktower

CHINATOWN, A PIECE OF ASIA IN AMERICA
From above: a streetlamp in Grant Avenue, Chinatown Gate, and a shop sign in Chinese characters

the following words are inscribed: "My Son, Observe the time and fly from evil", a precept no doubt aimed at parishioners with a mind to visit one of the adjoining establishments. The church was one of the few buildings here to escape destruction in the 1906 fire.

SACRAMENTO STREET. This street was known for many years as Chinamen's Street, being the first thoroughfare in the city where immigrants from China had the right to rent rooms. Later Dupont and Jackson Streets were also opened to the Chinese, and became the core of the future district.

The neighborhood is full of restaurants and food shops.

DONALDINA CAMERON'S CRUSADE. At no. 220 Sacramento Street stands a building named after Donaldina Cameron, whose original mission house here was destroyed in 1906. Donaldina was a youthful adherent of the Presbyterian Mission Home; horrified by the "Yellow Slave Trade" and the ill-treatment of its girl victims, she launched a crusade against the *Hip Yee Tong*, which was the association that controlled Chinese prostitution in San Francisco. By sheer tenacity, *Lo Mo* ("Little Mother") managed to rescue hundreds of girls, many as young as ten, and played an important role in the adoption of the Red Light District Act in 1914 to impose strict regulations on prostitution. To this day her house is the headquarters of an active religious community.

COMMERCIAL STREET. This small street, which leads off to the right north of Sacramento Street and links Chinatown to the financial district, owes its name to the quay built in 1849 for unloading ships anchored in the Yerba Buena Cove. Commercial Street was cut through in 1850 and runs perpendicular to the former shore. The quayside, filled in during the Gold Rush, was then extended into the Bay and twice renamed: first as Central Wharf, then as Long Wharf.

DOUBTFUL COMMERCE
The Chinese came to the US in the hope of enriching themselves and one day returning home. Married men could not pay for their wives' crossings, so the Chinese population of San Francisco was almost entirely male. Between 1848 and 1854, the Chinese community numbered 45,000, with only 20 women. But the female population grew quickly later on, due to prostitution; a "yellow" slave trade developed, in which girls were kidnapped in China or bought for a few dollars, then resold for a high price in the US. Gambling and opium dens (above) eventually gave Chinatown an evil reputation. Far from hiding the opium dens away in dark basements, their owners frequently set them up in restaurant back rooms, where they were comfortably furnished and fitted out.

157

THE CHINESE QUARTER
In 1880, Chinatown occupied six blocks between California, Broadway, Kearny and Stockton. In 1920, the neighborhood extended over eight blocks, from Bush to Broadway and from Kearny to Powell.

EMPEROR NORTON
One night in 1880, Emperor Norton, one of the city's greatest eccentrics, died on a Chinatown street. An English merchant who first arrived in San Francisco in 1849, Norton quickly made a fortune in real estate. After a business disaster which drove him insane, Norton vanished; a few months later he resurfaced, wearing a military uniform and a hat with a white plume (right), and announcing that he was Norton the First, Emperor of the United States and Protector of Mexico. The *San Francisco Bulletin* published this news and the San Franciscans, who were fond of Norton, went along with the joke for a full 25 years. Some shopkeepers even accepted the coinage Norton struck, and when he died a crowd of thirty thousand attended his funeral.

In 1850 Commercial Street was invaded by gaming houses, and then by brothels. These have long since vanished, and today it contains nothing more exciting than a pair of museums. One, the PACIFIC HERITAGE MUSEUM at no. 608, stands on the site of the first San Francisco Mint. The other, maintained by the CHINESE HISTORICAL SOCIETY at no. 650, recalls the history of the first Chinese immigrants and shows their contribution to California's development. Among the objects on display here are weapons from the Tong war ▲ *161*, an old yearbook of the neighborhood written in Chinese, and some fine papier-mâché dragons.

PORTSMOUTH SQUARE

This plaza existed in Spanish days and in 1839 the Swiss navigator Jean-Jacques Vioget ● *91* platted around it. It was originally intended as the heart of the city and Vioget was commissioned by the mayor to produce a rough town plan to make sense of the village that was then developing spontaneously around Yerba Buena Cove. At that time the shore of the cove reached present-day Montgomery Street ▲ *146*. When the cove was filled in, commercial activity

moved away and the square lost much of its importance. Since the 1970's it has regained a certain vitality with the appearance of tables at which retired Chinese sit and play cards or *mah-jong*, the latter being a very popular pastime hereabouts. On sunny afternoons grandmothers crowd the benches, and children invade the playground. In the northeast corner of the square stands a monument to Robert Louis Stevenson, the Scottish poet and novelist who lived with his wife in a small apartment overlooking Bush Street from 1879 to 1880. Stevenson is said to have spent days on end observing the passing crowds in Portsmouth Square and the ships moving in and out of the port.

BUDDHA'S UNIVERSAL CHURCH. At no.720 Washington Street, on the corner of Kearny Street, stands Buddha's Universal Church, also known as the "Church of a Thousand Hands". In 1950 the Buddhist congregation bought a former nightclub here to use as a temple; but as soon as the sale was concluded, the municipal authority ordered the demolition of the building on the grounds that it was too dilapidated. Since they had no money to pay for its reconstruction, the Buddhists themselves undertook to build a new temple, which was completed in 1961: it remains one of the largest Buddhist sanctuaries in the United States.

THE CHINESE CULTURAL CENTER. The Chinese Cultural Center is located on the third floor of the HOLIDAY INN HOTEL, at no. 750 Kearny Street, which may be reached from Portsmouth Plaza by way of a concrete bridge. Opened in 1973, the center mounts exhibitions of contemporary Chinese and Chinese-American artists; it also maintains a library and a theater seating six hundred. The Holiday Inn Hotel stands on the site of the former JENNY LIND THEATER, one of the city's most popular saloons at the time of the Gold Rush, which was named after the celebrated Swedish singer (who, as it happens, never visited San Francisco). The city later bought the saloon to build a courthouse on the plot, which provoked an outcry. The 1906 fire destroyed the entire block.

THE CHINESE TELEPHONE EXCHANGE. At no. 743 Washington Street stands the former central telephone exchange of the Pacific Telephone and Telegraph Company. This beautiful pagoda, completed in 1909, was the first Chinese-style building constructed in San Francisco. It was designed along the lines of a Chinese temple and stands on the exact site where Sam Brannan printed California's first newspaper, the *California Star* ● *70*. In 1960 the Bank of Canton bought the pagoda, which had been out of use since 1949, and set up a branch there.

THE PLAZA
A whole network of streets met in the square in front of Yerba Buena Cove, where visiting ships dropped anchor, and it became a favorite site for public meetings. On July 9, 1846, Captain Montgomery ● *44* disembarked from his ship the *Portsmouth*, and planted the US flag in the middle of the Plaza, which was renamed Portsmouth Square.

FROM MOTHER TO DAUGHTER
The Chinese Telephone Exchange receptionists (below) had to know five Chinese dialects and learn the numbers of the 2,800 subscribers: in Chinese circles it was considered rude to refer to a person by a number. This job, passed down from mother to daughter, was much prized. The new automatic telephone system forced the closure of the Exchange in 1949.

159

JENG SEN TEMPLE
This temple is located in Waverly Place, over the *Potsticker Restaurant*. In exchange for a donation, the visitor receives a red good luck calendar.

Though Chinese-Americans live in several different parts of town, Chinatown is still the cultural and commercial center of their community, where everyone goes to do their shopping. Today, a new Chinese neighborhood has emerged in the Richmond district ▲ 246. A shrine to Chinese gastronomy, the old Chinatown attracts food-lovers of all nations. The shops and alleys of these few tightly knit blocks form a world apart.

WAVERLY PLACE

Waverly Place, an alley that runs parallel to Grant Avenue, is chiefly remarkable for its green, yellow, red and gold balconies. Formerly Pike Street, it was nicknamed "15 Cents Street" at the turn of the century, 15 cents being the fee demanded for a haircut by the Chinese barbers who worked there.

TIEN HAU TEMPLE. The first floor of nos. 123–9 Waverly Place contains one of the two Chinese temples in the neighborhood which is open to the public. Located on an upper floor ("far from the street but near to heaven") this sanctuary betrays its presence by an odor of burning incense. Follow the red carpet and ring the bell to be admitted. The red and gold altar is dedicated to Tien Hau, goddess of the sea and the wind, and patron of travelers, actors and prostitutes. Its tiny sanctuary was built by Chinese mariners in gratitude for their safe passage across the Pacific to San Francisco in 1852.

FIRST CHINESE BAPTIST CHURCH. This church, which occupies the corner of Waverly and Sacramento Streets, was founded in 1880 and rebuilt with scorched bricks after the fire of 1906. A large number of churches in Chinatown were constructed by missionaries, who were particularly active here; in general they concerned themselves with setting up schools, the only places where the immigrant Chinese could learn English and thus hope to integrate themselves into American society. This helps to explain why many Chinese were converted to Christianity.

STOCKTON STREET

CHINESE SIX COMPANY. The headquarters of this Chinese secret society, founded in 1862, was at no. 843 in the busy commercial thoroughfare of Stockton Street. The segregation imposed on them obliged the Chinese to fall back on their own resources in Chinatown, which then covered six blocks, and to form a community similar to the ones they had left behind in Asia. They set up family associations, composed of people linked by name or shared ancestors, whose function it was to settle disputes, care for the sick and bury the dead. District associations were also established to maintain contacts between people born in the same villages and regions of China. The Chinese Six Company, which represented all the Chinese in California, served as an unofficial governing body within Chinatown and as an umbrella for the district associations, its main function being to promote projects for the common weal. The Company also

WAVERLY
天后廟街

controlled the importation of Chinese goods and manpower into San Francisco and was largely responsible for bringing over thousands of "coolies". Lastly, the Chinese Six Company was responsible for resolving internal conflicts within the community. Today the organization has been reduced to a purely social role. Toward 1880, fighting broke out between the various clans for control of Chinatown, and the Tongs set to murdering one another with hatchets. The Tongs were a highly organized group of Chinese immigrants, without family or regional ties, who had formed groups specializing in drugs, prostitution and racketeering. The "hatchet-killers", as they were called, instituted a reign of terror that lasted from 1880 to about 1921, with a brief revival in 1970. Originally they were easily recognizable by the way they wore their pigtails high on their heads, the better to elude the grasping hands of the police. In 1921, when the "Tong Terror" was at its height, Police Inspector Jack Manion was assigned for three months to Chinatown. He was to remain there until his retirement in 1946; thanks to Manion's work the district was cleaned up, and the inspector himself was adopted as its unofficial mayor.

THE "ALLEYS"

Ross Alley, the "gamblers' street", used to be called Li-Po-Tai's Alley, after a well-known Chinese herb doctor. At no. 52, the Golden Gate Cookie Factory turns out 200,000 of its famous fortune cookies every year. SPOFFORD ALLEY, by contrast, has little character, but a full history. Sun Yat Sen lived in exile here, at no. 36, and used the newspaper of the Chee Kung Tong, the *Chinese Free Press*, to propagate his reformist ideas. At no. 33 is the headquarters of the Laundry Association, one of the largest trade unions in Chinatown.

CHINESE OPERA HOUSE
The first Chinese theater in San Francisco opened in 1852 on Dupont Street. The "sung theater" (opera) was one of the community's few diversions.

ARNOLD GENTHE
Around 1895, the young Arnold Genthe left for San Francisco rather than enrol in the Kaiser's Prussian Army. Ignoring warnings not to do so, he went alone into Chinatown with his camera, and obtained fantastic pictures, of incalculable quality and historical importance because they constitute a unique visual record of pre-1906 Chinatown.

▲ NORTH BEACH

✹ Half a day

This itinerary may be combined with the Chinatown ▲ *152*, or Northern Waterfront ▲ *172* tours.

The white mists drifting off the Pacific which often envelop San Francisco during the morning and evening ■ *18* seldom rise farther than the spurs of Russian Hill. For this reason North Beach is regularly bathed in

soft sunshine not unlike that of the Italian Riviera. This climate makes the neighborhood, known as "Little Italy", one of the most pleasant in the city.

HISTORY

Until the beginning of the 19th century most of North Beach consisted of a sandy beach that extended up to today's Francisco Street, with a small lagoon fed by a tiny creek behind. As the city grew, landfill was deposited in the creek at North Point Cove, until by 1880 the strand at North Beach had disappeared beneath a layer of stone, allowing four extra blocks to be built seaward (Francisco Street to Jefferson Street). The first occupants of this new neighborhood were Chilean prostitutes, who were soon replaced by Irish and Mexicans. Before long, industry had taken hold at North Beach, with the establishment of sawmills, warehouses, a cotton mill (later converted into the Ghirardelli Chocolate Factory ▲ *176*) and Selby's Smelter and Lead Works, which stood on the cannery site until 1885. At the same time jetties, wharves and railway depots sprouted all over the area.

MEIGGS' WHARF. In 1852 an unscrupulous, big-spending entrepreneur named Harry Meiggs bought North Beach and

THE COBWEB PALACE
The *Cobweb Palace* saloon, popular in the 1850's, was known for the amazing spider population for which it was named; their webs covered its inside walls.

During the Gold Rush, Telegraph Hill ▲ *169*, overlooking North Beach, was a sea of tents.

FILBERT STEPS TELEGRAPH HILL PIONEER PARK COIT TOWER GREENWICH STEPS LEVI PLAZA

built a quay some 650 yards long at the foot of Powell Street, specifically for his own ships to unload lumber from Mendocino. Meiggs' Wharf became one of the liveliest spots in old San Francisco. Cheap hotels, saloons and bawdy houses abounded; San Franciscans came on Sundays to take the air, see the ships, eat clam soup and visit ABE WARNER'S COBWEB PLACE menagerie.

View of Meiggs' Wharf around 1860.

Greenwich Street steps in the 1890's.

THE ITALIANS. After 1860 the district changed entirely. With the steady stream of Italian immigrants, the atmosphere became much more family-oriented. Attracted by the gentle climate, the cheap real estate prices and the proximity of the port, Italian families began to move to North Beach in droves, quickly surpassing in numbers the Irish and Mexicans who had preceded them. From 1860 to 1880 Italian immigrants to San Francisco were mainly Genoese, who started shops or small businesses. Toward 1890 large numbers of southern Italians, especially Sicilians, settled in the vicinity of Meigg's Wharf ▲ *180.* Since 1970 the second and third generations of Italians have tended to prefer the Marina District ▲ *235* or the west slope of Russian Hill, and "Little Italy" is being gradually overrun by its Chinese neighbor. In any case North Beach retains its warm, southern, Bohemian flavor and is still a pleasant place to stop off for a pastry, a coffee – or perhaps some fried noodles or dim sum.

163

The blue fresco which covers the façade of the *Vesuvio Café* (above) invites passersby to have a drink and forget the hostile world around us.

BOB KAUFMAN
Among the Beat generation writers who hung around the North Beach bars was Bob Kaufman. Known to the French contingent as the Black Rimbaud, Kaufman was a visionary poet who systematically used hallucinogenic drugs, yelled his poetry in public and was often arrested. After the assassination of President Kennedy in 1963 he took a vow of silence, which he stuck to until Nixon's impeachment twelve years later. Apart from his *Golden Sardine* and *Ancient Rain*, published by his wife and friends, Kaufman wrote next to nothing. Today his biographers are still trying to put together his life's work, with only scribbled pieces of paper to go on. A Beatnik, surrealist and Dadaist, Kaufman proclaimed himself "against" everything.

COLUMBUS AVENUE

Constructed relatively late (1873) in comparison with other streets in the vicinity, Columbus Avenue slices diagonally across a network of older streets. The main thoroughfare of the North Beach district, it is probably the only one in San Francisco that fully respects the contours of the terrain. This is where some of the city's parades and processions are held, and where most of the Italian restaurants, cafés, groceries and pastry shops are located; in general, the avenue is highly animated, with plenty of Mediterranean charm. From the Transamerica Pyramid it is a walk of several blocks to the heart of "Little Italy".

COLUMBUS TOWER. The domed edifice, green, white and copper-colored, which stands against a backdrop of skyscrapers on the corner of Columbus and Kearny Streets, is one of the few Flatiron buildings ● *96* still standing in San Francisco. Just after it was built in 1907, the tower's top floor contained the offices of the notorious city official Abe Ruef, who was later sentenced to fourteen

"THE HILLS AND VALLEYS PRESERVE A CERTAIN MEMORY INTACT: ONE OF VIVACITY, ALACRITY; OF THE SMELL OF COFFEE, WINE , AND LEAVENED BREAD IN THIS THOUSAND-VISAGED PACIFIC PORT."

H. GOLD

years in prison after being found guilty of various charges involving bribes he paid and accepted while in a position of power. In 1970 Francis Ford Coppola bought and restored the Columbus Tower, which is now the headquarters of his film production company.

THE CRADLE OF THE BEAT GENERATION. The first Beatnik is said to have made his appearance on Columbus Avenue between Pacific Avenue and Broadway. Whether this is legend or not, the Beat generation who frequented the neighborhood during the 1950's have left a deep mark upon it. At the TOSCA CAFÉ (no. 242) poets with beards, black clothes and berets would sit for hours at a time discussing the major political and cultural issues of the day. Musicians, writers and celebrities still do. There is a gleaming cappuccino machine at the Tosca, and you can listen to opera arias on the old jukebox while you sip your "brandy cappuccino" (without coffee), which is the house specialty . It is best to go there in the afternoon, when you will not be bothered by the din from the neighboring Palladium disco whose dance floor is downstairs.

"VESUVIO". This bar (no. 255) was one of the shrines of the Beat generation, "hungry for jazz, sex and marijuana". Worth a visit, if only to see the portrait of Henri Lenoir, French Beatnik and former owner of the establishment, the poster of a typical Beatnik family, and the alcove reserved for "lady psychiatrists".

"CITY LIGHTS" BOOKSTORE. At no. 261, opposite the *Vesuvio*, a portrait of Baudelaire glares down on passers-by from the façade of the celebrated *City Lights* bookstore, headquarters of the Beat generation, and named after the Charlie Chaplin film. Its founder, the poet, writer and publisher Lawrence Ferlinghetti, still presides. Ferlinghetti spent much of his youth in France, where he obtained an arts doctorate at the Sorbonne in 1951. A founding member of the Beat movement, he opened his bookstore in 1953 to provide backing for a literary review, which he named *City Lights*(now published 2 or 4 times a year). Later Ferlinghetti became the first publisher of the Beat poets and a relentless popularizer of texts and ideas. Such ideas eventually overwhelmed the artistic and social conventions of the US and brought about the hippie explosion of the years 1965 to 1970. Nevertheless, *City Lights* is mainly known as the first American bookstore to sell only paperbacks. It is still going strong and even expanding. Ferlinghetti and his original partner, Shigeyosh Murao, still have a magnificent selection of poetry on offer, as well as philosophy, classical and avant-garde literature, political texts, and above all books which have been disdained or shelved by the East Coast publishing establishment.

ABE RUEF
This native of San Francisco was a brilliant law student who joined the California bar at twenty-two. He went into politics, quickly forgetting the principles of his thesis ("Purity in politics") and giving idealism second place to the corrupt practices of local politicians. He saw in the new leader of the Labor

Party, the handsome Eugene Schmitz, a perfect puppet for his ambitions. As Ruef said "Electors are like children or primitive people; given the choice between two candidates they'll always choose the strongest and handsomest." Within three years he became Schmitz's éminence grise, and when Schmitz was reelected mayor in 1903 he became San Francisco's number two figure. All bribes and payoffs were organized by Ruef. In 1908 he was sent to prison for fourteen years for extortion and corruption.

THE BEAT GENERATION

THE ORIGINALS. The Beat movement, which reached its peak in San Francisco during the 1950's, began in New York in about 1944 with the meeting of Jack Kerouac and Allen Ginsberg with the writer William Burroughs, ten years their senior. Kerouac and Ginsberg were students whose escapades had scandalized Columbia University. Burroughs had not yet published *Junkie* and *Naked Lunch* but was already questioning every form of convention, including those of contemporary literature. He became the mentor of Kerouac and Ginsberg, who were later to symbolize counter-culture in the USA. The three men led a nocturnal existence (surviving on odd jobs and above all drugs) between Times Square and the Harlem jazz clubs, where they listened to Monk, Parker and Gillespie at the *Milton Playhouse*. Soon they were joined by Gregory Corso, then aged only seventeen, who had taught himself English literature during a spell in jail. This jazz period is described by John Clellon Holmes in *Go* (1952), the first Beat novel.

ON THE ROAD. In 1946 the legendary Neal Cassady arrived in New York, fresh out of prison. Hungry for action, he was ready to try anything; with Kerouac and Ginsberg he set out "on the road" westward, following in the footsteps of the pioneers. Both food and gasoline were very cheap at the time, and Kerouac, who declared he could feel the "blood of Jack London pumping through his veins", traveled the United States in search of the real America, which he believed was gradually being replaced by the uniform "American Way of Life".

On the road, and later in San Francisco, Kerouac and Cassady (below) talked and talked.... Kerouac jotted down his thoughts, which later became the basis for his *On the Road*. Written between 1944 and 1952, the book was not published until 1957, at which time it became the bible of Beat generation.

THE REBEL POETS. "Beat", a word used to describe the hoboes who rode the rails of 19th-century America, was also used by black jazzmen to mean "broke, finished". According to Kerouac, Beat was associated with music, for obvious reasons, and also with the "Beatitudes" of Jesus, which condemn a life motivated by ambition. In part a reaction to the excesses of political conservatism, the Beat movement extolled life on the fringes of society; the idea was to cut conventional moorings, to go out in search of a different philosophy of being, and generally circumvent all social and artistic conventions. The Beat poets used words randomly, singing, dancing and shouting them as the spirit dictated. They acknowledged no formal or grammatical constraints and they routinely altered their perceptions with hallucinogenic drugs. John Clellon Holmes proclaimed a "cultural revolution on the march". The search for an authentic language, diametrically opposed to the smug America of President Eisenhower, was also expressed in jazz music (Bebop

"I HAVE SEEN THE ETERNAL DISTRIBUTOR FROM A WHITE HILL IN SOUTH SAN FRANCISCO"

L. FERLINGHETTI

emerged at about this time), in the plastic arts (Action Painting), in the theater and in literature.

THE INFLUENCE OF ZEN PHILOSOPHY. Since it had been founded by adventurers, San Francisco was fertile terrain for protest. In 1950 Jack Kerouac, Alan Ginsberg and Gregory Corso joined forces with the poets of the San Francisco Renaissance, a modest movement which had been launched in the 1930's by Kenneth Rexroth. An anarchist and pacifist influenced by Zen philosophy, Rexroth was one of the first men to read his poetry to the accompaniment of jazz. He played a catalytic role in the Beat movement and (despite his vehement denials) became known as the father of the Beat generation.

THE BEATNIKS OF NORTH BEACH. The young, penniless Beat poets, who survived on spaghetti and wine, lived at North Beach, where the rents were more or less affordable. They listened to jazz and poetry at *Minnie's Café*, the *Black Cat* and the *Iron Pot*. Their headquarters was Ferlinghetti's bookshop. In 1955 the Beat movement was officially founded with the reading of *Howl*, a long, rambling, rhythmical litany shouted out by its author Allen Ginsberg, and punctuated with a throbbing "who" refrain. A year later, *City Lights Books*, a publishing company linked to the bookstore of the same name, published the text, and the ensuing court case brought against them for obscenity swiftly called the Beat movement to the attention of a wider public, bringing a breath of fresh air to American literature. The publication of Kerouac's *On the Road* two years after, and of *Go* (1952), in which John Clellon Holmes exhorted his readers to travel the world and meet people, incited thousands of young Americans to take to the road. The main gathering points were New York, Chicago and of course San Francisco. In 1958 Herb Caen, a journalist at the *San Francisco Chronicle*, coined the word "Beatnik", which could be vaguely associated with the Sputniks of Communist Russia then orbiting the earth. Nevertheless, right-thinking Americans continued to view the devotees of Beat as nothing more significant than a bunch of strange-looking marginals with loose sexual habits.

"CITY LIGHTS BOOKS" Ferlinghetti (below) soon launched his own collection of paperback volumes, *City Lights Books*, with a view to offering an alternative to the 'cultural diktat' of the East Coast publishing houses and universities. The first collection he published was Allen Ginsberg's *Howl*. Printed in Britain, the books were intercepted by US Customs and Ferlinghetti was prosecuted for publishing obscenities. The trial mobilized artists and intellectuals all over the US, and Ginsberg won. The *City Lights Books* catalogue (above left) today includes over a hundred titles by American and foreign authors.

167

TOPLESS
The fashion for topless clubs was launched in 1964 by Carol Doda at the *Condor Club*, and survived well into the 1970's. Today, there are a few striptease cabarets, notably the *Finocchio Club* with its transvestite shows.

There are still plenty of jazz clubs (*Jazz Workshop*) and rock clubs.

NORTH BEACH MUSEUM
This little museum occupies the mezzanine of the Eureka Bank, 1453 Stockton Street. Old photographs and other items trace the history of the Italian community and of Chinatown, offering an unusual glimpse of the private side of San Francisco life.

BROADWAY

Originally the main access road to the Embarcadero (the port), Broadway has always been a more or less seedy street full of slums, gaming houses, squalid bars, bug-infested hotels and whorehouses. During World War One the district was cleaned up somewhat, but later on, during Prohibition, it became a bootleggers' resort. In the 1950's the Beat generation frequented smoky Broadway bars and jazz clubs like *Morty's* and the *Purple Onion*, while Lenny Bruce and Barbra Streisand appeared at the *Hungry i* (i for "intellectual"), Johnny Mathis at *Ann's 448*, and the folk music contingent at *On Broadway*. In 1962 the construction of the Embarcadero Freeway made Broadway more easily accessible from the outside, and a rash of bars, restaurants, cabarets and striptease joints cropped up. The avenue was flooded with bright neon lighting, which earned it the nickname "The Great White Way". These garish street lamps are still there, but many of the old Broadway clubs have made way for restaurants, giving the street more respectability than ever before.

COLUMBUS AVENUE

At the crossroads of Broadway and Columbus Avenue an astonishing fresco, completed in 1988, adorns the façade of the restaurant *New Sun Hong Kong*; it amounts to a kind of résumé of the history of San Francisco.
ST FRANCIS CHURCH. Walking down Columbus Avenue toward Vallejo Street, you pass by St Francis Church, the oldest Catholic sanctuary in San Francisco after Mission Dolores ▲ *292*. Built in 1860, this church was almost entirely gutted by the 1906 fire and was heavily restored in 1913. It closed in July 1994.

WASHINGTON SQUARE

The block between Powell, Stockton, Union and Filbert Streets was turned into a park precinct in 1862 and named in honor of the first president of the United States. This project had been under discussion ever since it was first suggested by Jasper O'Farrell in 1847 ● *91*. In fact Washington Square is more of a lawn with big trees all round than a park. During the 1906 earthquake local families sought refuge here, camping in the open while they waited for their houses to be repaired. In 1972 a crowd of terrified elderly Chinese rushed to Washington Square, believing a huge earthquake was about to take place in fulfillment of a bogus prophecy. The STATUE OF BENJAMIN FRANKLIN in the middle of the park was presented to the city in 1879 by Henry Cogswell, a dentist who

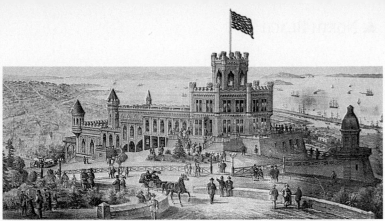

had made a fortune fitting pioneers with gold teeth at the time of the Gold Rush. As an active member of a temperance society, Cogswell had a scheme to install in whiskey-drenched San Francisco as many water fountains as there were drinking establishments. The bronze statue of three firemen in action, beside the playground off Columbus Avenue, was given to the city in 1933 by Lillie Hitchcock Coit, who also donated the Coit Tower ▲ *170*.

SAINTS PETER AND PAUL. The twin towers of the Church of Peter and Paul loom, white and serrated, over Washington Square. Ferlinghetti once called this the "marzipan church". The style of Saints Peter and Paul is ponderously neo-Gothic, and the elements of it are reinforced concrete. Consecrated in 1924 as an "Italian cathedral", it testifies to the affluence of the Italian contingent in San Francisco, which has mainly prospered in the fishing and market gardening businesses. Today at the church mass is said in three languages: Italian, English and Cantonese. Every year Saints Peter and Paul, the traditional "fishermen's church", with its statue of Santa Maria del Lume, patroness of fishermen, is the departure point for the procession of the same name, which goes down Columbus Avenue to Fisherman's Wharf on its way to bless the Italian fishing fleet. On STOCKTON STREET, toward Lombard Street, look in at the LIGURIA BAKERY for a slice of foccaccia with tomatoes or raisins, and then make a detour as far as the MAYBECK BUILDING (1736 Stockton Street), which was built by the famous architect of the same name at the turn of the century ▲ *238*.

TELEGRAPH HILL

Originally called Alta Loma by the early Mexican colonists, the 290-feet-high Telegraph Hill dominated the northeast quarter of San Francisco. Goats grazed on its slopes, and so for a while it was known as Goat Hill. Then in 1853 the city built a semaphore at its summit, in which was installed the first morse transmitter and receiver on the West Coast. This installation could register signals from a lookout near Point Lobos, so the whole city knew in advance when a brig, schooner or steamship was on its way into port. Goat Hill became Signal Hill, and later Telegraph Hill. Up until 1914 the east slope was regularly dynamited for rocks to fill in the Bay and pave the sidewalks and streets of the city.

THE TOWER ON TELEGRAH HILL
This contained a restaurant, a bar, a dance hall and an observation tower, all in one. A ground-level cable car that followed a zig-zag track up Greenwich Street (west side) was built to bring visitors to the top of the hill. Both cable car and tower burned down in the 1900's.

In 1927, the church of Saints Peter and Paul (below) was the target of a bomb attack by anarchists. The police managed to ambush the terrorists in the park, and they received the last rites on the steps of the church they had sought to destroy.

FIREBELLE LILLIE
This was the nickname given to Lillie by the firemen of the company whose mascot she was. Lillie liked to wear the firemen's uniform and made herself a feminine version of it: this consisted of a red flannel shirt, a black tie and a skirt that was scandalously short for the time, held up by a broad leather belt. There was also a helmet, stamped with Lillie's insignia.

In 1890 the semaphore was replaced by a huge wooden edifice nicknamed the "castle" which burned down at the beginning of the 20th century. Over the years Irish, Peruvians, Swiss and other foreign communities settled here, usually living in wooden cabins. Toward 1860 a wave of Italians arrived in San Francisco and moved to the hill because it overlooked the fishing port and no doubt reminded them of their native land. Several generations later the Italian colony had largely moved away and was replaced for a spell by penniless artists, who appreciated the panoramic views. Nowadays Telegraph Hill has become one of San Francisco's most expensive neighborhoods, for exactly the same reason.

COIT TOWER

The summit of Telegraph Hill is crowned by a gray concrete tower, which stands above the city like a gigantic Roman column (above). It is called Coit Tower after Mrs Lillie Hitchcock Coit, the generous donor who paid for it. Mrs Coit, who died childless in 1929, bequeathed two-thirds of her fortune to the universities of California and Maryland, and one-third to build a monument to San Francisco's firefighters at the top of Telegraph Hill. The committee appointed to oversee her project selected a design by the architect Henry Howard for a tower. The decision was controversial and a petition signed by five hundred people was raised to block it. Nevertheless, the work went ahead, and by 1937 the 70-yard-tall tower was completed, with extra funds supplied by the city as part of the public works sustained by Roosevelt's New Deal. The architects' main concern was to erect, in the small space allowed them, a monument combining Art Deco and classical styles.

LILLIE HITCHCOCK COIT. Lillie Coit was one of the more flamboyant characters in San Francisco's history. The daughter of an army doctor, she arrived in the city aged eight in 1851. While still a child she narrowly escaped death in a fire and from that time on nourished a profound respect for the courage of the men who worked for the fire department. Later she was associated with the Knickerbocker Engine Company No. 5, of which she was an honorary member. She scandalized good society with her eccentricities, living like a man, wearing trousers, gambling, smoking cigars and finally eloping with Howard Coit, a wealthy man a few years her senior. Coit married Lillie against her mother's wishes, and when he died in 1885 his widow left San Francisco and went to live in Paris, where she became a favorite in society. She returned to her beloved San Francisco to die, in 1929.

THE FRESCOES. All the walls on the ground floor of the Coit Tower are covered in frescoes. These were executed in 1933 by about thirty local artists, most of whom were only allotted an area of approximately 9 feet square each in which to deploy their talents; the better-known painters were offered larger spaces. These frescoes were created as part of the Federal Art Project set up by the Roosevelt administration's New Deal, by which artists and craftsmen received about 90 dollars a week to take part in the drive to embellish America's cities. Probably under the influence of Diego Rivera ▲ *118*, the founder of "social realism", each of the Coit frescoes depicts an aspect of the Great Depression in northern California. The city government strongly objected to their subversive content and decided to close the building to the public. This decision was taken during the dockers' strike of 1934 ● *64*.

THE FILBERT STEPS

After walking round the Coit Tower, go back to the road, continuing down from there by way of the Filbert Steps. Leading off this wooden stairway are some small alleys full of cottages, also made of wood, and half-hidden by greenery (DARRELL PLACE and NAPIER LANE). Halfway down you can stop at "THE SHADOWS" RESTAURANT, which occupies a 1920's grocery store, or at "JULIUS' CASTLE" restaurant, the name of which should be well-known to readers of the detective novels of Dashiell Hammett ▲ *132*. One particular section of the wooden houses that cover the hill was saved from the 1906 fire because their residents refused to accept the advice of the firemen to abandon the area, opting instead to stay and fight for their properties with all the means at their disposal.

LEVI PLAZA. At the foot of the hill is a pleasant square with fountains designed by Lawrence Halprin. As its name indicates, this is the headquarters of the firm of Levi Strauss, the world-famous jeans manufacturer ● *66*, which occupies the brick-and-glass office buildings around the Plaza. From here you can carry on down to the waterfront and follow the Embarcadero to the left. This will bring you to Pier 39 and Fisherman's Wharf.

The Filbert Steps are among the very few wooden staircases still maintained by the municipality. There used to be hundreds.

SOCIAL REALISM
In the early 1930's, the social and economic state of the nation and the major decoration projects started by the New Deal brought to the fore a generation of painters who were less interested in leftist politics (like the Mexicans Rivera, Orozco and Siqueiros) than in reproducing the American Scene with truly American realism. A fresco by Zakhein, called *Library*, showing a man reading Marx's *Das Kapital*, was considered to be subversive.

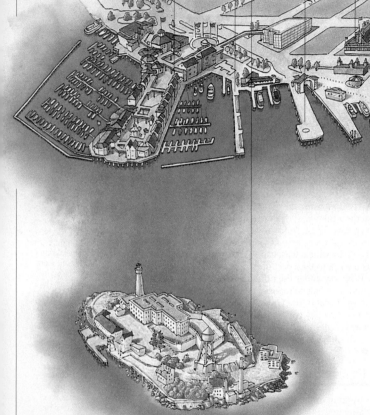

PIER 39
PIER 41
ALCATRAZ
PIER 43
WAX MUSEUM
JEFFERSON ST
EMBARCADERO
GRANT AV.
STOCKTON ST
MASON ST
PIER 45

🏃 Half a day

Entrance to the National Maritime Museum, on Beach Street.

A QUATIC PARK is a haven of green tranquility for San Franciscans. Here they can picnic on the grass, lounge on the small beach, bathe (if they do not mind cold water) and fish off Muni Pier. They can also visit the MARITIME NATIONAL HISTORICAL PARK, which includes the National Maritime Museum and the old ships tied up at Hyde Street Pier. Aquatic Park, which formerly belonged to the Golden Gate National Recreation Area (GGNRA) ▲ 234, has been independent since 1988.

NATIONAL MARITIME MUSEUM ★

The beach east of Van Ness Avenue was created on the site of an old railway bridge after the shoreline had been rebuilt to accommodate the National Maritime Museum in a setting worthy of its splendid Art Deco architecture. The building, originally a casino, has a handsome white silhouette that dominates Aquatic Park; it was conceived in 1939 by the architect William M. Mooser Jr on the model of a luxury liner, with portholes and steel bulwarks. The structure has two levels, laid out like the decks

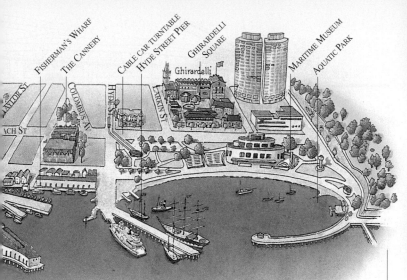

of a ship. After lying vacant for years following the casino's closure, it was taken over by the National Maritime Museum in 1951; the hallway is decorated with frescoes of underwater life by Hilaire Hiler.

THE COLLECTIONS. These include navigational instruments, paintings, photographs, postcards and model ships, notably of the *Preussen* (the largest sailing vessel ever built) and of the many crafts that frequented the port of San Francisco at the time of the Gold Rush. These objects trace the history of the port, the evolution of shipping, the development of the whaling industry and river navigation, the birth of yachting as a pastime, and the lifestyle of sailors and their families.

HYDE STREET PIER

The ferries from Sausalito and Berkeley used to put in here before the construction of Golden Gate Bridge. Today a number of older ships, maintained by the National Maritime Museum, lie moored along this pier. Some are open to the public, offering a variety of displays which give an idea of what life was like aboard ship. The "C.A. THAYER", a three-masted, wooden-hulled vessel (1895), was the last commercial sailing ship in use on the West Coast. She remained in commission until 1950 and was mainly used for freighting construction timber from the Pacific Northwest. The "EUREKA", a paddle steamer built in 1890, was in her time the world's largest passenger ferry, running between San Francisco and Tiburon. Today she contains a collection of vintage cars and trucks. The "BALCLUTHA" ★ was a steel-hulled three-master built in Scotland in 1883, and is the National Maritime Museum's prize exhibit. She carried wine and coal between Europe and San Francisco until 1900, then switched to freighting timber to Australia, bringing back cargoes of coal. From 1902 to 1930 she carried salmon fishermen and canning equipment to Alaska during the netting season. After 1933 the *Balclutha* was used for parties and other entertainments, before being purchased and restored by the National Maritime Museum.

MUNICIPAL PIER
A long jetty, built in the 1930's, runs round Aquatic Park and offers a fine view of the port.

MARINE EXHIBITS
Among the items displayed at the National Marine Museum is this carved sperm-whale tooth, or *Scrimshaw*, representing a whaler moored in the port of San Francisco at the close of the last century. *The Fall of the Clyde* is by William A. Coulter (1849–1986), a celebrated Irish seascape painter who moved to San Francisco in 1869 after several years at sea. Coulter completed about 5,000 seascapes in his long career.

173

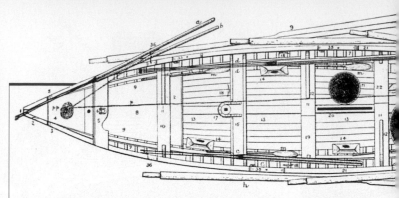

Before 1840, the ports of the California coastline were seldom used. Only a few British merchants and the odd whaler ever dropped anchor in these waters. The discovery of gold in 1848 made San Francisco an important port overnight; nevertheless it was the timber trade that underpinned the immense expansion of the city in the late 19th century. The real wealth of the region lay in its potential for agriculture and its reserves of forest land. The completion of the transcontinental railroad, in 1869, was a heavy blow to sea commerce with the East Coast; thenceforth San Francisco's maritime activities were redirected toward the Pacific Basin. The port went into steep decline during the 1960's, losing much of its trade to Oakland which had better container facilities.

"BALCLUTHA"
Post 1865, three-masted square-riggers replaced the great clipper ships, which were unsuitable for bulk cargoes.

STEAMSHIPS
After the 1850's, steamers took over river commerce and the trans-Pacific trade routes.

YACHTING
Isidor Gutte was one of the first chairmen of the San Francisco Yacht Club Yachting for pleasure developed quickly in the bay.

DESIGN FOR A WHALER

From 1882 to 1908, San Francisco was the largest whaling port in the world because of its easy access to Arctic waters.

"SCOW SCHOONER"

From 1880 to 1900, the lumber and grain trades were very lucrative. Steamers or "scow schooners" loaded up grain in the San Joaquin valley and made their way down the Sacramento River to San Francisco where the cargo was transferred to ships bound for Europe. The "scow schooners" were two-masters with flat bottoms which were built to sail in the bay and up the rivers (some did, however, manage to sail up to Alaska in the next gold rush). They were built locally after 1850 and were a common sight in the bay (left). The *Alma* is the last surviving schooner of this design.

NAVAL DOCKYARDS

At the close of the 19th century, there were about a dozen dockyards in and around San Francisco, specialising in three-masted ships and "scow schooners."

ALASKA PACKERS ASSOCIATION

In 1893, H. Fortmann merged several salmon fisheries and canning plants to form the Alaska Packers Association, situated in Alameda, across the bay from San Francisco, in 1920 (right).

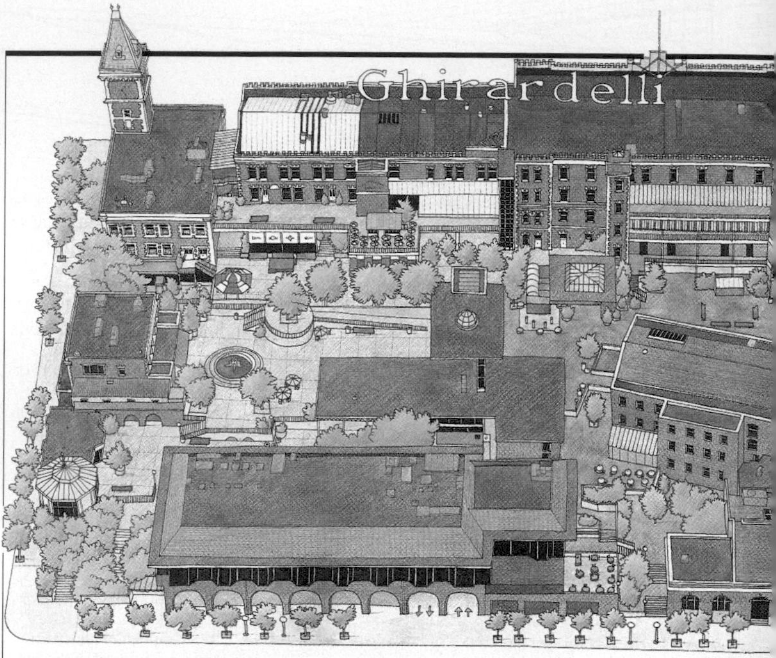

Ghirardelli

Ghirardelli

BEACH STREET
One of the busiest streets on the Northern Waterfront. Every weekend artisans come here to sell their products, while street artists (conjurors, mimes, jugglers, musicians and dancers) exercise their talents for the pleasure of passers-by. Don't miss the *Buena Vista Café* on the corner of Hyde Street, a splendid 1900's construction with projecting windows that faces Victorian Park. "Irish coffee" is supposed to have been invented here.

GHIRARDELLI SQUARE

After leaving the National Maritime Museum, cross Beach Street to Ghirardelli Square (900 North Point Street), a commercial complex installed in the buildings of a former chocolate factory; its 1926 electric sign is spectacular. This was the first of San Francisco's major industrial buildings to be converted in this manner, and indeed is one of the most successful post-industrial ventures in the USA. The conversion took place between 1962 and 1967. In devising their maze of passages and patios amid successive green terraces overlooking the bay, the architects were careful to preserve the best features of the one-time factory.

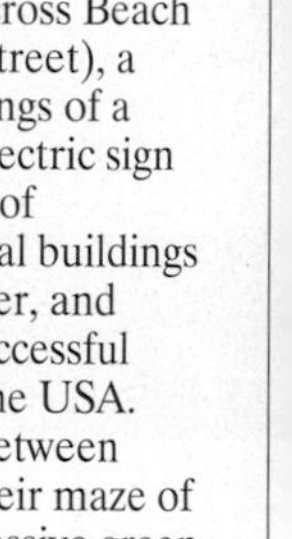

THE CHOCOLATE FACTORY. Domenico Ghirardelli (right) arrived in San Francisco from Italy in 1850, at the height of the Gold Rush. He set up a chocolate shop on Jackson Street ▲ *150*, where he prospered, and in 1893 his sons acquired a former wool factory, the Pioneer Woolen Mill, with a view to expansion. The mill building was enlarged by the architect William Mooser Sr (father of the William Mooser who built the National Maritime Museum) with new crenelated brick wings, between 1893 and 1916. The Ghirardelli factory was a model of its kind, built around a lawn on which the workers could sit and have lunch on fine days. The clocktower that crowns the factory's administrative offices (corner of North Point and Larkin Street) was modeled on the clocktower of the Château de Blois in France.

Ghirardelli chocolate, which has been famous here ever since 1850, has had innumerable advertising logos.

THE TRANSFORMATION. In 1960 the Ghirardelli family built a new, more modern plant on the far side of the bay at San Leandro, leaving the old building on North Point Street vacant. The block was scheduled for demolition, to make way for some residential apartment buildings, but at the last minute William M. Roth, heir to the Matson transport company, bought the entire block. Roth then called in the architects Wurster, Bernardi and Emmons to convert the buildings into a commercial complex that would respect their original function. New red-brick constructions were added to those of the factory, and a garage was built beneath it. Then Lawrence Halprin and Associates designed a series of tree-covered terraces, and John Matthias came up with the idea for the red-brick central pavilions. The result is a harmonious blend of old and new, which has been awarded a prize for merit by the American Institute of Architects. The mermaid fountain on the central plaza was sculpted in 1968 by Ruth Asawa.

CABLE CAR TURNTABLE The terminus of the Powell–Hyde Street Line is in Victorian Park, Beach Street, where there is a turntable for switching the vehicle's direction ● 68.

PRESERVING THE FACTORY. Roth was concerned that what remained of the factory's former activity should be preserved. Thus, in the hall under the clocktower, behind the GHIRARDELLI ICE CREAM PARLOR, one can still see the German-made machines once used here for making chocolate: mills, roasters, mixers and presses. The cocoa beans were first roasted and shelled, then crushed to a paste or cocoa "butter". White chocolate would be made by adding milk and sugar to this "butter". Cocoa paste, mixed with different quantities of sugar and afterwards with milk, would then be re-crushed until it was very fine and refined. After a lengthy mixing process it was turned into bars of hard chocolate.

WINDOW-SHOPPING. Throughout Ghirardelli Square's warren of passages and arcades there are many first-class shops of all kinds, displaying everything from craftwork to food, jewelry, clothes, books and toys. There are also a number of restaurants: a detailed guide to the commercial center is available at the information desk in the central plaza, which provides descriptions of the various other facilities available. Especially recommended are the *Mandarin* Chinese restaurant and the *Ghirardelli Chocolate Manufactory*, which serves delicious old-style hot fudge sundaes, but several others are worth a try.

"now vacuum packed"

Strictly Pure "A Meal in A Minute"

GHIRARDELLI'S SWEET **GROUND CHOCOLATE** AND COCOA **MADE INSTANTLY** PACKED IN VACUUM

Ghirardelli's Ground Chocolate Say "GEAR-AR-DELLY"

177

CRAB SOUP
In the old days fishermen and market staff had to sell their perishable goods as quickly as possible. They took no time off to sit down and eat at a table, preferring to gulp down a simple fish soup at a kiosk. The little stalls of Fisherman's Wharf perpetuate this tradition, selling takeaway crab soup.

THE CANNERY

Coming back to Beach Street along the seafront in the direction of Pier 39, the road leads past the Cannery, another commercial arcade. In 1968 promoters set out to repeat the architectural triumph of Ghirardelli Square by restoring the premises of the canning plant built by William M. Mooser Sr for the California Fruit Canners' Association on the site of the old Selby's Smelter and Lead Works (Selby's, a highly polluting complex, had been forced to move out in 1885). In 1909 the structure was taken over by the Del Monte Company, which operated it as a peach cannery until 1937. After this, the buildings were left empty for thirty years, until Leonard Martin saved them from demolition in 1963 and set about restoring them. Nowadays, although the cannery looks like a rehabilitated industrial plant, in reality it consists of a modern concrete structure on three levels designed by Joseph Esherick, hidden within the four red-brick walls of the original cannery.

SHOPS AND MUSEUMS. The cannery contains a large number of shops, as well as the Cannery wine cellars (on the ground floor, where there is an excellent choice of wines and liquors), bars, restaurants, art galleries, a movie theater, a cooking school, a TOY MUSEUM (mechanical toys and videos), the brand new Museum of the City of San Francisco, and the Cobb's Comedy Club theater (entrance from gardens) which mounts comedy shows every night. The upper floor of the center, which has been converted into a terrace, offers a spectacular panorama of the Bay, while the avenue below, which is planted with flowers, is the haunt of mime artists, musicians and other street performers, many of whom are very talented.

ANTIQUES. Among the decorative elements in the center are authentic antiques that once belonged to the press magnate William Randolph Hearst ● *70*. These include the ceiling of the *Great American Short Story* boutique (13th-century Byzantine painted marquetry), and the wood paneling, stucco ceiling and staircase of the *Chart House* bar and restaurant on the ground floor, taken from an English manor house dating from the early 17th century.

A fisherman repairing his net on Fisherman's Wharf in the early 20th century.

MUSEUM OF THE CITY OF SAN FRANCISCO. Parts of this museum, which was opened in 1991, are still under construction. Its purpose is to bring together various collections that recall San Francisco's past, such as souvenirs and relics of the Midwinter Fair ▲ *258*.

ALONG JEFFERSON STREET

During the summer Jefferson Street, which passes along the seafront between Aquatic Park and Pier 41, is one of the most crowded promenades in the city: it is said there can be as many as three thousand walkers at a time. The street is also full of artists at work. On the seafront are clothes shops and souvenir stalls, seafood restaurants (very touristy) and fish sellers hawking boiled crabs, caught beyond Golden Gate Bridge, straight from the pot. A walk along the quays past the seagulls, cormorants and seals (between Hyde and Taylor Streets) will give you the full flavor of the old fishing port.

FISH ALLEY. This section of Jefferson Street between Jones and Hyde Streets is very lively in the early morning, when the fish brought in by the trawlers are processed and loaded into trucks at the quayside. By 10 o'clock the job is finished, and the fishermen and dealers go home, leaving the waterfront to walkers.

ATTRACTIONS. Between Powell and Mason Streets is the JEFFERSON STREET AMUSEMENT ZONE, a Mecca for children which is full of video games and merry-go-rounds. Also, before you arrive at Pier 39, there are several museums worth visiting. The GUINNESS MUSEUM OF WORLD RECORDS (no. 235) contains a collection of objects mentioned in the *Guinness Book of Records*; the RIPLEY'S BELIEVE IT OR NOT! MUSEUM (no. 175) displays an array of weird items collected by Robert Ripley, who wrote the well-known syndicated newspaper feature; and the WAX MUSEUM (no. 145) has four floors of lifesize waxworks of famous people.

❝ Fisherman's Wharf, in San Francisco, is an Eldorado of restaurants, shops selling tourist trinkets and beautiful seashells, Italian stands where you can have a crab cooked to order, or eat a lobster or a dozen oysters, all with sourdough French bread. On the sidewalks, blacks and hippies improvise concerts, against the background of a forest of sailboats on one of the world's loveliest bays, which surrounds the island of Alcatraz. At Fisherman's Wharf you find, one after another, four waxwork museums. Paris has only one, as do London, Amsterdam, and Milan, and they are negligible features in the urban landscape, on side streets. Here they are on the main tourist route. And, for that matter, the best one in Los Angeles is on Hollywood Boulevard, a stone's throw from the famous Chinese Theatre. The whole of the United States is spangled with wax museums, advertised in every hotel – in other words, attractions of considerable importance.❞

Umberto Eco,
Travels in Hyperreality

179

The fishing trade in San Francisco reached a high point after the Gold Rush. Among those who came to make their fortunes were fishermen from Italy, Greece, Dalmatia and China, who eventually left the mines and fell back on their traditional trade, by which they managed to supply the city's burgeoning population. In the Bay the main harvest was salmon, crab and prawn; each different community used its own kind of boat and its ancestral fishing techniques (Italian *feluccas* and Chinese junks, for example). The bay also contained a number of oyster beds, which Jack London describes pillaging in *The Pirates of San Francisco* ▲ *310*.

FISHERMAN'S WHARF

In 1853 the entrepreneur Harry Meiggs, who had bought and converted North Beach ▲ *162*, built a 1,800-foot quay near Powell Street which came to be known as Meigg's Wharf. The area was soon filled with cheap bars and restaurants

competing for the custom of the waterfront habitués. In 1900 the fishing port established by Italian immigrants near Union Street was transferred to the Taylor Street zone, near Meiggs' Wharf, creating the present Fisherman's Wharf.

ITALIAN FISHERMEN. Genoese sailors who had no luck in the quest for gold formed San Francisco's first Italian fishing community in the 1850's. Ten years later they were joined by a new wave of immigrants, this time from southern Italy and Sicily. Skillful as the Genoese were at their trade, the southerners quickly supplanted them and the Chinese. Their fast little craft raced to and fro across the Bay; the fishing was excellent, and Fisherman's Wharf quickly became the main supply point for fishmongers and restaurateurs all over San Francisco. Meantime citizens came to walk along Meigg's Wharf, and watch the boats and the fishermen mending their nets. Since the 1960's fishing has declined, and tourism has usurped Fisherman's Wharf, which is now greatly changed. Though the fisherfolk nowadays are of many different nationalities, the quarter still retains its distinctive Mediterranean atmosphere.

THE FISHING FLEET. In 1970 the fleet was 300 vessels strong; nowadays there are about 140, only a third of which fish regularly all year round. The port, which is sandwiched between commercial centers and museums, is nonetheless relatively active behind Restaurant Row. The wooden chapel at the end of Pier 49 still watches over the returning fishermen, and in October the Sicilian parishioners of the Church of Sts Peter and Paul ▲ *169* (the "fishermen's church") carry the statue of Maria Santissima del Lume in procession from Washington Square to Fisherman's Wharf, for the annual blessing of the fleet that made their fathers rich ● *81*.

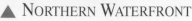

THE "MONTEREY" CLIPPER
Fisherman's Wharf can show a number of Monterey-type clippers (above) which were still being built in the 1930's. They derive from the *felucca* craft used by Italian fishermen in the bay during the 19th century ■ *20*.

MODERNIZATION OF FISHING METHODS.

In the early 20th century the hitherto profitable fishing trade underwent a recession, on account of shortages caused by overfishing and pollution. With the introduction of motor-powered trawlers, and seine nets and dragnets instead of harpoons and lines, production rose once again. The Chinese were expert at prawn-fishing, in which Europeans were largely uninterested.

When the weather was foggy, the Bay rang with the voices of Italian fishermen, who bellowed arias from popular operas to warn one another of their presence on the water and avoid collisions.

Because of its strategic position facing the Golden Gate straits, the formerly uninhabited *Isla de los Alcatraces* (Pelican Island) was garrisoned with troops and a hundred cannon in 1853. Supplanted by Fort Point in 1861, the base was transformed into a military prison; in 1907 soldiers under sentence of hard labor were put to work constructing new cell blocks on the island's high ground and laying out gardens on its formerly sterile rock surface. In 1933 Alcatraz became a federal penitentiary for hardened criminals. It was abandoned in 1963, then occupied by Native Americans from 1969 to 1971. The 12-acre island has now been turned partly into a nature reserve by the GGNRA, its owner since 1972.

WARDENS' QUARTERS

CELLS

CASEMATES · JETTY · THEATER, BOOKSHOP · LOOKOUT · SALLY PORT · CHAPEL

THE LANDING STAGE
The quay, built in 1854, is the only point on the island where visitors can disembark without risk. The prisoners, transferred to Alcatraz, would arrive in a special truck, towed by a barge up to the landing stage.

The jetty is overlooked by casemates which housed the cannons when Alcatraz was a military stronghold. The batteries became obsolete in 1891, and the casemates have now been converted into a theater and bookshop.

CELL BLOCKS

On its completion in 1911, the old prison building at Alcatraz was one of the largest reinforced concrete structures of the time. It consists of four independent cell blocks so arranged that not one of the 5-foot by 9-foot individual cells has a wall or ceiling immediately abutting the exterior. The corridor between blocks B and C, which was the one most frequently used by convicts, was known as Broadway.

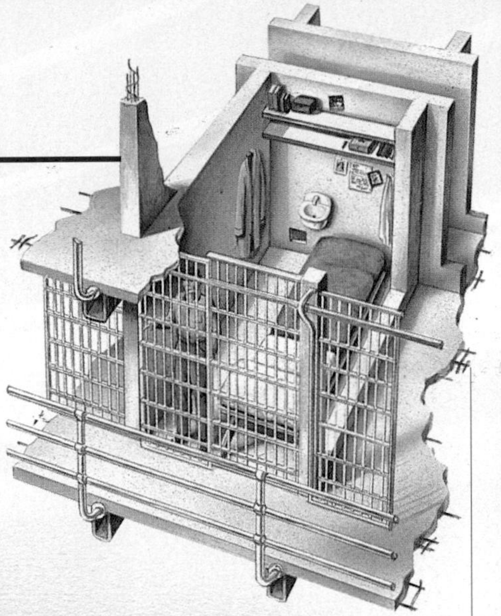

COURTYARD

WORKSHOP

WAREHOUSE

SALLY PORT
The Sally Port (1857), the former garrison building, is the oldest on the island. Beside a steep path leading to the cell blocks stands a building where the warders' chapel and school used to be; adjoining are the ruins of the bursar's office and the quarters of the staff and the prison governor (gutted by fire in 1970).

THE LIGHTHOUSE
Alcatraz lighthouse was the first of its kind on the Pacific Coast (1884). The keepers lived in a house at its foot and climbed the stairs every day to clean and refuel the lamps. When the prison buildings were built, they obstructed the old light, which was replaced in 1909 by a taller, electrically powered construction located at the cell block entrance.

AL CAPONE
Probably the all-time most famous inmate of Alcatraz was Al Capone, who spent the years 1934 to 1939 in the prison. The former Chicago Mafia chief died in Florida in 1947 at the age of forty-eight.

GARDENS ON THE ROCK
The gardens maintained by the soldiers and their families, and subsequently by the convicts, were the only green areas on the island. They still are.

REGULATIONS

Food, clothes, a roof over his head and medical care were every convict's inalienable right; but the other consolations of prison life (work, exercise, access to a library) were all privileges that had to be earned by good conduct. At Alcatraz any breach of discipline was punished by the loss of one or several of these privileges. The more serious offenses earned a spell in the "hole", Block D, where there was a row of solitary confinement cells.

ROBERT STROUD

While doing time for murder at Leavenworth prison, Robert Stroud, the "Birdman of Alcatraz", became an expert in ornithological diseases. His nickname is misleading, for he was never allowed to keep birds at Alcatraz; he was transferred there in 1942. Eventually going insane, Stroud spent seventeen years between Block D and the prison hospital, where he finally died aged seventy-two.

ALVIN KARPIS

"Public Enemy" Alvin Karpis was arrested in 1936 after pulling off two spectacular kidnappings. Sentenced for a term of twenty-seven years, nine months, he was to remain at Alcatraz for longer than any other inmate in its history. Karpis died in Canada in 1979, after being paroled.

NO ESCAPE

Every precaution to prevent escapes was taken; thirteen roll-calls per day, a warder for every three to five convicts, impromptu checks with metal detectors, body searches at the workshop exits, and many other controls. Of the fourteen escape attempts between 1939 and 1962, not one was successful.

RESTAURANT ROW

In 1960 port activity went into decline as steeply as tourism was increasing. The commercial centers of Ghirardelli Square and the Cannery opened in 1968; Pier 39 followed in 1978. At this time many of the Italian fishermen decided to switch to the restaurant business. Their names may now be seen on the signs of Restaurant Row, which includes Taylor Street between Beach Street and Pier 45. The restaurants serve seafood and fish, as well as "Dungeness crab

soup", a local specialty and a traditional Christmas dish in San Francisco.

FISHERMAN'S WHARF TO PIER 39

PIER 45. Like Fish Alley, Pier 45 is invaded by fishermen and dealers from the early hours of the morning. The submarine *USS Pampanito* is moored to the east of the jetty and is open to the public; during World War Two this vessel, which could cruise 600 feet below the surface, sank six Japanese warships and on several occasions she too was nearly sunk. Several other US Navy ships anchored along this jetty are also open to the public.

PIER 43. This is the embarkation point for Alcatraz ▲ *182*; buy tickets well in advance, especially if you plan to go on a weekend. You can also sign up here for a cruise outing, and pedicabs for visiting the port and adjoining areas can be rented at the same spot.

PIER 39. Formerly an unloading dock, Pier 39 is the northernmost point of the San Francisco peninsula. In 1978 a complex of restaurants and shops selling clothes, souvenirs, gadgets, craftwork and pastries was established here, with the general look of a "fishing village". Constructions in recycled wood designed by the architect Walker Moody stand on either side of an alley where jugglers regularly perform. This center is a favorite for family outings.

THE MARINA. Large numbers of yachts and sailing boats are docked at the landing stages of Pier 39, from which you can see, and hear, the colony of seals that has migrated to this spot from the Seal Rocks off Land's End ▲ *252*. From the end of the jetty the entire bay comes into sight: Alcatraz, Golden Gate Bridge and Marin County. The same view can be had from the restaurants of Pier 39, unless you prefer to picnic in the gardens by the water. Children will love the playground and the big merry-go-round in the central alley of Pier 39.

THE HILLS OF
SAN FRANCISCO

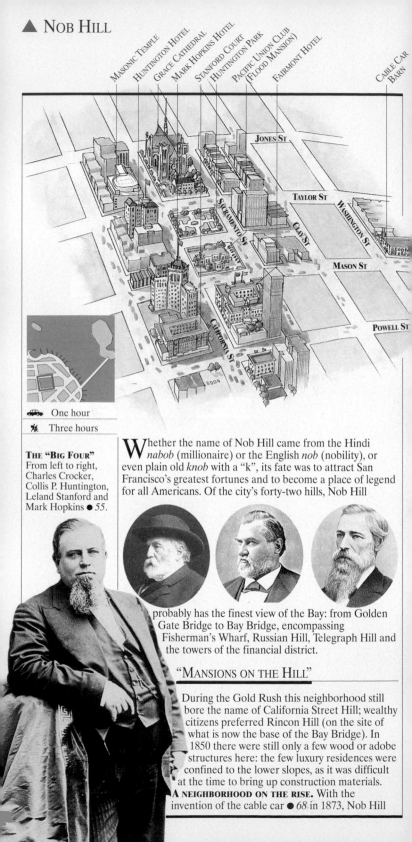

MASONIC TEMPLE
HUNTINGTON HOTEL
GRACE CATHEDRAL
MARK HOPKINS HOTEL
STANFORD COURT
HUNTINGTON PARK
PACIFIC UNION CLUB (FLOOD MANSION)
FAIRMONT HOTEL
CABLE CAR BARN

JONES ST
TAYLOR ST
WASHINGTON ST
CLAY ST
SACRAMENTO ST
MASON ST
POWELL ST
CALIFORNIA ST

🚗 One hour
🚶 Three hours

THE "BIG FOUR"
From left to right,
Charles Crocker,
Collis P. Huntington,
Leland Stanford and
Mark Hopkins ● 55.

Whether the name of Nob Hill came from the Hindi *nabob* (millionaire) or the English *nob* (nobility), or even plain old *knob* with a "k", its fate was to attract San Francisco's greatest fortunes and to become a place of legend for all Americans. Of the city's forty-two hills, Nob Hill probably has the finest view of the Bay: from Golden Gate Bridge to Bay Bridge, encompassing Fisherman's Wharf, Russian Hill, Telegraph Hill and the towers of the financial district.

"MANSIONS ON THE HILL"

During the Gold Rush this neighborhood still bore the name of California Street Hill; wealthy citizens preferred Rincon Hill (on the site of what is now the base of the Bay Bridge). In 1850 there were still only a few wood or adobe structures here: the few luxury residences were confined to the lower slopes, as it was difficult at the time to bring up construction materials.
A NEIGHBORHOOD ON THE RISE. With the invention of the cable car ● 68 in 1873, Nob Hill

quickly became a favorite zone for San Francisco's millionaires, who, far from the puritanism of New England, indulged in every possible excess. Vast fortunes were being made, notably from the profits of the huge Comstock Lode silver deposits discovered in Nevada ● *45*. The real boom on Nob Hill began with the construction of James Ben ali Higgins' villa on Taylor Street, a sixty-room house with its own stable block. Then came the palaces of the magnates responsible for the Southern Pacific Railroad ● *55*, better known as the "Big Four". Leland Stanford and Mark Hopkins shared the block formed by California, Powell, Pine and Mason Streets, a site which they reinforced with a granite retaining wall. Charles Crocker built himself a palace for the tidy sum of two million dollars, on the site of the present-day Grace Cathedral. As for Colton, the minority partner of the "Big Four", he built an Italianate palace opposite which was bought by Huntington after his death. In the wake of the railway magnates came Flood and Fair, the "Silver Kings". James Clair Flood and his associate William S. O'Brien had started out running a saloon on Commercial Street ▲ *157*, adjacent to the financial district. Little by little they managed to infiltrate the stock exchange milieu, to which most of their clients belonged. Here they pulled off several spectacular coups. In the late 1860's they went into partnership with Fair and MacKay to buy up the Comstock Lode silver mines and exploit the old seams, which everyone thought had been worked out. In 1873 they discovered a fabulous new vein; subsequently, the four partners became phenomenally rich and settled in San Francisco, where they founded the Nevada Bank of California in competition with William Ralston's Bank of California ▲ *210*. Flood built his villa between those of Colton and Hopkins, on California Street. But Fair only had time to build a gigantic granite retaining wall before his death: he never came to live on Nob Hill. Amongst other early settlers, William Walton, a rich merchant, had a house built at the corner of Taylor and Washington Streets; William T. Coleman commissioned a Roman-style villa and George Hearst moved into a white stucco Spanish-style villa on Jackson Street, after making his fortune in the mines. The day after the 1906 earthquake, nothing remained of the great palaces of Nob Hill except Flood's

THE "OCTOPUS"
The "Big Four", who had invested in the cable car and secured the monopoly of the railroad, tried to tighten their hold on San Francisco by buying the port installations. But William R. Hearst the newspaper magnate and Adolph Sutro the populist mayor of San Francisco ● *252* led an outcry against them, denouncing their business dealings as the strangulation of "octopus tentacles".

The caricaturists of *The Wasp*, along with the writer Frank Norris, were quick to exploit this vivid image and devoted a whole novel to them entitled *The Octopus*.

Foyer of the Mark Hopkins Hotel.

MARK HOPKINS HOTEL
This twenty-floor tower block in the Gothic style is basically a framework of steel girders faced with terracotta. Its penthouse bar, the *Top of the Mark*, is world famous; decorated in Art Deco style in 1936 by Timothy Pfleuger, it has recently acquired plate glass windows to make the most of the phenomenal view.

THE "SPITE FENCE"
In 1876 Charles Crocker commissioned a mansion (opposite, c. 1870) from Arthur Brown, who built him a huge palace in the style of the French Second Empire. But Crocker was never fully able to enjoy his sumptuous home, because a neighbor, Nicholas Yung, refused to sell him the lot on which he had built his own much more modest house. In retaliation, Crocker built a thirty-foot fence all around three sides of Yung's property, known as the "Spite Fence". Yung moved to Broderick Street in the late 1980's but retained the property. The fence came down in 1904 when Yung's widow finally sold the property to the Crocker family.

villa (which was built of stone, not wood) and the walls of the properties of Stanford, Hopkins and Fair.

TOUR OF NOB HILL

The intersection of California and Powell Streets, which is served by two cable car lines, is the best place to begin a tour of Nob Hill.

UNIVERSITY CLUB, 800 POWELL STREET. Constructed in 1912 by Bliss and Faville, this building in the style of the Florentine Renaissance is typical of the architecture favored by gentlemen's clubs at the beginning of the century. It stands on the site of Leland Stanford's stables, which were destroyed during the 1906 earthquake.

STANFORD COURT HOTEL, CALIFORNIA STREET. This building was erected in 1916 by the architects Curtis and Davis, and from the start was one of San Francisco's finest hotels. The only vestige from Stanford's time is the granite wall on which stood a severe-looking Victorian villa. The interior décor was highly original, with Chinese, Indian and Pompeïan reception rooms and a Gothic library. There was also a gallery in which, at the press of a button, a thicket of plants filled with exotic birds could be made to materialize. The other half of the site was taken up by the villa of Mark Hopkins, Stanford's partner in the transcontinental railroad venture.

MARK HOPKINS HOTEL. Designed in 1925 by the

architects Weeks and Day, the Mark Hopkins Hotel stands on the site of the magnate's former villa (999 California Street). This house, built by Hopkins' wife, was the most extravagant and certainly the most overwhelming of all the mansions on Nob Hill. It was, in effect, a Norman château with Victorian overtones and Gothic towers. The main floor contained a picture gallery 90 feet long and 45 feet high, a medieval-style music room, and thirty Louis XV and Gothic guest bedrooms. Mark Hopkins, who was known for his frugality, refused point blank to live in this palace and in fact died before its completion in 1878, leaving a vastly wealthy widow. In 1893 the Hopkins Mansion became the headquarters of the San Francisco Art Association ▲ 199. The palace and its thousands of wooden moldings were utterly consumed in the fire of 1906.

MASON STREET TOWNHOUSE ROW. At nos. 831, 837, 843 and 849 stand a series of small houses built by the architect Willis Polk in 1917. They are representative of ordinary pre-war private homes in San Francisco.

PACIFIC UNION CLUB, 1000 CALIFORNIA STREET. Flood's villa, which was the only one to escape the 1906 earthquake, is now the Pacific Union Club, one of San Francisco's most prestigious clubs. The forty-room building was constructed by James Flood in 1886 of brownstone specially shipped from Connecticut. Designed by the English architect Augustus Laver, this sober Renaissance-style mansion used to be surrounded by expensive bronze railings, the maintenance of which alone required a full-time employee. Willis Polk in 1908, and George Kelham in 1934, were commissioned to redecorate the interior. The result was extraordinarily luxurious, rivalling the finest clubs on the East Coast or in London. As its name indicates, the Pacific Union Club arose from the merger of the Pacific Club (founded 1852) and the Union Club (founded 1854). Annual membership fees for this highly exclusive institution are in the region of two thousand dollars – and there is a four-year waiting list.

STANFORD HOUSE, c. 1870
The hall, three floors high, was crowned by a transparent dome reflecting all the signs of the zodiac, which were encrusted in black stone on the white marble floor below.

JAMES FAIR AND THE "SILVER KINGS"
Born in Ireland in 1832, James Fair emigrated to the USA in 1844 with his parents, arriving in San Francisco at the height of the Gold Rush. But Fair eventually became more interested in the apparently exhausted Comstock Lode silver mines than in gold. In 1860 he went into partnership with Flood, O'Brien and MacKay, the latter being a former miner like himself. In 1872 the four men bought the Consolidated Virginia Mine. Thanks to the perseverance of Fair, who was known as "Bonanza Jim", they discovered a fresh lode of silver, the richest ever found in the USA, from which they made profits of well over 100 million dollars.

Entrance of the
Fairmont Hotel.

FAIRMONT HOTEL
Before his death
James G. Fair had
time to stabilize his
building site on
California Street
between Powell and
Mason Streets with a
massive concrete
wall. In 1902 his
daughter Tessie built
a hotel there,
employing the
architects James and
Merritt Reid. But the
enterprise ruined
Tessie Fair, and she
was forced to put the
project on the
market just
before the 1906
earthquake. The
furniture for the
Fairmont's six
hundred
bedrooms was
delivered only a
few days before
the fire began.
The hotel burned
merrily for over
three days.

FAIRMONT HOTEL AND TOWER, 950 MASON STREET. Toward the end of the 1940's Dorothy Draper was given the job of redecorating the foyer, and the designs she came up with subsequently established the interior as a classic example of post-war luxury. Among its notable guests from around that time, the Fairmont includes the signatories of the United Nations Charter, who stayed at the hotel in 1945. The hotel has an impressive collection of historical photographs, a succession of richly decorated public rooms and also a transparent elevator from which guests can enjoy a fine view of the Financial District during the ride.

HOTEL FAIRMONT

HUNTINGDON PARK, CORNER OF TAYLOR AND CALIFORNIA STREETS. This park, which covers the site of the former Colton Mansion, is one of the few public areas on Nob Hill. It was here that David Colton, the minority partner of the "Big Four", built his grandiose Italianate palace, with the inside walls painted to imitate white marble. In 1892 Huntington bought the house after being attacked by Colton's widow, who set out to prove that the "Big Four" had embezzled funds on a huge scale during the building of the railroad. Her husband, a close associate of Huntington's, left a devastating correspondence which was gleefully seized upon by the contemporary press. The Colton Mansion, like the others, was reduced to ashes in 1906.
HUNTINGTON HOTEL, 1075 CALIFORNIA STREET. Constructed in 1924 by Weeks and Day, this is an elegant hotel. With its collection of old photographs and its restaurant *The Big Four*, this is in a way a museum of Nob Hill in the 19th century.
MASONIC TEMPLE AUDITORIUM, 1111 CALIFORNIA STREET. Designed by Albert F. Roller in 1958, the Masonic Temple is a fine example of post-war San Francisco architecture. In reference to the Temple of Solomon, two imposing marble columns guard the entrance to the building, which is lit by a stained-glass window featuring a mason in his ceremonial apron, with the Masonic eye above. The Auditorium is used for musical performances, lectures and meetings. A small museum of Masonic history is on the top floor, and there is a superb view across the city from the terrace.

Reconstructed by
Julia Morgan, it
opened a year later.

Masonic Temple.

192

GRACE CATHEDRAL

Grace Cathedral with (below) the copy of a 16th-century Roman fountain in Huntington Park.

Situated in the block formed by California, Taylor, Sacramento and Jones Streets, Grace Cathedral, a replica of Notre Dame in Paris, was built on the site of William and Charles Crocker's former properties, made over by their heirs to the Episcopal Church. The nave stands on the site of the Queen Anne-style house built by William's son Charles, and the choir on what was once the site of William Crocker's own mansion. The construction works began in 1925, under the direction of Lewis P. Hobart, but were not completed until 1964, at which time the architects were Weihe, Frick and Kruse. Concrete and steel were used instead of stone, as they were considered to be more resistant to earthquake tremors. The altar (California granite) and the baptismal font date from 1964. The stained-glass windows are by Charles Jay Connick and date from 1930–66; the Willet windows date from 1966, and the Gabriel Loire windows date from 1964 and 1970. Some of them show "latter-day saints" such as Albert Einstein and the astronaut John Glenn. The rose window in the façade, made in Chartres in France, is also by Loire and dates from 1964. One of the towers, "The Singing Tower", has a carillon of forty-four bells made in Croydon, England, in 1938. The *Gates of Paradise* are replicas of those of the Baptistery in Florence. The CHAPEL OF GRACE, funded by the Crocker family, is surrounded by a handsome wrought-iron grille and contains a 15th-century French altar. William Crocker was a talented banker who also built up a fine private collection of paintings; during the 1906 fire most of these were saved by his faithful Chinese majordomo, who unfortunately omitted to bring out a score of pictures of dancers by Degas, which he judged to be of little value.

SKYSCRAPERS. Nob Hill, one of the areas of San Francisco most severely damaged by the 1906 earthquake, took a while to recover and it was many years before the first skyscrapers appeared there. The Art Deco CLAY-JONES TOWER on the top of the hill, at the Clay-Jones intersection, is one of the finest of those that were eventually built there.

CABLE CAR POWERHOUSE, CORNER OF MASON AND WASHINGTON STREETS. Built in 1887, the powerhouse was severely damaged in 1906 and was later renovated. It is still possible to visit the machine room which hauls the cables ● 68, and there is a small adjoining museum.

🏃 Half a day

R ussian Hill is more remarkable for its topography than for any special ethnic or social peculiarity. The hill is part of a long ridgeline extending from north to south, interrupted by a saddle at the level of Pacific Street which separates it from Nob Hill. A traffic tunnel runs beneath Broadway. Steep streets, lush gardens and panoramic views make this one of the most charming districts in San Francisco.

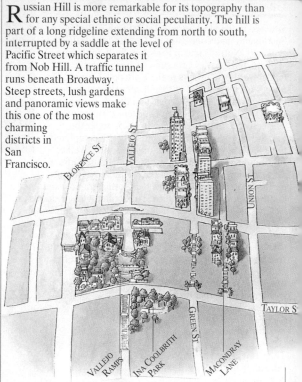

THE GREAT FIRE
In 1906 about 400 acres on Russian Hill were saved from destruction by the occupants, who kept coming back to battle the flames even though driven away several times by soldiers. The inhabitants of block 1000 in Green Street persuaded the army to help them save their homes, instead of dynamiting them to stop the spread of the fire.

The naive painting (1887) above by Percy Gray ● 110 is a view of the Bay from Russian Hill. In the background smoke is seen rising from the chimneys of the Selby Smelting and Lead Company ▲ 287, which stood on the site of today's Cannery. Pollution laws later forced the works out of town.

HISTORY

RUSSIAN HILL. The district was so named during the Gold Rush, because of seven gravestones that were found on top of the hill (between today's Broadway, Florence, Vallejo and Jones Streets). These stones bore Cyrillic inscriptions and probably marked the graves of Russian trappers from the colony at Fort Ross ● 44, or else of sailors from Russian warships which anchored in San Francisco Bay between 1806 and 1847. In 1850 eighteen unlucky "Forty-Niners" ● 49 joined the Russians in their cemetery, but over the following ten years all twenty-five graves disappeared without trace when the zone began to be built up.

DEVELOPMENT. Less steep, and oriented toward the center of town, the eastern flank of the hill was the first part of it to be developed. During the 1850's, a quantity of wooden rowhouses ● 92 were built on the terrain between Taylor and Powell Streets, from Broadway to Union Street, where the immigrants lived. The remainder of Russian Hill was gradually built up between 1850 and 1880, with the levelling of Union Street in 1860, which made it easier to climb the hill, and the establishment of cable cars on Union Street (1880), Mason Street (1887) and Hyde Street (1891). Nevertheless,

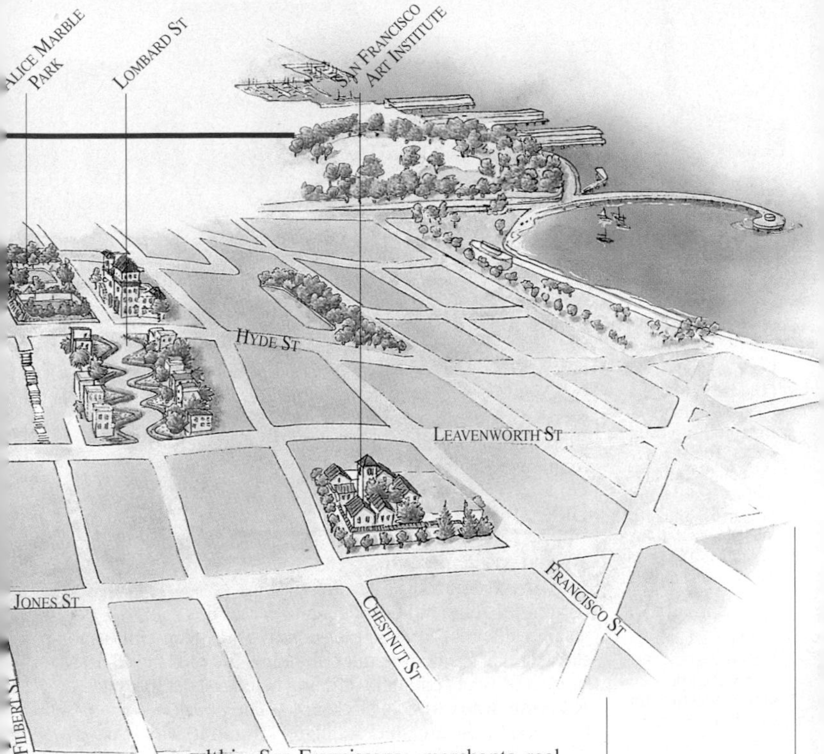
Alice Marble Park
Lombard St
San Francisco Art Institute
Hyde St
Leavenworth St
Jones St
Chestnut St
Francisco St
Filbert St

wealthier San Franciscans – merchants, real estate speculators and other leading citizens – did not wait for these improvements; from 1860 onward they were building splendid houses on the north flank of the hill, some of which escaped the 1906 fire and are still standing. To the south rose more modest homes, as exemplified today by the 1000 block on Green Street. At the beginning of the 20th century rowhouses predominated, and buildings each containing two or three apartments began to take the place of single-family houses. Many buildings dating from the Gold Rush vanished in the 1906 fire, along with huge numbers of Victorian houses, with only the hilltop and block 1000 in Green Street being saved. Because of the high price of building land, Russian Hill was rebuilt in 1900's style, the best examples being on Union Street between Mason and Jones Streets. At the same time several magnificent shingled Mediterranean-style houses were erected in the neighborhood. Between 1910 and 1920 a number of

View of Russian Hill and Washington Square in 1865.

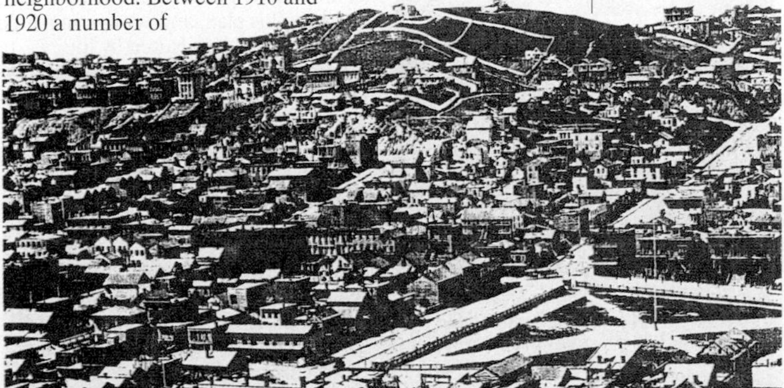

taller residential blocks were raised, which are still highly appreciated by local buyers. Their successors, the modern towers of 1950–60, caused such an outcry that the city was obliged to impose a height limit of 120 feet.

BROADWAY TO FLORENCE STREET

JOSEPH ATKINSON HOUSE, 1032
BROADWAY. From 1853 onward a group of architects and builders began to create a small residential zone on the summit of Russian Hill. Among the original five houses still remaining, the oldest and best-preserved is an Italianate building belonging to Joseph Atkinson, who owned a brickworks. The house was probably designed by the architect William H. Ranlett, with whom Atkinson worked in partnership on several San Francisco projects. During the 1890's Atkinson's daughter held parties in the house, as well as literary meetings.

INA COOLBRITH PARK. From 1869 to 1875, when the city's schools were desegregated, this site at the corner of Vallejo and Taylor Streets was occupied by a school for black children. In 1908 an old wooden cabin was set up here containing an experimental wireless station, after which the city paid for a park to be laid out and named it after a local poet.

The Golden Gate Bridge (above top) and Alcatraz (above), both seen from Russian Hill.

VALLEJO STREET STEPS AND RAMPS. In 1894 Willis Polk suggested that the goat-track leading up to Vallejo Street should be made into a road and then "...if we fix up those plots tastefully, the place will be one of the most charming in San Francisco". Ten years later Horatio P. Livermore and a few neighbors resolved to execute this plan, and it was completed in 1914 after a delay caused by the earthquake. The balustrades on Taylor and Jones Streets and the traffic circle at the center of the block lend a satisfactory unity to the ensemble.

POLK-WILLIAMS HOUSE, 1013–19 VALLEJO. This is one of the most remarkable shingle houses in California. In reality it is made up of two adjacent buildings, of which the one on the west side once belonged to the painter Dora Williams, widow of the head of the School of Design ▲ *199*. Designed with an admirable regard for unity by the architect Willis Polk, this construction with its slightly curved gables is modeled on the medieval wooden architecture of northern France.

REVEREND WORCESTER'S BUILDINGS, 1030–6 VALLEJO. San Francisco's first shingle houses ● *96* were designed by the Reverend Joseph Worcester, a member of the Church of the New Jerusalem, a believer in Swedenborg's illuminist theory, and a great lover of architecture. He designed three houses on Vallejo, nos. 1032, 1034 and 1036, in 1888 for a member of his congregation who wanted to make an investment in real estate. A year later the reverend built a house for himself next door at 1030 (the present Hermitage). Painters and architects such as William Keith, Bruce Porter, Willis Polk and Daniel Burnham frequently visited Worcester here to discuss esthetics.

FLORENCE STREET ★

The summit of Russian Hill is to the east of Florence Street on Vallejo Street, at the top of the steps. From 1894 to 1897 the writer GELETT BURGESS (author of *I never saw a purple cow* and *Goop*) lived in a house that once stood on Florence Street.

THE LIVERMORES. Between 1912 and 1916 Horatio Livermore and his son Norman built approximately ten houses at the top of Russian Hill, four of which are on Florence Street (nos. 35, 37, 39 and 40). Inspired by a trip to Italy, father and son asked the architects to model their work on that of Italian hill villages; the result occasionally looks more like the adobe houses of the Pueblo Indians of the southwestern US. No. 1 Russian Hill Place, a superb composition of Mediterranean elements designed by Willis Polk, is perhaps the most interesting of the group.

MACONDRAY LANE

Macondray Lane, formerly known as Lincoln Street, was opened in 1852 by the owner of the block, Seth S. Lincoln, and after 1906 was renamed for a prominent local merchant. Though never intended as a thoroughfare for vehicles, the lane eventually had to be leveled because its slope was so abrupt. Nos. 15–17 constitute the former house of Giuseppe Cadenasso, a landscape painter of Italian origin who lived here at the turn of the century and was known as the "Corot of the West Coast". After studying at the School of Design in the 1880's, Cadenasso went on to exhibit his work and became famous for his treatment of the silvery surfaces of eucalyptus leaves. The writer Armistead Maupin chose Macondray Lane as the main setting for his novel, *Tales of the City*.

GELETT BURGESS (1866–1951) Expelled from Berkeley for misconduct, Burgess proclaimed himself a poet of the Art Nouveau and set out on a career as a dilettante writer in the mold of Oscar Wilde. In 1895 he founded a group known as *Les Jeunes* with Bruce Porter, Ernest Peixotto and other artists. At his home on Florence Street the group produced a magazine called *The Lark*, which mostly dealt in humorous drawings, burlesque poems (like Burgess' celebrated "Purple Cow") and his strip cartoon *Goop*. Later Burgess went to New York, where he continued to write but was never successful. His house on Russian Hill was destroyed in the 1906 fire.

A. MOOR JR HOUSE
The house of the lawyer A. Moor Jr, which stood on the intersection of Chestnut and Hyde

Streets, strongly resembled a Piranesi engraving, with classical ornaments and ivy-covered walls. Designed in 1902 by Bliss and Faville, it was demolished and replaced by a modern building in 1954.

LOMBARD STREET
In the 1920's this street, between Hyde and Leavenworth Streets, was a two-way thoroughfare. Most of the blocks were occupied by the extensive gardens of Carl Henry's house. At his death these were divided into lots; Montclair Terrace was created in 1937, and new houses added.

GREEN STREET

Block 1000 of Green Street was built over a period of thirty years (1850–80). The northern section of the street burned down in 1906, but the owners of about five houses at the south end managed to save their property. These are still standing today.

FEUSIER OCTAGON HOUSE, 1067 GREEN STREET. In the mid-19th century Orson Fowler's book *A Home for All* started a nationwide fad for octagonal houses. San Francisco acquired five of these; the second to be constructed was the one in Green Street, built in the 1850's by George Kenny, who had arrived from New York with his friend Howe Bancroft to found a bookshop. In 1890 a new owner added a Victorian-style mansard roof.

BELLAIRE APARTMENTS, 1101 GREEN STREET. During the 1920's the architect H.C. Baumann built hundreds of new residences in San Francisco. In 1928 he invested his personal fortune in this project, a majestic tower with high curved porches and stucco ornamentation. Baumann was ruined by the collapse of the luxury real estate market during the Depression.

At an early stage the people living in Lombard Street
started growing flowers within each curve of the street.
When he moved into the neighborhood, Peter Bercut
planted hydrangeas along the road, which gives this
section of it a charming unity.

An old house in the
neighborhood.

**HISTORY OF AN
INSTITUTION**
In 1874 the San
Francisco Art
Association founded
a fine arts school,
the School of Design,
which soon attracted
talented teachers and
pupils. Its first
director (1875–86)
was the landscape
painter Virgil
Williams ● *314*, who
had run the
Woodward's Gardens
Art Gallery ▲ *296* for
many years. His
successors – Thomas
Hill (1886–7) ▲ *110*,
Emil Carlsen
(1887–9), Raymond
Yelland (1889–90)
and Arthur Mathews
(1890–1906) – were
also celebrated
painters.

LOMBARD STREET, THE "CROOKEDEST STREET" ★

Blocks 2100 and 2200 of Lombard Street, renowned as the
"World's Crookedest Street", have been in existence since
1922, at which time the public works department tore out the
paving stones of the block and relaid the road in a series of
hairpin bends to admit motor traffic.

SAN FRANCISCO ART INSTITUTE

A neo-colonial Spanish-style building at 800 Chestnut Street
is the home of what is now called the San Francisco Art
Institute, completed in 1926. Going against the usual practice
of the time, Arthur Brown Jr, the architect, left the concrete
exterior unrendered, foreshadowing the fashion of forty years
later. Stafford Keating Clay designed the modern addition to
the building. The school's exhibitions of young artists' work
and its temporary shows (right) are open to the public.
THE GEORGE STERLING GLADE. In 1936, after the suicide of
one of San Francisco's most famous poets, the Spring Valley
Water Company decided to landscape an empty lot on the hill
next to the reservoir, at the intersection of Larkin and
Greenwich Streets, and dedicate it to him. George Sterling
published several collections of poetry which made his
reputation in San Francisco, but not beyond; even at the time
of his death his work was distinctly outdated.

In 1893 the School
moved to Mark
Hopkins' former
home on Nob Hill
▲ *190*. In 1906 it was
destroyed and in 1920
the site was sold to a
hotel. The school
then acquired the lot
on Russian Hill,
where the present
building stands. In
1913 it was renamed
the San Francisco Art
Institute.

| 🚶 | Three hours |
| 🚗 | One hour |

MEMORIES OF THE FIRE
Pacific Heights, which escaped the 1906 fire, was immediately afterwards invaded by hordes of refugees. One former resident

remembered hearing for days on end "the scrape of trunks and suitcases being dragged along the streets".

Pacific Heights, clamped to the hillside north of California Street between the Presidio to the west and Van Ness Avenue to the east, is now the most exclusive neighborhood in San Francisco. Elegant Victorian houses, Italianate villas, smart schools and foreign consulates succeed one another along tree-lined streets that have dizzying views across the bay. Every architectural period imaginable is represented here, and some of the buildings are an extraordinary mixture of styles.

HISTORY. The first settlers in the zone, who were dairymen, used to invite their friends out from the city to hunt on the land. In 1867, City Hall incorporated into the city all the acreage between Lafayette Park, Alta Plaza Park and Alamo Square. But this quarter, known as the Western Addition ▲ *230* because it extended San Francisco westward, hardly evolved at all before the appearance of the cable car in 1878. At the time private mansions were being built around Lafayette Square, Van Ness Avenue, Franklin and Gough Streets. In the next ten years opulent new houses appeared on the block corners. But it was not until the 1906 earthquake that the area really got into its stride; at that point high society abandoned Nob Hill ▲ *190*, which was devastated, and moved to Pacific Heights, which had been spared major damage and which still had large building sites available. During the 1930's concrete Spanish-style buildings replaced the old corner mansions; the new rich tended to travel about more, and they discovered that an apartment was less expensive to maintain than a fully staffed mansion. About a third of these new luxury buildings, which are sometimes really sumptuous, were built by the architect C.A. Lewsdorfer. The automobile had by now begun to take over from the cable car, and the Pacific Avenue line was

SMITH HOUSE   ALTA PLAZA PARK   PALACE OF FINE ARTS   FLOOD MANSIONS   BOURNE MANSION   SCHUBERT HALL   LAFAYETTE PARK   SPRECKELS MANSION   OCTAGON HOUSE   HAAS-LILIENTHAL HOUSE   LOMBARD ST

STEINER ST   LAGUNA ST   CALIFORNIA ST   SACRAMENTO ST   WASHINGTON ST

closed down in 1929. The residents of the
area formed an even more exclusive, élitist clique than ever.
At the beginning of the 1970's the influential Pacific Heights
Association imposed regulations limiting building heights to a
maximum of five floors. At the foot of the hill, meanwhile, the
storekeepers of Union Street were transforming residential
buildings into shops and offices.

FROM ALTA PLAZA PARK TO PACIFIC AVENUE ★

Alta Plaza Park occupies the summit of the hill between
Jackson, Clay and Fillmore Streets. Jackson Street, at the
northwest corner of the park, is the best place to begin a tour
of the splendid residences of Pacific Heights.
GIBBS HOUSE, 2622 JACKSON STREET. This Italian Baroque
villa, now known as Stonehouse, was built in Oregon
sandstone with a roof of varnished tiles and was the architect
Willis Polk's first commission in 1894. The client was the
industrialist George Gibbs, who intended it to be a country
house: but the Heights were built up so rapidly that the
terraced gardens provided for in the initial project were never
laid out. For a while Gibbs House
was used as the Japanese consulate,
which closed down during World War
Two. From 1947–93 it belonged to
the Institute of Music and
Arts. Today it is a private
residence and is undergoing
restoration after damage
caused by marine erosion
and the 1989 earthquake.

**THE VIEW FROM THE
EAST.** This view from
Steiner and Clay
Streets (Alta Plaza
Park) takes in Pacific
Heights, the Fillmore
neighborhood,
Alamo Square,
Lone Mountain,
Haight-Ashbury
and Twin Peaks.

DIVISADERO
To get from Mission
Dolores ▲ 294 to the
Presidio ▲ 240,
Spanish soldiers and
travelers once took a
path called
Divisadero, or
"lookout path".
Despite a number of
alterations,
Divisadero Street still
exists, with a
panoramic view over
the Pacific Ocean.

Left, Smith House
▲ 202.

201

SMITH HOUSE, 2600 JACKSON STREET. A little farther on is the red brick house (right) which was given by Irving M. Scott to his daughter Alice, after her wedding to Reginald Knight Smith. It was built in 1895–7 by Ernest Coxhead in a mixture of Jacobean and Georgian styles, with outer walls three feet thick. The red bricks had to be imported specially, substantially increasing the building cost. The house was used as a soup kitchen for refugees after the 1906 earthquake and was one of the first in the neighborhood to be wired for electricity.

JAMES IRVINE HOME. On the way down Pierce Street to Pacific Avenue, look out for no. 2415–21, a neo-Tudor-style house built in 1897 for the Irvine family who owned a third of Orange County in southern California at that time. This wood and plaster house was planned by Edgar Matthews, whose style is evident in the distinctive design of the windows.

PACIFIC AVENUE

Turning right along Pacific Avenue, you come to Shreve House (no. 2523). This fine peach-colored construction was designed by Willis Polk in 1905. The moldings and projections of the upper floors are particularly attractive.

MONTEAGLE HOUSE, 2516 PACIFIC AVENUE. A *Blue Book* member of high society, Louis F. Monteagle commissioned this neo-Gothic mansion (completed in 1923) from Lewis Hobart, the architect of Grace Cathedral ▲ *193*. The red brick section of it, on the right, was a later addition. This building now houses the British Consulate.

LEALE HOUSE, 2475 PACIFIC AVENUE. Raised in 1853, this house was originally a four-room farmhouse belonging to a cattle rancher. John Leale, a ferryboat captain famous for his autobiography *Recollections of a Tule Sailor,* bought it in 1883 and added the porch and façade. The Italianate garage was added in 1980.

BOURNE MANSION, 2550 WEBSTER STREET (PACIFIC/ BROADWAY). An imposing Georgian building in dark brick, Bourne Mansion was designed by Willis Polk in 1896 for William Bowers Bourne, who would be San Francisco's richest citizen during the 1930's.

FROM BROADWAY TO LAFAYETTE PARK

From the intersection of Fillmore Street and Broadway, there is a view taking in the bay, Alcatraz Island, Angel Island with its abundant vegetation, and the blue hills of Tiburon beyond. This part of Broadway is lined with magnificent houses.

GRANT MANSION, 2200 BROADWAY. This red brick building was constructed in 1910 for Joseph Grant, president of the Columbia Steel Company, to plans drawn up by the New York architects Hiss and Weeks. Since 1948 it has been a girls' school, the Convent of the Sacred Heart.

> "THE SIGHT OF A HILL ALWAYS GIVES ME AN IRRESISTIBLE
> YEARNING TO CLIMB TO THE TOP OF IT . . . WHICHEVER
> WAY YOU TURN, THERE'S A SLOPE OR A DESCENT
> OF SOME KIND." JOHN DOS PASSOS

THE TWO FLOOD MANSIONS. On Broadway, between Fillmore and Webster Streets, are two houses built by Flood, the wealthy "silver baron" ▲ *191*. The one at 2222 was erected soon after the earthquake of 1906. For greater security, Flood had promised his wife that he would build on granite. The architects Bliss and Faville designed a Renaissance-style house entirely of pink Tennessee stone, which was built on a granite base. The granite had to be imported, because it does not occur naturally in the area. The works were completed in 1916. The earlier building at no. 2120 had been built in similar Renaissance style for Flood's son James Leroy in 1901. Made of wood throughout, it was painted in trompe l'oeil to give the impression of a stone palace. After this, turn back up Buchanan Street to Pacific Street.

SCHUBERT HALL, 2099 PACIFIC AVENUE (BUCHANAN/LAGUNA STREETS). Built in 1905 for John D. Spreckels, this wood and stucco structure has contained the library of the CALIFORNIA HISTORICAL SOCIETY for thirty years.

WHITTIER MANSION. Turning right into Laguna Street, note the massive building in pink sandstone at no. 2090. The architect Edward R. Swain designed this in 1896 for the financier William Whittier. The inside walls are covered in paneling of mahogany and light oak, carved and inlaid. This was the first house in San Francisco to be equipped with central heating. Now being restored, it belongs to a Japanese industrialist. Continuing via Laguna Street, the road is fairly steep until the intersection with Washington Street, at which point you enter Lafayette Park.

SPRECKELS MANSION ★

At no. 2080 Washington Street (corner of Octavia Street) stands one of the most elegant private houses on the West Coast. This huge white building with its Ionic columns was commissioned in 1913 by Adolph Spreckels, a mega-rich sugarcane magnate, and his wife Alma, and designed by the couple's friend George Applegarth, architect of the Palace of the Legion of Honor ▲ *248*.

The Palace of Fine Arts, above.

ADOLPH B. SPRECKELS
Claus Spreckels, father of Adolph, made friends with King Kalakaua while on a trip to Hawaii, and won most of the island of Maui from his host in a game of poker. He became the "sugar king" by building refineries on the island and in San Francisco. Adolph, heir to the sugar king's fortune (and title) married Alma de Bretteville in 1908. Adolph was heavily involved in the development of Golden Gate Park and financed, among other things, the building of the museum at the Palace of the Legion of Honor.

The elegant Spreckels Mansion at no. 2080 Washington Street.

"PARTHENON OF THE WEST COAST". Spreckels Mansion soon became known by this term. Occupying an entire block between Jackson, Gough, Octavia and Washington Streets, it contained no fewer than twenty-six bathrooms, as well as a swimming pool, visible at the end of the park. Alma Spreckels ▲ *248* bathed here daily even when she was well into her eighties. The house has been featured in a number of films, including George Sidney's *Pal Joey*; today it belongs to the popular novelist Danielle Steel, who lives there with her thirteen children.

LAFAYETTE PARK
This park covers the top of the hill, facing the Spreckels Mansion. In the clump of trees surrounded by broad lawns there once stood a house belonging to the squatter Samuel Holladay, the site's first occupant. In 1879 the pioneer western scientist George Davidson built California's first astronomical observatory, which remained in use until 1907.

MUSEUM
Preserved by the National Society of Colonial Dames of America, Octagon House moved here from its original location on the far side of the street and was transformed into a museum (entrance free).

HAAS-LILIENTHAL HOUSE

The huge Victorian house at no. 2007 Franklin Street was built in 1886 by Peter Schmidt in the style of Stick Lake. Formerly the residence of the Bavarian trader William Haas and his family for over eighty years, it is now the headquarters of the Foundation for San Francisco's Architectural Heritage and is furnished throughout in Victorian style (right). (It is open to the public Wednesdays and Sundays.) Farther along Franklin Street and to the left of Vallejo Street, are several fine examples of Arts and Crafts-style cottages ● *98*, which date from 1909; and beyond these, at no. 1772, stands an eclectic building with a mansard roof which blends influences from both Italian and French styles of architecture. This building, designed in 1875 by the architect Edmund Wharff, was given by Mayor Ephraim Burr as a wedding present to his son.

OCTAGON HOUSE

At no. 2645 Gough Street, between Union and Green Streets, stands a pale blue, octagonal building erected in 1861 by a kidney specialist, who was convinced that this shape was ideal for the health of the occupants because every room received a maximum amount of sunlight. The interior is decorated throughout with colonial-style furniture. After this, continue into UNION STREET, a busy commercial thoroughfare between Gough and Steiner Streets which is full of smart boutiques, antique dealers and luxury restaurants in restored Victorian houses. No. 2040 (recognizable by the palm tree in front of it) is the old COW HOLLOW farmhouse after which this neighborhood, formerly a cattle pasture, is named.

FINANCIAL
DISTRICT

▲ FINANCIAL DISTRICT

BANK OF AMERICA

TRANSAMERICA PYRAMID

BANK OF CALIFORNIA

MILLS BLDG

345 CALIFORNIA

ALCOA BLDG

SHELL BLDG

101 CALIFORNIA

EMBARCADERO

HYATT REGENCY

JUSTIN HERMAN PLAZA

SOUTHERN PACIFIC BLDG

RUSS BLDG

CLAY ST

SACRAMENTO

CALIFORNIA ST

PINE ST

BUSH ST

SUTTER ST

POST ST

SANSOME

MARKET ST

CROWN ZELLERBACH

P.G. & E. BLDG

MATSON BLDG

FEDERAL RESERVE BANK

FERRY BLDG

MONTGOMERY

KEARNY ST

LOTTA'S FOUNTAIN

CROCKER GALLERIA

HOBBART BLDG

SHERATON PALACE HOTEL

Three hours

A 19th-century lithograph, taken from *The Wasp*, which shows the New Pioneer Building (opposite page, below).

The Financial District, San Francisco's commercial hub for nearly 140 years, contains the principal banking institutions and skyscrapers of the city.

BEGINNINGS OF THE FINANCIAL DISTRICT. The Financial District dates from 1852, when the first three banks were established on California and Montgomery Streets. By 1897 the Bank of California, the Merchants' Exchange and the Fireman's Fund, among many others, had established themselves on California Street. Between 1860 and 1870 the discovery of silver in the Comstock Lode ● 45 revitalized the region's economy. At this time the mining companies of Nevada established their headquarters in San Francisco, injecting new money into the city's banks, which proliferated in response to the mushrooming demand for their services. Some of these banks were branches of leading British and French institutions, but most were founded by California financiers. Soon the streets of the Financial District were filled with substantial Italianate stone buildings, three or four stories high. Insurance companies,

brokerage houses specializing in mining shares, private libraries and office buildings with shops on their ground floors appeared alongside the banks, and eventually the *Russ, Lick* and *Cosmopolitan* hotels, which had opened on Montgomery Street in the early 1860's, were joined by Market Street's *Grand Hotel* and *Palace Hotel*.

THE FIRST SKYSCRAPERS ● *104.* The first steel-frame skyscraper appeared in the Financial District in 1889. Burnham and Root, architects from Chicago, designed the Romanesque Chronicle (1889) and Mills (1892) buildings; both owe much to Henry Hobson Richardson and both have the tall windows that distinguish the Chicago School. The skyscrapers built later, such as the Kohl Building (1900) or the Merchants' Exchange (1903) are more classical in style; this became the norm after 1906. In the years following the earthquake and fire the new buildings became taller and taller, culminating in the twenty floors of the Standard Oil Building (completed in 1922). In the late 1920's yet another style was sought for a new generation of skyscrapers: Chicago again served as an example to San Francisco, with the Russ, Shell and PT & T buildings (1925–9) displaying the same soaring outlines and split-level top floors as the magnificent architectural design submitted by Eliel Saarinen for the 1922 Chicago Tribune competition. After World War Two many more office buildings were built, in a style that was resolutely modern ● *106.* Nowadays the most recent buildings of the Downtown Plan have returned to forms of architecture that resemble the materials and graceful lines of the Financial District as it used to be in the 1860's.

EMBARCADERO CENTER
This L-shaped complex designed by John C. Portman and Associates (1971–82) stands between Sacramento and Clay Streets. It includes four office towers, two hotels and has

stores in each building. Though the entrance is not very attractive, the maze of catwalks and staircases within are worth exploring. Embarcadero Four boasts a sculpture three stories high, with delicate outward-vaulting arcs at its summit. Like the center itself, the material (reinforced concrete) is a disappointment, but the form of the sculpture is remarkable. The HYATT REGENCY HOTEL (1973) is famous for its twenty-floor atrium, with another sculpture: *Eclipse* by Charles O. Perry.

207

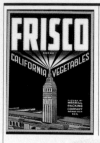

FERRY BUILDING

Constructed between 1896 and 1898 by the architect A. Page Brown, the Ferry Building represents an era when there were still neither bridges nor freeways in San Francisco. Its outstanding strategic position at the end of Market Street has become much more clearly defined since the demolition of the Embarcadero Freeway, in the wake of the 1989 earthquake.

HISTORY. After the completion of the Transcontinental Railroad in 1869 ● *54*, with its terminus at Oakland, the volume of sea traffic between the two cities grew apace. In 1873 the Central Pacific Railroad Company set about building its own port facility, a long, gloomy building with a clocktower, which was quickly found to be inadequate in size. The present building, erected by the State of California, is composed of a central pavilion topped by an imposing clocktower modeled on the Giralda tower in Seville; this is flanked by two wings, each with eighteen arches. Like many other constructions of the period, the Ferry Building is built of grey Colusa sandstone reinforced by a steel framework. From the day of its opening in 1898 until the inauguration of Bay Bridge in 1936 ▲ *306*, this was the busiest place in San Francisco. Passengers on the bay ferries mingled here with transcontinental travelers, as they emerged from the concourse to take their streetcars in front of the building. The ferries ceased to function altogether in 1958; but in the 1970's the service to Marin County and Vallejo was re-established.

On the corner of California and Front Streets stands one of the last groups of small Victorian buildings constructed in the Financial District. The venerable *Schroeder's* (founded in 1893) is at 240 Front Street and the *Tadich Grill*, the oldest restaurant in San Francisco is at 240 California Street. There is also a concrete building with a curious green terracotta façade, and windows with small panes and bronze frames.

ALONG MARKET STREET

A VITAL ARTERY. This street links the seafront with Twin Peaks; for many years it was recognized as San Francisco's main street. Taverns and sheds selling food were the first constructions here; they were soon replaced by office buildings, movie theaters, banks and department stores. In 1948 the historian Robert O'Brien described Market Street as the "lowest common denominator of San Francisco". Post-1880 the Market Street streetcar route marked the boundary between the affluent northern quarter and the working-class south (South of Slot) ▲ *146*.

The skyline in 1958.

This service, which was later doubled by the municipal authorities, was for many years an exceedingly awkward obstacle for automobiles. The Irish engineer Jasper O'Farrell, who laid out Market Street in 1847 parallel to the old route to Mission Dolores, must have known what he was doing, for it has remained the most logical and popular way of getting to San Francisco's outskirts. Nowadays it would be hard to imagine the city without it.

SOUTHERN PACIFIC RAILROAD BUILDING, 1 MARKET STREET. The Southern Pacific Railroad Building, along with the other older edifices nearby (the Ferry Building, the Matson Building and the Pacific Gas and Electric Building) lend an agreeably warm accent to this sector of town, which is

otherwise dominated by cold glass and steel. With its red brick, its arcade of fine brownish ocher and Renaissance-Baroque décor, this 1916 building by Bliss and Faville used to be the headquarters of the company that controlled regional transportation and agricultural policy from 1869 to the beginning of the 20th century. The economic stranglehold of the giant railroad, known as the "octopus" ● *54*, was so pervasive that it was many years before California was able to break free of its tentacles.

FEDERAL RESERVE BANK BUILDING, 101 MARKET STREET. Finding its premises at 400 Sansome Street too cramped, the Federal Reserve Bank demolished an entire block of older buildings and replaced them with this composition of glass and pink concrete. The entry hall, with its white portico, contains a museum that with an exhibit demonstrating how the Federal banking system operates.

MATSON BUILDING, 215 MARKET STREET. This 1921 building by Bliss and Faville was at one time visible from the bay. Polychrome varnished terracotta moldings (fish, waves, whales, shellfish and rigging) adorn its façade; the porch roof is marked with a large "M". Together with the Dollar Line and the Spreckels Oceanic Steamship Line, the Matson Navigation Co. was one of the biggest shipping companies in the history of San Francisco. Its founder, a Swede named William Matson, began by transporting cargo and passengers between Hawaii and California. The company expanded hugely under the management of his son-in-law, William P. Roth, whose luxury liners operated in the South Seas.

PACIFIC GAS AND ELECTRIC BUILDING, 245 MARKET/77 BEALE STREETS. Here terracotta is used to imitate granite. The

"PATH OF GOLD"
The line of street lamps along Market Street was installed in 1916, during the *City Beautiful* campaign. Willis Polk ▲ *196* designed the lamp-post base and trunk to fit the sculptor Leo Lentelli's triple-globed lanterns, while the bas-reliefs are by Arthur Putnam.

THE FLOOD BUILDING
The building shown in the upper picture, at the corner of Market and Powell Streets, was completed in 1904 to plans by Albert Pissis. It was commissioned by James Flood, son of a "Bonanza King" ▲ *209*. With its glazed brick walls and Renaissance-Baroque décor, it matches the Emporium Building.

The skyline in 1972.

building, constructed in 1925 by Bakewell and Brown, is richly decorated with sculptures on its ground floor and crowned with columns and urns.

CALIFORNIA STREET

(Turn right into Front to make your way back to California Street.) At the end of the 1970's there was a boom in skyscraper construction in San Francisco. A Houston promoter, Gerald Hines, demolished the block at 101 California Street, including the superb Oceanic Steamship Building designed by George Applegarth. He then commissioned the New York architect Philip Johnson to build the glass cylinder that now occupies the site. At no. 255 in the same street, the INDUSTRIAL INDEMNITY BUILDING (formerly the John Hancock Building), created in 1959, has twelve floors of smoked glass. It has had its moment of glory, as one of San Francisco's first skyscrapers. The NEWHOLT BUILDING at 260 California Street, designed by Lewis Hobart, is an interesting composition of red brick with terracotta moldings.
DOLLAR BLOCK, CALIFORNIA, PINE SANSOME AND BATTERY STREETS. The neo-Gothic, steel-and-concrete structure at 311 California Street was built in 1919 as the new headquarters of the Robert Dollar Steamship Lines, a shipping company that began by freighting lumber and then expanded into commerce with Asia. At no. 351 note the red brick façade of the J. HAROLD DOLLAR BUILDING (1920). Between these two constructions is one of San Francisco's tallest tower blocks (forty-two floors), built in 1987. The *Mandarin Hotel* occupies the top eleven floors, which divide into two towers linked by glass sky-bridges; the spires of these towers are illuminated at night. The foyer and the shops within the complex are paneled in wood. The façade of no. 350 CALIFORNIA STREET, which dates from 1977, is embellished with a series of granite walrus heads salvaged from the old Alaska Commercial Building (1908), which formerly occupied this corner site.
MERCHANTS' EXCHANGE, 465 CALIFORNIA STREET. During the Gold Rush the merchants of the city paid large sums to receive early notice of the arrival of ships loaded with merchandise. In San Francisco's Merchants' Exchange, traders, exporters, shipowners, investors and speculators began their negotiations as soon as a fresh arrival was spotted by the lookout point on the roof of the building. This exchange (now called the Grain Exchange Hall) was the commercial nerve center of the entire West Coast; visitors will admire the fine seascapes by William Coulter ▲ *173*, an Irish-born painter and former sailor, illustrating the importance of San Francisco's maritime activity in the early years. Willis Polk designed the exchange early in his career, when he was managing the San Francisco offices of Daniel Burnham ▲ *224*, the famous Chicago architect. The cornices of the exchange echo those of the Insurance Exhange Building

WILLIAM RALSTON Founder of the Bank of California ▲ *216*, he financed a number of the prosperous firms that helped to consolidate California's economic independence. The bank went heavily into debt to buy the Comstock Lode mines and Ralston built the *Palace Hotel* in an attempt to increase the value of his real-estate investments, but it only made matters worse. His partner William Sharon finished him off by ceding his own shares in the Comstock Mines. Depositors tried to withdraw their money from the bank, forcing its closure. Two days later Ralston drowned while swimming in the bay at Aquatic Park.

(1913) at 433 California Street, also by Polk. At the turn of the century the Merchants' Exchange and the Kohl Building ▲ *214* dominated the Victorian edifices of the Financial District with their tall silhouettes.

BANK OF CALIFORNIA, 400 CALIFORNIA STREET. Founded in 1864 by William Ralston and D.O. Mills, the Bank of California quickly became a major force in San Francisco's financial affairs. A magnificent building inspired by St Mark's Library in Venice was originally built here in 1867, only to be pulled down in 1906 when the bank needed more space. The 1908 classical monument raised in its stead by Bliss and Faville is very well proportioned, with tall Corinthian columns topped by a generous coping. The office tower adjoining (by Anshen & Allen, 1967) is clad in rectangular panels which form a counterbalance to the colonnaded building.

BANK OF AMERICA WORLD HEADQUARTERS, 555 CALIFORNIA STREET. Constructed between 1968 and 1971, the world headquarters of the Bank of America towers over GIANNINI PLAZA, a windy square with a stone sculpture in the middle nicknamed the "Banker's Heart". In the evening the misty rays of the setting sun play on the facets of the bank's red granite exterior, making it gleamingly visible for miles around. When he founded the Bank of Italy in 1904, Amadeo P. Giannini cannot have imagined that one day its headquarters would be one of San Francisco's tallest buildings. To begin with, Giannini targeted the Italian immigrants whom other banks ignored; within a few years his tactics paid off, and by 1920 the Bank of Italy was one of the principal financial powers in California. In the 1920's it bought so many local California banks that several holding companies had to be created to help manage them. By 1945, four years before Giannini's death, his bank (renamed the Bank of America) had become the largest in the US.

300 MONTGOMERY STREET, SOUTHEAST CORNER OF CALIFORNIA STREET. Of the American National Bank Building built in 1922 by George Kelham, nothing remains except the hall and colonnade. Purchased in 1941 by the Bank of America for its main office, the construction has now been completely remodeled and modernized from the first floor upward.

AMADEO P. GIANNINI In 1902, at thirty-two years old, Amadeo Giannini succeeded his father-in-law as head of John Fugazi's Columbus Savings and Loan Society. Unable to convince the directors to liberalize the bank's policy regarding low-income Italians, Giannini decided in 1904 to open his own bank, the Bank of Italy, in a former saloon on Columbus Avenue. He then launched a campaign aimed at Italians, including those who had no more than a dollar at a time to invest. The Bank of Italy was the first to create branch offices so as to come closer to its clientèle. In 1930, the entire organization was consolidated as the Bank of America.

456 MONTGOMERY STREET

456 MONTGOMERY STREET

The somewhat ugly result of an attempt to integrate historic buildings into a modern architectural ensemble, this sleek, glistening twenty-four-floor skyscraper overlooks two small banking establishments set up in 1908. The building on the corner of Sacramento used to be the Italian-American Bank, founded 1899, which was absorbed by the Bank of Italy during the 1920's, along with many other Italian banks. The other building, with Corinthian columns, was the Antoine Borel Bank, built to plans by Albert Pissis, one of San Francisco's leading architects at the beginning of the century. In 1891 the Swiss financier Antoine Borel was one of the investors in the Hyde Street cable car line.

WELLS FARGO

WELLS FARGO BANK HISTORY ROOM, 420 MONTGOMERY STREET. This museum evokes the role of Wells Fargo in the history of California. It contains, among other things, mementos of "Black Bart", the bandit who held up over a score of coaches; he is famous for his curious habit of leaving poems at the scene of his exploits, announcing that his aim was to rob the rich and give to the poor. The museum also possesses specimens of the coinage struck by Emperor Norton ▲ *158*, paintings, old photographs, strongboxes, minerals, gold nuggets and an original stagecoach, which today is the symbol of the Wells Fargo Bank.

WELLS FARGO: BEGINNINGS. In July 1852 the New York bank founded by Henry Wells and William G. Fargo opened a banking and transportation service in a small brick building on Montgomery Street. Their service became famous for freighting gold from the mines and shipping supplies back to miners and pioneers. Within three years Wells Fargo had set up fifty-five branches in California and was the region's largest transport agency. The San Francisco office then moved into solid-looking granite premises on the corner of California and Montgomery Streets, where it remained until 1876. But although Wells Fargo with its stagecoaches may have been the best-known bank in the West, it was by no means the biggest in San Francisco during the late 19th century.

THE FIRST BANKS. During the Gold Rush San Francisco underwent a phenomenal economic expansion. For a while the town was sunk in indescribable chaos, and banking facilities were rudimentary, to say the least. Some banks, among them Wells Fargo, began as rapid transportation companies, supplying capital to traders in the town who dealt in goods from the East Coast and serving as intermediaries for the payment of shipping fees. They also accepted deposits and loaned money at high rates of interest. The Californians stood in great need of bankers, but they had learned to mistrust them following the bankruptcies of 1847, when notes distributed by the banks had lost all value. In 1849 the California State Legislature made it against the law for banks to merge, to issue checks and promissory notes, or to print paper money. Thus until 1864 California's banks were no more than savings institutions that loaned money and were the property of a single individual or a few associates. In 1864 William Ralston's Bank of California ▲ *210* was the quickest to take advantage of the repeal of this law, outstripping all the others. In 1870 the First

National Gold Bank, owned by the "Silver Kings" ▲ *189*, became the first bank in California to subscribe to the national charter and issue paper money backed by gold reserves. In 1875 James Flood and W.S. O'Brien, who had amassed huge fortunes in the mines of the Comstock Lode ● *45*, opened the Nevada Bank of California; Charles Crocker, president of the Central Pacific Railroad ● *54*, founded the Crocker-Woolworth Bank in 1883. The Anglo-Californian Bank opened an agency in 1873, as did the London, Paris and American Bank in 1884: these institutions brought international financial expertise, as well as capital, to San Francisco. The competition was intense, but Wells Fargo continued to prosper by developing its courier service. Agencies opened in the mining communities of the Sierra Nevada and Oregon, and Wells Fargo stagecoaches were soon moving goods, mail and passengers all over the West. Between 1860 and 1869 the company absorbed all its rivals, until the opening of the transcontinental railroad ● *56* forced it to change its policy. The two giants eventually formed an alliance, with Wells Fargo exchanging one-third of its stock for a monopoly of goods and mail transportation on the new railway.

New Mergers. After this coup Wells Fargo continued to grow by merging with other banks: with the Nevada Bank of California in 1905, the Union Trust Co. in 1923, and the American Trust Co. in 1960. Finally, the 1986 fusion of Wells Fargo with the Crocker Bank (which had itself absorbed First National Gold Bank and Anglo-California National Bank) completed the union of the eleven major institutions which had, in a manner of speaking, "created" San Francisco. Over the years the name of Wells Fargo won out because it was the oldest bank in California, and because the memory of its red and black stagecoaches remains indelibly associated with the city's rollicking beginnings.

"Black Bart"
In the 1870's the Wells Fargo mail coaches loaded with gold and coins were a favorite target for robbers. The most famous of these, "Black Bart", had a grave, authoritative manner which made coachmen do exactly as he ordered. In the space of eight years (1875–83) his courtesy and the pithy poems he left in his wake made "Black Bart" famous. Finally, after twenty-eight hold-ups, he was caught thanks to a handkerchief he had dropped, the laundry mark on which led the Wells Fargo detective to a small family hotel and a mining engineer, Charles E. Boles (or Bolton). After a spell in St Quentin, the elegant poet-bandit was freed for good conduct in 1887 and dropped out of sight.

▲ FINANCIAL DISTRICT

RUSS BUILDING, 235 MONTGOMERY STREET
It was on this site that Russ, a German-American jeweler, built his house in 1847. This house was demolished to make way for shops, and then for the elegant

Russ Hotel, one of the city's best establishments during the 1860's. It burned down in 1906. Constructed in 1927 by George Kelham, the present skyscraper rises in successive, apparently dislocated levels which emphasize an impression of verticality; in this it is similar to Eliel Saarinen's entry in the competition for the Chicago Tribune Tower. The Gothic decoration is in molded, glazed terracotta. For several decades the Russ Building was San Francisco's tallest construction; today one can barely see it from Bay Bridge.

MONTGOMERY STREET.

KOHL BUILDING, 400 MONTGOMERY STREET. With its giant columns and mannerist upper stories embellished by sculpted garlands and heads of animals, this 1901 building served as a model for all other San Francisco skyscrapers until 1920. It was at once the last major project undertaken by George W. Percy, a highly reputed architect during the Victorian era, and the first skyscraper built by Willis Polk; the two men were commissioned by Alviza Hayward, a former prospector who had invested his vast fortune in banking, property, railways, coal and various other industries. Alviza Hayward died shortly after the completion of the building, which now bears the name of its second owner.

MILLS BUILDING AND TOWER, 220 MONTGOMERY STREET. This edifice was one of the last examples of the period in which the façades and lobbies of buildings were embellished with richly sculpted stone. Here stone columns support the great entrance porch of sculpted white marble, which echoes the Roman arch motif of the upper stories. Constructed in 1892 by Burnham and Root, this landmark of the Financial District is a faithful reflection of the man who commissioned it, Darius Ogden Mills (1825–1910), a great banker of Gold Rush days and co-founder of the Bank of California.

The Mills Building was restored by Willis Polk after the 1906 earthquake, then enlarged on the Bush Street side between 1914 and 1918. The tower built at 220 Bush Street, to plans by Lewis Hobart, respects the style of the original construction.

HALLIDIE BUILDING, 130–50 SUTTER STREET. Though it is not quite the oldest glass and steel building in San Francisco (see the Glass House, 266–70 Sutter Street, built in 1908 by George Applegarth), the Hallidie Building is probably the most interesting of its type in the city, with its Gothic cornices and elegant fire escapes. Constructed in 1917 by Willis Polk, it bears the name of the inventor of the cable car ● 68.

MECHANICS' INSTITUTE, 57 POST STREET. This private library was founded in 1855, at a time when there were pitifully few public libraries in San Francisco. Its chess club was for many years one of the largest in the US. The building itself was constructed in 1866, destroyed by the 1906 fire, and then rebuilt in 1909 by Albert Pissis.

HUNTER-DULIN, 11 SUTTER STREET
This Romanesque-style, 1926 skyscraper by Schultze and Weaver is reminiscent of a French château, with its mansard roof and copper roof ridge.

NEWSPAPER CORNER, MARKET, THIRD AND KEARNY STREETS. The three main San Francisco newspapers installed themselves in this area in the 1890's. Built in 1890 by Burnham and Root, the CHRONICLE BUILDING (690 Market Street) was the city's first skyscraper. The *Chronicle*'s editorial offices occupied the upper floors, and the presses were in the basement. The original Romanesque ornamentation on the Market Street façade and Willis Polk's neo-classical additions on the Kearny side were obscured in 1962 by metal panels. Today the *Chronicle*'s offices are on Fifth and Mission Streets. In 1847 William Randolph Hearst put up the EXAMINER BUILDING at 691–9 Market Street. These premises, which were gutted by fire in 1906, were replaced in 1909 by a more interesting construction designed by Kirby, Petit and Green of New York. Note the "H" monogram of the paper's founder in the brightly colored foyer. The CALL BUILDING, built in 1898 by Reid Brothers (703 Market Street, now known as Central Tower) was by far the most elaborate and highly finished construction of the three. Commissioned by the sugar baron Claus Spreckels for his newspaper the *Call*, it was modernized by Albert Roller in 1938, at which time its splendid classical entrance and richly decorated dome were removed.

CROCKER GALLERIA
Built in 1982 by Skidmore, Owings and Merrill, this three-level ensemble of shops with a cylindrical glass roof was part of a single project that included the adjoining skyscraper on Post and Kearny Streets.

LOTTA'S FOUNTAIN
The actress and dancer Lotta Crabtree (1847–1924) gave this fountain on the corner of Kearny and Market Streets to the city in 1875. As a child, "Miss Lotta" earned a good living performing in the mining communities; in 1864 while living on the East Coast she had a fountain cast in Philadelphia and

brought to San Francisco as a mark of her affection for the city. The base of the fountain was raised in 1916 to harmonize with Market Street's "Path of Gold" lamps. On April 18 every year, at exactly 5.13 am, the ever-fewer survivors of the 1906 earthquake meet here to commemorate the event.

SHERATON PALACE HOTEL

The first *Palace Hotel* (633–65 Market Street) shimmered with hundreds of windows; its post-1906 successor was to be much more austere and elegant. Opened in 1875, the first *Palace* was conceived by the rich banker William C. Ralston as a luxury hotel with seven floors, seven hundred windows, seven staircases and five hydraulic elevators, with fireplaces and toilets in every bedroom, exotic wood paneling and European marble, Irish linen, Bavarian china, French tableware and Turkish carpets. Its vast circular inner courtyard (Grand Court) could accommodate horse-drawn carriages, which turned in off Market Street. Grand Court was later endowed with its own glass dome, girdled by a catwalk overlooking fountains and tropical gardens, where receptions were held. Ralston brought over the finest chefs from Paris; the salad dressing called *Green Goddess* was invented here, and artichokes were served for the first time in San Francisco at the *Palace Hotel*. Having begun his project right after the great earthquake of 1868, Ralston spared no expense to preserve his masterpiece from future natural catastrophes, allowing for four artesian wells, fire pumps, a huge reserve of water, thermostatic electric bulbs in the rooms and corridors, and over two thousand ventilation ducts. But not even these precautions could stop the *Palace* burning down in 1906. It was rebuilt almost immediately, with a glass-domed Garden Court very similar to the old Grand Court. In one of the bars there is a huge fresco, painted by Maxfield Parrish in 1909, entitled *The Pied Piper*. Between 1989 and 1991 the hotel was restored at a cost of $150 million.

SHELL BUILDING, 100 BUSH STREET
George Kelham built this modern skyscraper in 1919 for the Shell Oil Co. It is clad on the outside with a handsome glazed terracotta. The foyer, lifts and façade are richly embellished with shells, the emblem of the firm.

MECHANICS' MONUMENT, BATTERY/MARKET STREET. This sculpture created by Douglas Tielden in 1894–5 (below) was placed here in honor of Peter and James Donahue, San Francisco's first great industrialists, who founded the Union Iron Works and the city's first gasworks.

MARKET, FROM MONTGOMERY TO BUSH STREET

1 MONTGOMERY ST. This building was designed by Willis Polk in 1908 for the First National Gold Bank. It later became the headquarters of the Crocker Bank when the two establishments merged in 1926, and finally a branch of the Wells Fargo Bank in 1986. The top ten floors of the tower were demolished in 1980; the architecture of both exterior and interior is highly refined.

HOBART BUILDING, 58–92 MARKET STREET. This richly embellished 1914 skyscraper is an original example (like the Hallidie Building) of Willis Polk's best work.

1 SANSOME STREET. The original building here was constructed in 1910 by Albert Pissis for the London-Paris and American Bank. When this organization merged with the Anglo-Californian National Bank in 1921, George Kelham was commissioned to add a north wing to double its size. Integrated in 1956 with the Crocker Bank network, the building was truncated in 1984 to make room for the entrance courtyard of the new CITICORP CENTER designed by William Pereira. The latter contains a sculpture by Alexander Stirling Calder, *Star Figure*, created for the Panama-Pacific International Exhibition.

CROWN ZELLERBACH BUILDING, 1 BUSH STREET. Built in 1959 by Hertska and Knowles in association with Skidmore, Owings and Merrill, this was one of the first "International Style" buildings in San Francisco. It was also the first office tower in the city to maintain its own gardens, designed by Lawrence Halprin, which distance the building from the rest of the urban fabric.

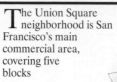

The Union Square neighborhood is San Francisco's main commercial area, covering five blocks

adjacent to the Financial District. Here are the principal department stores, luxury boutiques, big hotels and theaters in what is in effect the center of town.

MARKET STREET TO UNION SQUARE

Two of the city's largest shopping centers are on Market Street. The SAN FRANCISCO SHOPPING CENTRE contains about a hundred shops on ten levels, the four highest being occupied by *Nordstrom,* a vast department store. Whole trucks are raised by a huge elevator to unload merchandise on these upper floors. The EMPORIUM is easily recognizable by its fine neo-classical façade designed by Joseph Moore (1896). Opposite is the turntable of the Powell–Hyde cable car line ● *68* which serves Nob Hill, Chinatown and Fisherman's Wharf. The first intersection on the way up Powell Street toward Union Square, Ellis Street, is the site of *John's Grill* (on the right), a restaurant dedicated to Dashiell Hammett. The walls are covered in photos and posters from film versions of detective novels by Hammett, who spent nine years of his life in San Francisco and wrote most of his books here ● *131.*

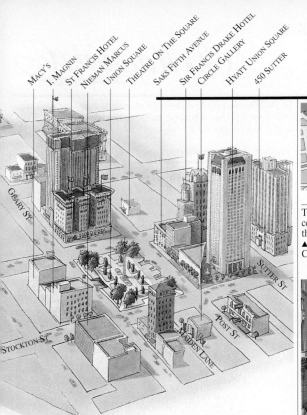

MACY'S
I. MAGNIN
ST FRANCIS HOTEL
NIEMAN MARCUS
UNION SQUARE
THEATRE ON THE SQUARE
SAKS FIFTH AVENUE
SIR FRANCIS DRAKE HOTEL
CIRCLE GALLERY
HYATT UNION SQUARE
450 SUTTER

GEARY ST

SUTTER ST.

STOCKTON ST.

MAIDEN LANE

POST ST.

🏃 Two hours

This itinerary can be combined with that of the Financial District ▲ 206 or of the Civic Center ▲ 224.

TURNTABLE
This contraption makes it possible for a single operator to swivel an 18-foot cable car so that it points back in the direction from which it came. The Powell–Hyde Street line is the most impressive of the three cable car routes still in use.

UNION SQUARE

HISTORY. This green square planted with palm trees, which occupies the block between Post, Geary, Powell and Stockton Streets, lies at the heart of the commercial quarter. In effect Union Square was one of the two original green areas included in Jasper O'Farrell's 1847 street map ● 91. The site was ceded to the municipality by John W. Geary, the city's first American mayor, and named on the eve of the Civil War (1861–5) because of the many demonstrations of support for the Union's troops that were held here at a time when California was deeply divided over whether to support North or South. The Protestant churches, the synagogue and the gentlemen's clubs (these were the first of their kind in San Francisco) installed around the square were gradually squeezed out by offices and stores.

Union Square's character was definitely established by the construction of the *Hotel St Francis* in 1908.

NAVAL MONUMENT. This imposing Corinthian column in granite, 90 feet high, was raised in the middle of Union Square in 1903 to celebrate Admiral Dewey's naval triumph in the Bay of Manila during the Spanish-American War of 1898. It is crowned with a bronze Goddess of Victory sculpted by Robert Aitken, who took the young Alma de Bretteville Spreckels ▲ 248 as his model.

The square in 1870.

219

J. Magnin & Co.
INCORPORATED

In 1942 the world's first multi-level underground car park was built beneath Union Square. In the early days shoppers' cars would be brought out by "grooms" to the exits of the stores.

THE BIG DEPARTMENT STORES

I. MAGNIN AND CO., 233 GEARY STREET. Founded in 1876, this is the oldest major store in San Francisco. The present building was designed by Timothy Pfleuger in 1946, on the steel structure of an office building constructed in 1905.
"NIEMAN MARCUS", 50 STOCKTON STREET. Neiman's has replaced the old *City of Paris*, which was demolished in 1982. It was the city's most elegant store at the beginning of this century, and vigorous protests from the citizenry forced the builders to preserve the 1900 rotunda and the fine amber-colored skylight above it. This skylight bears the arms of the city of Paris, a ship with a Latin motto, *fluctuat nec mergitur*.

Made by the United Glass Company, it is a testimony to the art of American glassworkers in the early 1900's.
"MACY'S", 101 STOCKTON STREET. This famous chain of department stores had to be present in Union Square.
"SAKS FIFTH AVENUE", 384 POST STREET. The entrance to *Saks* is on the corner of Powell and Post Streets. Its architecture is modern (1981) but beautifully integrated into the surroundings. *Saks* is renowned for the quality of its ready-to-wear range.
"GUMP'S", 250 POST STREET. Founded in 1865 by two brothers who had emigrated from Germany, Gump's is famous for its oriental antiquities, especially jade and pearls, and other decorative goods. In 1948 its interior design department, the Design Studio, became famous under the aegis of Eleanor Forbes and the McGuires, who designed furniture in rattan and wood, using innovative shapes. Gump's will move to 135 Post Street in spring 1995.

MAIDEN LANE

Morton Street, where prostitutes solicited passers-by from their open windows and where at least two serious crimes

were reported every week, was a place of very ill repute until 1906. After the earthquake it was renamed Maiden Lane, probably in the hope that this would give it a little respectability. Today Maiden Lane is mostly occupied by smart boutiques and restaurants.

CIRCLE GALLERY BUILDING, 140 MAIDEN LANE. This contemporary art gallery, designed in 1947 by Frank Lloyd Wright, is like an early small-scale version of the Guggenheim Museum which the architect later built in New York in 1956. The spiral plan is exactly the same, as is the masterly use of both natural and artificial light.

THE BIG HOTELS

"WESTIN ST FRANCIS HOTEL". This luxury establishment, constructed by the millionaire Charles T. Crocker as a place where visiting dignitaries could be "properly entertained" while in San Francisco, first opened its doors on March 12, 1904. Since then crowned heads and celebrities have been perennial guests here. Seriously damaged during the earthquake, the *St Francis* was reconstructed by the architects Bliss and Flaville, who preserved the surviving steel structure and greatly enlarged it. Today the *Westin St Francis* occupies the entire front of the block between Geary and Post Streets on Union Square. The tower and elevators were added in 1972. In addition to its twelve hundred rooms, the hotel operates a huge ballroom, seven restaurants, including the famous *Victor Hirtzler* restaurant on the 32nd floor, and several exterior glass elevators, from which there is a view of the entire city. A favorite rendez-vous point for San Franciscans is "under the clock" in this lobby, the clock in question being a rosewood article that has been here since 1907. The handsome Compass Rose room overlooking the same lobby serves as a bar and tea room. According to a century-old tradition, the coins used for change here are carefully washed so they will not soil ladies' gloves.

"GRAND HYATT HOTEL", 345 STOCKTON STREET. This hotel offers a number of services to business people (translation, office equipment, communication services) and contains a glass-domed restaurant (the *Plaza*) and a jazz club (the *Club 36*) on its top floor, with superb views across the city. At the foot of the Hyatt is a fountain by Ruth Asawa, assembled from bronze plates with designs relating to various aspects of San Francisco.

"SIR FRANCIS DRAKE HOTEL", POWELL AND SUTTER STREETS. Smaller in scale than its giant neighbors, the *Sir Francis Drake* also offers more personalized service and surroundings: notably a marble staircase, frescoes, mirrors and crystal chandeliers in the great 1930's tradition. The porter, dressed

Union Square is famous for its flowerstalls. With M.H. de Young's approval the florists arrived in the late 19th century and obtained an official license to trade in 1904. Since then San Franciscans have fiercely resisted all attempts to dislodge them.

"VICTOR HIRTZLER"
The restaurant on the 32nd floor of the Westin St Francis hotel bears the name

of one of its greatest chefs, who reigned in the kitchen from 1906 to 1926. Prior to this, Hirtzler had been in the service of the king of Portugal, for whom he invented a host of exquisite dishes, notably his celebrated *Passion Lucullus* mousse.

This canvas by Paul Ferenzy (below right), entitled *Meeting of the Bohemian Club*, was painted between 1874 and 1879. It shows the first members of the club, which was founded in 1872. Farther right is, *The Critics* (1915) by Frank Van Sloun.

in the uniform of a halberdier of the Royal Guard, is here to honor the memory of Sir Francis Drake, the first Englishman to visit this region. *Sir Francis Drake Hotel* is currently undergoing refurbishment.

"FOUR SEASONS CLIFT HOTEL", GEARY AND TAYLOR STREETS. In the center of the theater district, the *Clift Hotel* is famous for its cuisine and service. For over seventy-five years the *Clift* has boasted the city's most loyal clientèle; don't miss the *Redwood Room* here, which is one of the finest bars in San Francisco.

ISADORA DUNCAN (1878–1927)
Paradoxically, the dancer Isadora Duncan (a child of Union Square) was discovered in New York, not San Francisco, which gave so many other artists their first break. All the same, a plaque bearing her name reminds us that Isadora was born at no. 501 Taylor Street, in a house that has since vanished.

THE CLUBS

"OLYMPIC CLUB", 524 POST STREET. This exclusively male club was founded in the 1850's by a group of German mericans who wanted to maintain their German gymnastic traditions. The statues of athletes in the foyer of this Renaissance palace testify to this, as does the superb swimming pool surrounded by high columns and overtopped by a broad skylight. For years this pool was filled with seawater specially piped from the ocean.

"BOHEMIAN CLUB", 625 TAYLOR STREET. The 1900's building covered in ivy which adjoins the *Olympic Club* is the home of the *Bohemian Club*, founded in 1872 by a group of journalists, writers and painters. As an artists' club it had its Golden Age at the beginning of the 20th century, when Ambrose Bierce, Joaquin Miller, Frank Norris, Jack London, Sinclair Lewis and the photographer Arnold Genthe were among its members. Since then the *Bohemian* has reverted to a more staid membership of businessmen and industrialists, while retaining its cultural vocation; performances are given all year round at its small theater, and in summer at *Bohemian*

Grove, the club's property on the Russian river, north of San Francisco. A superb bronze plaque depicting an owl, the emblem of the *Bohemian Club*, may be seen on the corner of Post Street; this plaque is by the sculptor Haig Patigian. There is also a fine art collection on the premises.

THEATER DISTRICT

A VENERABLE TRADITION. San Francisco's zeal for the theater has a history that goes back to the Gold Rush.

Some of San Francisco's theaters (above).

Many of the Forty-Niners were culturally sophisticated, with an appreciation of poetry, opera and Shakespearean drama. In 1848 there were astonishing numbers of small theaters in the city, notably the *Tivoli Opera House*, the *Baldwin*, the *California*, the *Bush Street Theater* and the *Alcazar*; between 1850 and 1859, 1,105 performances of various kinds were staged in San Francisco, of which 907 were plays, 48 operas and 85 ballets or pantomimes. The social diversity of the gold-miners was conducive to the development of all kinds of theatrical performance, and this quickly became San Francisco's favorite pastime. Much more than a simple diversion, the theater enabled San Franciscan society to construct a fabric of its own, by giving spectators an awareness of community.

THE THEATER DISTRICT. A number of theaters are concentrated in the Union Square district, principally on Mason and Geary Streets, which together form the theater district. The THEATRE ON THE SQUARE (450 Post Street) mounts off-Broadway avant-garde shows. Not far away are the IMPROVISATION THEATRE (401 Mason Street) and the CABLE CAR THEATRE (430 Mason Street), a small seventy-seat auditorium where the comedy *Greater Tuna*, which ran from 1983 to 1991 when it closed to go on tour, has now reopened. The CURRAN THEATRE (445 Geary Street.), the façade of which was designed in 1922 by Alfred Henry D. Jacobs, features Broadway shows, some of which are well worth seeing even if the seats are expensive. The GEARY THEATRE (415 Geary Street) is a handsome establishment with an ornamental façade built in 1900 by Bliss and Flaville. It is the headquarters of the famous, and extremely serious, American Conservatory Theatre (ACT).

TENDERLOIN
A few streets away from the shops and big hotels of Union Square, between Larkin, Mason, O'Farrell and Market Streets, is the seedy neighborhood known as the Tenderloin. This area has a reputation for having the highest incidence of crime in the whole of San Francisco.

ALAMO SQUARE
DAVIES SYMPHONY HALL
CIVIC AUDITORIUM
OPERA HOUSE
CITY HALL
CIVIC CENTER PLAZA
WAR MEMORIAL VETERANS' BUILDING
NEW STATE BUILDING
PUBLIC LIBRARY
OLD STATE BUILDING
OLD FEDERAL BUILDING

FULTON ST.

VAN NESS AV.

MCALLISTER ST.

LARKIN S.

POLK ST.

GROVE ST.

HYDE ST.

AN AMBITIOUS PROJECT

🏃 Two hours

James Rolph, nicknamed "Sunny Jim", was mayor of San Francisco for twenty years. In 1930 he became governor of California.

With the acquisition of Hawaii and the Philippines, which were ceded by Spain in 1898, the United States became the predominant power in the Pacific basin. From that time on, San Francisco ceased to consider itself an ordinary frontier town, aspiring instead to become the principal port on the West Coast. The city authorities set out to build a new metropolis of world importance with administrative buildings worthy of its rank. Europe, and more specifically Paris, served as the model for this headlong drive to make San Francisco a great capital. In 1899 the architect B.J.S. Cahill suggested the grouping of political and cultural institutions around City Hall (which at that time stood on the site of the present Main Library) to form an administrative center. Cahill's proposal was supported by the city's aristocratic mayor James Duval Phelan, who had taken office in 1897.

BURNHAM'S MASTER PLAN. Phelan left office in 1901, his project still unrealized. Nevertheless he continued to support it, and three years later commissioned a Chicago architect, Daniel Burnham, to rethink the entire city plan and devise a brand new "imperial" design. The result was unveiled in 1905; it provided for parks, monuments and a series of boulevards,

JAPANTOWN PEACE PAGODA

rather like Haussmann's Paris. The civic center, modeled on the the Place de l'Etoile at the top of the Champs-Elysées in the French capital, was to be built at the intersection of the two main throughfares of San Francisco, Market Street and Van Ness Avenue. In other words, Burnham visualized Market Street as the Champs-Elysées of the West Coast. However, when City Hall was badly damaged by the 1906 earthquake, the breakneck speed of reconstruction and grave doubts about the city's future combined to kill the project.

GEARY BLVD

DANIEL BURNHAM
A Chicago architect, Burnham spent two years in a house on Twin Peaks from which he could see the whole of San Francisco spread out before him while he worked on plans for the new city. Throughout his life he remained true to his principle: "avoid small projects, they leave no mark on people's memories."

JAMES ROLPH'S MANDATE. When James Rolph Jr. became mayor in 1911, he announced that the building of a civic center was to be a priority of his term, along with the construction of a new City Hall and the organizing of a trade fair in San Francisco ▲ 236. This fair was dubbed the Panama-Pacific International Exposition and was intended to celebrate both the opening of the Panama Canal and the rebirth of the city. The charismatic Rolph was usually able to extract what he wanted from his constituents, and indeed, by 1912 the citizens had overwhelmingly approved a bond issue of $8.8 million to finance the projected works.

THE BIRTH OF THE CIVIC CENTER. Several different architects participated in the planning of the new civic center, among them John Galen Howard, Frederick H. Meyer and John Reid Jr. A local firm, Bakewell and Brown, designed the City Hall. Completed shortly after the closure of the Panama-Pacific Exposition in 1915, City Hall turned out to be neatly geared to the grand ambitions of Rolph; from its balcony the mayor could survey the huge square of Civic Center laid out before him. Geometrically perfect, San Francisco's Civic Center is today recognized, along with Washington D.C., as one of the finest American interpretations of French baroque ideals. In 1930 a new mayor, Angelo Rossi, continued the program of Rolph and the architect Arthur Brown Jr with the construction of the War Memorial and Federal buildings. The Civic Center was declared a historic site in 1987.

Top to bottom: City Hall, the Civic Auditorium and the War Memorial group.

MARKET STREET TO CIVIC CENTER PLAZA

UNITED NATIONS SQUARE. This square, which commemorates the 1945 signing of the UN Charter in the opera house nearby, was one of the key elements in the

Lick Monument.

embellishment of Market Street, at the time when a project was afoot to turn it into a prestigious avenue ● *91*. The present square was designed in 1975 by the architect Larry Halprin, who conceived it as the principal means of access to the Civic Center and placed a modern fountain in the middle of it – a jumble of concrete blocks from which no water ever seems to emerge. Twice a week a farmers' market is held here.

OLD FEDERAL BUILDING. A pedestrian alley leading through to Hyde Street takes you past the old Federal Building. With its massive Doric columns, this neo-classical edifice built in 1936 symbolizes the expansion of the bureaucracy under Franklin D. Roosevelt. Designed by Arthur Brown Jr, who also took contributed to the development of City Hall and the War Memorial Group, it is in many ways similar to the Federal Triangle in Washington, which the same architect built for President Roosevelt.

AROUND CIVIC CENTER PLAZA

FARMERS' MARKET
Held twice weekly, many different ethnic groups and an astonishing variety of Californian agricultural products can be seen here.

CIVIC CENTER PLAZA. This broad esplanade at the heart of Civic Center marks the main entrance to City Hall on Polk Street. What with the windows of the mayor's office opposite and the square's capacity of 100,000 people, this area became a favorite place for political demonstrations; previously, demonstrators had foregathered on Newspaper Corner at the intersection of Third and Market Streets ▲ *215*. Conceived as a garden in the French style, the square was transformed in 1958 by the addition of an underground car park and a conference center, the Brooks Hall. San Franciscans agree that these alterations have disfigured the square, but for financial reasons its modification is not on the current agenda. Today the square is a popular hangout for homeless people.

MAIN LIBRARY. Completed in 1917, the municipal library on the corner of Fulton and Larkin Streets is a perfect example of the architectural principles that guided the

The new library, designed by I.M. Pei, completes the Civic Center by rounding off its original symmetrical plan. The original library is destined to house the Asiatic Museum ▲ 270.

planning of the Civic Center. The library was designed by George Kelham, who organized it symmetrically around a monumental staircase leading to large reading rooms. As for the Panama-Pacific International Exhibition, for which he supervised the works, Kelham used travertine (limestone) to cover the walls of the stairwell. This contributes to the atmosphere of Roman grandeur, an impression further enhanced by the granite statues on the façade by Leo Lentelli, which are inspired by Michelangelo. The library was never finished for lack of money, and soon proved to be manifestly inadequate, given the number of users; the municipal authorities issued bonds to finance the replacement on the other side of the street. The third floor of the present establishment contains the Historical Archives of the city, and includes a number of interesting objects and documents.

OLD CALIFORNIA STATE OFFICE BUILDING. This federal office in the style of the Italian Renaisssance has been a bone of contention ever since its construction in 1926. The people of San Francisco were strongly opposed to it from the start, because its cornices in no way matched those of the library and City Hall; indeed, they spoiled the whole effect of the ensemble. The state of California replied that the city would have to like it or leave it. Faced with this ultimatum, the city backed down, and the new state office building was designed to specifications by Bliss and Faville, architects of the *Saint Francis Hotel*. It was enlarged in 1957 and today it extends as far as Golden Gate Avenue, thus occupying practically the entire block.

CITY HALL. The construction of a city hall was begun in 1912, and in the event not one of Burnham's suggestions for it was adopted. Recognized as the finest monument in San Francisco, City Hall is the key element of the Civic Center and the masterpiece of its architects, Bakewell and Brown, who also built the Coit Tower ● *171* and the city halls of Berkeley and Pasadena. All the entrances lead through an immense, bare hall to the rotunda, which is crowned by a majestic dome. The staircase, in pink Tennessee marble, leads down from the mayor's office, its rounded steps descending to the

BAKEWELL AND BROWN. These two architects from the University of Berkeley also trained at the Ecole des Beaux-Arts in Paris.

French sculptors were called in to decorate City Hall. Henri Crenier did the statues on the exterior façades. The ones on Polk Street represent Wealth, Trade and Navigation; those on Van Ness symbolize Work, Industry, Truth, Study, the Arts and Wisdom. Jean-Louis Bourgeois (who was killed on the Western Front in 1918) decorated most of the dome.

227

THE SOCIETY OF CALIFORNIA PIONEERS.
The museum of the Society of California Pioneers at 450 MacAllister Street is well worth a detour. Among its many attractions are a display and video on the history of California.

DAVIES SYMPHONY HALL
The décor and acoustics of the Davies Symphony Hall were strongly criticized from the outset. Leonard Bernstein, who came there to conduct a concert given by the Vienna Philharmonic, declared that the auditorium made a nonsense of sound. Alterations to the tune of ten million dollars (paid for by private donors) were eventually begun in 1991; the hall reopened on September 12, 1992, with new acoustics designed by Kirkegaard and Co. of Chicago.

paved floor of the hall. At its inauguration Mayor James Rolph repeatedly bragged that the dome (modeled on that of St Peter's in Rome) was a good 3 feet higher than the dome of the Capitol in Washington, D.C. Indeed, San Francisco's City Hall stands as a testimony to the determination of San Francisco's leaders that their city should be the focus of a Pacific empire, with a destiny that promised to be "grander than Ancient Rome's". Unfortunately, the building suffered considerable damage during the 1989 earthquake, and today its arches are supported by wooden struts carefully painted in trompe-l'oeil.

CIVIC AUDITORIUM. This building, which looks curiously like a railroad station, was designed by John Galen Howard, Frederick H. Meyer and John Reid Jr. It was donated to the city by the committee responsible for the Panama-Pacific Exposition ▲ 236, which intended it to fill the need for a public meeting place; this is why it is occasionally referred to as the Exposition Auditorium. Planned as a hall for concerts, conferences and other events, the Civic Auditorium was the first element of the Civic Center to be completed, even before City Hall itself. It was renamed in 1992 in honor of Bill Graham, a legendary rock impresario of the 1970's ● 78, who was killed in a helicopter accident in 1991. There are two small museums in the Auditorium building: the Boxing Museum, which is situated on the third floor, and the Police Museum, on the fourth.

DAVIES SYMPHONY HALL

The symphony hall, financed by the millionaire philanthropist Louise Davies, was inaugurated on September 16, 1980. It stands on the corner of Grove Street and Van Ness Avenue and was designed by Skidmore, Owings and Merrill, architects of the NEW STATE BUILDING, its twin on the other side of the opera house, where Van Ness meets MacAllister. Both of these modern constructions are particularly striking due to their thin, curved glass façades blend.

THE WAR MEMORIAL GROUP

In 1920 the city made the decision to construct a municipal opera house. The works had scarcely begun when a violent controversy brought them to a grinding halt. Veterans of World War One, in alliance with various wealthy citizens, demanded the construction of a monumental group instead, in memory of the Americans killed in the Great War. In 1931 the city launched a public loan to finance the monument as a part of the major building works then in progress. Finally it was agreed that two identical buildings, the Opera and the Veterans' building, should be constructed side by side, prolonging the Civic Center west of City Hall on the far side of Van Ness. This double project was assigned to Arthur Brown Jr and Albert Lansbergh. Unfortunately, the granite used for the other façades of the Civic Center had become prohibitively expensive by 1931.

WAR MEMORIAL OPERA HOUSE. The Opera opened its doors in late 1932 and witnessed the signing of the United Nations Charter on June 26, 1945. It is the home of America's oldest dance company, the San Francisco Ballet. The ballet school and rehearsal studios moved to a separate building on the corner of Fulton and Franklin Streets in 1978. Today the Opera maintains one of the finest opera companies in the world, the San Francisco Opera, founded by Gaetano Merola. It gave its first performance on September 26, 1923, at the Civic Auditorium, and was established at the opera house in 1932.

WAR MEMORIAL VETERANS' BUILDING. This building serves as the headquarters of several veterans' associations; it also houses the HERBST THEATER, situated on the ground floor (with a balcony extending up to the second floor) and has frescoes by Frank Brangwyn dating from the 1915 fair. From 1935 to 1995 the building housed the MUSEUM OF MODERN ART ▲ 287, which is now installed in its new premises in the South of Market neighborhood.

ALONG HAYES STREET
The Hayes Valley neighborhood, with its galleries and restaurants open day and night, owes much to the revival of this part of the city.

SAN FRANCISCO BALLET
Founded in 1933, the San Francisco Ballet is the oldest professional dance company in the USA. Highly innovative from the start, it has produced the US premières of many works, notably *Coppelia* in 1939, *Swan Lake* in 1940 and *The Nutcracker* in 1944 under the direction of William Christenson. In 1991 the San Francisco Ballet company appeared for the first time in New York, earning rave reviews.

MAMMY PLEASANT
Born of a black
mother and a
Cherokee father,
Mary Ellen Pleasant
arrived in San
Francisco during the
Gold Rush. A true
abolitionist, she spent
her life championing
the Afro-American
cause. Many fugitive
slaves found refuge
with her, and in 1865
she won a court case
against a racist
tramway company.
Her house, at the
intersection of Bush
and Octavia Streets,
is no longer standing,
but the six eucalyptus
trees she planted still
grow beside the spot
where the African-
American Cultural
Society erected a
plaque in "Mammy"
Pleasant's memory.

WESTERN ADDITION

This was the name given to the district built to the west of Van
Ness Avenue in 1870. The Jewish community settled here in
the early years of the century, but from 1909 onward Japanese
immigrants began to take over those blocks around Post
Street that had survived the earthquake. After the Japanese
were interned during World War Two, the neighborhood
changed identity again, this time becoming occupied largely
by black workers employed in the munitions factories and
naval dockyards of the city. In 1945 the black community was
badly hit by the closure of the war factories. During the 1960's
City Hall launched an urban renewal campaign to clean up
the Western Addition slums, at which time many black
families were relocated to the outskirts of San Francisco
around Hunter's Point. Part of the Western Addition was then
demolished to make way for soulless concrete blocks, which
replaced the original Victorian buildings; nonetheless, a few
Victorian enclaves have survived, notably Cottage Row
(between Sutter and Bush Streets), east of Fillmore Street,
and Alamo Square (above).

JAPANTOWN

The Japanese quarter of San Francisco has shriveled from
forty blocks to six since 1945. Even though it is still a rallying
point for Japanese-Americans, only about 4 percent of them
actually live there. Right after the 1906 earthquake the San
Francisco Japanese who had previously lived in Chinatown
and South of Market moved into the Western Addition
quarter, which had been left relatively unscathed by the
calamity. The low rents encouraged them to settle in large
numbers; and thus the Post and Sutter Street zones, from
Franklin to Fillmore, became the backbone of an authentic
Japanese quarter.

JAPANTOWN, THE JAPANESE QUARTER OF SAN FRANCISCO IS STILL A RALLYING POINT FOR THE JAPANESE-AMERICANS, EVEN THOUGH ONLY A FEW OF THEM STILL LIVE THERE.

THE JAPANESE COMMUNITY

THE "ISSEI". In the 19th century Meije Japan developed a strong admiration for America and operated a careful selection process in regard to the men it sent there. Most of the *Issei* (first-generation immigrants) were manual workers who could read and write Japanese, and attached great importance to acquiring knowledge. The first *Issei* arrived around 1860 in small numbers, but this trickle became a flood by the beginning of the 20th century. As agricultural laborers, domestics and gardeners, the Japanese formed an efficient and valuable workforce.

XENOPHOBIA. Despite the substantial contribution made by the Japanese to the city's recovery after the 1906 disaster, a wave of anti-Japanese sentiment swept through California in the early 1900's. In 1906 Japanese children were banned from public schools, and a law was passed forbidding the Japanese local ownership of property. Following military victories against China and Russia, Japan became a power to be reckoned with and a treaty was drawn up in 1908 whereby Japan agreed to curb emigration to the US in return for Washington's consent for Japanese wives to join their husbands in America and for Japanese children to attend American schools. In 1907 the Japanese represented only 3 percent of the total quota of immigrants; nevertheless their community quickly increased in size and influence. The living conditions of the *Nisei*, or second generation of Japanese immigrants, were very different from those of their parents; as Americans they were entitled to own property and gradually became fully integrated into US society.

INTERNMENT CAMPS. When America entered World War Two after the bombing of Pearl Harbor in December 1941, the Japanese-Americans of California were rounded up and interned in camps, regardless of their citizenship. In January 1943 the pressure on them was relaxed slightly, and the army began recruiting *Nisei*, who seized this opportunity to prove their loyalty to the land of their birth. No fewer than 300,000 *Nisei* soldiers fought on the American side during this war.

THE POST-WAR ERA. On their return from the internment camps, those Japanese who had been forced to sell off their possessions in a hurry found that they had lost virtually everything. Many of the *Issei* were obliged to work as gardeners, but the *Nisei*, who usually spoke English and tended to be better educated, contrived to overcome these obstacles.

PEACE PAGODA
This monument, given to the community by the Japanese, stands in the heart of Japantown.

A SENSE OF HONOR
With its attachment to American values and ideals, the Japanese community took great trouble over its children's education. Within the family, emphasis was placed on study and reflecting honor on the community. Gang wars, prostitution and crime were virtually non-existent: anyone who broke the law was automatically repatriated to Japan by the community itself.

Golden Gate Avenue, c. 1870.

"Urban renewal" poster for the Western Addition.

NEW CITY *SAN FRANCISCO REDEVELOPED*

SAN FRANCISCO CITY PLANNING COMMISSION

Every April the Cherry Blossom Festival is celebrated in Japantown with sumo wrestling, tea ceremonies, traditional dancing and parades ● *81*.

Racial prejudice towards Asiatics declined greatly in the post-war years. Economic change and mixed marriages dispersed Japanese born on US soil among the rest of the population.

JAPAN CENTER

This commercial center was opened in 1968. It covers three blocks, bordered by Post, Sutter, Laguna and Fillmore Streets, and backs on to Geary Boulevard. By way of Post and Buchanan Streets there is an entrance to the PEACE PLAZA GARDEN overlooking the PEACE PAGODA, a gift from the Japanese to the community. Inside the KINESTSU BUILDING, west of the square, the RESTAURANT MALL contains a variety of Japanese restaurants, while the main gallery is occupied by shops. The Japan Center has a number of stores, mostly selling books, groceries, clothes and souvenirs. The MARUMA grocery store on Post Street stocks a wide range of authentic Japanese products. At the end of the mall is WEBSTER BRIDGE (a copy of the 'Ponte Vecchio' in Florence), which crosses Webster Street to the KINOKUNIYA BUILDING.

NIHONMACHI MALL

TEA HOUSE
The Nichi Bei Kai Cultural Center (1759 Sutter Street) contains a room specially designed for

Designed along the lines of a traditional Japanese village, this shopping center stands to the left of Buchanan Street. The two fountains and colored concrete benches are by the sculptor Ruth Asawa. The various shops here offer a wide range of products much appreciated by the Japanese-American contingent in *Soko*, as they call San Francisco.

TEMPLES AND CHURCHES. Japantown has many Shinto and Buddhist temples, as well as Christian churches. The more interesting of these include SAINT FRANCIS XAVIER ROMAN CATHOLIC CHURCH (on Octavia Street), a blend of Victorian architecture and Japanese décor; the SAN FRANCISCO BUDDHIST CHURCH, which holds a relic of the Buddha; and the KONKO KYO (further along Bush Street), the shrine of a Shintoist sect founded in 1859. This is in traditional Shinto style, with a fine altar in pale wood that is often laden with offerings of food and flowers. By contrast, the SOTO ZEN MISSION on the corner of Laguna and Sutter Streets has a spartan interior to

the tea ceremony. Small and intimate, this room is built entirely of natural materials, with windows placed according to the direction of the light; the décor, which is austere and simple, varies according to the season.

encourage meditation, though its public ceremonies can be extremely lavish. On the east side of the neighborhood, on the corner of Geary and Gough, stands SAINT MARY'S CATHEDRAL. Destroyed by fire in 1962, this elegant building was built in contemporary style. On the other side of the street is the FIRST UNITARIAN CHURCH, the headquarters of Pastor Thomas Starr King, who led California into the abolitionist camp during the Civil War. King was buried here following his death in 1864.

GOLDEN GATE PROMENADE

OCEAN BEACH   SEAL ROCK   THE CLIFF HOUSE   RICHMOND DISTRICT   LAND'S END   LINCOLN PARK   PALACE OF THE LEGION OF HONOR   CHINA BEACH   SEACLIFF   BAKER BEACH

🚗 One day

🚶 Four hours, Fort Mason to Fort Point.

MARINA GREEN
This broad lawn edging the Marina Small Craft Harbor as far as the St Francis Yacht Club is a favorite promenade of San Franciscans, who also come here to watch the kite-flying. Marina Boulevard is rich in Mission Revival-style houses ● 88, many of which have splendid views across the bay.

Fort Mason.

FORT MASON

Fort Mason stands on the site of the former *Punta Medanos*. In 1797 the Spaniards fortified this point, positioning five cannon there and renaming it the *Bateria San José*. In 1850, when it was known as Black Point, the fort officially became the property of the American army; but the absence of military personnel to occupy it encouraged civilians to settle there. During the Civil War the military expelled all civilians from the point and installed artillery to defend the approaches to the port. In 1882 the outpost was renamed in honor of Colonel Richard Barnes Mason, the military governor of California from 1847 to 1849. Fort Mason quickly became an important supply base for the US Pacific fleet; after the attack on Pearl Harbor it was used as the headquarters of all military operations in the Pacific war theater. During the conflict 1.6 million men and 23 million tons of material passed through Fort Mason, which continued in service throughout the Korean and Vietnam wars. The army finally left in 1972. Since 1977 Fort Mason has been the seat of the Golden Gate National Recreation Area (GGNRA). Theaters, workshops, galleries, museums and restaurants have moved into its four disused warehouses, and on the third floor of C Building is the library of the Maritime National Historic Park, the J. PORTER SHAW LIBRARY, which contains a wealth of information on the maritime history of the West Coast.
"LIBERTY SHIPS". Just before reaching Fort Mason, coming from the Maritime Museum ▲ *172*, you can see the *USS Jeremiah O'Brien*, one of the last "Liberty ships" still afloat.

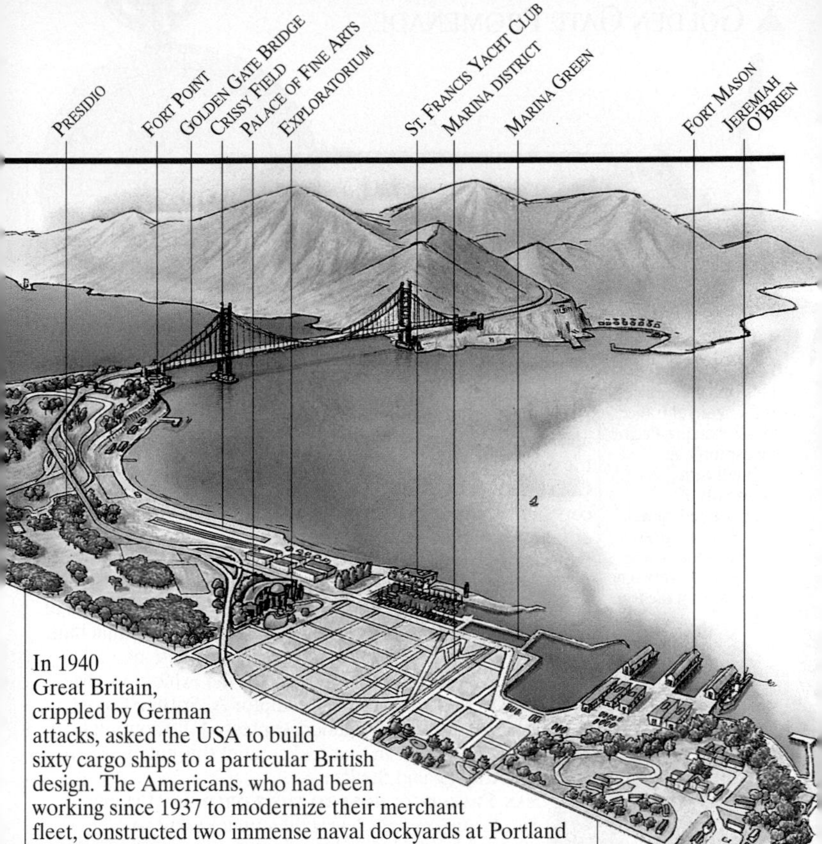

In 1940
Great Britain,
crippled by German
attacks, asked the USA to build
sixty cargo ships to a particular British
design. The Americans, who had been
working since 1937 to modernize their merchant
fleet, constructed two immense naval dockyards at Portland
and Richmond on the West Coast. In December 1941
H. J. Kaiser was directed to build the first of these Liberty
ships, and achieved the task in the record time of 226 days.
The bombing of Pearl Harbor and the threat from German
submarines in the Atlantic forced the pace to be speeded up
still further: before long construction time had been reduced
to twenty-seven days, and in 1942 the Kaiser shipbuilding
yard succeeding in building one of the vessels in just four
days, fifteen hours, and twenty-nine minutes. Between 1941
and 1945 the eighteen yards produced 2,710 ships, an
astonishing feat. Two hundred Liberty
ships were sunk between 1942 and 1945,
five hundred were sold to European
companies at the end of the war, and
the rest were scrapped after the
Vietnam War.

MUSEUM SHIPS
The *Liberty Ships,* like
the *Jeremiah O'Brien,*
supplied the Allies
with tanks, vehicles,
gasoline and other
material for the war
against Germany and
Japan.

MARINA DISTRICT

A residential area that is fast gaining
prestige, the Marina district (known
simply as the Marina) began to emerge in the 1920's on a
marshy site between Black Point and the Presidio. This site
had been drained to receive the 1915 Panama-Pacific
International Exposition. Because of its unstable subsoil, a
combination of drained land and landfill, the Marina was
severely damaged by the 1989 earthquake.
MARINA BOULEVARD is lined with Mission Revival-style houses
● 88, which have a wonderful view over the bay. Most of them
are stucco and are painted in pastel shades, reinforcing the
Mediterranean atmosphere.

**ST FRANCIS YACHT
CLUB.** Founded in
1927 on a promontory
overlooking the
Marina district, the
club has a small,
sheltered harbor and
a fine view of the bay.
The building, designed
by W. Polk, was
substantially modified
after a 1976 fire.

TOWER OF JEWELS
This Italianate tower at the main entrance to the Panama-Pacific exposition was studded with thousands of multicolored "jewels" of Bohemian glass. The baritone Roy la Pearle sang every day at noon from the top of it.

ART SMITH
The intrepid aviator Art Smith, in company with some Blackfoot Indians. The biplanes and monoplanes whose terrifying acrobatics were such an attraction are on view at the Palace of Transportation along with a locomotive, bicycles and motorcycles, including a Harley-Davidson.

PANAMA-PACIFIC INTERNATIONAL EXHIBITION

This year-long international exhibition was organized in 1915 to celebrate the opening of the Panama Canal, and the flats and creeks of Harbor View were drained and filled to receive the exhibits.

CELEBRATION OF THE PANAMA CANAL. After the failure of a corps of French engineers, who underestimated the technical difficulties presented by the project, and a financial scandal that resulted in the disgrace of Ferdinand de Lesseps, it was left to the Americans to complete the Panama Canal. As the main West Coast port, San Francisco was vitally concerned in the opening of the waterway, which, like the Suez Canal built by the French in 1869, hugely advanced the cause of international trade. At the entrance to the exhibition, the FOUNTAIN OF ENERGY by the sculptor A. Stirling Calder (father of Alexander Calder) expressed the boundless vigor and optimism that had created this link between the Atlantic and the Pacific.

SAN FRANCISCO: HOST TO THE WORLD. For the city of San Francisco, which was then undergoing an unprecedented boom in real estate values, the exposition was an opportunity to celebrate its own rebirth only six years after the 1906 catastrophe ● *58*. Every important personality in San Francisco – Reuben Hale of the Merchants' Association, William H. Crocker, M. H. de Young (founder of the *San Francisco Chronicle*), Mayor James Rolph and C. C. Moore, among many others – was associated with the project and sat on its board of governors. Subsidies from the state of California and private contributions flowed in. While war raged in Europe, San Francisco threw all its energy into the task of surprising and delighting visitors with the very latest products of art, craftsmanship, industry and agriculture.

A CAREFULLY BALANCED PROJECT. The architectural committee for the exposition was made up of the San Franciscans Willis Polk, Clarence Ward, W. B. Faville, George Kelham and

The entrance to the Palace of Machinery, painted by Sheldon Pennoyer during the exhibition.

THE ZONE

A huge amusement park full of merry-go-rounds, games, dioramas and replicas of parts of the Panama Canal and Yellowstone Park, the Zone occupied the east side of the exposition park. Visitors ate at restaurants and bought souvenirs: handfuls of earth from Panama, imitations of the Bohemian glass gems in the Tower of Jewels (below, left), teaspoons and watches. Some of the latter are still in working order.

Louis C. Mullgart, assisted by several New York architects. George W. Kelham produced a unified plan comprising eight domed exhibition "palaces", all of a conventional type, to surround the Palace of Machinery (for industrial machines) and the Palace of Fine Arts. The scintillating Tower of Jewels dominated the ensemble, the various avenues of which were punctuated by pools of water, colonnades and gardens beautifully laid out by John McLaren, the brilliant landscape architect of Golden Gate Park ▲ 254. The pavilions contributed by foreign countries and other states of the Union were grouped beyond the Palace of Fine Arts. Sculptures by artists from all over the world adorned the various buildings and gardens, and the exposition was lit throughout by electricity. The famous muralist and illustrator Jules Guérin took charge of the decorations and color overall.

BERNARD MAYBECK
Born 1848 in New York, of German parents, Maybeck spent five years in Paris studying carpentry design and

architecture at the Ecole des Beaux-Arts. On his return to America he worked in New York and Kansas City. In 1889 Maybeck left for San Francisco, where he led a bohemian life; charismatic and talented, his special gift was for decorative detail. His best-known work is the First Church of Christ Scientist in Berkeley.

AFTER THE PARTY. All told, about eighteen million visitors came to the exposition. When it was over, the huge Festival Hall with its excellent acoustics became the Civic Auditorium ▲ *228*. The French pavilion, a copy of the Palais de la Légion d'Honneur in Paris, was to serve as a model for San Francisco's own Palace of the Legion of Honor, a museum in Lincoln Park ▲ *248* dedicated to European art, founded by Alma and Adolph Spreckels. Behind the great hedge (John McLaren's "vertical lawn") everything was demolished, dismantled, sold or dispersed. By the end, all that remained of the exposition was a memory – with the exception of a few odds and ends in junk shops, and Bernard Maybeck's astonishing Palace of Fine Arts, which was left intact.

PALACE OF FINE ARTS ★

For his imitation of Roman ruins reflected in a pool of water, the architect Bernard Maybeck drew inspiration from a monument in a painting by the Swiss artist Arnold Böcklin entitled *L'Ile des Morts*, and from the engravings of Piranesi. The result is dreamlike, unreal and beautiful, consisting of an elegant rotunda with high arches open to the sky and Corinthian columns. Each colonnade is topped by a stone container; these were originally meant to contain plants, over which statues of nymphs sculpted by Ulric Ellerhusen were supposed to scatter blossoms. These nymphs, with their bent

238

heads and swathed bodies, are meant to symbolize the "melancholy of life without art." The dome of the Palace of Fine Arts is decorated with allegorical painted panels showing a female nude, the embodiment of art, defended by naked men (idealists) against the onslaught of centaurs (materialists): a symbolism that was echoed in many of the other buildings of the exposition. After the closure of the Panama-Pacific Exposition, the Palace of Fine Arts was used for an exhibition of paintings in 1918, and subsequently forgotten. For the next half-century San Franciscans watched the elegant plaster palace crumble away, until in 1959 a neighborhood resident came up with funds to restore it, which were matched by contributions from the city and the state of California. The edifice was reconstructed in reinforced concrete between 1962 and 1975; today it still stands on Baker and Beach Streets between the Bay and the Presidio, a reminder of the great exposition and a perennial favorite with the people of San Francisco.

EXPLORATORIUM SCIENCE MUSEUM ★

Behind the rotunda and colonnades is the half-moon-shaped pavilion in which a number of exhibitions of paintings and sculpture were held during the 1920's. Since 1969 this building has housed an astonishing museum which allows visitors to experience and understand a wide variety of physical effects. The Exploratorium Science Museum was founded by Frank Oppenheimer (brother of the physicist J. Robert Oppenheimer) to promote knowledge of advanced technology and to demonstrate the interdependent nature of art and science. Children of all ages enjoy operating the various machines here and trying out the wide range of active exhibits (over six hundred) related to sound, light and other phenomena in the various laboratories and rooms. In the Vidium, for example, an oscilloscope with a microphone turns all kinds of sounds into visual impressions, while the Shadow Box throws participants' shadows on phosphorescent screens where they linger for the space of thirty seconds. Opening hours vary according to the time of ycar, and the Tactile Dome can be visited only by prior arrangement and reservation.
AUDITORIUM. The auditorium in the Palace of Fine Arts can hold up to a thousand spectators.
THE COAST PATH. The northwest side of San Francisco forms a kind of outpost before the entrance to Golden Gate. The coast path, a favorite walk for San Franciscans, overlooks the Pacific. From here, in all, there are three parks

THE "WEEPERS"
These strange figures on the tops of the palace's columns, with their backs turned to visitors, were designed to water (with their tears) the plants beneath them.

239

PRESIDIO
A classified historical monument since 1963, the Presidio tracks the development of American architecture from 1850 to the present day: administrative

in the area: the Presidio to the north, the GGNRA's Lincoln Park and Golden Gate Park ▲ *254* further to the south. The northwest side also includes Richmond ▲ *246*, the city's most extended, most residential, and foggiest neighborhood and Seacliff ▲ *252*, probably its grandest, in a rocky promotory above the strait.

PRESIDIO

Founded in September 1776 by José Joaquin Moraga to defend the bay entrance and Mission Dolores ● *43*, ▲ *292*, the Presidio was originally a small fortified camp of adobe buildings ● *88*. From 1822 to 1835 it was the northernmost garrison of the fledgling Mexican republic; the United States army took it over in 1847. By the late 1850's wooden barracks had replaced the original adobe ones, which by then were falling down. In 1862–3, during the Civil War, the Presidio was given a broad parade ground flanked on the east side by twelve cottages that served as officers' quarters, with wooden cantonments and a hospital on the east side. From 1865 to 1890 it was the US Pacific army's headquarters. In the 1870's the entire precinct was opened to the public, and in March 1883 Major William A. Jones decided to lay out a 1,383-acre park on the windswept dunes adjoining the Presidio. The valleys were sown with grass for lawns, and the higher areas planted with some sixty thousand cypresses, acacias and eucalyptus trees to give the illusion of a dense expanse of forest. No other American army camp, before or since, has ever been environmentally landscaped in this manner. Between 1890 and 1914 most of the wooden buildings were replaced by brick and concrete structures in the Spanish colonial or Mission Revival style ● *88*. From 1910 to 1912, on a height to the northwest of the Presidio, Fort Winfield Scott was built as a military camp to protect the coastline, with its parade ground surrounded by concrete and stucco barracks, also

residential buildings in the Spanish or Georgian colonial style, industrial design shops and warehouses, and the hangars of the Crissy Army Airfield, cradle of American military aviation.

in the Mission Revival style. During the 1930's new Georgian-style cottages were erected here to provide housing for officers and their families. From 1946 to 1990, the Presidio was the headquarters of the Sixth Army and was also an important medical center, comprising a hospital and research laboratory. The Presidio is due to be transferred to the Golden Gate National Recreation Area, although a small military presence (approximately 700 people of the Sixth Army) will be maintained here.

PRESIDIO ARMY MUSEUM. This museum may be found on the corner of Lincoln and Funston Avenue, in the former military hospital built in 1857. It displays uniforms, weapons and other military items, along with dioramas and old photographs. Admission free.

NATONAL MILITARY CEMETERY. The National Military Cemetery contains the remains of about fifteen thousand American soldiers killed in action as well as many graves of their family members. Among the veterans' graves are those of the Indian scout Two Bits, and of Pauline Cushman Fryer, an actress who spied for the Union during the Civil War.

FORT POINT ★

In March 1776 the men of Juan Bautista de Anza's expedition raised a cross on a hilltop overlooking the Golden Gate to signify Spain's sovereignty over San Francisco Bay; later, in 1794, the Castillo de San Joaquín was built to defend this strategic site. Like the Presidio, the Castillo had bastions of adobe; designed to house only very few soldiers, it fell into disuse around 1810 when the Spaniards abandoned their California missions and returned to Mexico to fight the revolutionaries. The strategic value of the site was not lost on the US army, which in 1847 demolished San Joaquín and built a solid brick, steel and granite fortress in its stead. The construction went on from 1853 to 1861; but by the time it was finished, the fort was already obsolete, since the bricks offered no protection against shells or the newly invented repeating cannon, a prototype of the machine gun. In any event not one of the fort's 126 cannons ever fired a single shot in anger, and the only physical assault it ever experienced was that of the 1906 earthquake, which it survived with honor. Today Fort Point lies in the shadow of the south piling of Golden Gate Bridge; it was restored during the 1970's and serves as a small museum displaying paintings, uniforms and weaponry. Visitors can also watch one of the cannon being loaded, primed and fired. The top of its windy parapet, from which the swiveling cannon would be sighted on suspect vessels, offers a fine view of the bay, the rocks and any surfers crazy enough to ride the rollers under Golden Gate Bridge.

Storm over Golden Gate, by Nils Hagerup, showing Fort Point at the entrance to the bay.

COASTAL BATTERIES
Muzzle-loading cannon, central to the defence system of the bay, became obsolete in the 1890's when the American army adopted the new steel breech-loading model. Concrete casemates for the new artillery, some of which had a range of up to 3 miles, were installed along the coast between 1893 and 1908. Four of these installations, to the northwest of the Presidio, are open to the public.

241

The wildly ambitious project of spanning the Golden Gate with a suspension bridge between Marin County and San Francisco was brought to fruition in 1937. This, the second-longest single-span bridge on the planet, with 745-feet-high pilings bearing 1.86 miles of roadway 220 feet above the boiling waters of the bay, has become the absolute symbol of San Francisco. For over sixty years its pure, red-orange silhouette has soared above the green, ocher and blue waters of the bay, withstanding seismic tremors, high winds and increasingly dense traffic.

JOSEPH B. STRAUSS (1870–1938)
The designer of the Golden Gate Bridge first attracted attention in 1893 at the University of Cincinatti with a project for a bridge across the Bering Strait. His plan for the Golden Gate was scarcely less ambitious, and it was only by dint of great tenacity and persuasiveness that he was able to push it through at a time of economic difficulty. A bronze statue of the man who "conceived and gave shape" to the Golden Gate Bridge now overlooks the bay. All the same, it was the calculations made in 1930 by Strauss' aide, a brilliant engineer named Charles Alton Ellis, that allowed him to overcome many of the technical problems posed by the construction of a bridge on such an unusual site. Strauss (who was not a public works engineer) commissioned Ellis to draw up the bridge plans in 1921, and employed him to put them into execution in 1929. But later, in December 1931, fearing that his much-admired protégé would steal the glory, Strauss sacked Ellis, on the pretext of a disagreement over the cost and timing of the work.

Diagrammatic Study
Of San Francisco Pier
Showing Caisson And
Fender Construction

JOSEPH B STRAU
Chief Engineer

THE GOLDEN GATE BRIDGE
AT SAN FRANCISCO

The construction of the Golden Gate Bridge, as seen in oil paintings by Chesley Bonestell.

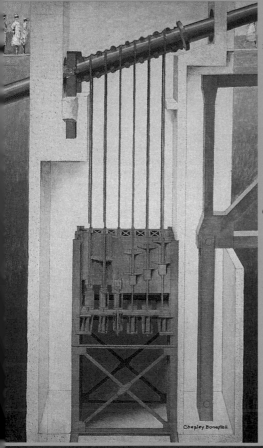

Chesley Bonestell

A TECHNICAL TRIUMPH

The building of a suspension bridge at the mouth of a great port, anchored in a difficult, rocky site dangerously prone to earthquake tremors and buffeted by strong winds and sea currents, was a gamble of heroic proportions: 676,000 cubic yards of concrete, a million tons of steel and over eighty thousand miles of metal cables were used in the construction work. The two parallel cables, 3 feet in diameter, which supplied the main support for the roadway, were anchored to the two gigantic pilings of the bridge and sealed into monster concrete blocks at either end of it. The construction of the north piling on the Marin County side posed no insuperable difficulties, but the south one took two years to build. The first stage involved grounding a concrete border in 60 feet of water, which was then pumped out. The piling was built inside this border. When the work was finished, conduits were added to allow the seawater to circulate freely within the border, thus cushioning the highly exposed structure from tremors and high tides. Apart from the collapse of a platform beneath the roadway which killed nine men, there were no other fatal accidents during the five years it took to build the Bridge.

245

A COSMOPOLITAN NEIGHBORHOOD
With its avenues of middle-class houses and gardens, the Richmond is a peaceful residential district enlivened by groupings of shops and restaurants. In this ethnically mixed community it is possible to buy groceries in a Russian store, down a beer in an Irish pub, then sit down to dinner in a

RICHMOND

At the beginning of the last century what is now the Richmond district was no more than a windy stretch of sand, indicated on contemporary maps as "Outside Lands". The construction in 1853 of a toll road from Point Lobos on the coast and the 1858 founding of an elegant restaurant, the *Cliff House*, brought San Francisco's high society out in droves, on horseback or in carriages, to this previously overlooked corner of the city. Following the 1906 earthquake a few San Franciscans decided to build houses in the area, and the toll road was renamed Geary Boulevard in honor of the first mayor of San Francisco. In 1912 a tramway was laid the length of Geary Boulevard, triggering a real estate boom in this part of town.

THE FIRST RESIDENTS. After World War One a number of Slavic immigrants came to the Richmond, where they set up tearooms, grocery stores and bagel bakeries. The Orthodox Church, on the corner of Geary and 26th Avenue, is still packed with worshippers at Easter and is well worth visiting to view its murals.

Chinese restaurant, all within yards of each other. The neighborhood was named by George Turner Marsh after the town in Australia where he was born.

GRAND MANSIONS. North of Lake Street most of the avenues come to a dead end alongside the Presidio gardens; this is the area where many of the neighborhood's finest houses are located. On Pacific Avenue, between Presidio Avenue and Walnut Street, there is an interesting group of houses with brown shingles, black moldings and steeply slanting roofs. These houses, in the best Bay Area traditional style, were designed by Coxhead, Maybeck and Polk.

NEW CHINATOWN. Clement Street, near Arguello Boulevard, is the main thoroughfare of the new Chinese quarter. When the laws forbidding Chinese to own property outside Chinatown were abolished in 1940, many of them moved to the Richmond. Since 1970 Thais, Vietnamese, Koreans and Japanese have arrived to swell the ranks of the Chinese population. The daily influx, to this day, of immigrants from Hong Kong and Southeast Asia steadily reaffirms the cultural and commercial links between San Francisco and the opposite shore of the Pacific.

A funeral at the Richmond cemetery in 1850.

SEACLIFF

This residential district began to be built up at the turn of the century. Many of its pastel-colored houses (there are no apartment blocks) are in the Mediterranean style that was

fashionable at that time. With its large, well-maintained villas, private mansions, winding streets and magnificent views from the cliffs, Seacliff is a favorite stop on the celebrated SCENIC DRIVE along CAMINO DEL MAR between Golden Gate Bridge and Lincoln Park's Palace of the Legion of Honor. But Seacliff is even more admirable viewed from the cliffs of Marin County on the far side of the narrows. From there it looks as if the white city of San Francisco were tumbling into the waves between the dark, rocky promontories.

LINCOLN PARK

This park, with its golf course and clumps of pine trees which dominate both the city and Golden Gate, stretches away to the west of Seacliff.

THE GOLDEN GATE CEMETERY. In 1868 the city acquired this site for use as a graveyard. Chinese, Greeks, Italians, Japanese and immigrants of many other nationalities were buried here over the years. A 19th-century journalist once wrote of this ". . . sinister spot, haunted by poor wretches who fed on the offerings left by the Chinese for the spirits of their dead." In fact, most of the Chinese contingent were only temporarily buried here before being carried across the ocean to the land of their ancestors, as was customary. In 1909 the municipality transferred the graves to Colma, and the former "paupers' cemetery" was turned into a golf course.

THE GOLF COURSE. The entrance to this eighteen-hole course is on 34th Avenue and Clement Street; its gates are open every day of the year. At the first and fifteenth holes are Chinese tombstones left over from the cemetery. The park roadways are much frequented by joggers and bicyclists.

Born 1881 in San Francisco, in modest circumstances, Alma Spreckels' maiden name was aristocratic: Emma Charlotte Corday le Normand de Bretteville. She never forgot that she was the descendant of a French general. At fourteen, she gave up delivering the laundry her mother took in, to study plastic arts at the Mark Hopkins Art Institute. But it was her marriage to

the rich sugar baron Adolph Spreckels that made her dreams of greatness a reality. In 1914 she went to France to buy furniture worthy of the enormous house she had built for herself ▲ 203. In Paris she discovered Art Nouveau and met the sculptor Rodin. Shortly afterwards, she began collecting art works and persuaded her husband to finance her museum project.

CALIFORNIA PALACE OF THE LEGION OF HONOR ★

This museum, built in the 1920's by the hugely rich Alma de Bretteville Spreckels to promote French art in California, stands elegantly profiled at the top of a hill overlooking the Golden Gate narrows. Currently closed for renovation, the building is scheduled to reopen in 1994. It contains theaters, a library and a restaurant, and maintains a highly active cultural service.

AN EXACT COPY. The museum was inspired by the Palais de la Légion d'Honneur in Paris, built in 1786 by the architect Pierre Rousseau. When Alma Spreckels saw a copy of this erected by the French delegation to the 1915 International Exhibition ▲ 236, she had the idea of asking France's government for permission to build a much larger replica dedicated to French art. The municipality donated the site, and the work was assigned to architect George Applegarth, a former student at the Paris Ecole des Beaux-Arts, who was able to adapt modern construction techniques to French classical architecture of the 18th century.

THE INAUGURATION. The opening of the Palace took place on November 11, 1924, Armistice Day, and was attended by French Marshals Foch and Joffre. The building was officially dedicated to the thousands of Californian servicemen who fell in France during World War One. Alma Spreckels had instigated a search of the military archives so that their names could be inscribed in a golden book, which was then signed by the two French commanders. On the day of the inauguration seven hundred works of art were exhibited, including thirty-one Rodin sculptures loaned by Alma Spreckels.

THE PRINCIPAL DONORS. In addition to her loan of the Rodin sculptures, including one of five models of *The Thinker* (pictured on the opposite page), Alma Spreckels donated her collection of Egyptian art, bronzes by Arthur Putnam, sculptures by

Théodore Rivière, and original drawings of the décors and costumes of the Russian ballet. The French government produced Gobelins tapestries and Sèvres china.

Alma Spreckels was also able to galvanize a group of other generous donors, notably Henry K. Williams, Archer M. Huntington, Moore S. Achenbach and Helen Irwin Fagan. For the rest of her life Alma Spreckels took a prominent hand in developing the various concerns of the Palace of the Legion of Honor, contributing to its refurbishment and to its ambitious educational and cultural program, *Patrons of Art and Music*, launched in 1955. On her death in 1968 thousands came to pay their respects before the embalmed body, sitting in an armchair, of the "woman who brought Europe to the people of San Francisco".

THE MUSEUM COLLECTIONS. Following changes decided for the sake of efficiency in 1972, the Palace of the Legion of Honor and the M.H. de Young Memorial Museum in Golden Gate Park ▲ *266* were merged. Both now form a single institution, the FINE ARTS MUSEUMS OF SAN FRANCISCO. Through this arrangement the M.H. de Young Museum acquired most of the American art, while the European art was grouped in the Palace of the Legion of Honor.

EUROPEAN ART. In the field of painting, the following are well represented: the Florentine school (Fra Angelico), the early Venetian school (Bellini, Titian, Tintoretto), 17th- and 18th-century Italian painting (Magnasco), the Flemish school (Herri met de Bles, Joos van Cleve, Rubens), Spanish painting (El Greco), Dutch painting (Pieter de Hooch, Rembrandt, Frans Hals), the British school (Gainsborough, Raeburn) and German painting (Lucas Cranach).

FRENCH ART
The collection consists mainly of sculptures and tapestries of the 16th century, and Limoges and St Porchaire porcelain. The 17th century is represented with works by Simon Vouet, Nicolas Poussin and Georges de la Tour. The richest section of the museum contains furniture, Gobelins, Beauvais and Aubusson tapestries, Sèvres and Chantilly china, Biennais silver, and paintings by Fragonard, Watteau and Boucher. From the 19th and early 20th centuries there are paintings by David, Corot, Manet, Monet, Renoir, Degas, Seurat and Cézanne. There is a whole roomful of Rodin sculptures, 106 in all, including the *Age of Bronze* and *Head of John the Baptist*.

249

Entrance to the
Sutro Heights park at
the beginning of the
century.

LAND'S END ★

From the parking lot at Lincoln Park, a path leads to the cliff
trail around Land's End. The unforgettable view of the strait
from here has made this sector of the Coastal Trail a great
favorite with those who enjoy walking. Passing from sunshine
to shade to mist and back again, the path winds for almost a
mile through fields and cypress woods and then along the
promontories overlooking the ocean. In the spring yellow
lupines and rock flowers with bright red petals lend color to
the landscape. In summer this exposed place is often cold and
foggy. The breeze off the Pacific, which blows throughout
the year, has tortured the vegetation along the coast,
twisting the shapes of the cypresses which were planted
during World War One to hide the guns mounted on this site.

"USS SAN FRANCISCO" MEMORIAL. At the point where
the Coastal Trail rounds Point Lobos and rejoins Merry Way,
there is a flight of steps leading right to the top of the cliff.
Here stands the bridge of the *USS San Francisco*, a warship
that was torpedoed by the Japanese during the Battle of
Guadalcanal in 1942. The names of the 107 seamen killed
in the incident are engraved on a nearby memorial.

OCTAGON HOUSE. It is now used as a private residence, but
the octagonal building just above Vista Point used to be a
telegraph relay station, the function of which was to signal the
arrival of shipping to the port authorities.

MILE ROCK LIGHT. This light stands on a rock that once
represented a serious menace to vessels passing through the
Golden Gate. Its construction was something of a feat; the
first team hired to do it refused the job at the very sight of this
breathtakingly sheer, slippery, barnacled rock emerging from
the waves. Finally , in 1904 a crew of experienced seamen
succeeded in erecting a 39-foot foundation of reinforced
concrete and the three-tier lighthouse atop it. However, the
only access was by means of a rope ladder which was
constantly lashed by the wind and spray; this was so
dangerous that one of the keepers named the place "Devil's
Island". In 1966 the upper structure was dismantled and
replaced by a helicopter pad and an automatic signal light.

SEAL ROCK
The Spaniards called
the farthest
promontory of Land's
End *Punta Lobos*, on
account of the seals
(*lobos marineros*),
whose roaring
mingled with the
thunder of the waves.
Adolph Sutro was a
great protector of
Seal Rock and was
adamant that nobody
should hunt the
animals there for
their fur. The colony,
with pups and mother
seals is still on Seal

SHIPWRECKS. The configuration of the
coastline, as well as the fog, wind, tides
and currents, combine to make the
approaches to San Francisco Bay
extremely hazardous. Some ninety-five
vessels have gone down over the years
and at least a hundred more have barely
escaped foundering while approaching or
passing through the mile-wide bottleneck
that is Golden Gate. The most celebrated
shipwreck was that of the *Parallel* in 1887.
This ship, its hold full of gunpowder,
struck the rocks below the Cliff House in
the middle of the night; the resulting

rock, although some
seals have now moved
to Pier 39.

Lands End Beach and
Hermit Rock (above).

explosion awoke the entire city. At low tide the wreck of the
Coos Bay (1937) can still be seen from the clifftop; this
merchant vessel broke up in thick fog off China Beach with a
cargo of timber. Fourteen of her thirty-two crew members
were hoisted up the cliff by cable.

SUTRO HEIGHTS

The grounds of the elegant Land's End park were opened to the people of San Francisco in the 1880's by the millionaire Adolph Sutro. Eleven gardeners contrived to establish on this bare, windswept shore an arboretum comprising exotic varieties collected from all over the world by Sutro, along with parterres of flowers, well-kept lawns, a greenhouse and a long parapet overlooking the ocean. Sutro Heights Park, as it is now called, was given to the city in 1938. Today care of the gardens has been taken over by the GGNRA.

THE PARAPET. This astounding construction overlooking the Pacific resembles the upper levels of a medieval castle. Its thirty crenellations were formerly studded with statues, and equipped with seats where people could sit and contemplate the view ● *119*.

ROCK GARDEN. Sutro also laid out a rock garden north of his house on Sutro Heights. The house has now disappeared but the flowered rock face, a vertical collage of dark stone, spiky aloes, delicate tea roses and hibiscus amid a riot of foliage, is still maintained.

"DIANA AND THE LIONS". Adolph Sutro, like Alma Spreckels, was concerned that the people of San Francisco should know as much as possible about European art. He imported from Belgium about two hundred life-size plaster statues (mushrooms, animals, elves, Greek gods and a range of historical figures), which still crowd his gardens. Vandals have defaced most of them, but the national park authorities have replaced many, most notably the two majestic lions which stand at the north entrance to the gardens. A great favorite with San Franciscans is the statue of the goddess Diana, whose devotees place garlands of leaves around her shoulders and bring offerings of food and flowers to lay at her feet.

SUTRO BATHS
In 1896 Adolph Sutro built what was then the world's largest public swimming bath establishment: seven heated pools under a giant glass canopy. For 10 cents anyone could rent a bathing suit and towel and use the pools, trampolines, slides and trapezes installed there, before going up to eat on the terrace. The original complex was closed in 1952, renovated, and finally destroyed by fire in 1960. Today its ruins may be seen at the far end of the Golden Gate Recreation Area.

THE CLIFF HOUSE

Since 1863 tourists and San Franciscans alike have come to this restaurant to drink and eat above the Pacific surf. The Cliff House has been rebuilt three times, and the present building bears no resemblance whatever to its predecessors. Apparently, though, much on offer there remains the same: shops for tourists, indifferent food, expensive drinks and a wonderfully sheltered place to sit and admire the view. In

1881 Adolph Sutro bought the Cliff House, a single-story shingled building constructed in 1863. At that time San Francisco high society had abandoned the place to gamblers, drunks and prostitutes; Sutro, who sternly disapproved of such elements, ordered his new manager to convert it into something more suitable, without beds everywhere and without locks on the doors. In 1894, after the old building was gutted by fire, Sutro decided to replace it with a Victorian palace complete with turrets, spires and elaborately carved pinewood décor. His restaurants, shops, private offices, art galleries and huge bay window overlooking the sea attracted San Franciscans to the Cliff House in droves, along with famous personalities such as Mark Twain, Sarah Bernhardt and President Roosevelt. This

system. In 1879 he sold his shares to buy land in San Francisco and began building public amenity areas such as Sutro Heights Park, the second Cliff House and the Sutro Baths. In his role as benefactor, Sutro convinced Southern Pacific to lower the price of its tickets to the seashore. Though he was "more concerned with poor people than wealthy ones", he routinely entertained personalities such as President Harrison, Andrew Carnegie and Oscar Wilde.

establishment was destroyed by fire shortly after the death of Sutro, and was again replaced: this time by a more modest construction, in neo-classical style, which was designed by the architects of the *Fairmont Hotel*. Today's building on the Great Highway is a modified version of this third Cliff House. Just below it are two curiosities that are well worth a visit. The MECHANICAL MUSEUM, which houses a collection of old mechanical toys that can be made to work with 50-cent coins, and the CAMERA OBSCURA, a replica of the darkroom invented by Leonardo da Vinci.

OCEAN BEACH

This 4-mile-long beach stretches away to the south of Cliff House. Though bathing is forbidden, the strand is very popular with San Franciscans, especially on sunny days. At the beginning of September Ocean Beach is the location of kite-flying championships, kite-flying being a very popular pastime all along the West Coast.

GOLDEN GATE PARK
AND HAIGHT-ASHBURY

MURPHY WINDMILL
OCEAN BEACH
BEACH CHALET
DUTCH WINDMILL
THE CLIFF HOUSE
NORTH LAKE
BUFFALO PADDOCK
GOLDEN GATE STADIUM
SPRECKELS LAKE
LINCOLN WAY

🚲 One day
🚗 Half a day

A ribbon of green over 3 miles long and 870 yards wide, Golden Gate Park stretches from the Pacific Ocean to the center of San Francisco, crossing the crowded districts of Richmond and Sunset ▲ 246.
Its thousand-odd acres are the city's green lung, forming one of the world's largest urban parks. This lush oasis coaxed from the barren sand is also something of a horticultural masterpiece, a triumph of human ingenuity over nature. Its existence mirrors the interest that San

THE PARK'S BEGINNINGS
Frank McCoppin, was one of the first to suggest a huge park in this part of town, which had no green areas whatever, since development during the Gold Rush ● *90* had occurred too quickly and chaotically to allow for them. The plan was backed by the local press and prominent citizens. In 1868, an editorial in the local paper complained that Portsmouth Square, Union Square and Washington Square were San Francisco's only green areas. "Soon our streets will seem to shrink and there will be a desperate need for more space" was the conclusion. The idea quickly caught on.

Franciscans have always taken in their environment, an interest that is underpinned by today's active and concerned ecology movement.

BEGINNINGS. Officially, San Francisco had only been in existence for two decades when the city fathers drew up plans for a municipal park on a scale to rival anything in New York, Paris or London. In 1866, with the Civil War drawing to a close, Mayor Frank McCoppin asked the landscape architect Frederick Law Olmstead to investigate the feasibility of a municipal park in the dunes west of Divisadero. Olmstead, who had already designed Central Park in New York, made no attempt to hide his skepticism; he doubted that respectable trees could ever be made to grow in these sandy wastes and advised the authorities to look for a different site

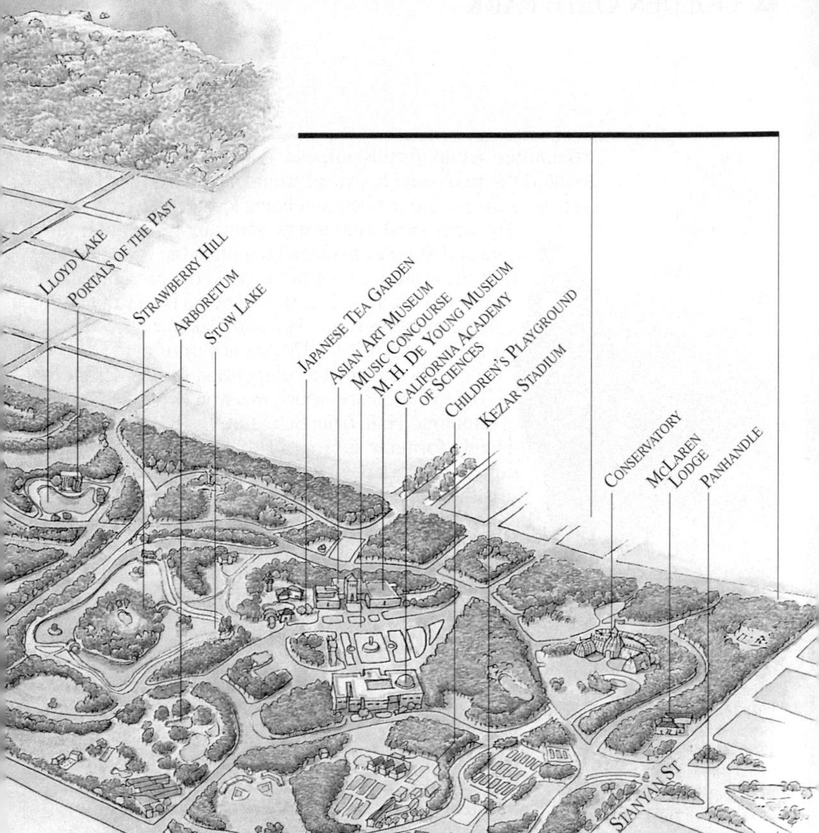

Labels on illustration (left to right):
LLOYD LAKE
PORTALS OF THE PAST
STRAWBERRY HILL
ARBORETUM
STOW LAKE
JAPANESE TEA GARDEN
ASIAN ART MUSEUM
MUSIC CONCOURSE
M. H. DE YOUNG MUSEUM
CALIFORNIA ACADEMY OF SCIENCES
CHILDREN'S PLAYGROUND
KEZAR STADIUM
CONSERVATORY
MCLAREN LODGE
PANHANDLE
STANYAN ST

from that which the newspapers were soon gleefully deriding as "The Great Sand Park". But before long, as the newly planted trees began to flourish, Olmstead was forced to admit that the new park was surpassing his wildest expectations.

LEGAL PROBLEMS. Administrative responsibility for the dunes outside San Francisco belonged to the municipality. It was assumed that they were a part of the common land of Yerba Buena, the former Mexican village whose mayoral authority assumed legal title to the zone. However, difficulties arose as to the geographical definition of this land, because San Francisco had for some years been expanding in a more or less uncontrolled manner. The municipal officers, under the impression that the dune land outside the city was worthless, had assigned a number of free lots on it to newly arrived immigrants. When the park project brought these handouts to an end, an argument ensued between City Hall and the "sand-lotters"; interestingly, while some of these sand-lotters actually resided on the dunes, most were in fact shrewd speculators who had foreseen the inexorable westward spread of the city. McCoppin, by now firmly resolved to create his park on this land, finally managed to negotiate a compromise solution ▲ 274.

A DIFFICULT BIRTH. Next came the establishment of plans for the park, and there were acrimonious debates within the

THE ARCHITECT OF GOLDEN GATE PARK
W.H. Hall was only twenty-four when his design for Golden Gate Park was accepted. In 1871 he began planting trees, building roads and laying out areas for sports, always taking care to respect the natural topography of the site. This firm stance made him a number of enemies, and he was forced to resign in 1876 on a trumped-up charge of embezzling public funds. Nevertheless, he was recalled to manage the park ten years later, in 1886.

255

committee set up for this purpose. Ashbury and Clayton wanted the park zone to extend from Divisadero right across to the ocean, the best soil being located between Divisadero and what is now Stanyan Street. Stanyan, Cole and Shrader managed to obtain the concession that the eastern sector of the park, the present Panhandle zone ▲ 280, should be no larger than a single block, between Fell and Oak Streets. Finally, on April 4, 1870, the governor of California launched a competition for the design of Golden Gate Park, which was won by William Hammond Hall, from Stockton. In 1871 Governor Haight formally approved Hall's project, and in the same year work commenced on the Panhandle sector. Less than ten years later the new park had become the favorite promenade for San Franciscans: one sunny day in 1886, an estimated fifty thousand people (a quarter of the city's population) visited Golden Gate Park. Until the end of the century the appointment of the park's administrators was the responsibility of the governor of California, not the mayor of San Francisco.

MCLAREN, HALL'S WORTHY SUCCESSOR
Born in Scotland in 1846, John McLaren arrived in California in the early 1870's. A peerless botanist and landscape gardener who had studied in Edinburgh, he administered the park from 1887 to 1943 and is largely responsible for its present form. McLaren was a passionate nature-lover, who introduced several hundred new varieties of trees and plants to Golden Gate. In the early 1890's he supervised the construction of buildings for the Midwinter Fair ▲ 258.

STABILIZING THE SOIL. Nobody had found a solution to the problem of stabilizing the sand dunes so that trees and plants could take firm root. The answer came to William Hammond Hall by chance. In the early 1870's his horse spilled some barley from its nosebag on to the sand. On returning to the same spot a few months later, Hall discovered green shoots growing. He proceeded to mix barley with the seeds of slow-growing lupines, and sowed this mixture in several of the areas to be reclaimed. The months that it took for the nurse crop of barley to grow gave the lupines time to take root. In the areas of the Park where the sand was impregnated with salt water, Hall used sand grass instead of barley and lupines; and eventually he was able to reclaim all the sandy parts of Golden Gate Park by the same method. Meantime, Hall built a 6- to 9-foot wall along the seafront as a barrier against sand being blown off it; this wall is now buried beneath the Great Highway. After the architect's forced resignation in 1876, the maintenance of the park deteriorated so badly that only ten years later the governor of California, George Stoneman, recalled him to act as an adviser. Hall undertook to rehabilitate the park and to improve the horticultural techniques used there, but he was only to remain in office for one year; time enough, fortunately, to choose his successor, John McLaren.

"UNCLE JOHN". John McLaren was the kind of person that people either adored or loathed. His fierce autocratic ways, crude oaths, rough manners, fondness for whisky and broad Scottish accent were as delightful to some as they were infuriating to others. Nevertheless his botanical genius was

beyond doubt, as was his astonishing skill at outfoxing the politicians he despised; and these qualities quickly won the hearts of San Franciscans. So great was Uncle John's charisma that he was able to convince all kinds of philanthropists to give money for the embellishment of his beloved park. In 1916 the citizens of San Francisco demonstrated furious opposition to the forced retirement of Uncle John, then aged seventy, by petitioning the park's Board of Administration. As a result of this McLaren was able to retain his function until his death during World War Two. He was given an official funeral by the city, and as a last homage to the "man who dedicated his life to planting a million trees" the procession passed through Golden Gate Park.

THE 1906 EARTHQUAKE. Golden Gate Park came through the 1906 earthquake virtually unscathed, and over 200,000 people took refuge there when the great fire broke out. Despite its distance from the main flashpoints, which were about 3 miles away, burning ash rained down on the survivors sheltering under the trees and shrubs. The Red Cross established emergency facilities throughout the park, and the United States army sent the world's largest tent from St Louis by railroad for use as a makeshift hospital. A few days after the catastrophe there were still 40,000 people sleeping in the park. The tent was to remain occupied for a year after the catastrophe, at which time the de Young memorial was reopened; within only a few months the flowers and shrubs trampled by the soldiers and the homeless had been replanted.

"NO" TO THE CABLE CAR
John McLaren had a major bone to pick with the municipality over its proposal to push a tramline slap through the middle of his park. To obtain McLaren's agreement, the tram promoters had made a legal engagement not to damage any of the park's plantations. On the night before the works were scheduled to begin, the crafty Scotsman planted a whole row of trees along the path of the future line. He won his point: the project had to be abandoned. This caricature from the satirical San Francisco newspaper *The Wasp* shows Crocker, the principal shareholder of the cable car company, laying waste the park with his new tramway.

257

MIDWINTER FAIR

Michael Harry de Young, co-founder of the daily *San Francisco Chronicle*, was a commissioner at the 1893 Universal Exhibition in Chicago. When that exhibition was over, he had the idea of organizing something similar in his own city. De Young brought home a few examples of what could be shown, obtained financial contributions from his wealthy friends, presented his proposal to the park commission, and won its agreement. Thus the Midwinter Fair opened in Golden Gate Park in January 1894, the first international exhibition ever held in California. As a public relations exercise, its goal was to advertise the gentle climate of San Francisco, even in wintertime, and the wealth of the state of California. In a year of severe economic recession, it also aimed to stimulate business enterprise. No fewer than thirty-seven foreign countries took part in this show and the hundred-odd pavilions, which were originally planned to cover about 7 acres, eventually sprawled over a total of about 180 acres.

THE ELECTRIC TOWER. In the early 1890's, electricity was the new thing, so naturally the Electric Tower set up in the central esplanade was one of the fair's principal attractions. The beam radiating from its turret was so powerful that one could read a newspaper by it at night 6 miles away.

FANTASY AND EXOTICA. Around the central esplanade stood the five principal pavilions of the exhibition, including

the Fine Arts Museum and the Japanese Village. But beyond these structures, the main purpose of which was to highlight the latest technological developments, a certain exotic atmosphere reigned at the Midwinter Fair. In the event, most of the pavilions were of Asiatic or Middle Eastern inspiration. Outside, there were sideshows galore; perhaps the most famous of these was a troop of belly-dancers from Cairo, among whom the legendary "Little Egypt" made her US début. There was even an Eskimo village in the middle of an artificial pool of water, round which hired Inuits perpetually paddled their kayaks. But the most successful attraction of all was Boone's Arena, a wild animal show which became enormously popular after one of the lions happened to kill his trainer in the middle of an act.

A SPECTACULAR SUCCESS. The Midwinter Fair was a resounding triumph; over a period of six months it attracted no fewer than 2½ million visitors and gave a phenomenal boost to local business. But although the fair was a source of great pride to San Franciscans, it caused havoc in Golden Gate Park and was ridiculed by East Coast observers for its "incoherent organization and mediocre architecture", proof (to them) of the "provincialism" of San Francisco. The Electric Tower remained in the park until 1897, at which time John McLaren characteristically had it blown up, since the exhibition organizers firmly refused to pay for its removal. The only complete features of the fair that have survived to this day are the Japanese Tea Garden ▲ 263, the Fine Arts Museum (now the M.H. de Young Memorial Museum ▲ 264) and the Music Concourse esplanade ▲ 262. Other traces of the event include the wine press and the stone lions that stand at the park gates, along with a few other odds and ends and memorabilia now on display at the San Francisco City Museum.

"The universal expositions were not only market places where the commercial and industrial powers showed off their prowess; they also favored the emergence of new values and allowed the crowds that saw them to find out about other, little known or even unknown societies. For some visitors the expositions were merely picturesque; for others they constituted a change to call home-grown esthetic criteria into question."
M.N. Pradel de Grandry

259

FROM McLAREN LODGE TO THE ARBORETUM

McLAREN LODGE. This attractive sandstone building, designed by Edward R. Swain, was constructed in 1896 on Stanyan and Fell Streets as a home for McLaren and his family, as well as for the Recreation and Park Commission. In 1950 an annex was added to it, from which the city's 215 other parks and playgrounds are now administered. In front of McLaren Lodge grows a very tall cypress which San Franciscans still call "Uncle John's Christmas Tree". In 1943, when the old Scotsman was dying, he asked for it to be covered in Christmas lights, a request that nobody had the heart to refuse even though there was a wartime blackout in force. The cypress has been lit with colored lights every December since, in memory of McLaren.

CONSERVATORY OF FLOWERS ★. In 1875 the American millionaire James Lick ordered a conservatory from Ireland, stipulating that it be identical to the one in London's Kew Gardens. He planned to install this conservatory on his property at San José, south of San Francisco. But the magnate died in the following year, and his huge greenhouse, which had only just been put in place, was purchased by a group of San Franciscans who presented it to the city's new park. This generosity was not entirely innocent, given that the group was controlled by Leland Stanford, who at the time was fighting to obtain a permit to run his Park and Ocean Railroad across the southeast end of Golden Gate Park. Erected on its new site in 1878, the conservatory was severely damaged by fire in 1883, after which the original panels were replaced by a much larger central dome encrusted with polychrome glass, designed by John Gash. It survived the 1906 earthquake unscathed and today contains an immense and resplendent collection of flowers, notably waterlilies, cyclamens, begonias, cinerarias, azaleas and calcedarias. The ambient heat and humidity are constantly adjusted to simulate different tropical environments and flowering seasons. From the outside this gem of Victorian architecture seems to be couched in a lush bed of blossoms. The Conservatory of Flowers is not only the oldest building in Golden Gate Park, but also the oldest public greenhouse in California.

CHILDREN'S PLAYGROUND. If you cross Kennedy Drive and continue down Bowling Green Drive, you eventually reach the children's playground, the oldest facility of its kind ever built in an American public park. Inaugurated on December 22, 1888, it was renamed Mary B. Connolly's Children's Playground on March 22, 1978, as a tribute to the lady who for many years was secretary to the park's Recreation Commission. The playground has soda fountains distributing ice water and ice cream, stables, gymnasiums, lawn tennis courts, swings and merry-go-rounds. Children can also take part in a number of creative activities (drawing, pottery, painting on glass, and so on) at the Sharon Art Studio.

STRYBING ARBORETUM

The arboretum and botanical gardens together form a park within a park. No fewer than six thousand plant species are represented, in an area that covers nearly 70 acres. The arboretum, which is located by 9th Avenue and Lincoln Way, was designed by a Californian university professor, Robert Tetlow, and paid for by funds bequeathed by Helen Strybing. Open seven days a week, it also contains the Helen Crocker Horticultural Library, designed by Gardner Dailey in 1967.

THE BOTANICAL GARDENS. A vast array of plants from every corner of the planet can be viewed in the various thematic gardens, which have evocative names such as SUCCULENT GARDEN, BIBLICAL GARDEN, ASIA GARDEN, CONIFER WALK, etc. Every August, a flower show is mounted in the HALL OF FLOWERS.

GARDEN OF FRAGRANCE. This area was designed with blind people in mind, as a place where they might appreciate flowers through their senses of touch and smell. It contains a collection of scented and medicinal plants, the names and properties of which are indicated in braille. The walls of the garden were built of limestone blocks from a 12th-century monastery brought from Spain by the press magnate William Randolph Hearst; the remainder of the building itself may be seen behind the Japanese Tea Garden.

CONIFER WALK
Fifty-four varieties of native conifer are represented here, among them the Monterey cypress (*Pinus radiata*), the Lambert cypress (*Cupressus macrocarpa*) and the giant sequoia (*Sequoiadendron giganteum* ● *30*).

SHAKESPEARE GARDENS
In this garden on the far side of Martin Luther King Drive, just behind the California Academy of Sciences, the plants on show are confined to the 150-odd species mentioned in the plays and poems of Shakespeare. This garden was laid out in 1928 by the California Spring Blossom and Wildflower Association. A bust of Shakespeare by Gerard Jensen overlooks the plantation.

C.9.

STATUES

McLaren, who detested statues, would only allow them in the park under duress, and even then would go to great lengths to conceal them behind bushes. After his death, his successors went so far in their disregard for Uncle John's preferences that they put up a statue of McLaren himself in the park. Today there are a number of statues on view, notably in the area round the Music Concourse. The three assassinated US presidents (James A. Garfield, Abraham Lincoln and John F. Kennedy) are thus commemorated. The "Doughboy" statue, by Earl Cummings, pays homage to the American heroes of the World War One. The Italian composer Giuseppe Verdi (1813–1901) is also featured, in a bust by Orazio Grossoni executed in 1914. At the corner of the Music Concourse another well-hidden statue commemorates Thomas Starr King (1824–64), a Boston pastor and fervent Unionist, who was the first American priest to open his church to all denominations. His monument in bronze was sculpted by Daniel Chester French in 1892.

MUSIC CONCOURSE

This esplanade lies between the Academy of Sciences and the M.H. de Young Memorial Museum. With its thoroughly French appearance and its fountains and deciduous trees (the only ones of their kind in the park), the Music Concourse is in direct contrast to the more romantic English temper that prevails elsewhere. The Concourse is the scene of the Opera Concert in the Park which takes place on the Sunday following the Friday night opening of the Opera and attracts artists of international repute. Other concerts are held throughout the summer.

SPRECKELS TEMPLE OF MUSIC. This Colusa sandstone pavilion, built in 1900 opposite the Japanese Tea Garden, dominates the Music Concourse. It was commissioned from the sculptor Robert Ingersoll Aitken by Claus Spreckels, the "Sugar King", who donated it to the park. The municipal orchestra, which is the oldest municipal musical group in the United States, gives a concert here every Sunday afternoon.

FRANCIS SCOTT KEY MONUMENT. The (substantial) funds to pay for this monument to the author of America's national anthem were provided by the millionaire James Lick. Sculpted in Italy by William M. Story, it was inaugurated on July 4, 1888, Independence Day.

MONUMENTS. Several statues and monuments can be seen around the Music Concourse. The JUNIPERO SERRA MONUMENT is dedicated to the Franciscan missionary who participated in the expedition of Gaspar de Portolá in 1769, and who evangelized the southern California coast, founding twenty-one missions ▲ 293, among them that of San Francisco. Created by Douglas Tilden, the statue was presented to the city in 1907 by the former senator and mayor James Duval Phelan. The SOLAR DIAL, sculpted by Earl Cummings in 1905, was a gift of the Daughters of the American Revolution. The ROMAN GLADIATOR, with his cloak, helmet and sword, was sculpted in 1881 by Guillaume Geefs. The two concrete sphinxes facing the gladiator replaced those sculpted in bronze by Arthur Putnam (1903), which originally crouched on either side of the Egyptian-style Fine Arts Museum, a legacy of the Midwinter Fair. THE WINE PRESS made by Thomas Shields-Clarke for the French pavilion at the Universal Exhibition, remains one of the few features of that event still on public display.

JAPANESE TEA GARDEN ★

During the Midwinter Fair the "Japanese Village" was such a success with the public that the Golden Gate Park Administration decided to keep it on. With its pools, wooden bridges and miniature trees, this garden is still one of the most attractive parts of the park, especially at the end of March when the cherry trees come into blossom. The Japanese Tea Garden was originally designed in 1894 by George Turner Marsh, an Australian officer who had spent

his childhood in Japan. Nevertheless, it was a Japanese gardener, Makato Hagiwara, who defined its contours, its clumps of conifers and its waterfalls. Hagiwara's family subsequently maintained the garden from 1895 to 1942, when they were interned in camps by order of President Roosevelt, along with all the other Japanese inhabitants of California. At the end of the war the Hagiwaras were refused permission to move back to the park ▲ *230*; their devotion to the garden was not fully recognized, or recompensed, until 1974, when a bronze statue was erected in their honor. The TEA HOUSE, near the five-tier pagoda, is a delightful place to stop, in which hostesses in kimonos serve cups of green tea accompanied by rice cakes.

FORTUNE COOKIES
In 1909 Makato Hagiwara invented the fortune cookie, a hollow cookie containing a piece of paper inscribed with a maxim or cryptic piece of advice. Brought to the public's attention for the first time at the Midwinter Fair, these cookies went on to achieve worldwide success. The restaurants of the Chinese quarter quickly began to serve fortune cookies and exported the recipe to China, with the result that nowadays people believe that this San Francisco invention is of Chinese origin ● *86*.

A 9-foot-tall Buddha known as Amazarashi-no-hotoke – the Buddha who sits unsheltered from the wind and rain – overlooks the Japanese Garden. This bronze statue dates from 1790.

The M.H. de Young Memorial Museum.

CALIFORNIA ACADEMY OF SCIENCES

Set up in 1853 in the city center and subsequently destroyed by the 1906 fire, the California Academy of Sciences relocated in Golden Gate Park in 1910. The one or two rooms saved from the flames by the Academy's staff later formed the kernel of its new collection. Today the Academy maintains an aquarium, a planetarium and a museum of natural history. In the south wing of the museum, the WATTIS HALL OF MAN traces mankind's evolution from prehistory down to the present time, while the section entitled "LIFE THROUGH TIME" offers an interesting collection of fossils. In the eastern part of the building, the AFRICAN HALL displays dioramas of African fauna. For a deeper understanding of the formation of the solar system and planet Earth, visit the EARTH AND SPACE HALL. Other rooms are variously dedicated to Californian flora and fauna, mineralogy, and so on.

M.H. DE YOUNG MEMORIAL MUSEUM ★ ● 266

When the Midwinter Fair came to an end, M.H. de Young presented the municipality with the neo-Egyptian building that had harbored the fine arts section. Later he steadily enriched the collections, which were at first largely composed of purchases made during the fair. Enlarged soon after the San Francisco International Exhibition, again mostly with funds contributed by M.H. de Young, the museum was officially named after its benefactor in 1921. De Young had time to add a west wing before his death in 1925. Four years later the original building was pulled down, and it was not until 1949 that it achieved its present form. The museum's central tower, 48 yards in height, is reflected in the POOL OF ENCHANTMENT, the surface of which is dotted with waterlilies.

ASIAN ART MUSEUM★ ● 270

The Asian Art Museum, which is in the left wing of the same pink sandstone building, houses the Avery Brundage Collection and is the only establishment in America entirely dedicated to Asiatic Art. The collection covers six thousand years of history and forty countries, including all the great artistic traditions from Iran to Japan and from Mongolia to Indonesia. About twelve thousand different objects (paintings, sculpture, ceramics, architectural elements) form the basis of a display that is constantly changing because the 5,380 square yards of space available can only accommodate 15 percent of the collection at any given time.

SPORTS AND RECREATION

Golden Gate Park offers visitors a wide range of sporting activities, ranging from jogging and bicycling to archery, riding, golf, tennis, basketball, handball and bowls. More romantic spirits will opt for an outing in a

boat or pedal-craft on one of the many lakes. For those less interested in sport, there are three museums, an arboretum and many separate gardens to visit. On Sundays some of the park's main avenues, notably Kennedy Drive between Stanyan Street and 19th Avenue, are closed to automobile traffic. Rollerskaters, skateboarders and "ultimate frisbee" buffs take over.

The 1972 merger of the M.H. de Young Memorial Museum and the California Palace of the Legion of Honor resulted in a redistribution of their collections. Everything under the heading of European art was moved to the institution founded by Alma Spreckels, while African, Pacific and American art went to the museum created by M.H. de Young. The donation of John D. Rockefeller III in 1979 and more recently a legacy from his widow have enriched an already handsome collection of pre-'45 North American painting, sculpture and decorative art.

FAVRILE. This special form of glass is the hallmark of the American Art Nouveau artist Louis C. Tiffany (1870–1921).

"MRS ROBERT S. CASSATT". Mary Cassatt (1844–1926) painted this portrait of her mother in about 1889. A harmonious composition in beige and black, this canvas is [the o]nly American painter who was a part [of t]he original Impressionist group.

"FROM THE GARDEN OF THE CHÂTEAU" (1921). Charles Demuth (1883–1935) was, with Charles Sheeler, one of the most prominent advocates of "Precisionism", which used limpid colors and jagged shapes to convey the spirit of modern life.

CLOCK. Made in Pennsylvania between 1810 and 1820, this elegant clock is decorated with a replica of the seal of the United States.

"BOATMEN ON THE MISSOURI" (1846)
The painter and politician George Caleb Bingham (1811–79) became famous on the East Coast for his paintings of what was then the Western Frontier. With its subtle tones and sober outlines, this scene of daily life on the Missouri shows the wood-sellers who supplied fuel to the steam-powered ships along the river.

"THE HARVEST SUPPER"
This 1934 painting by Grant Wood (1891–1942) evokes the *Last Supper*. The painter set out to extol the simple life of farmers in Iowa, where he himself was raised. The colors and the triptych composition of this work echo the early Italian Renaissance, when simple treatment was similarly appropriate to contemporary themes.

KING SAUL (1882). Resident in Rome from 1855, sculptor William Wetmore Story (1819–95), popular in the US during the 1870's, drew his subjects from the Bible, Greek mythology, or literature, which were calculated to please the puritanical home public.

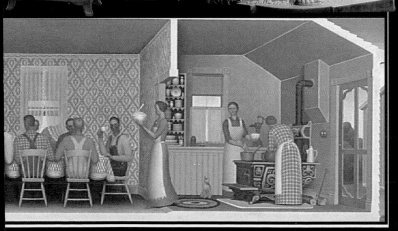

"The Bright Side"
Winslow Homer (1836–1910) was hired to cover the Civil War by the magazine *Harper's Weekly.* He avoided battle scenes, preferring to concentrate on the day-to-day existence of ordinary soldiers, especially black soldiers. The title of this painting is significant: the soldiers are seen resting before returning to combat, a theme rarely pictured during the war. Painted in 1865, *The Bright Side* was shown at the 1867 Universal Exhibition in Paris.

**"STEELWORKERS:
THE MIDDAY BREAK"**
Thomas P. Anshultz
(1851–1912) was a
pupil of Thomas
Eakins who had been
trained in the French
naturalist tradition.
In this 1881 painting
he achieved a
remarkable frieze
composition, using
studio models. The
choice of subject
demonstrates his
deep interest in
everyday working life.

"AN ARCADIAN"
In 1883, Thomas
Eakins (1844–1916)
began a series of
studies for paintings
and sculptures which
attempted to recapture
the spirit of classicism.
This one was cast by
his widow in 1930.

"SUFFOLK STALLION". The son of a famous painter,
Herbert Haseltine (1877–1962) became a
specialist in sculptures of horses. This piece is
of gilded bronze, encrusted with lapis lazuli,
onyx and ivory
(1921–37).

Inaugurated in 1966, the Asian Art Museum (or Avery Brundage Collection) is the only major American museum devoted to the art of Asia. More than half of the collection is dedicated to Chinese art, but Southeast Asia is also extensively represented among its twelve thousand or so pieces. The items are exhibited in rotation, though the rarer works are those most often on view.

CHINESE WINE PITCHER (11TH CENTURY BC)
This wine pitcher in the form of a rhinoceros (above) is unique in the art of the Shan dynasty. Though these animals seem to have been common in northern China during the 11th century, likenesses of them are very rare: this little bronze is superbly realistic.

BRAHMI (SOUTHERN INDIA, 9TH CENTURY)
Brahmi is the female aspect of Brahma, the creator; she is represented with four heads crowned by the ascetic's crown of tresses and holding a rosary, a pitcher with a spout and the four books of the *Veda*. The sensual features, narrow waist, ample bosom and restrained elegance of this granite figurine are characteristic of Dravidian art during the Chola period.

SHIVA AND UMA (CAMBODIA, 11TH CENTURY)
Sculptors of the Baphuon created these terracotta statuettes reflecting feminine beauty.

MOGUL MINIATURE (INDIA, 18TH CENTURY)
A delicate rendering of a maharajah and his wife watching a fireworks displ▮▮

"HANIWA" WARRIOR (JAPAN, 16TH CENTURY)
Haniwa terracotta "cylinders" used to be placed on burial mounds during the period of the *kunfun,* or "Great Tombs" (3rd–6th centuries). They often included human or animal figures and served to stabilize the mound and indicate the social status of the deceased.

CHINESE▮ TIBETAN "DAKINI" (18TH CENTURY)
This lion-headed female sentinel of Tantric Buddhism is one of the "celestial walkers" who guide human beings along the way of the just and unite the earthly and heavenly spheres.

DURGA (JAVA, 10TH–11TH CENTURY)
Durga is the martial form of Parvati, consort of the Hindu god Shiva. On this basalt relief she is depicted brandishing in her many hands the weapons given to her by the gods to help her defeat the buffalo demon Mahisha, shown here in his double form, as both human and animal.

NEPALESE RELIQUARY (LATE 18TH CENTURY)
This silver box encrusted with mother-of-pearl, coral, rubies, turquoises and tourmalines, represents the god Vishnu astride his mount, the eagle Garuda, who crushes two serpent gods as they fly over the Himalayas.

STOW LAKE

The park includes eleven lakes, seven of which are artificial. Stow Lake, with 1,602,000 acres and 9,140 feet of shoreline, is the largest of all. In 1895 the lawyer W.W. Stow, president of the Park Commission, succeeded in convincing Collis Huntington, of the "Big Four" ▲ *189*, to finance the construction of this huge reservoir, which can hold thirty million gallons of water. It was decided that the lake should be built around abedrock hill some 370 feet high, named STRAWBERRY HILL, which constitutes the park's highest point. Before 1906 an observatory stood at the top of this hill, which owes its name to the wild strawberries that used to grow on it. A path leads around the lake to a small wooden chalet where visitors can rent boats and pedal-craft.

HUNTINGTON FALLS. This cascade, which was inaugurated on April 9, 1894, runs down the green slope of Strawberry Hill to the lake. Damaged in 1906, it was restored in the late 1980's, to the delight of San Franciscans. The little bridge of flat stones that spans the waterfall was built by Ernest Coxhead in the 1890's.

CHINESE PAVILION. The pagoda, known as the Chinese Pavilion, was a gift of the city of Taipei, the capital of Taiwan. It was erected at the foot of the waterfall in 1976; the roof of varnished tiles, which was originally intended to be yellow, was finally painted gray-green because the San Francisco Arts Committee insisted that the building blend harmoniously with its surroundings.

PRAYER BOOK CROSS. This 50-foot high Celtic cross, made by Ernest Coxhead for the Midwinter Fair, commemorates the first Anglican communion celebrated by Sir Francis Drake's chaplain, Francis Fletcher, in what is now known as Drake's Bay ● *42*. It overlooks RAINBOW FALLS, an artificial cascade built c. 1930.

PIONEER LOG CABIN. After the 1906 earthquake destroyed their meeting house, the members of the Association of Pioneer Women of California held monthly picnics in the park instead. The mayor, P.J. McCarthy, came across them one day as he was riding in the park and gallantly proposed the construction of a log cabin for their exclusive use. The cabin was built in 1911 and enlarged in 1932.

LLOYD LAKE TO OCEAN BEACH

THE LAKES. Not far from Rainbow Falls is LLOYD LAKE, the third-largest artificial lake in Golden Gate Park. SPRECKELS LAKE, farther west, is a favorite meeting place for model boat buffs. From this stretch of water one can see the Richmond neighborhood beyond a thin screen of cypresses.

THE STADIUMS. South of SPRECKELS LAKE is the GOLDEN GATE STADIUM or POLO FIELD, inaugurated on May 12, 1907.

Polo, cricket and rugby matches are held here, along with concerts and other public events. On January 14, 1967, fourteen thousand hippies came to this stadium for a "Gathering of the Clans" ▲ 277. Golden Gate Park also possesses a football stadium, known as the KEZAR STADIUM. Opened in 1925, this facility was the home of the local team, the Forty-Niners, until the opening of Candlestick Park.

BUFFALO PADDOCK. This bison enclosure may be found along Kennedy Drive, on the west end of the park. The first group of bison brought here from Wyoming in 1892 was decimated

PLAYLAND. This spacious amusement park used to be in the Haight-Ashbury neighborhood ▲ 275. It was moved to Ocean Beach by Golden Gate Park in 1902, and then again further to the south, before it closed down.

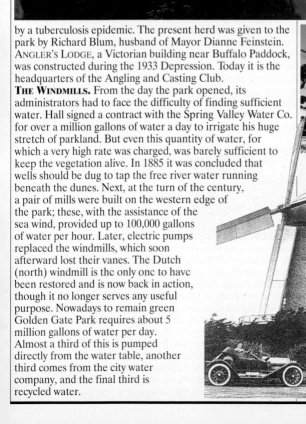

by a tuberculosis epidemic. The present herd was given to the park by Richard Blum, husband of Mayor Dianne Feinstein. ANGLER'S LODGE, a Victorian building near Buffalo Paddock, was constructed during the 1933 Depression. Today it is the headquarters of the Angling and Casting Club.

THE WINDMILLS. From the day the park opened, its administrators had to face the difficulty of finding sufficient water. Hall signed a contract with the Spring Valley Water Co. for over a million gallons of water a day to irrigate his huge stretch of parkland. But even this quantity of water, for which a very high rate was charged, was barely sufficient to keep the vegetation alive. In 1885 it was concluded that wells should be dug to tap the free river water running beneath the dunes. Next, at the turn of the century, a pair of mills were built on the western edge of the park; these, with the assistance of the sea wind, provided up to 100,000 gallons of water per hour. Later, electric pumps replaced the windmills, which soon afterward lost their vanes. The Dutch (north) windmill is the only one to have been restored and is now back in action, though it no longer serves any useful purpose. Nowadays to remain green Golden Gate Park requires about 5 million gallons of water per day. Almost a third of this is pumped directly from the water table, another third comes from the city water company, and the final third is recycled water.

SPENCER HOUSE BUENA VISTA PARK BUENA VISTA AVE WEST PANHANDLE

ASHBURY S.

HAIGHT ST

PAGE ST

BAKER ST

OAK ST

THE FIRST FAMILY OF HAIGHT
In the 1850's the Langes, a German immigrant family, bought a 10-acre tract in the present Cole Valley and installed a dairy on the corner of Sutter and Divisadero Streets. By 1879 the zone was overrun by encroaching urban

sprawl, and the dairy was surrounded by "civilization". Nevertheless, until 1893 the Langes' cows continued to drink at the Laguna Seca and to graze in the meadows that have now made way for Cole, Stanyan, Carl and Gratton Streets.

The Haight-Ashbury district, as it has been known officially since 1965 ▲ 276, grew up on a broad expanse of dunes to the west of town, along the road built by the first Spanish colonists to link Mission Dolores ▲ 294 to the Presidio ▲ 240. Between 1854 and 1865 the pioneers established four cemeteries in the dunes that undulate between Fulton and California Streets; of these, nothing remains save the Columbarium of Lorraine Court and one or two headstones that were reused for the construction of drainage canals in Buena Vista Park. In the early 1860's squatters attempted to occupy the dunes but were thwarted by the municipality, which was plannint to create a park on the site ▲ 254. After a period of bitter negotiations the mayor finally yielded a section of the dunes to the squatters, retaining the rest for his park.

A SUNDAY PROMENADE. At an early stage the Haight area was already a semi-rural zone visited by Sunday strollers; in the 1880's, after the opening of Golden Gate Park, it became one of San Francisco's favorite promenades. In August 1883 the Southern Pacific Railroad inaugurated the first tramway linking the center of town to the park. The development of this new means of transport caused a rise in real-estate prices, with saloons, restaurants and hotels crowding the dunes overlooking Haight Street. At the same time several rows of Victorian houses were constructed ● 92, and Haight gradually acquired residential status.

THE EARTHQUAKE. The earthquake and fire of 1906 caused relatively little damage to the Haight area. During reconstruction ● 62 all the surrounding sites were divided

STANYAN ST

SHRADER ST

COLE ST

CLAYTON ST

✻ Three hours

into lots; later, in the 1920's, the appearance of more prestigious housing around the Sunset district and west of Twin Peaks ▲ *304* led to a fall in Haight's standing. The amusement parks were dismantled and reinstalled along Ocean Beach, while the big Victorian buildings of the Haight area, abandoned by their owners, were divided into apartments. Populated for the most part by tenants of immigrant Anglo-Saxon, Asiatic and black origin, Haight-Ashbury soon became a middle-class neighborhood.

POST-WAR IMPROVEMENTS. In the 1950's and 1960's the district changed radically. With a view to enlarging its campus, the University of California pulled down hundreds of buildings in the surrounding area, and black families moved in consequence from Fillmore to the middle of the Haight area. Real-estate values and rents plunged; Beatniks and artists seized the chance to move to Haight from North Beach, which had become much too expensive ▲ *166*. The year 1965 marked a decisive turning-point for what was now known as Haight-Ashbury; in that year the hippies arrived en masse, attracted by the fine old Victorian buildings, the very low rents and the proximity of Golden Gate Park. Also in 1965 the first hippie café, the *Blue Unicorn*, hoisted its sign at 1927 Hayes Street, near the intersection of Haight and Ashbury Streets. This establishment became a kind of headquarters for the community, where cheap black coffee and secondhand books and records were always available.

RECREATION AREAS
The proximity of the park made Haight an ideal area for recreation. In 1887 the California Baseball League stadium was built on Stanyan and Waller, with a capacity of twenty thousand spectators.

THE "CHUTES"
This amusement park opened in 1895 between Cole and Clayton Streets. The main attraction was a toboggan with gondolas on it, which shot 100 yards downhill into the lake. The park also had a miniature railroad, a zoo and a theater. Eventually the "Chutes" were

moved to Ocean Beach, near Golden Gate Park, in 1902.

At the start of the 1960's small communities of students and artists were already settled around the intersection of Haight and Ashbury Streets. This advance guard was swamped by a tidal wave in 1967, the legendary "Summer of Love" when half a million young people from all over America converged on San Francisco. After this, Haight-Ashbury declined from its status as a model for alternative living, quickly falling prey to drug dealers and violence. On October 6, 1967, on Haight Street, the media-invented word "hippie" was symbolically buried. Since the end of the 1980's the district has to some extent revived, though it is still only a shadow of its former self. Nevertheless, it has its place in history as the neighborhood where San Francisco's reputation for tolerance, radical ideas and excessive behavior was forged in the joyous 1960's.

"FURTHER"
The legendary psychedelic bus in which Ken Kesey and the *Merry Pranksters* made their LSD crossing of the US in 1964.

HIPPIES
The Beatniks ▲ *166* called the new generation "hippies", a mildly insulting term which implied that the 1960's kids were aping their elders, the "hipsters". Like Beatniks, hippies felt alienated by consumer society, but their rebellion took a different form: they preferred hallucinogenic drugs to alcohol, far eastern philosophies and pacifism to poetry, and rock and folk music to jazz.

OHIO TO SAN FRANSICO

PEACE JOY

"HUMAN BE-IN"

On January 14, 1967, Golden Gate Park was the scene of the "Gathering of the Clans", to which the Bay hippies came to dance and to listen to music, poetry readings and speeches. The hippies of Haight-Ashbury announced that the entire summer would be dedicated to love, peace and LSD, a proclamation that attracted half a million young people to San Francisco. This was the "Summer of Love" made famous by Scott McKenzie's song.

FROM MARIJUANA TO "ACID TESTS"

The use of hallucinogenic drugs (especially LSD) spread rapidly among hippies. Timothy Leary, a former Harvard professor, recommended the use of LSD as a means of attaining spiritual enlightenment. But it was Ken Kesey, author of *One Flew over the Cuckoo's Nest*, who, with his LSD "happenings", made "acid" part of the hippie vocabulary.

THE "LOVE GENERATION"

The slogan "Make Love, Not War" crystallized the beliefs of the hippies; the newspapers christened them the "Love Generation".

HIPPIE ART. Alton Kelley, Wes Wilson, Rick Griffin, Victor Moscoso and Stanley Mouse (left to right) were among the leading artists who created "new graphics" in the 1960's, initially through posters advertising rock concerts ● 78.

PSYCHEDELIC. This new word, meaning literally "that which opens the mind", spread like wildfire all over the world. By extension it was used to define anything outlandish (sounds, images or smells), and specifically the effects of hallucinogenic drugs.

THE SAN FRANCISCO MIME TROUPE. In 1965 Bill Graham became manager of this avant-garde mime troupe, which specialized in politically charged routines in the style of the *Commedia dell'arte*. To finance the troupe, Graham launched the Trips Festivals, huge dance concerts that were a steady success in San Francisco for six years running.

"MISTER NATURAL" This character, created by cartoonist R. Crumb, personifies the shrewdness and guile of "aging" hippies.

GRAPHIC ART

Wes Wilson created a new typographical style by squashing inflated letters together, a style that was immediately copied by other psychedelic artists. For a while these artists were much in demand to design posters and record covers: R. Crumb worked for *Big Brother* and Janis Joplin, Rick Griffin for *Quicksilver Messenger* and the *Grateful Dead*. The poster at center is by Griffin. Later on the psychedelic artists turned their attention to underground comic strips.

A CULTURAL MELTING POT

San Francisco in the 1960's was at the center of a cultural adventure, relayed by music and graphic art and popularized by the press and underground radio. For each new concert artists produced innovative posters in a style that fixed the world's attention on what was going on around the Bay and reinforced the legend of psychedelic San Francisco. Larry Miller, a D.J. on one of the local radio stations (KMPX radio), had a huge success with the first 100 percent rock program in February 1967.

THE "SAN FRANCISCO ORACLE"

The *Oracle* was a monthly magazine launched by Allen Cohen, Ron Thelin, Steve Levin and Michael Bowen in 1966 as the mouthpiece of the psychedelic movement. It published poems, news, concert and theater listings and dates of "happenings". Allen Cohen has recently republished a complete collection of *Oracle*s in a single volume.

THE "DIGGERS" From left to right: La Mortadella, Emmett Grogan, Slim Minnaux of the San Francisco Mime Troupe, Peter Berg and Butcher Brooks. As anarchist "Diggers", they dreamed of a society where essential goods would be free for all; they put their ideas into practice with a shop that supplied free clothes and other objects collected around town. The Diggers also organized a soup kitchen.

THE END OF THE HIPPIE MOVEMENT Proclaiming that their ideals had been perverted by materialism and the media, the Diggers organized a "funeral" for the hippie movement in October 1967. This ceremony, involving the burial of a clay coffin in Buena Vista Park, marked the shatteringly sudden end of a dream. Dealers in hard drugs had infiltrated the community; violence and crime had become endemic. Most of the shops, theaters and concert auditoriums closed down as the hippies gradually drifted away.

FROM THE PANHANDLE TO HAIGHT STREET

THE PANHANDLE. This strip of green extending along the bottom of Pope Valley, at the eastern end of Golden Gate Park, was a major hippie stronghold, where the "Diggers" distributed free meals and where concerts were held frequently. (On the way up Baker Street to Haight Street is a statue of *Justice*, sculpted by Robert Ingersoll Aitken in 1904.)

SPENCER HOUSE. No. 1080 Haight Street, on the corner of Baker Street, is a Queen Anne mansion that is unusual, in that it is freestanding ● *94*. Constructed in 1887 for the Irish millionaire Spencer, it has now been converted into a bed-and-breakfast by its present owners. The Victorian interior has been perfectly preserved (visits by appointment).

BUENA VISTA PARK. Buena Vista Park is sited on a sand-covered bedrock hill; it has its own natural spring and stream, which was crossed by the old road between Mission Dolores and the Presidio. Certain flowers and plants native to this piece of land (notably coastal oaks) still flourish here.

BUENA VISTA AVENUE WEST. This avenue which runs alongside the park boasts a number of interesting houses. The most spectacular of these, the SPRECKELS MANSION at no. 737, was built in 1897 by Edward Vogel for Richard Spreckels, nephew of the sugar magnate ▲ *203* and a noted philanthropist and art lover. Jack London ▲ *310* wrote his *White Fang* in this house, and Ambrose Bierce ▲ *132* spent several years here.

MASONIC AND PIEDMONT STREETS. At no. 1526 Masonic Street stands a weird-looking building designed by Maybeck in 1910. No. 11 Piedmont, farther along, is one of the oldest houses in San Francisco (1860). The original Lange farm was located nearby.

DELMAR STREET. Delmar Street is a breathtaking hotch-potch of architectural styles: Mission Revival style at no. 182, Tudor at no. 187, Arts and Crafts at no. 141, Stick at no. 168, Sunset at no. 164, Queen Anne (with an extra floor) at no. 159, neo-classical at no. 152. As for no. 130, this house is mainly remarkable for having been the headquarters of the *Jefferson Airplane* fan club; connoisseurs will know that it featured on the back of the group's album *Surrealistic Pillow*.

HIPPIE FASHIONS
The basic idea was to invent new combinations from day to day, using cheap or free elements. Everything was recycled as a gesture against consumerism, though this did not stop specialist shops from proliferating all over Haight-Ashbury. The important thing was to parade one's uniqueness and, above all, to look as though one were irrecoverably outside the system. The hippies loved velvet and lace dug out of Victorian wardrobes, along with miniskirts, flared pants cut very tight around the hips, and Oriental jewelry and clothing (especially from India).

Poster for the
Haight Street Fair.

MASONIC (BETWEEN FREDERICK AND HAIGHT STREETS). No.
1200 was formerly the studio of the painter Michael Bower;
the first numbers of the *San Francisco Oracle* were put
together here.

ALONG HAIGHT STREET

This is the busiest throughfare in the neighborhood. Closely
associated with the hippie movement in the 1960's, it remains
one of the liveliest and most unconventional places in San
Francisco, with its many cafés, cheap restaurants, booksellers
and secondhand clothes shops. It is worth remembering that
today's Haight-Ashbury is a hybrid neighborhood,
where the marginals in and around Haight Street
live side by side with professionals who inhabit
restored Victorian homes in adjoining residential
streets. The northwest corner of Haight and
Masonic Streets was once the site of the famous
DRUGSTORE CAFÉ, a favorite hippie hangout; now
a restaurant called *Dish* is located there. Fans of
the *Grateful Dead* ● *78* should make a detour to
no. 710 Ashbury Street where they were based for a
long time. At no. 1535 *Cybelle's Pizza* has taken the
place of the PSYCHEDELIC SHOP, which specialized in
psychedelic gear and tickets to avant-garde concerts. The
PRINT MINT, which sold posters, was nearby at no. 1540. At
no. 1601 note the discreet signboard of the HAIGHT-ASHBURY
FREE CLINIC, a dispensary founded in 1965 to treat local
hippies. The clinic is still active today, helping AIDS
sufferers. At no. 1635 Haight Street is the FIRST
INTERSTATE BANK, built in 1869 by a German and
now displaying old photographs of Golden Gate
Park in its foyer. The secondhand clothes shop
WASTELANDS, at no. 1660, has taken over the
old Superba Theater and perpetuates the
hippie style with its masses of used clothing.
The 1600–1700 block was where the "Chutes"
▲ *275* were located, while the old RED VIC
MOVIE THEATER is at no. 1727. *Taming of the
Shoe* stands on the site of the former *I-Thou Coffee
Shop*. Turning right into Shrader Street, then left
down Page on your way to the park, you go by
several fine old houses, notably a replica of the
Spreckels Mansion on Buena Vista Avenue.

SOUTH OF MARKET STREET

OLD US MINT

MARRIOTT HOTEL

MOSCONE CONVENTION CENTER

ANSEL ADAMS CENTER

PACIFIC TELEPHONE BUILDING

MARKET ST

FREMONT ST

MISSION ST

FIRST ST

HOWARD ST

SECOND ST

FOURTH ST

FIFTH ST

STORES
In the 19th century the people of South of Market did their shopping in the 2nd Street stores, which were served by the horse-drawn trams going up and down 3rd Street.

RINCON HILL
Buildings on the hill were completely razed to make way for the Bay Bridge approach ramp in 1936.

I n 1851, Happy Valley (Mission Street between 1st and 3rd Streets) and Pleasant Valley (Howard, Folsom, 1st and 2nd Streets) were no more than encampments, full of tents and shanties built from the hulls of abandoned boats ▲ *146*.

URBAN CONSTRUCTION. The South of Market neighborhood developed in the 1870's as wharves, warehouses, brickworks, sawmills, foundries, refineries, ironworks and flour mills turned the portside area into an industrial center. Workers lived in modest wooden dwellings which sprang up all over this zone. Rincon Hill became the first genuinely smart neighborhood, and at the foot of Rincon Hill, South Park grew up into a small, fashionable square of English-style houses. But before long the Rincon Hill enclave was found to be impeding expansion of the industrial zones, as well as access to the future Central Pacific Railroad Terminal. City Hall therefore voted to level 2nd Street, and build a road through to the center of Rincon Hill; affluent inhabitants retreated to the nobler, and quieter, heights of Nob Hill ▲ *188*, which the new cable car system had made accessible in 1873. Meanwhile, farther south, near the present Potrero Hill, a working-class sector had begun to develop. Irish immigrants concentrated around St Patrick's Church, while Germans gathered on 6th and Harrison Streets. Toward 1883, coinciding with the arrival of the cable car on Market Street, this precinct was baptized "South of the Slot", a reference to the pit running between the rails which housed the traction cables ● *68*. The neighborhood was devastated in 1906 ● *58* between the seafront and 11th Street, the only buildings left standing being the Main Post Office, the Old Mint, the Audiffred Building and the Southern Pacific Railway Depot.

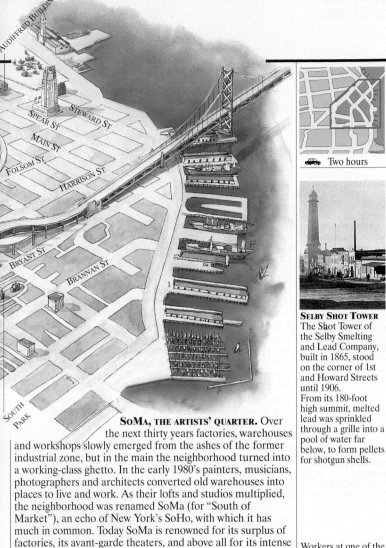

AUDIFFRED BUILDING

SPEAR ST
STEWARD ST
MAIN ST
FOLSOM ST
HARRISON ST
BRYANT ST
BRANNAN ST
SOUTH PARK

🚗 Two hours

SELBY SHOT TOWER
The Shot Tower of the Selby Smelting and Lead Company, built in 1865, stood on the corner of 1st and Howard Streets until 1906.
From its 180-foot high summit, melted lead was sprinkled through a grille into a pool of water far below, to form pellets for shotgun shells.

SoMa, THE ARTISTS' QUARTER. Over the next thirty years factories, warehouses and workshops slowly emerged from the ashes of the former industrial zone, but in the main the neighborhood turned into a working-class ghetto. In the early 1980's painters, musicians, photographers and architects converted old warehouses into places to live and work. As their lofts and studios multiplied, the neighborhood was renamed SoMa (for "South of Market"), an echo of New York's SoHo, with which it has much in common. Today SoMa is renowned for its surplus of factories, its avant-garde theaters, and above all for its intense nightlife, fashionable bars, restaurants and clubs ◆ *385*.
YERBA BUENA GARDENS. Situated between Mission and Howard, 3rd and 4th Streets, this new commercial development includes a Center for the Arts, six acres of gardens, the popular Moscone Convention Center and a major new cultural center.

Workers at one of the many factories in South of Market Street, c. 1900.

FRANK & HYMAN INC.
MANUFACTURERS OF SHOES

Office of
FRANK & HYMAN INC.

THE SAILING SHIP RESTAURANT, PIER 42
This vessel, built in Bordeaux, France, in 1862, has been a popular restaurant and cabaret for the last twenty years. Before her arrival here, the sailing ship voyaged all over the world and had many adventures. At the beginning of the century she was chartered by Jules Verne, becoming his inspiration for *Twenty Thousand Leagues under the Sea*. During World War One she was used for Allied spy missions; and during Prohibition, she ran liquor from Canada to the US. Finally the sailing ship was used as a prop for a number of films between 1930 and 1950, notably *Mutiny on the Bounty, Treasure Island, Moby Dick* and *Captain Blood*.

PACIFIC TELEPHONE BUILDING
This L-shaped Art Deco building (140 New Montgomery Street, shown right) was designed in 1925 by the architect Timothy Pflueger and was the first skyscraper built in San Francisco ● *106*. Inside is a small museum, The Telephone Pioneer Communications Museum, which traces the history of telecommunications in the US.

THE "GRANITE LADY"
The former mint is now open to the public, with exhibits commemorating the Gold Rush in addition to the original strongrooms.

A tour of SoMa, which at first may seem somewhat gray and austere, should begin on the waterfront by Mission Street.

AUDIFFRED BUILDING, MISSION AND STEUART STREETS. Built in 1889, this is the only building on the south waterfront that survived the 1906 fire. Apparently its owner, who kept the ground floor *Bulkhead Saloon*, managed to stop the firemen from dynamiting his building by passing out free whisky and wine. Burned down in 1981, it has since been restored.

RINCON CENTER, SPEAR STREET.
This is a combination of the renovated Rincon Annex (the Old Post Office) and two new mixed-use towers, which was completed in 1929. It remains a fine example of 1930's architecture, containing a number of shops, restaurants, offices and apartments. In the old foyer opening on Mission Street are twenty-seven historical frescoes by Anton Refrigier.

PACIFIC GAS AND ELECTRIC SUBSTATION, 222 JESSIE STREET.
Utilitarian but nevertheless extremely stylish, this building was designed by Willis Polk in 1907. Its brick and terracotta façade and its beautifully worked portal make it one of the neighborhood's principal architectural features and a showcase for Polk's uncanny ability to blend disparate styles.

THE OLD UNITED STATES MINT, 88 5TH STREET BY MISSION STREET. This neo-classical building, the "Granite Lady" (above), was erected in 1874 to strike coins out of California gold and Sierra Nevada silver. Built largely of California Colusa sandstone, its walls (over 3 feet thick) and its steel shutters saved the Mint from destruction in 1906 ● *58*.

ANSEL ADAMS GALLERY, 250 4TH STREET. A non-profit cultural institution and photography gallery since 1987, the Ansel Adams Gallery is the headquarters of the Friends of Photography group ▲ *290*, founded in 1967 by historian

SOUTH PARK
This oval square
between 2nd, 3rd,
Bryant and
Brannan Streets
was created
in 1854 by the
Englishman George
Gordon to house
San Francisco's
high society. South
Park was modeled
on London's
Berkeley Square; at
the time it was
closed off from the
rest of the city with
iron gates, to which
only the residents
had a key. To
complete the
"European"
atmosphere,
Gordon imported
several dozen
London sparrows.
Now being
extensively
restored, the
square is home to
several fashionable
restaurants.

Beaumont Newhall and renowned photographers Brett
Weston and Ansel Adams. The center is also used for
temporary exhibitions.

FRANCIS "LEFTY" O'DOUL BRIDGE, 3RD AND BERRY STREETS.
The only swing bridge still in service in San Francisco, it spans
what remains of Mission Creek, a once-busy canal. The
engineer who sits in a cabin at one end of the bridge operates
a counterweight of 500 tons to raise the steel roadway, though
this is now very seldom done. When it does occur the
spectacle is so impressive that the O'Doul Bridge has been
several times featured in Hollywood films. Another swing
bridge on the corner of 4th and Berry Streets, the PETER J.
MALONEY BRIDGE, was built in 1916 by Joseph B. Strauss.

ORIENTAL WAREHOUSE, 1ST AND BRYANT STREETS. South
Beach, the section of waterfront north of Bay Bridge, has
been heavily renovated since 1985. Dilapidated sheds, sailors'
bars and docks have been replaced by tall modern buildings,
and the neighborhood now boasts a yacht marina and many
restaurants. Nonetheless, many vestiges of the old quarter still
survive. For example, behind the ultra-residential BAYSIDE
VILLAGE APARTMENTS, on 1st and Bryant Streets, one can still
see the façade of the Oriental US BONDED WAREHOUSE, built
in 1867. Next to the wharves of the PACIFIC MAIL STEAMSHIP
COMPANY ▲ 155, where ships from Asia and Central America
were once unloaded, this warehouse and store specialized in
products from the Orient. The façade of the
Oriental Warehouse was all that survived a fire
during the 1980's.

MUSEUM OF MODERN ART. The modern
art collections were moved from the
Veteran Building ▲ 229 to a site
designed by Swiss architect Mario
Botta and opened in January 1995.
The total space given over to
collections, new exhibitions and
academic activities comprises the
SFMOMA, America's second
museum devoted to modern art.

YERBA BUENA CENTER
Completed in 1995,
this complex houses
the Moscone
Convention Center
and the new Museum
of Modern Art
(below) ▲ 288 .

The San Francisco Museum of Modern Art, which opened in 1935, was the first museum on the West Coast entirely devoted to 20th-century art. Its collection of 14,000 works, contains fine paintings by the German Expressionists (Marc, Beckmann, and Jawlensky), excellent examples of early Matisse and Fauves, extensive Klee holdings , an important array of sculpture by Brancusi, Giacometti, and Arp (among others), and a strong collection of California art (Diebenkorn, Bischoff, Still, Park). In addition there is an collection of over 7,000 photographs. The museum, which reopened at its present location in 1995, now has room to display even more of its possessions.

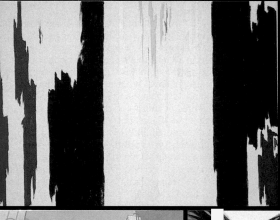

RICHARD SHAW
Born in 1941, Shaw has always worked with ceramic, but draws inspiration from everyday objects, as in his *Melodius Double Stop* (1980, above).

CLYFFORD STILL
(1904–80) Still gave twenty-eight of his paintings to the museum in 1975. The vivid colors and sheer power of *Untitled* (1960, above right) demonstrate a form of expressionism that has been sublimated by abstract art.

CHARLES SHEELER
(1883–1965) Sheeler painted and photographed things of monumental scale with g   precision. *Aerial Gyrations* (1953, right) shows a geometric landscape of industrial architecture.

RICHARD DIEBENKORN (1922–93). In 1963, Diebenkorn lived in Berkeley. His *Cityscape I* (above) is a painting of San Francisco. The composition of this figurative theme illustrates the painter's researches into the abstract.

MAX BECKMANN (1884–1950). *Landscape, Cannes* (1934, left) adds a quasi-Californian style to the incisiveness of German Expressionism.

JEAN ARP (1887–1966). Arp concentrated nature's essence in the forms he invented. *Human Concretion Without Oval Bowl* (1933) synthesized the morphology of the human body.

Photography reached California in the 1860's when photographers were hired to help with railroad projects and geological surveys. Many studios were set up in the US at that time, especially in San Francisco, which became a base for professionals such as Muybridge and Watkins. These men explored unknown areas and magnificent landscapes like the Yosemite Valley, which first came to be known on the East Coast through their photographs. The profession was already firmly established in the 1920's when a group of young artists, determined to shake off the yoke of "pictorialist" photography, founded a group known as "F 64".

The F 64 group was originally formed around Preston Holder and Willard van Dyke, and its more prominent members included Edward Weston, Ansel Adams, Imogen Cunningham and Sonya Noskowiak. A modernist trend, it set out to create an artistic pole of attraction in the West that would acknowledge international development in art while at the same time promoting a specifically Californian vision of life. The group's first exhibition was held in 1932 at the De Young Memorial Museum, and a gallery was founded the same year. The name "F 64" itself refers to the minimal aperture of a camera, the one that allows maximum depth of focus. F 64 advocated the use of large cameras (20–5cm in the case of Weston), contact printing of the image, absolute clarity of focus, and the avoidance of any manipulation that might alter the image as recorded by the lens. This strict credo even called into question the personal arrangement of still lifes. Behind all F 64's principles lay a philosophy of artistic rigor, craftsmanship and acceptance of natural beauty. The influence of the Bauhaus and of German photography are very evident in the tendency to magnify the subject matter, in the use of close-up, the monumental treatment of the merest rock or artifact, and the emphasis on the relationship between the natural world and industry. By 1935 the group's members (especially Ansel Adams) had gone their different ways. Represented above all by the work of Weston and Cunningham, F 64 had served to bring the West Coast into the artistic mainstream while preserving its cultural individuality.

"PHOTOGRAPHY AS AN ART FORM MUST BE DEFINED IN RELATION TO THE REALITIES AND PRINCIPLES OF THE PHOTOGRAPHIC MEDIUM AND MUST REMAIN UNINFLUENCED BY THE IDEOLOGICAL CONVENTIONS OF ART AND ESTHETICS." F 64

1 *Self-portrait*, 1932, Alma Lavenson (1897–1989).
2 *Rubber Plant*, 1929, Imogen Cunningham (1883–1976).
3 *Rollers and Stacks*, 1932, Preston Holder (1907–80).
4 *Cypress, Point Lobos*, Sonya Noskowiak (1900–75).
5 *Cabbage Leaf*, 1931, Edward Weston (1886–1958).

TWIN PEAKS

CASTRO

🚗 Half a day

JUNIPERO SERRA
Born in Majorca in
1713, the thirty-six-
year-old Serra arrived
in Mexico as a
Franciscan priest. In

1767 the viceroy of
Mexico assigned him
the task of converting
Upper California and
setting up a series of
missions along the
coast. In 1769 the
small, physically frail
Serra undertook the
800-mile journey
between Mexico and
San Diego on a mule.
He soon became
known for his fervor;
in particular he liked
to carry chains about,
with which he would
flagellate himself. His
cell at the Carmel
Mission, where he
is buried, is a model
of austerity. His
ardent desire to
save the souls of
Indians drove
him to use
methods that
St Francis himself
might not have
cared for;
nevertheless his
contemporaries
viewed him as
a saint; he was
beatified in 1988,
allowing him to be
known as Blessed
Junipero Serra.

$\underset{\text{San Francisco, evolved on the site of an}}{\text{M}}$ ission District, the Spanish quarter of
Indian village called Alta-Mo, which lay in a valley cleft
sheltered from the wind and mists of the bay. Today it is still
the only part of town that is never fog-bound.

HISTORY

The area owes its name to the Mission Dolores, founded in
1776 by the Spanish Franciscans who came to colonize the
region with Juan Bautista de Anza's expedition ● *43*. The
soldiers built a fortress at the entrance to the Golden Gate,
called the Presidio ▲ *242*, and the colonists built adobe
houses along the road (now 16th Street) to the little village of
Yerba Buena. These were the first European occupants of the
site of San Francisco. In 1834 the Franciscans, whose land had
been appropriated by the nascent Mexican Republic,
abandoned the Mission. After this the zone remained rural in
character, only developing after 1860 with the construction of
a road linking the present 3rd and 16th Streets, the line of
which cut across the present Mission Street. All along the new
thoroughfare saloons and gambling houses appeared, along
with a racecourse and an arena for horse-fighting and bear-
baiting. In this way the original countryside was transformed
into an amusement resort for the inhabitants of the Barbary
Coast ▲ *148*. Germans and Scandinavians began
to move in, followed (after the 1906 earthquake)
by Italians and Irish. From this ethnic and linguistic
mix resulted an accented English, peculiar to the
Mission District and known as the *mish*, which is
similar in many respects to the Brooklyn accent. In
the 1960's, with the influx of new migrants and
political refugees from Mexico, South America
and Central America, the Mission District, with its
low rents, became the Hispanic quarter
of San Francisco. In the 1980's the
Hispanics were joined by marginals
and artists in quest of low rents.
INDIANS. San Francisco's first-
known inhabitants, the Ohlones
(known in Spanish as
'Costanoans') camped on the
Bay shore around South Beach
and Mission. Huge mounds of
shells unearthed by archeologists

The map shows streets: DOLORES ST, CHURCH ST, GUERRERO ST, VALENCIA ST, LIBERTY ST, 17TH, 18TH, 19TH, 21ST, 22ND, MISSION DOLORES, MISSION HIGH SCHOOL, DOLORES PARK

have

● 42

FRANCISCO PALOU
A former student and friend of Junipero Serra, Francisco Palou took holy orders and came to Mexico at the same time as his master. Palou wrote an admiring biography of Serra, larded with tales of miracles. He was also the founder of the Mission Dolores, which he led for nine years; his tomb is in the cemetery, and his leather-bound breviary is displayed in the mission museum.

shown that at least 425 Ohlone encampments existed here four thousand years ago. Before the arrival of Christian colonists, the Bay Indians (a mosaic of tribes speaking different languages) lived here by fishing, hunting and gathering ● 42. They greeted the strangers in a spirit of friendship, but over the 18th century they were gradually converted and reduced to slavery. Twenty-one missions were established between Mexico and Sonoma, north of San Francisco. Forced to do heavy work, confined within mission walls, decimated by the diseases of the white man and driven from their hunting grounds, the Indians died in droves. Their number, which had been estimated at ten thousand in 1776, was reduced to almost nothing by 1856. There are over five thousand unmarked Costanoan graves in the cemetery of Mission Dolores.

EL CAMINO REAL

"EL CAMINO REAL". This "royal way", some 650 miles long, formerly linked the twenty missions established along the coast of California by members of the Franciscan order, who were sent by King Carlos III of Spain in 1769 and the years following. The official goal was to "convert the savages", but the real purpose was to colonize and defend the outer limits of the Spanish empire, on which Russia, England and the United States were beginning to cast greedy eyes. Exploratory missions made up of detachments of soldiers accompanied by colonists and priests were sent to San Diego (where the first mission was founded in 1769) and Carmel, by the Franciscan

Bull-fighting and bear-baiting were among the favorite pastimes of Californians. An arena specifically for these activities was built on the road which linked the Mission Dolores with the village of Yerba Buena.

superior, Junipero Serra. When they had selected a site, they set up a mission with a military garrison to protect the missionaries and hunt down fugitive Indians. In 1833 the Mexican authorities ordered the secularization of mission lands, which by then had become rich farms and the land was distributed among the ranchers and soldiers. After this the missions were abandoned and ransacked. General Vallejo even dug up the trees in the orchard of the mission at San Rafael Arcángel and removed them to his own land. The pitiful remains of the old missions were finally returned to the church during the 1860's.

Interior of the mission church.

MISSION DOLORES ★   ● 88

As the sixth out of twenty-one in California, the San Francisco mission began with a mass said in a temporary shelter by Father Francisco Palou on June 29, 1776, a few days before the American Declaration of Independence. In one of his texts, Father Palou dèscribes the inaugural ceremony, which was celebrated with fireworks and booming cannon in the presence of the terrified Indians. Officially baptized Mission San Francisco de Asís, it later became known by the name of a small lake nearby, the *Laguna de Nuestra Señora de los Dolores* (Our Lady of Sorrows). The present mission site is a few blocks west of that of the first mission.

"The missions were generally built with four sides, about 150 yards in length, with an inner courtyard containing fountains and trees and a cross at its center. All around was a covered cloister, into which the lodgings, schoolroom and workshops opened. The church occupied one wing of the building; the lodgings of the fathers, adjoining it, were connected to a common room that was used for meetings and festivals, events that were rare. A few more rooms served as a monastery. On either side of the main corpus of the mission were cells lived in by those Indians who were true converts, separated according to their sex. Finally, at the back of the mission stood the stables, barns and sheds used for sheltering cattle and storing farm implements. Each mission had a garrison of four dragoons and a sergeant, whose upkeep was paid for by the monks.**"**
Léon Lemonnier

THE CHAPEL. Built with Indian labor in 1782, this is the oldest building in San Francisco and one of the oldest churches in California. Adobe walls ● 88, 3 feet thick, pink rooftiles, sequoia beams attached by leather thongs, and ceiling decorations with Indian themes painted in vegetable dyes were all preserved when the chapel was restored in 1891. The façade, the hand-carved altars and the statues were brought here on mules from Mexico. The chapel survived the 1906 earthquake (the thickness of the walls and flexibility of the leather holding the beams in place had something to do with this), while the neighboring church, built in 1876 to mark the mission's centenary, collapsed completely. The architect Willis Polk, who restored the chapel with great sensitivity in 1918, took care to reinforce the original beams with steel girders. All the same, following heavy damage caused by the 1989 earthquake, the chapel is again in need of restoration.

BASILICA. Designed in the exuberant Churrigueresque style (after the three Churriguera brothers, 18th-century Spanish architects and sculptors), this building replaced the demolished brick church in 1913. It forms a striking contrast to the simpler mission beside it. Pope Pious XII endowed the structure with the status of basilica in 1952 (left, facing page).

MUSEUM. In the former mission classroom are displayed the first baptismal register (1776), sacred objects bequeathed to the mission by Father Junipero Serra, and everyday implements used here in the early days.

CEMETERY. The cloister, store, barn and other original mission buildings vanished long ago, leaving only the chapel and the cemetery. In the midst of lush vegetation, a statue of Junipero Serra keeps vigil over the graves of the Spanish, Italian and Irish pioneers, and of the five thousand poor nameless Indians buried here.

DOLORES PARK
The skyscrapers of the Financial District can be seen from the highest points of the park.

"The Californian ladies wore blouses with embroidered sleeves that were richly hung with lace, muslin skirts with red ribbons cinched at the waist by broad red sashes, slippers of blue velvet or satin, shawls, and pearl necklaces or earrings; their hair fell about their shoulders in long tresses.**"**
Léon Lemonnier

DOLORES STREET ★

Palm trees planted in 1910 cast a cooling shade over this broad, undulating street, lined with low buildings and Victorian houses. In all, Dolores Street covers twenty-four blocks, parallel to Mission Street.

MISSION HIGH SCHOOL, DOLORES/18TH STREETS. This is one of the many schools built by the architect John Reid in the Mission Revival style, which was fashionable in the 1920's ● 88. It has white adobe walls and a red tile roof, the basic features of Spanish colonial architecture.

DOLORES PARK, DOLORES/CHURCH/18TH/20TH STREETS. Dolores Park is a former Jewish cemetery that has been converted into a public garden (above). This is a good spot to pause and admire the superb view of downtown San Francisco, notably from the corner of 20th and Church Streets.

295

WOODWARD'S GARDEN

This garden on Mission Street at 14th Street was one of San Francisco's principal attractions between 1866 and 1894. Its creator, Robert B. Woodward, was a Forty-Niner who made his fortune in the hotel business. In 1857 he bought 4 acres of land in the Mission District which he then landscaped, planting rare tree species and constructing buildings (below). In 1860 Woodward went to Europe, where he was deeply impressed by the cultural heritage of the Old World and decided to found a collection of copies of works of art. The best of his pieces were displayed in his Mission Street property, quickly arousing the interest of his fellow citizens. Finally, Woodward opened the garden to the public (1866) and converted his home into a museum of natural wonders. In addition to other attractions, there were a bandstand and a fairground theater; the latter earned Woodward the nickname "Barnum of the West". The park was closed down in 1894.

DOLORES TO VALENCIA STREET

If you take LIBERTY STREET on the left toward Mission Street, you eventually come to one of San Francisco's prime historic neighborhoods, the LIBERTY HILL DISTRICT. Within the perimeter bordered by Dolores, Mission, 20th and 23rd Streets no renovation is permitted without permission from the municipal authorities. This wise measure has saved a number of the fine turn-of-the-century buildings that escaped the 1906 earthquake. The Italianate style is much in evidence (no. 159, built in 1878) ● 95, along with those of the Arts and Crafts movement (nos. 151–3) and Stick-Eastlake (nos 120–1 and 110). Other interesting buildings are to be seen in GUERRERO STREET (take a right), with turn-of-the-century façades (nos. 850–2) and a Moorish–Queen Anne house ● 94 (no. 827). Take another turn to the left into 21st Street and continue toward Mission Street. At no. 3243, on the corner of 21st and BARTLETT STREETS, stands the Victorian house of George Pattison.

VALENCIA STREET. From Liberty Street continue to Valencia Street, a low-rent enclave that has become a stronghold of the feminist movement and several alternative and/or leftist organizations. Unions and left-leaning political groups are well entrenched in the Mission District, which has always been fundamentally working class. The *Modern Times Bookstore* (no. 968) offers literature and miscellaneous political publications, particularly from Latin America.
"Casa El Salvador" (no. 988) is the headquarters of one of the neighborhood's many pacifist groups.

THE "LEVI STRAUSS" FACTORY. At no. 250 Valencia Street is a factory where the authentic Levi Strauss blue jeans are made ▲ 66. Visits by prior arrangement only.

MISSION STREET

This commercial thoroughfare is the backbone of the Hispanic quarter. On its busiest sector, between 15th and Army Streets, are several interesting stores;

these include the *Rainbow Grocery and General Store* (no. 1899), an alternative cooperative that offers natural, ecologically sound products (bring your own baskets and wrapping paper); *Oh's Fine Food* (no. 1904), one of the best healthfood stores in the entire region; and *El Rio* (no. 3158A), a salsa and world music disco which features a live band on Sundays. SAN JOSÉ AVENUE (between 22nd and 24th Streets), which can be reached by way of a detour west down 22nd Street, follows the line of the old Camino Real. Farther along, in 22nd Street (no. 3126), is ST JOHN'S LUTHERAN CHURCH, surrounded by handsome Victorian private houses. On 24th Street, between Mission and Potrero Streets, you find yourself in the heart of the Latin-American quarter (note the colorful wall paintings); here live large numbers of exiled Latin Americans, escaping war and repression in their own countries. Many have opened restaurants and shops, which

"MISSION DISTRICT" An 1874 painting by Thomas Ross. This district remained rural for a long time.

297

CAPP STREET
Between 22nd and
23rd Streets is a row
of identical Victorian
houses, most of them
very well preserved
with beautifully
carved woodwork.
This street has also
retained its fine
1920's streetlamps.

Balmy Alley.

The Galeria de
la Raza, founded
in 1971. exhibits
Latin-American
arts and crafts.
Precita Eyes Mural
Arts Center (348
Precita Avenue/
Folsom Street)
arranges guided
tours of Mission
District murals.

*Tribute to Archbishop
Romero (Balmy Alley).*

are priced competitively. The *sauterias* of the quarter
specialize in magic plants and potions, which are offered for
sale to the public.

THE MURALS OF THE MISSION DISTRICT

The Mission District is famous for its murals, huge painted
scenes on the walls and the façades of buildings, which are
part of a long-established San Francisco tradition. There
are nearly 600 murals in San Francisco, with the richest
concentration in this neighborhood.

THE COMING OF THE MURAL. Throughout the world, there
have been murals on walls as long as there have been
people to paint them, since the earliest pre-historic
cave paintings dating back to 20–30,000 years BC.
Murals from ancient civilizations in Egypt, Greece,
Rome and Asia, as well as North and South
America, still remind us of the earliest traditions
of this art form. In the early 20th century, encouraged
by "Los Tres Grandes", the three great Mexican
muralists Diego Rivera, José Clemente Orozco and
David Alfaro Siqueiros, mural art depicting "social
realism" is executed by the people, for the people.
An explosion in the genre occurred in the 1930's,
when two events combined to favor it: the arrival of
"Los Tres Grandes", and the New Deal's financing
of artworks. Soon murals were adorning the walls
of schools and buildings all over the nation. Diego
Rivera painted the major frescoes for the city of
San Francisco, Maxine Albro completed the first of the
Coit Tower murals in 1934. In San Francisco the genre had
a second lease of life during the 1970's, when the walls and
façades of buildings in the Mission District were painted
with social and political images, as well as life-affirming
scenes reflecting the needs, hopes and dreams of a vibrant
and thriving community.

TOUR OF THE MURALS. On the corner of 22ND STREET and
SOUTH VAN NESS AVENUE there is a multi-cultural "musical"
mural, painted by Michael Rios in 1987 to honor Carlos
Santana, entitled *Inspire to Aspire*. In BALMY ALLEY, near
Harrison and 24th Streets, there is an ongoing series of
murals enlivening this quiet side street,
including the 1984 murals by the
"Placa" group (*Placa* means a mark
that requires a response). At 23rd
and Mission Streets is a handsome
mural entitled *Homenaje a
Siqueiros* (*Homage to Siqueiros*)
inside the Bank of America
building, painted by Michael
Rios and Chuy Campusano.
The mural at the BART
station at Mission and 24th
Streets and the composition
at the corner of 24th and
South Van Ness Avenue
(*Carnaval/ A Golden Dream
of the Mission*) are both well
worth a visit.

Tiny Thumb (Balmy Alley)

Balance of Power (Mission Pool)

On the Way to Market (Balmy Alley)

Carnaval (24th and South Van Ness)

Changes (Balmy Alley)

Placa mural (Balmy Alley)

▲ *New World Tree*   Mural, Mission Pool ▼

▲ *Quetzacoatl*   *Five Sacred Colors of Corn* ▼

The Castro neighborhood lies between Church, 17th, Twin Peaks and 30th Streets, and includes Noe Valley.

VICTORIAN HOUSES
On Castro Street, between Liberty and 20th Streets, is a group of Victorian houses in Queen Anne and Stick styles designed by Fernando Nelson. All told, Nelson designed nearly four thousand San Francisco houses; in 1897 he built a home of his own here, the cottage at number 701 Castro.

The Sisters of Perpetual Indulgence are four young men who parade the streets of the Castro district dressed as nuns; droll as this may seem, it is worth remembering that twenty years ago the Castro, now the world's most famous gay enclave, was the fief of the strictly Catholic "Most Holy Redeemer Parish". Back then, nobody in the street would have looked twice at a genuine nun. In the early days the part of Eureka Valley that includes the Castro belonged to a Mexican ranch, as some of the street names (Sanchez, Castro, Alvaro) recall. In 1854 a real-estate speculator bought most of the land here then subdivided and resold it in lots. The neighborhood stagnated until the arrival (1887) of the Market Street Cable Railway in Castro Street. At around this time working families began to move to the new suburban area, attracted by its low rents. Catholic churches (and bars) proliferated and for nearly 100 years provided the main meeting places for a blue-collar, mostly Irish population, who lived in a style that was as modest and conventional as the picturesque Victorian houses that were a characteristic of the area.

THE "VILLAGE" OF CASTRO. In the early 1970's service industries began displacing San Francisco's old manufacturing firms, and workers were obliged to look for employment outside the center of the city. Their exodus coincided with the decline of the hippie movement in Haight-Ashbury ▲ 276. At this time the homosexual wing of the "Flower-power" generation moved into the nearby Castro area, where houses were cheap, and they were shortly joined by legions of other homosexuals of both sexes from all over the US. Many blue-collar families moved out as the "invaders" set about restoring the old Victorian houses, pushing prices up by as much as 400 percent between 1973 and 1976. Nowadays the "Most Holy Redeemer Parish" on 18th and Diamond Streets continues to serve the gay community. Like the rest of the Castro district, it has earned an exemplary reputation for tolerance.

The legendary Harvey Milk, San Francisco's first openly gay city supervisor ▲ *302*, used to say that the name Castro Street made him think of a "Cuban seaside resort". Nevertheless, the neighborhood is genuine picture postcard San Francisco, with the characteristically steep streets and brightly painted Victorian houses. The Castro is something of a Mecca for American gays; but with its rainbow-colored banners flying from every window, this village is much more than a series of bars, home improvement shops, boutiques and body-building establishments. There is a real community spirit here, with grocery stores, laundries, pharmacies and churches serving the needs of the local people. One need only turn off Castro into one of the side streets to see this spirit at work, though obviously Castro Street and Upper Market remain the liveliest precincts.

MARKET STREET

"CAFÉ FLORE", 2298 MARKET STREET. For several years now the *Café Flore* has been a favorite meeting place for San

Francisco's gays, where regulars sip their decaffeinated cappuccinos with one eye on a book and the other on the people at neighboring tables. But you don't necessarily need to be a homosexual to stop in for a drink at the *Flore:* it is sufficient just to be good-looking.

NAMES PROJECT, 2362 MARKET STREET. This is the workshop of the Names Project, an organization that co-ordinates the creation and display of an enormous and ever-growing quilt made up of thousands of large panels, each commemorating a person who has died of AIDS and made by surviving family and friends. Some panels are made at the workshop; others are sent there to be added to the quilt. Sections of the quilt are sent on tour each year throughout the US to be displayed as a memorial and to raise AIDS awareness.

SHOPS IN THE NEIGHBORHOOD. All kinds of novelties, from electronic gadgets to clothes, accessories, furniture and unusual decorative objects, can be found in the old shops at the end of Market Street, in the area located between 16th and 17th Streets. In particular there are a lot of shops specializing in home-decoration.

"CONDOMANIA" (541 Castro) Today safe sex is a matter of life and death, hence this down-to-earth condom shop.

THE ALL AMERICAN BOY CLOTHING STORE (Corner of Market and Castro Streets).

CASTRO CLONES
In the 1970's, San Francisco gays delighted in mocking the cliché of the effeminate, dandified homosexual.

THE GAY COMMUNITY

"The love that dare not speak its name" has always been more freely expressed in San Francisco than elsewhere in the US. In 1849, the young adventurers of the Gold Rush had to live in an overwhelmingly masculine society. Local newspapers at the time told of the exploits of the "Lavender Cowboys", a gang of homosexuals who traveled the region on horseback, and some of the city's smarter restaurants were routinely provided with comfortable private rooms reserved exclusively for male couples. But it was with the systematic purging of homosexuals from the ranks of the US Army during World War Two that San Francisco became a real gay enclave. As an important military port, it received a flood of servicemen carrying demobilization papers stamped with the shameful blue 'H'. Many of these men dared not go home to their families and decided to remain in San Francisco forming the first gay enclaves of Tenderloin, Polk, Gulch and Folsom Streets. During the 1950's, after the purges of the administration conducted by the McCarthy Commission, there was a second wave of homosexual immigration. In 1972 the community, which was essentially focused around Castro Street, was further expanded, with bars and saunas starting up all over. In 1977, the election of a gay militant, Harvey Milk, to the city board of supervisors gave the community a final badge of respectability. But the following year Milk and the mayor, George Moscone, were assassinated by a notorious gay-hater,

TRANSVESTITES
With their extravagant hairdos, tight dresses, fishnet stockings and stiletto heels, San Francisco's transvestites are a familiar sight at events like the Gay Freedom Day Parade.

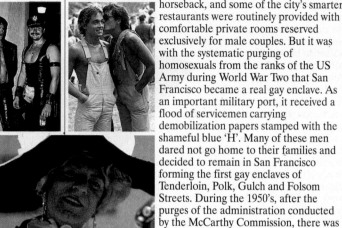

and the euphoria vanished. In 1981, the first AIDS cases appeared and everything changed completely. The community was forced to close ranks and organize. Federal funds were obtained for research into AIDS and treatment of the different diseases resulting from it, and the gay community set up special hospitals and home treatment facilities for those suffering from the last stages of AIDS. Huge information drives on safe sex were launched. Today, the gay community has a pre-eminent influence in San Francisco's administration and economy. Certainly this is a long way from the "summer of gay love" but the extravagances of the 1970's still resurface on occasions like Halloween, the Castro Street Fair and the Gay & Lesbian Freedom Day

● *80*. On these days Castro and Upper Market are invaded by a multicolored horde – girls and boys in leather, exhibitionists in G-strings, passersby in jeans, and drag queens in fishnet stockings and stiletto heels. Everyone hugs, toasts are drunk to AIDS victims, and people meet and get to know each other around drinks stands and stalls distributing AIDS literature.

HARVEY MILK PLAZA

During the 1970's San Francisco was the first American city to punish discrimination against homosexuals in housing or employment. In 1975, a former Wall Street financial analyst who had moved to San Francisco obtained a quarter of the votes in the municipal elections. In 1977, he was the first openly homosexual member of the city board of supervisors, where he represented his community, the gay citizens of Castro. His career was tragically cut short in September 1978 when Dan White, a former police officer who had recently resigned from the board of supervisors, burst into City Hall and shot Harvey Milk, as well as the pro-gay mayor George Moscone. The particularly indulgent sentence – only ten years in prison – which was given to the killer six months later caused widespread rioting, with several thousand San Franciscans taking to the streets to protest. Anticipating his death, Milk had left a will in the form of a recorded cassette, in which he designated his successor, Harry Britt (another gay leader who did, in fact, succeed him in politics) and declared "If I'm going to get a bullet in the head, make it a bullet that bursts all our chains". At one point Harvey Milk had proposed that all municipal functionaries should do a spell of work in the the underground systems; thus it may not be entirely fortuitous that City Hall placed a commemorative plaque to the gay community's martyr above the Castro Street Metro line entrance. There is no memorial at no. 575 Castro Street, where Milk lived and kept his small photography shop under his famous sign, which read "Yes, we are very open".

Liberty Street boasts a fine succession of gabled cottages dating from the late 19th century. At the intersection of Liberty and Noe Streets, a flight of steps leads to the top of the hill, from which the view is spectacular.

ELEPHANT WALK, 500 CASTRO

This bar-restaurant frequented by local people is a quiet, convivial backwater, well worth a visit. In 1979, after the controversially lenient verdict handed down to Dan White, the murderer of George Moscone and Harvey Milk ▲ *302*, demonstrators set fire to a dozen police cars. Police raided the Castro area, beating up a number of passers-by, including several clients of the *Elephant Walk*. The owner sued the municipality and was awarded damages.

MOUNT SUTRO

Recognizable by the TV antenna at its summit, Mount Sutro used to belong to Adolph Sutro, who owned about one-twelfth of the city.

CASTRO STREET★

CASTRO THEATER, 429 CASTRO. This is a Spanish-Gothic cinema (1924) with ceiling stucco of valances, ropes and pompoms that create the illusion of a Bedouin tent. The Castro Theater is a symbol of the neighborhood's renaissance in the 1970's; it projects experimental and art films and is part of the group of cinemas that puts on the annual San Francisco Film Festival. Every weekend, during the interval, an organist on a dais plays melodies from favorite gay shows, with the audience singing along and clapping.

"CLIFF'S VARIETY", 479 CASTRO. "Guppies" (Gay Upwardly Mobile Professionals) spend much of their time and money on renovating their homes. At *Cliff's Variety* has you can find everything you need for restoring a Victorian house.

"A DIFFERENT LIGHT BOOKSTORE", 489 CASTRO. Like its sisters in New York and Los Angeles, this bookshop specializes in works written by, or about, homosexuals. A prominent feature is *Betty and Pansy's Severe Queer Review*, a ferociously witty publication and a mine of information about the gay world in San Francisco.

TWIN PEAKS ★

The 900-feet Twin Peaks stand in the geographical center of San Francisco; in the old days the Spaniards called them *Los Pechos de la Chola*, the "Breasts of the Indian Maiden". Still uninhabited, they offer one of the loveliest views of the city. It was on the heights of these Twin Peaks that the architect Daniel Burnham ▲ *224* insisted on having his house, the better to survey San Francisco's topography. The best way to reach the peaks is by way of Castro Street to Clipper Street, then up Woodside Drive to Twin Peaks Boulevard.

TANK HILL. Going east down Twin Peaks Boulevard, on the righthand side after Clarendon Avenue, look for a shingle house (no. 192) flanked by wooden steps. Take these steps to reach the outcrop of Tank Hill, overlooking the city. There used to be a water tank here, as the name implies.

AROUND
THE BAY

ALAMEDA SAN FRANCISCO OAKLAND PIEDMONT THE BAY BRIDGE

THE BAY BRIDGE
Completed in 1936,
work on the bridge
(directed by the
engineer Purcell)
took three years.
With a length of over
8 miles (nearly 4½
miles of which is
above the water), the
structure consists of a
first bridge between
San Francisco and
Yerba Buena Island,
prolonged by another
leading on to the east
shore. Four steel
pylons support the
two decks. Traffic on
the upper deck flows
west; traffic on the
lower flows east. An
intermediate anchor
block is set midway
between Yerba Buena
and San Francisco.

On the eastern
shore of the bay (East Bay) sprawl two rival cities whose
pasts are closely associated with that of San Francisco:
Oakland and Berkeley.

THE SAN FRANCISCO–OAKLAND BAY BRIDGE

This steel structure linking the two cities across the bay is, like
the Golden Gate Bridge ▲ *242,* a masterpiece of elegance and
simplicity erected by the engineers and architects of the
1930's. More heavily used than the Golden Gate Bridge, the
Bay Bridge carries about 250,000 automobiles per day on its
two superimposed, five-lane roadways. Unlike the Golden
Gate, it is closed to pedestrians. It is especially lovely at night,
because of the lights on the bridge cables.
A FRAGILE CONSTRUCTION. Several projects for a bridge
between San Francisco and the far side of the bay were
mooted in the 19th century. Some of these were fantastical,
such as the one presented by Emperor Norton ▲ *158.* The
dream had to await the 20th century, when it became clear
that the ferries were no longer adequate for transporting
vehicles from one shore to the other. Less famous than the
Golden Gate Bridge, the Bay Bridge nonetheless made
headlines after the 1989 earthquake. During the tremor a
part of the cantilever bridge resting on mud-based wooden
pilings was severely damaged; because it was not bedded in
rock, it was bound to be highly vulnerable. The result was
that one end section of the upper deck abruptly collapsed on
the lower, leaving one car suspended precariously between
the two. Fortunately, no part of the bridge fell into the water,

🚗 One day

and only one person was killed. Within only a month the bridge had been repaired and reopened.

TREASURE ISLAND

HISTORY. This 500-acre artificial island lies to the north of Yerba Buena Island and is linked to it by a roadway. It was built to receive the 1939 international exhibition celebrating the opening of the two bridges. At that time there were plans to locate the San Francisco airport here, but in the end a site at San Mateo, south of the city, was preferred. Treasure Island is now a US Navy installation.

YERBA BUENA ISLAND
The island lies midway between the east and west shores of the bay, level with Oakland. Assigned to the county of San Francisco in 1850, it was known for a while as Goat Island; later, in 1898, it was handed over to the Navy, which used it for an officers' barracks. In 1933 a tunnel was driven through the island's hills; this project was designed to link the two spans of the San Francisco–Oakland Bay Bridge, the construction of which began in the same year. At the time, the tunnel (45 feet high and 69 feet broad) was the biggest of its type in the world. Part of Yerba Buena Island is now occupied by the US Coast Guard, which maintains surveillance and sea rescue stations here. A tour of the center demonstrates how ships are guided by radar from the bay entrance and along all the region's inland waterways.

INTERNATIONAL GOLDEN GATE EXHIBITION

The Treasure Island exposition, which was mounted to celebrate the completion of the Golden Gate and San Francisco– Oakland Bay bridges, opened in February 1939. It continued until September 1940 and attracted some seventeen million visitors; nevertheless, it was accounted a financial failure by its organizers. Practically nothing remains of its handsome Art Deco features (notably the "Sun Tower", the "Court of the Moon", and a fountain statue of the "Goddess Pacifica"). Still, the event is commemorated in the Treasure Island Museum, located in the Administration Building, which is one of the three buildings dating from the exposition to have survived. Sixteen statues from the exposition fountain now stand on either side of the gates here.

CONSTRUCTION.

Treasure Island was built from mud and sand dredged locally and filled in behind a rectangular rock dyke made of debris from the island tunnel. Financed by the Works Progress Administration, work was begun in 1936 and completed in 1939. The place owes its name to Robert Louis Stevenson's book; it is also said that the landfill used to create it contained traces of gold.

"CHINA CLIPPER". Not far from the Treasure Island Museum is a display devoted to the legendary amphibian plane that was based here. From 1939 to 1946 this seaplane crossed the Pacific Ocean once a week – during the war, it stopped at Hawaii – carrying a maximum of twelve passengers and mail. There is a scale model in metal of the China Clipper, and photographs of the people (all of them wealthy, because the trip was very expensive) who traveled aboard this comfortable, spacious aircraft.

OAKLAND

HISTORY. During the 1830's, when this part of California was still a Mexican possession, the site of Oakland on the east shore of the bay was mostly occupied by Rancho San Antonio, the property of the Peralta family. In 1851, during the Gold Rush, Oakland was only a small town linked to San Francisco by a ferry that plied to and fro three times a day. In 1855 the city inaugurated the College of California, the first university in the West to offer an education comparable to that available in the great universities of the East Coast. The first graduates of this college received their diplomas in 1864, and in 1868 the college was incorporated into the University of California.

The completion of the Transcontinental Railroad in 1869 ● *54* marked a decisive turning point in the life of Oakland, the line's terminus. The town now found itself in a key position and its commercial and industrial expansion was immediate. The sector acquired important new industries, immigrants arrived in droves, and the ferries found themselves carrying large numbers of workers from San Francisco to Oakland each day. The 1936 opening of the San Francisco–Oakland Bay Bridge ▲ *306* gave an even greater boost to the economy. Oakland's administrators shrewdly developed its port facilities, which have now supplanted those of San Francisco, making Oakland one of the leading container terminals in the United States. Today the shipping companies and naval dockyards of the area are all based on this side of the bay. Industry and commerce mostly occupy the lower districts of the town, where there is plenty of room and the terrain is level; the hillside neighborhoods are more residential in character. For many people, present-day Oakland is synonymous with drugs, crime, ghettos, poverty and urban decline. The large working-class section of town has indeed been hard hit over the years by a series of economic crises; nevertheless, although there are still serious difficulties in some areas, Oakland is above all a highly dynamic town, in which administrators, businessmen and black investors have been working together for renewal ever since the end of the 1970's. Financial and administrative offices have burgeoned, and some of the best museums of the entire West Coast are now to be found here. Even tourism is making headway for Oakland's climate is, if anything, better than that of San Francisco. The center of town, which can be accessed easily by BART, has been extensively restored and is now developing fast, with pleasant parks, buildings on a human scale, bold construction work, and new business and cultural activities.

THE BLACK COMMUNITY
Since 1869 Oakland has been a melting pot of different races. Many communities are represented there today, notably Chinese, Koreans, Vietnamese, Italians, Mexicans, Portuguese, Greeks and above all Afro-Americans. The mayor, the chief of police and the owner of the main local newspaper tend nearly always to come from the majority Afro-

Lake Merritt.

THE BLACK PANTHER PARTY
Militants of this party, founded in Oakland, incited black people to defend themselves against police brutality; their action led to a virtual state of warfare. One of the co-founders, Huey Newton, was arrested in 1967 and became a symbol of resistance for blacks. Later the party treasurer, Bobby Hulton, was killed and Eldridge Cleaver, arrested and released for lack of evidence, became another symbol of resistance. The FBI began to harass Black Panther leaders; they were systematically killed in shootouts, imprisoned, divided and dispersed. However, the militants continued to work on behalf of blacks and found their persistence rewarded in 1977 by the election of Oakland's first black mayor.

THE BLACK PANTHER

ALL POWER TO THE PEOPLE

THE BLACK PANTHER

▲ JACK LONDON

Born in 1876 in San Francisco, Jack London was the child of a brief liaison between an itinerant astrologer and a medium. He was raised with his stepfather's surname and it was not until his later youth that he learned, to his deep dismay, that he was a "bastard", as he termed it. He grew up on the waterfront in Oakland, and at sixteen bought a sloop, becoming "King of the Oyster Raiders" in San Francisco Bay. But the wider world soon beckoned and he went to work as a seal hunter on the ice-floes; he then became a hobo riding the railroads, a gold prospector, an investigative reporter in London's slums, and a war correspondent. Hemingway, Fitzgerald, Kerouac and others followed in his footsteps, but Jack London was the first American writer to transform his own life, fiascos and all, into a legend.

His real career began with the Klondike. In 1897 Jack joined the horde of men who sailed from San Francisco to try their luck in the new Gold Rush, this time in Alaska. He spent a whole winter in the mountains, barely surviving the sub-Arctic temperatures. He returned, declaring he would strike his own brand of gold by writing an account of his adventures. With *The Son of the Wolf* (1900) he became the "Kipling of the Klondike". Then came *The Call of the Wild* (1902). The young writer's success was immediate and his rise meteoric: he was only twenty-four. Next came *The Sea-Wolf* (1904), *White Fang* (1906) and the extraordinarily prophetic *Iron Heel* (1907). In a few years London earned a million dollars, which he immediately squandered.

Raised in poverty, London stood as a socialist candidate for mayor of Oakland; but in his heart he saw himself as a born aristocrat. There was something of the Great Gatsby in him: through his belief in his own stories he virtually reinvented himself. His most spectacular folly was *The Snark*, a 55-foot ketch whose construction cost him a small fortune. At her helm London cruised to the Marquesas Islands, following the trail of Robert Louis Stevenson.

For years Jack London was viewed as a rebel who had managed to drag himself up by his bootstraps, an American Gorky whose version of the steppes was Alaska. But the truth was more paradoxical. A prophet of the revolution, he harangued the proletariat to bring about the "Red Dawn": yet was also fascinated by the predators of the capitalist jungle. Photographs of London show a man with a handsome face and mocking, impetuous charm, but he lived in constant dread that his muscular body would disintegrate, debilitated by "John Barleycorn" (whiskey) and weakened by the "sordid debauches" of his youth. Little by little, his dark side overwhelmed him. Did he mean, like his character Martin Eden, to "slip away into the wide ocean"? Jack London died at the age of forty of a morphine overdose.

The business sector of town includes City Hall (intersection of Broadway, 14th Street and San Pablo Avenue), John B. Williams Plaza with its fountains, the *DeLauer Newstand* (1310 Broadway), a shop selling imported newspapers that stays open night and day, the Tribune Tower (13th Street and Franklin), the offices of the *Oakland Tribune* since 1923, and *Holmes Books* (274 14th Street), Oakland's huge bookstore, which dates from 1906.

The Paramount Theater, a 1930's Art Deco building.

American community. Starting out as sleeping-car stewards or dining-car chefs, many of the first blacks to arrive here were blue-collar employees of the railway company. After World War Two the black population of Oakland grew considerably. In 1966, 70 percent of them were living on the city's West Side, but little by little Afro-Americans acquired lodgings in East Oakland. It was in the black ghetto here that the Black Panther Party was founded, at a time when social tensions in America were at their height.

BRET HARTE BOARDWALK, 567 FIFTH STREET AND CLAY STREET. This small group of restored Victorian houses is named after the author of novels about the Gold Rush ● *126*, who lived here for a while in a building that has since been torn down.

IN THE FOOTSTEPS OF JACK LONDON ● *129* ▲ *310*. Heading south on Broadway beyond Nimitz Freeway, you reach the estuary and Jack London Square, where the writer once moored his boat, the *Razzle Dazzle*. Born in San Francisco, London grew up in Oakland and lived there for many years. He read his first books as a teenager in the city library, encouraged by the poetess (and librarian) Ina Coolbrith ▲ *306*. A saloon that he patronized, the *First and Last Chance*, is still in existence here, as is the shack (tracked down and brought to Oakland in 1960) where London lived during the Klondike Gold Rush of the 1890's. Here, and a little further to the south in Jack London Village, the redeveloped seafront with its many shops and restaurants resembles that of Fisherman's Wharf ▲ *178*, only without the huge crowds.

BROADWAY TO LAKE MERRITT

BROADWAY can be reached from north of Lakeside Park westward via Grant Avenue, a pleasant shopping street. On Broadway, heading south, and in the adjoining streets a warm, friendly atmosphere prevails, with small buildings and old-style shops and stalls.

PARAMOUNT THEATER, 2025 BROADWAY. This restored former cinema now puts on theater productions. The interior, designed by T. Pfleuger, is open for visits.

OAKLAND CITY CENTER. The City Center is at the heart of the revived business quarter ● *108*.

VICTORIAN ROW. A few streets lower down Broadway are two superb groups of brick and wood houses dating from 1860 and 1880, some of which are still in the process of renovation.

CHINATOWN, BROADWAY, 8TH, 11TH AND HARRISON STREETS. Oakland's Chinatown is both more welcoming to visitors and less tourist-oriented

Samuel Merritt.

than that of San Francisco ▲ 152.
Currently in the process of rapid
expansion, it attracts immigrants from all
over Asia and is gradually extending
toward Lake Merritt.

LAKE MERRITT. Both the idea and the
money for a project to build a dyke
around the northern arm of the estuary
(thereby creating a lake) originated with
one of Oakland's mayors, Samuel
Merritt. Completed in 1869, this salt-
water lake, linked to the estuary by a
canal, became the first state nature
reserve in North America. Although
today it extends into the heart of the
business quarter, many thousands of
migrating birds still gather here. In winter
one can observe them from the Charles
Muckelroy Nature Trail, which follows
the canal by Lake Merritt Channel Park.
A footpath and cycle trail make the 3-
mile circuit of the lake; there are also

regular excursions by boat to visit the Cameron-Stamford
House (1418 Lakeside Drive), known as the "Lady of the
Lake", a large Italianate Victorian house than was restored
recently. Youngsters will enjoy Children's Fairy Land to the
northwest in Lakeside Park; this amusement park was opened
in 1950 and features the dozens of fairytales and legends that
inspired the creators of Disneyland.

Oakland
architecture.

**INFORMATIVE
DISPLAYS**
The section of the
Oakland Museum
concerned with
nature contains
various scale models

OAKLAND MUSEUM ★

100 OAK STREET. This street can be reached from the
seafront, heading eastward. The museum, which is not far

from the Lake Merritt BART station, is entirely dedicated to
the history, art and natural environment of California.
Founded in 1960, it is a handsome piece of modern
architecture, with most of its structure beneath the surface;
the architects were Kevin Roche, John Kinkeloo and
Associates, and the terraced gardens were landscaped by Dan
Kiley. The displays are highly educational, with instruction
panels, dioramas and computer screens.

representing
California's
ecosystems. In the
second section of the
museum are displays
that illustrate the
state's history, while
the floor devoted to
art possesses
important collections
of paintings,
photographs and
sculptures.

313

Mexico's ceding of California to the United States in 1848, followed by the 1849 Gold Rush, focused America's attention on the region. Painters and photographers rushed to this untouched and fascinating land. Albert Bierstadt (1830–1902), a landscape artist of German origin known for his large-scale mountain views, discovered California in 1863, when he painted several canvases of Yosemite Valley (3). He returned there in 1871, with a commission from Collis P. Huntington to paint a view of Lake Donner. Thomas Hill (1829–1908) and William Keith (1839–1911), both from England, were the two other great painters of the American West. Keith moved to San Francisco in 1859; a wood-engraver by training, he only turned to painting in 1868. This was exactly the time when Hill (1 and 2), then living in Boston, abandoned portrait painting to take up landscape work, using sketches from an 1862 trip to Yosemite with Keith (4). In 1870 Hill became vice-president of the San Francisco Art Association, with Keith also on the board. Julian Rix (1850–1903) a self-taught painter who later moved to the East Coast, was another artist who profited from the new-found public taste for Californian landscapes (5).

"AN AUTHENTIC BRANCH OF IMPRESSIONISM WAS BORN IN
AMERICA AND PRODUCED WORKS WHICH ARE REMARKABLE AND
TO THIS DAY GREATLY UNDERVALUED."

J.D. PROWN

The first Impressionist exhibition in San Francisco, which was organized in 1894 by M.H. de Young and the Paris dealer Paul Durand-Ruel, had no perceptible effect on local artistic production. It was not until the 1915 International Exhibition ▲ 236 that modern works of art, both American and European, began to have a decisive influence on five local painters: Selden Gile (5) (1877–1947), August Gay (3) (1890–1948), Maurice Logan (1) (1886–1977), Louis Siegriest (2) (born 1899) and Bernard von Eichmann (4) (1899–1970). These were joined in 1917 by the Canadian William Clapp (6) (1879–1954), who had encountered the Post-Impressionists and Fauvists in Paris. In 1923, at their first joint exhibition, these painters called themselves the Society of Six, in reference to a couple of other groups who had influenced the history of modern art in the United States (the Society of Ten and Society of Eight). In 1925 they came into contact with the German and Russian avant-garde and their work subsequently developed toward figurative Expressionism. Their final joint exhibition took place in March 1928 at the Oakland Art Gallery, which was then being run by Clapp according to the Bauhaus principles of interaction between the various branches of the arts.

	3
1	4
	5
2	6

In 1951 California began to react against the Abstract Expressionism of the East Coast when a group of artists from the bay abandoned abstraction in favor of a new, figurative approach. This trend, known as Bay Area Figurative Art, was to remain vigorous until 1965. This return to realism and the painting of the human figure as a vehicle for the expression of feeling appears to have been warmly welcomed.

David Park (1911–60) painted in broad, flat tints, depicting faces staring into nowhere and bodies silhouetted against a strong light, such as *Women in a Landscape* (1958) (1). As his *Figure on a Porch* (1959) (2) shows, Richard Diebenkorn (born 1922) presented the reality of things through basic, structural lines, rather than exploring their romantic inner qualities. Joan Brown, born in 1938, belongs to the second generation of the

movement and has continued Park's researches. Her figures (*Girl Sitting*, 1962) (3) are highly expressive, rich in color and dense in texture. Elmer Bischoff, born in 1916, places his figures in settings that are at once nebulous and drenched with light. *Figure in a Landscape* (1957) (4) has a symbolic overlay which resembles the work of Edvard Munch.

1	2
3	4

319

THE FREE SPEECH MOVEMENT
From 1960 to 1964 the Berkeley campus was in ferment. There were demonstrations in favor of civil rights and social reform, and against racial segregation, nuclear tests and the death penalty. On September 30, 1964, the leading figures of the North Beach counter-culture ▲ *166* crossed the bay to join the Berkeley protesters. A sit-in was organized at the university, and the Free Speech movement was launched to obtain the lifting of a ban on political propaganda on campus. The new American left was born.

HUBERT BANCROFT
A bookseller and publisher, Bancroft accumulated a huge collection of books, newspapers, manuscripts and documents. In 1905 he sold his library to the university, which has been adding to it and enriching it ever since.

BERKELEY ★

Berkeley extends from the flatlands to the hills ● *98*. It is named after Bishop George Berkeley, an Irish philosopher who came to the US to convert the Indians during the 18th century. The town itself, which is heavily influenced by its proximity to the University of California, was developed in the aftermath of the 1906 earthquake, when thousands of San Franciscans moved to the east side of the bay.

UNIVERSITY ART MUSEUM, 2626 BANCROFT WAY. This museum owns a particularly fine collection of Oriental and Western and modern art as well as housing the Pacific Film Archive.

TELEGRAPH AVENUE. South of the campus, after Sproul Plaza, is a real student enclave frequented by marginals of all kinds who appear to be living relics of the 1960's. There are also cheap restaurants, coffee bars and a multitude of bookstores, among them *Cody's* (2454 Telegraph Avenue), which as well as selling books serves coffee and arranges readings, and *Moe's*, which boasts that it is the biggest second-hand bookstore in the Bay Area.

PEOPLE'S PARK, BETWEEN HASTE, BOWDITCH AND DWIGHT STREETS. Today the denizens of this park are mostly dealers and hoboes, but in the 1960's it was a major rallying point for young protesters of the time. In 1969 the forcible eviction of hippies and leftist students from the park led to vicious rioting.

NORTHSIDE, EUCLID STREET. North of the campus there are some quieter zones. The lush hills of North Berkeley form a residential sector that is particularly pleasant, full of tree-lined alleys, gardens and old houses. This quarter is also well known for its remarkable restaurants.

UNIVERSITY OF CALIFORNIA ★

Founded in 1868 and built in 1873 on the green plateau crossed by Strawberry Canyon, the University of California, Berkeley, is the original campus of the University of California and remains the system's premier research institution. It occupies about 1,800 acres of land, and has some thirty-thousand students. As an important intellectual and scientific center, this university has for years been a training ground for Nobel prizewinners. Every aspect of avant-garde thought is represented at Berkeley, from scientific research to politics.

Affluent houses in
Berkeley at the turn of
the century.

FOUNDATION. Frederick Law Olmsted, the architect of New York's Central Park, was the first designer of the campus, where he juxtaposed a mosaic of architectural styles in the midst of woods and gardens. Toward the close of the 19th century Phoebe Apperson Hearst (mother of the newspaper magnate ▲ 70) decided to found a mining school in memory of her husband, George Hearst, who had made a fortune with a Comstock Lode silver mine concession ● 44. In 1899, at the suggestion of the architect Bernard Maybeck, Phoebe Hearst financed an international contest for a new campus design. The winner was Emile Bénard, a French architect influenced by the monumental style then in favor at the Ecole des Beaux-Arts in Paris. His laboriously composed plan for an "Athens of the West" ultimately became a reality thanks to an American architect (also trained at the Beaux-Arts) named John Galen Howard, who contributed a number of additional campus buildings ▲ 102.

The streets and shopfronts in the center of Berkeley sometimes evoke the psychedelic style of the 1960's.

THE PROTEST MOVEMENT. By the end of the 1950's America had safely emerged from the McCarthy era and was settling down in comfort to enjoy the "American Way of Life". But some of the nation's youth refused to go along with the previously held values of their elders. In 1960 John Fitzgerald Kennedy's arrival in power along with the desegregation social program he sought to enforce heralded the opening of a new political era, one in which all kinds of accepted standards were called into question. In San Francisco the Beat generation ▲ 166 broke all the literary, artistic and cultural rules of the status quo, savaging a conformist society bent on consumption: the "one-dimensional society", as it was described by Herbert Marcuse, whose thought galvanized rebellious American youth in 1968. At the same time the student milieu awoke to a new political consciousness and a protest movement began to develop, notably at Berkeley, where strong opposition to the methods of Senator Joe McCarthy and the House Committee on Un-American Acitivities had already surfaced during the 1950's. Linked as it was to the hippie and flower-power movement generation in Haight-Ashbury ▲ 274 and to the Black Power movement spearheaded by the Black Panther party ▲ 309, the protest movement gradually receded in the 1970's and finally vanished during the Reagan years. Nevertheless, a certain leftist tradition, according to which even the food one eats has to be "politically correct", has survived here: not for nothing is the city still known as the "People's Republic of Berkeley".

A NEW LIFE
Many students, and some of the teachers at Berkeley who shared the aspirations of the young people, did not directly confront the status quo but chose instead to create another society on the margins of society, which in theory was free and egalitarian.

UNIVERSITY HALL, UNIVERSITY AVENUE AND OXFORD STREET. At University Hall visitors can obtain documents and

"CAMPANILE"
The 300-foot-tall
Sather Tower was
built in 1914 by John
Galen Howard on the
model of St Mark's
campanile in Venice.
Twice a day the
carillon is played. The
bells were made in
England.

SPROUL PLAZA
This square in the
university was the
venue for the
meetings and sit-ins
that resulted in the
loosening of rules
governing political
propaganda on
Berkeley's
campus.

information about the university and campus, and sign up for guided tours.

EARTH SCIENCES BUILDING, UNIVERSITY DRIVE. This building contains a seismograph which records tremors all over the planet. The system operated here keeps a watch for developing epicenters, making early warning possible in the event of danger. In the same building there is a small MUSEUM OF PALEONTOLOGY displaying fossils of prehistoric animals and dinosaur skeletons.

LIBRARIES. The manuscripts of Mark Twain are preserved at the DOE LIBRARY, which is the central library of the University. The BANCROFT LIBRARY next door boasts a handsome collection of rare books and a museum rich in objects illustrating the history of California. Among other treasures, it possesses part of the vein of gold discovered on January 24, 1848, which sparked the San Francisco Gold Rush ● *48*.

SATHER TOWER. An elevator will take you to the top of this tower, which offers a view of Oakland, San Francisco, Marin County, the Golden Gate narrows and (in clear weather) far beyond ● *102*.

LECONTE HALL. This world-famous physics faculty was the scene of the invention of the cyclotron particle accelerator and the discovery of plutonium.

SOUTH HALL. The ivy-covered South Hall is one of the two original buildings of the university ● *102*.

HEARST MINING BUILDING. Completed by John Galen Howard in 1907, the granite-faced Mining School has a magnificent memorial vestibule with a glass vault arching above.

SATHER GATE. This bronze gate forged in 1909 was also designed by Howard, the campus architect; it marks the entrance to the university, giving on to Sproul Plaza at the heart of it. Mingling with the crowds of brightly dressed students, militants and distributors of political tracts still haunt this shrine of protest, where countless sit-ins and political meetings were held at the time of the Free Speech movement in 1964. The plaza was also the scene of demonstrations – some of them violently broken up – against the Vietnam War.

LOWIE MUSEUM OF ANTHROPOLOGY, BANCROFT WAY. Turn left along Bancroft Way and continue as far as College

MOUNT DIABLO
Snow-capped in winter, Mount Diablo is the highest peak in the
area and was considered sacred by the Bolgone Indians. It owes
its name to the "devil" who appeared among the ranks of the
Indians in 1806, putting to flight a Spanish force from San
Francisco that had come to annex their territory.

Avenue and Kroeber Hall, the Museum of Anthropology.
Here there is a display of craftwork of every kind, notably
created by Ishi, an Indian of the Yahi tribe, who was the last
California Indian to come down from the hills in 1911.
Opposite this building is the ART MUSEUM.
HEARST GREEK THEATER, GAYLEY ROAD. A detour eastward
across the campus leads to the Greek Theater (below) given
to the university by William Randolph Hearst and built in
1903 by John Galen Howard in imitation of the one at
Epidaurus in Greece. Sarah Bernhardt acted here on one
occasion. The botanical gardens above the theater contain
thousands of varieties from all over the globe, especially
flower species.
THE PHOEBE A. HEARST MEMORIAL GYMNASIUM. This
building was designed by Bernard Maybeck and Julia Morgan.
It has a swimming pool reminiscent of San Simeon.
LAWRENCE HALL OF SCIENCE, CENTENNIAL DRIVE. High above
the campus, this science museum is a place of fascination for
children. Like the Exploratorium
in San Francisco ▲ 241,
it mounts exhibitions
and conferences,
films, experiments
and other events,
using the most
modern techniques,
such as lasers and
holographs, to explain the basic
principles of various scientific disciplines, including atomic
theory, evolution and biology.

The Memorial
Vestibule in the
Hearst Mining
Building.

PARKS AROUND OAKLAND   ■ 30

TILDEN REGIONAL PARK. Bathing in Lake Anza, riding, golf,
botanical gardens: all these features are available in the park
behind the University of California.
SKYLINE NATIONAL TRAIL. This footpath follows the ridge of
the Oakland hills, offering superb views of the bay.
REDWOOD REGIONAL PARK. The people of Oakland are
specially fond of this park, which has numerous footpaths. A
new generation of sequoias has now replaced the giants that
were cut down to build the cities of the region.
JOAQUIN MILLER PARK. More or less integrated with the
Redwood Park, Joaquin Miller Park is named after a colorful
character who dreamed of greatness as a poet and was (to
some degree) lionized in England. Miller's house, The Abbey,
still stands among the trees he planted himself in 1880.
ANTHONY CHABOT REGIONAL PARK. Among these hills is Lake
Chabot, a fishing and canoeing paradise. (No bathing
allowed.)
NATURE RESERVES. The reserves of Las Trampas (Las
Trampas Regional Wilderness), further to the east, and the
Ohlone Trail (Ohlone Regional Wilderness) southeast of
Alameda County, are very wild. In the hills of Oakland
(entrance via Skyline Boulevard) is Huckleberry Botanic
Regional Preserve, a small (150-acre) reserve for rare plant
species.
MOUNT DIABLO. "Devil's Mountain" is the highest point in
the Bay region (nearly 4,000 feet).

**THE EAST BAY
REGIONAL PARKS**
In 1830, when the
country hereabouts
was still ruled by
Mexico, the hills of
Berkeley and
Oakland were
covered with giant
sequoias ■ 30.
Woodcutters arrived
at the time of the
1849 Gold Rush; the
sequoia lumber was
used to build town
houses, while the
oaks that gave
Oakland its name
served as firewood.
By 1857 these forests
were completely
devastated. The zone
was adapted first for
agriculture, then for
industry. Today it is
the center of heavy
industry in the Bay
Area, but a girdle of
national parks runs
round the crests of
the hills of Berkeley
and Oakland,
incorporating a
network of over 700
miles of trails and
footpaths. There are
also ample facilities
for volleyball, golf,
swimming, riding and
bicycling, in addition
to picnic areas.

323

POINT REYES LIGHTHOUSE

DRAKES BAY

TOMALES BAY

POINT REYES

INVERNESS

POINT REYES STATION

🚗 One–two days

ANGEL ISLAND
This island may be reached by ferry from Tiburon, or from Fisherman's Wharf ▲ *180* in San Francisco. In January 1910 a detention center was opened here for immigrants coming in from Asia and for Europeans arriving by way of the Panama Canal. Up to 175,000 Chinese passed through Angel Island between 1910 and 1940. Today the buildings here contain a museum that chronicles the period.

The Famous Double Bow Knot,
Mt. Tamalpais Railway, California.

Marin County extends northward from San Francisco between the Pacific coast and the bay. Mount Tamalpais (more commonly known as Mount Tam) marks the boundary between West Marin, a wild spot buffeted by the winds off the Pacific, and East Marin, which is more Mediterranean and urban in character. At the time of Spanish colonization the Franciscans at Mission Dolores used to send sick Indians to San Rafael, which is now the administrative center of the county, in the belief that the milder climate there would hasten their recovery. From the 1830's onward vacationers would travel to Mount Tam to spend the day there, and rich San Franciscans, attracted by the sunshine and varied landscape here, soon began to build second homes in the area. After the 1906 earthquake Marin County took in thousands of refugees from San Francisco, and many of the holiday houses there became main residences for the duration of the reconstruction program. The 1937 opening of Golden Gate Bridge ▲ *242* marked a decisive turning point in the county's history, which before that time had relied on a ferry service for its links with San Francisco. During World War Two several naval dockyards were built at Sausalito, attracting large numbers of workers to live in the region. Today the area continues to attract industry, and its population is still growing: however, the coastal zones, which were abandoned by the army after the war, have now been made into national parks as a part of the Golden Gate National Recreation Area. The present inhabitants of Marin County tend to be affluent white-collar workers with liberal tendencies, who have built attractive houses ranging from the spartan to the luxurious, with spacious gardens. They are fierce in their defence of the local environment, both natural and urban; no tower blocks are permitted to be built here. A number of artists who have remained in Marin County work hard to perpetuate the way of life and outlook that were particularly in vogue during the 1970's. In Bolinas, on the Pacific coast, for example, local people regularly remove the direction signs that are put up by the municipal authorities, with a view to discouraging tourists from coming to the district.

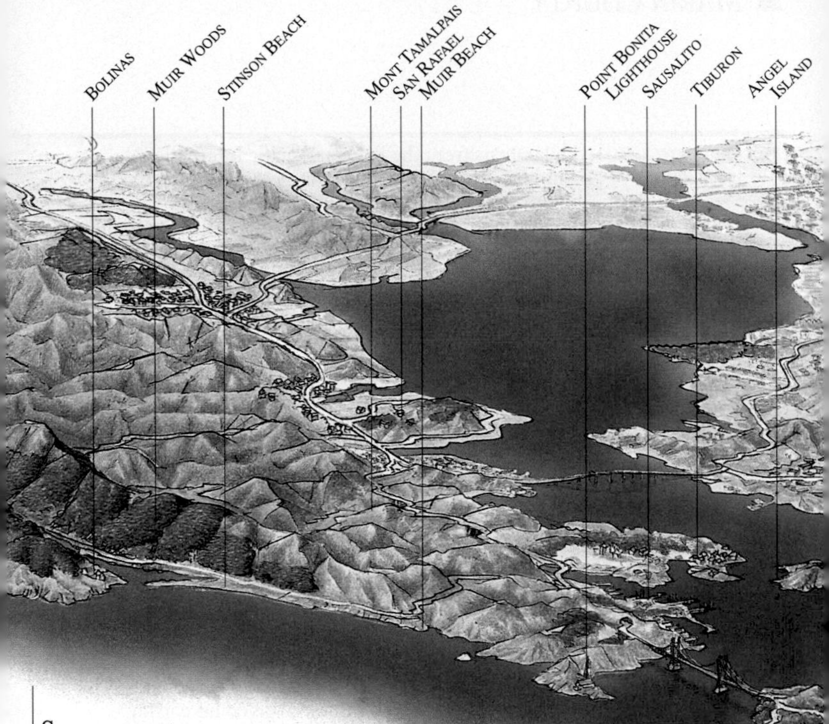

BOLINAS · MUIR WOODS · STINSON BEACH · MONT TAMALPAIS · SAN RAFAEL · MUIR BEACH · POINT BONITA LIGHTHOUSE · SAUSALITO · TIBURON · ANGEL ISLAND

SAUSALITO ★

To those taking Golden Gate Bridge across the bay, VISTA POINT offers a magnificent view of San Francisco. Though at times the wind and mist of the Pacific overwhelm Mount Tamalpais, the typically Mediterranean climate, together with the many seafood restaurants and craftshops, makes for a relaxed, holiday atmosphere in the little town of Sausalito, which clings to the hillside above the bay. The town (which should be avoided at weekends) owes its name to the willow woods the Spaniards found on the site. In the 19th century Sausalito became a whaling station; at the time, what is now Richardson Bay was known as Whaler's Cove. The Victorian houses on the slopes of the hill were constructed during the 1870's by the captains of British ships entering Richardson Bay to collect Californian fruit and vegetables intended for sale in Europe. William Richardson, after whom the bay is named, was the first American to become a naturalized Mexican around 1822. The government entrusted Richardson with the task of collecting dues from the ships that entered San Francisco Bay, and later ceded Sausalito to him. The main road through the town, Bridgeway Boulevard, is today lined with shops, hotels and restaurants with views over to San Francisco. Most of the terraced streets of Sausalito, many of which are connected by steep flights of steps, run into this boulevard. Near the landing stage the garden of the Plaza Vina del Mar has a fountain and two elephants

TROUBLED HISTORY
Around 1900 the bustling port had a bad reputation, with saloons, gambling dens and brothels all along Bridgeway Boulevard. During Prohibition many of San Francisco's bootleggers hid out in Sausalito. Since World War Two and the closure of the shipyards, the town has become quieter, and its inhabitants, like those of the rest of Marin County, enjoy a high standard of living.

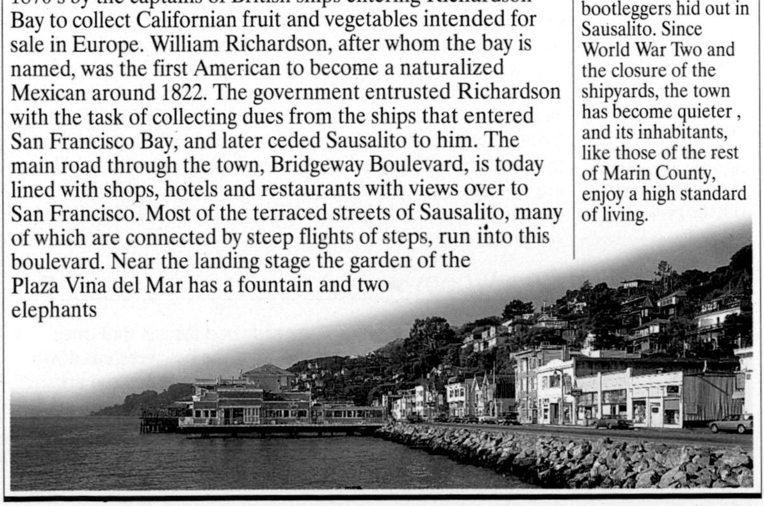

325

HOUSEBOATS
The site of the disused shipyard is now a village on the water, with houses linked by pontoons and constructed from materials taken from abandoned ships.

Beatniks and hippies once lived here and today the village is still a stronghold of unconventional artists. Such fanciful and chaotic architecture is surprising in the center of ultra-clean Sausalito, and the municipal authorities aim to demolish the village for reasons of hygiene. This has prompted real estate speculators to build another group of houses on the water, this time clean and neat, in conformity with the by-laws.

with lanterns from the Panama-Pacific International Exhibition of 1915 ▲ *236*. Not far away, between the Spanish-style Sausalito Hotel and the Sausalito Yacht Club, is the *Have a Drink on Sally* fountain. It is dedicated to the memory of Sally Stanford, a former San Francisco madam who in 1950 took over Sausalito's oldest restaurant, the *Valhalla*, now called the *Chart House* (located on Bridgeway, near Richardson Street). Farther north, at no. 2001 Bridgeway Boulevard, in a former army depot, is the BAY MODEL, an animated model of some 143 square yards representing the Bay Area. The geological evolution of the zone (sedimentation, salinity and rock formations) is cleverly simulated here ■ *16*, along with the shifting tides and sea currents of the Pacific Ocean in the vicinity of San Francisco.

MOUNT TAMALPAIS

According to Indian legend, the sun god, being obliged to return from earth to heaven, transformed his earthly paramour into a mountain; since then she has lain here on her back in an attitude of abandon, with her lovely hair shaken out to the eastward. Hence the name of "Sleeping Lady", by which Mount Tam is sometimes known. The attachment of the local people to this place has also earned it the title of "Sacred Cow of Marin County". At the beginning of the century a tourist railway was built up the mountain's south slope, leading to an inn at its summit. This railway, the "world's twistiest", had no fewer than 281 turns: the descent, in particular, was little short of hair-raising. The train, like the inn, disappeared following a fire in 1920, but it has left behind it one of the most beautiful footpaths on the entire West Coast: the OLD RAILROAD GRADE. It starts at Mill Valley, a former logging camp that is now a charming small town. From here many miles of trails crisscross the green slopes of Mount Tamalpais, across pastures, through forests of sequoias ■ *30* and cork oaks ■ *34*, and along tumbling streams. Everywhere on these walks, the visitor encounters a wide variety of plant species. Note, however, that it is forbidden to pick wildflowers here; they tend to wilt immediately after picking in any case. There are also cycle tracks and a road leading to the 2,400-foot summit, from which, in clear weather, the entire Bay Area is visible.

MUIR WOODS ★   ■ *30*

Close to Mount Tamalpais, the redwood forests that once clothed the slopes on the east side of the bay were cut down to build the cities that sprang up in the San Francisco area during the Gold Rush. All the same, in 1906 a businessman named William Kent bought Redwood Canyon, managing to save it from the loggers, and above all from the Redwood Canyon Water Company, which was planning to build a dam

POINT BONITA LIGHTHOUSE
Built in 1877, this lighthouse was the last in
California to be made automatic. It still uses
the great lens made by the French
manufacturer Fresnel in 1855 and brought
here by ship round Cape Horn.

on the site at that time. Kent, who ranks as one of the earliest ecologists, subsequently donated the forest to the state. It was given the new name of Muir Woods in honor of John Muir, a 19th-century philosopher and scientist of Scottish extraction (pictured below left) who devoted his life and

work to the study of nature. In 1908 Muir Woods was proclaimed a national monument by President Theodore Roosevelt; today one can still admire the Muir Woods National Monument on Mount Tamalpais, the last original forest of redwoods in Marin County. Some of these trees are eight hundred years old, and the tallest is some 240 feet high. This delightful forest attracts visitors in very large numbers every year.

MUIR BEACH. This beach at the mouth of Redwood Canyon is an ideal place to picnic, and perhaps go for a walk in Muir Woods afterward. The beach road passes in front of the PELICAN INN, a somewhat surprising (but nevertheless authentic) replica of a 16th-century English tavern.

STINSON BEACH ★. The western slope of Mount Tamalpais falls away steeply to the sea. Round its foot runs a 3-mile-long crescent of sand, the finest beach in the bay. If you don't mind cold water, you can bathe here without danger; there is also surfing and kayaking. During the summer months Stinson Beach is watched by life-guards.

BOLINAS LAGOON ■ *20.* At the far end of Stinson Beach is a sandy spit of land, where the sheltered, fish-filled waters attract thousands of seabirds, ducks and egrets. The road continues along this shore, past the AUDUBON CANYON RANCH, established in 1962, a mile or so north of Stinson Beach. Here, with the aid of binoculars, you can observe the herons and egrets that return to nest here every spring in the tops of the trees (over 125 nests have been counted). If you are willing to make the climb, you can also observe these birds and their young from an observation point known as Henderson Outlook that is located above their nests. Take binoculars with you. Pleasant picnic spots have been set aside on the ranch, which also maintains a permanent exhibition on the fauna, flora and geology of the entire region.

COASTAL HIGHWAY 1
Running parallel to the coast, this road offers a splendid view of the Pacific and Mount Tamalpais (the watercolor opposite is by Percy Gray ● *111*); the highway passes through peaceful villages nestling in the hills. The West Marin Chamber of Commerce in Point Reyes supplies a brochure, the *Marin Coastal Arts Trail*, which indicates the galleries you can visit en route. Thanks to the work of early ecologists and the pressure of public opinion, the Marin Headlands region was spared various plans for development in the 1950's and 1960's; it is now part of the great nature reserve network of the Golden Gate National Recreation Area.

The *Pelican Inn*.

POINT REYES LIGHTHOUSE
This lighthouse, built in 1870, stands some 150 feet above the ocean. Its lens, like that of Point Bonita, was made in France. It is an excellent point for watching migrating gray whales ■ *26*.

POINT REYES ★   ■ *24*

This peninsula, on the mistiest section of the California coast, is covered by a maze of paths across its prairies, marshes and woodlands, all of which are very carefully preserved. The beaches here tend to be hard to reach and dangerous on account of the tides, currents and high waves. (Information about conditions is available from the Bear Valley Visitor Center.) This is perhaps the best area for bird-watching in the entire region, with over 350 species to date identified here; it is also a paradise for botanists and nature lovers in general, who with a bit of luck may glimpse buck, elk, lynx, coyotes and falcons here.

SAN ANDREAS FAULT ■ *16*. The San Andreas fault, which runs from Bolinas Lagoon to Tomales Bay, marks the boundary between the Pacific and North American Plates. Located on the western (Pacific) plate of the two tectonic formations, this peninsula has shifted a total distance of 6 yards since the 1906 earthquake and is currently slipping northward at an average rate of about 2½ inches per year. You may wish to walk along Earthquake Trail or drive down Highway 1, which runs along the fault to the village of OLEMA at the entrance to Bear Valley. Certain differences in the landscape and flora of the two formations are clearly visible; for example, the redwoods that abound on Bolinas Ridge (which is on the North American plate) are conspicuously absent on Inverness Ridge, which belongs to the Pacific plate. On the other hand, pines seem to prosper on the granite soil of Point Reyes, but do not grow on Bolinas Ridge. Not far from Olema a narrow footpath leads to KUKU LOKLO, a beautifully reconstructed Miwok Indian village. The Miwoks welcomed the first Europeans to reach these coasts with great kindness; this was something of an error, since their society was quickly submerged by drink and disease. Today, like the Ohlones of the Bay Area, the Miwoks are practically extinct ● *42*.

INVERNESS. This pleasant little town a few miles north of Point Reyes Station, on the western shore of Tomales Bay, is an excellent staging point for hikers and visitors, featuring shops, bed-and-breakfast establishments and good restaurants.

SIR FRANCIS DRAKE BOULEVARD. This road stretches along the peninsula to its furthest point, which for years was much dreaded by mariners. Today it is marked by a lighthouse. Along the boulevard, there are a number of paths leading down to the various beaches.

PRACTICAL
INFORMATION

BY AIR

◆ There are several direct flights from London to San Francisco. British Airways (0181 897 4000) run two services a day, Monday to Saturday, and one flight on Sundays. United Airlines (0181 990 9900) offer a daily flight from London Heathrow and Virgin Atlantic (01293 562000) also operate a daily direct service. American Airlines offers a connecting service via New York or Chicago, while US Air flies to San Francisco via Charlotte, North Carolina. There are regular flights to San Francisco from most major US cities. The San Francisco airport (SFO) is 14 miles from the city center.

◆ To get to the city center from SFO airport tel. (415) 761 0800.

TAXIS

These are found at the lower level of the airport. Depending on the traffic, the ride to the center of town takes between 25 and 40 minutes. Prices vary from $30 to $35, without tip (obligatory in the US).

PRIVATE BUS SHUTTLE

Different private bus companies provide a service departing from the upper level of the

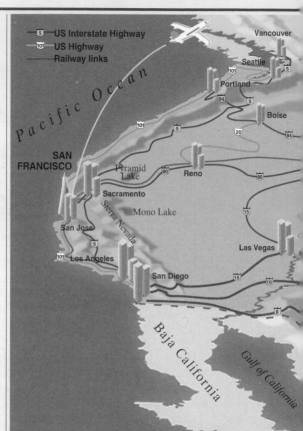

airport roughly every 20 minutes. The cost is $11 one way. The Yellow Airport Shuttle Service, tel. 415 282 7433 also serves Oakland; other lines include the Door to Door Airport Express, tel. 415 775 5121 and Super Shuttle, tel. 415 558 8500. To reserve a seat to

the airport, call at least one day in advance. The shuttle will collect you at the time you request.

BUS

The SFO Airporter Co, tel. 415 495 8404 goes directly to Union Square (downtown), thence to the big hotels in surrounding districts (Financial District and Nob Hill). Departures from the upper level of the airport are every 15 minutes, 6.20am to midnight. One way, this costs $9; return $18. The SamTrans Co, tel. 1 800 660 4287

offers a ride to Transbay terminal (Mission and 1st Streets), serving 3rd, 7th and 9th Streets; bus no 7b ($1) is an omnibus (one hour journey), and no 7f ($2.50) is an express service (half an hour). Departures are from the upper level of the airport, every 30 minutes from 6am to 40 minutes after midnight.

CAR RENTAL

It's easy to rent a car on arrival at the airport; the main agencies are all present. Dollar Rent-a-Car (tel.

330

tel. 1 800 872 7245, provides links with the main cities of the USA. There are two services from Los Angeles to San Francisco. The first departs daily, lasts 11 hours and costs $120 (return). The second lasts 9 hours and costs $82, with four departures daily. New York to San Francisco (via Chicago) lasts 3½ days and costs $442 (return). The service arrives at the Oakland Depot train station, where you will find buses to the Ferry Building, and sometimes also to Union Square and Pier 39.

BY COACH
Greyhound buses serve most American cities. The offices of the Greyhound Co. in San Francisco are at 50 7th Street, (tel. 1 800 231 2222). The coach station is also at Transbay terminal, tel. 415 558 6746.

BY CAR
The American Automobile Association (AAA), California State, tel. 1 800 922 8228 (membership fee $41–$118), offers members insurance, route information and a breakdown service. For the state of traffic on freeways, tel. 415 557 3755. Freeway 101, which crosses San Francisco downtown, links Seattle to Los Angeles along the coast. Interstate 5 goes from Vancouver to San Diego via Sacramento. Interstate 80 links New York with San Francisco.

Rent-a-Car (tel. 1 800 800 4000), Avis (tel. 1 800 831 2847), Budget (tel. 1 800 527 0700), Hertz (tel. 1 800 654 3131) and Thrifty (tel. 1 800 367 2277). The minimum age is 19–25 years depending on the agency, but allow for an insurance supplement for under 25's. An international driving license and a credit card are obligatory.

◆ To get from Oakland airport, tel. 1 510 577 4000

LIMOUSINE
Airport Limousine for You, tel. 415 876 1700.

TAXI
The taxi ride to Oakland will cost approximately $55, excluding the obligatory tip.
PRIVATE SHUTTLE
American Airporter Shuttle, tel. 415 546 6689. The trip to your hotel will cost about $15.

BUS
BART(Bay Area Rapid Transit)/Air BART (bus), tel. 510 562 7700, will take you to the BART Coliseum station (one way, $1) or downtown (price one-way $2, journey time 45 minutes). One bus every 15 minutes. The AC Transit Co, tel. 510 839 2882, runs bus no. 57 for the same destinations, with a service leaving every 30 minutes.

BY TRAIN
Amtrak, The Ferry Building, 31 Embarcadero,

MUNI PUBLIC TRANSPORT

The San Francisco Municipal Railway (MUNI) covers all the inner city public transport facilities, such as buses, MUNI metro and the cable cars. Maps of the various routes are available for $2.17 at the Visitor Information Center in Hallidie Plaza and also in some kiosks.

TICKETS

When you pay the driver, give him the exact sum because he will not give you change. You can ask the driver for a transfer ticket, which is valid for two changes until the time shown on it (about one hour and forty-five minutes after purchase). This applies to buses, trolley-buses and the metro.

SPECIAL TARIFFS

Several types of pass are available on public transport, which allow unlimited travel within San Francisco. These are:
–1 day ($6)

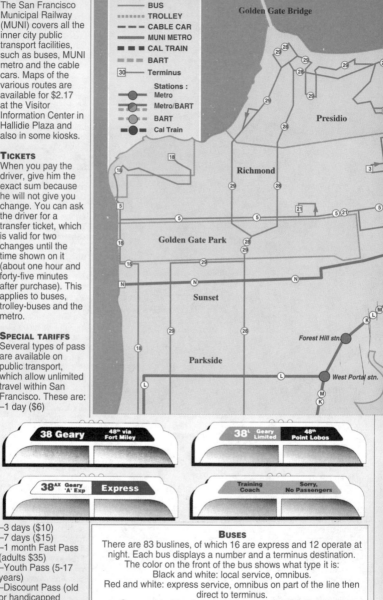

——	BUS
▪▪▪▪▪▪▪	TROLLEY
– – –	CABLE CAR
——	MUNI METRO
■ ■ ■	CAL TRAIN
▬ ▬ ▬	BART
30——	Terminus

Stations :
⬤	Metro
⬤	Metro/BART
⬤	BART
⬤	Cal Train

Golden Gate Bridge

Presidio

Richmond

Golden Gate Park

Sunset

Forest Hill stn.

Parkside

West Portal stn.

38 Geary — 48th via Fort Miley

38L Geary Limited — 48th Point Lobos

38AX Geary 'A' Exp — Express

Training Coach — Sorry, No Passengers

–3 days ($10)
–7 days ($15)
–1 month Fast Pass (adults $35)
–Youth Pass (5-17 years)
–Discount Pass (old or handicapped people).
These passes can be obtained at the BART/MUNI station on the corner of Powell and Market streets or at the Visitor Information Center.

BUSES

There are 83 buslines, of which 16 are express and 12 operate at night. Each bus displays a number and a terminus destination.
The color on the front of the bus shows what type it is:
Black and white: local service, omnibus.
Red and white: express service, omnibus on part of the line then direct to terminus.
Green and white: limited service, not all stops displayed.
Yellow and black: taking no passengers.
Buy your ticket aboard the bus. The normal tariff is $1.00. Local buses run 7 days a week, from 6am to 1pm (frequency about every 10 minutes). A night service operates on 12 lines from midnight to 6 am. Express buses operate 7am to 6pm all week, limited service buses Monday to Friday 7am to 6pm and Saturday 9am to 5pm.
Most bus stations have ramps for wheelchairs.
Tel. 923 6142 for information.

The three current cable car lines were classified as historical monuments in 1964. They are mainly used by tourists downtown.

TAXIS

These can obviously be hailed in the street, but there is no supplementary charge for telephone bookings. Veteran's Cab, tel. 552 1300; De Soto Cab Co, tel. 673 1414; Luxor Cabs, tel. 282 4141; Yellow Cab, tel. 625 2345; City Cab, tel. 468 7200; Pacific Cab, tel. 986 7220. Taxis are not particularly expensive: $1.70 for the first mile and $1.80 per mile thereafter.

BY BICYCLE

There are plenty of good bike rides in San Francisco, especially the one from Golden Gate Park to Lake Merced.
MOUNTAIN BIKE RENTALS: Golden Gate Park Skate and Bike

MUNI METRO

There are a total of five metro lines, all of which converge on the Embarcadero.
J (30th–Church Streets)
K (San Jose Avenue)
L (46th–San Francisco Zoo)
M (San José Avenue–Geneva Avenue)
N (Judah Street–Great Highway)
There is a train every 15 minutes on all these lines. Tickets are $1 and may be bought at machines in the metro stations; for the above ground service (after Van Ness Avenue) they can be purchased from the driver.

HOURS
Mon.–Fri. 5am–12.30am, Sat. 6am–12.30am, Sun. 9am–12.30am. A night service (owl service) exists on some lines.

CABLE CAR

There are three cable car lines, chiefly for tourists. The Powell-Hyde Line goes from Hallidie Plaza across Nob Hill and Russian Hill to Victorian Square beside the Aquatic Park; the Powell-Mason Line starts at the same place, crosses Nob Hill then goes down again to Bay Street by Fisherman's Wharf; and the California Street Line leaves from Market Street (Main Street), crossing Chinatown to Nob Hill (Van Ness Avenue). The cable cars operate roughly 15 minutes apart, and stops are made by request to the driver.

The normal ticket price is $2. MUNI passes are accepted.

HOURS
Cable cars run from 6.30am to 12.30am, 7 days a week.

SAFETY PRECAUTIONS
Wait until the car is stationary before getting on or off. Only two passengers may stand beside the driver. Do not stand beyond the zone marked in yellow, which is reserved for the driver.

3038 Fulton Street (6th Avenue) American Bike Rental, Fisherman's Wharf, 2715 Hyde Street, tel. 931 0234. Open all year 9am–10pm.

The *MTC Regional Transit Guide* ($5.50), which can be purchased at the San Francisco Visitor's Information Center in Hallidie Plaza, provides information on all the buses, trains and ferries operating round the bay. Telephone information is available on 1 510 464 7738.

BY BUS
Departures are from Transbay terminal.
◆ Samtrans serves the San Mateo area, including San Francisco airport and Palo Alto. Tel 1 800 660 4287.
◆ AC Transit serves the towns east of the bay (Treasure Island, Berkeley, Oakland)

Tel: 1 510 8 39 2882.
◆ Golden Gate Transit Buses serve the Marin and Sonoma areas. Tel. 332 6600.

Solano County

Contra Costa County

Pittsburg *Antioch*
Oakley
CONCORD
Brentwood

Contra Costa County

Alamo
Danville
Dublin
Castro Valley
Livermore
Pleasanton

FREMONT

Alameda County

SAN JOSE

Santa Clara County

BY TRAIN
The MUNI network is linked with the BART, Cal Train and AC Transit Intercity networks.
◆ The BART (Bay Area Rapid Transit) is a suburban railroad between San Francisco and the east bay towns (Oakland, Richmond, Concord, Fremont and Berkeley). There are four downtown stations, on Market Street. Tickets can be obtained from machines. Trains leave every 15–20 minutes. Prices vary according to destination but are generally between $1 and $4. Hours are Mon. to Fri. 4am–midnight, Sat. 6am–midnight, Sun. 8am–midnight. Tel. 1 (510) 464 7133.
◆ Cal Train links San Francisco with the peninsula and San José. Departure from Cal Train depot (4th and Townsend Streets) daily from 5am–10pm; night service weekends only. Tel. 1 800 660 4287.

BY FERRY
◆ Golden Gate Transit operates crossings to Larkspur and Sausalito. Departures are from the San Francisco Ferry Building 6am–9pm. Tel. 332 6600.
The Sausalito crossing takes about 30 minutes. Daily service (excluding Thanksgiving, Christmas and New

Year). Usual tariff: $4.25 (one way). The trip to Larkspur takes 50 minutes; daily service, Mon.–Fri. at rush hours; also weekends in summer.
◆ Red and White Fleet Ferry puts in at Sausalito ($5.50 one way) and Tiburon ($5.50 one way). It offers a one-day excursion through three vineyards, including wine-tasting ($47, tel. 546 2700). Departures (daily at 11am) from piers 41, 43 1/2 and San Francisco Ferry Building. For Muir Woods (pier 43 1/2) there is a combined ferry and bus fee ($28 adults). Tel. 546 2628.
◆ Blue and Gold Fleet serves Oakland ($4) and Alameda ($4 one way). Departures from pier 39 and at the Ferry Building. Tel. 705 5444.

BOAT RENTALS
◆ Club Nautique, 100 Gate 6 Road, Sausalito, tel. 332 8001. Sailboat rentals (prices vary from $150 to $795); instruction available. Those with no license can hire a "Skipper Charter" for $40 per hour (3 hours minimum).

BOAT EXCURSIONS
◆ Adventure Cat Sailing Charters. Pier 40, South Beach Harbor, tel. 777 1630. Works all year round. Excursions of 2½ hours by catamaran in the bay. Adults $20. Bookings possible.
◆ Let's Go Sailing. Pier 39,

tel. 788 4920. From April to November only. Charters. 1½-hour trips. Adults $25.
◆ Oceanic Society Expeditions. Fort Mason, Building E, tel. 474 3385. Reservations essential. Departures from Fort Mason. Day trips to the Farallon Islands (from $62) June to November, Fri. and weekends only. Also day trips to Point Reyes ($50) during the whale migration season December to April, Fri. and weekends only.

BICYCLE TOURS
There are some delightful bike excursions to be made in the Marin area, with Golden Gate Bridge as a starting point.
Start to finish, 1820 4th Street, San Rafael, tel. 459 3990. Open Mon.–Fri. 10am–8pm, Sat. 9am–6pm, Sun. 9am–5pm.
Sausalito Cyclery, 1 Gate 6 Road, tel. 332 3200. Open Mon.–Sat. 10am–6pm, Sun. 11am–5pm.

PIER 43 1/2
BAY CRUISE & FERRY TERMINAL
RED & WHITE FLEET

San Francisco has a total of twenty-seven neighborhoods, scattered over an area of 125 square kilometers. For San Franciscans, the suburbs include the entire zone south of Golden Gate Park, Twin Peaks, Noe Valley and the Mission. Forty-two hills, their heights varying from 200 to 938 feet, signposted "hill" or "grade", lend originality to this typically American city layout, a checkerboard of streets intersecting one another at right angles.

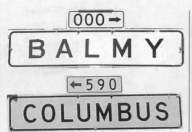

ADDRESSES

Most of San Francisco's streets are very long, with numbers typically ranging from 1 to 4000. Thus it is vital to know the name of the nearest intersecting street to the address you are looking for. To avoid covering long distances for no reason, the name of the nearest crossroads is always indicated in directions, for example, 152 Taylor Street (Turk-Eddy).

Street numbers get higher going from east to west, going away from Market Street. Distances are measured in blocks, with numbers rising by 100 from block to block. In the first block numbers will go from 1 to 99, in the second from 100-199, and so on. For example: 15 blocks separate the beginning of Stockton Street from its intersection with Union Street.

ORIENTATION

The city is divided in two by Market Street, which serves as a convenient landmark for visitors. A street's line may be broken by a hill, but will invariably continue on the far side of it under the same name.

DOWNTOWN

Downtown includes the Financial District, Union Square and Civic Center.

STREETS AND AVENUES

San Franciscans tend to call streets by their names without specifying "street" or "avenue" (Van Ness and Market), except when the street or avenue has a number, not a name: for example, 3rd Avenue, 24th Street. There is no 13th Street or 13th Avenue. Twenty-five parallel streets with numbers are concentrated in South of Market, while forty-six numbered parallel avenues (2nd to 48th) cross Richmond.

STREET NAMES

There are no street signs on buildings; only the panels at the intersections will tell you the name of the street you are on.

PRONUNCIATION

A number of San Francisco's streets have Spanish names, which point to the city's Hispanic origins. So Vallejo Street, for example, is pronounced as the Spanish, "Val-lay-ho".

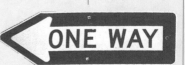

ONE-WAY STREETS

Throughout the northwest sector of the city (Downtown to Fisherman's Wharf) the streets are often one-way. When the traffic in a street goes one way (east to west or north to south) the traffic in the two streets either side of it will move in the opposite direction.

Traffic wardens (on motorized tricycles) go by regularly, marking tyres with chalk to show how long a car has been parked in a given spot.

The city maintains a highly organized public transport network, so it is not strictly necessary to have a car in San Francisco; moreover, parking can be a nightmare in Chinatown, Nob Hill, Fisherman's Wharf area, North Beach, Telegraph Hill and the Financial District. On the other hand, if you want to get out of town you will definitely need an automobile. But bear in mind that offences against the highway code are severely punished here; fines are heavy and applicable to everyone, tourists included. Police patrols and checks are very frequent.

PARKING METERS
These operate from Monday to Saturday, between 7am and 6pm; the length of stay permitted is limited to either half an hour or two hours, non-renewable. If there is no parking meter, a sign indicates the parking periods authorized.

PARKING RULES

It is against the law to park in front of a bus stop or a fire hydrant. One day a week the streets are cleared and all automobiles unlawfully parked are towed away. The rules are indicated by color bands along the sidewalk.
Red – no stopping or parking
Blue – parking

reserved for handicapped drivers
White – 5 minutes maximum
Green – parking 10 minutes maximum
Yellow or yellow and black – commercial deliveries only
Yellow, black and green – taxis only
The penalties for drunk driving are severe: high fines and even jail.

THE TOP TEN HILLS
The ten steepest hills in San Francisco can all be negotiated by car. Starting with the steepest, they are:

PARKING LOTS
These are expensive, with prices varying widely: some parking lots cost three times as much as others. Usual price: $3 to $6 per hour, $8 to $20 per day.

PARKING ON GRADIENTS
The rules here are very strict; handbrake engaged and front wheels turned towards the sidewalk.

DIRECTION SIGNS
Elevated signs near the curb indicate one-way streets, stops and compulsory turnoffs.

TRAFFIC LIGHTS
Where there are traffic lights, they are always installed on the far side of the crossing. A flashing yellow light means slow down. A flashing red light means stop. You can turn right even if the light shows red, but only after bringing your vehicle to a dead halt and checking that the road is clear.

TOW-AWAY SIGNS
If you are wrongly parked, your car will be clamped or towed to the pound. This will cost you the price of a release at the local police station, as well as a heavy fine (at least $110).

Filbert (Leavenworth/ Hyde), 22nd Street (Church/Vicksburg), Jones Street (Green/ Union), Webster Street (Vallejo/ Broadway), Duboce Street (Buena Vista/Alpine), Jones Street (Green/Union), Webster Street (Vallejo/ Broadway), Duboce Street (Divisadero/Alpine and Castro/Divisadero), Jones Street (Pine/California), Fillmore Street (Vallejo/Broadway).

The cost of living in San Francisco is much the same as in New York or Los Angeles. Hotels offer a wide range of prices; restaurants are very good value and are among the best in the United States. Value added tax is unknown (so far) in America, the substitute for it being a ubiquitous state tax, which currently stands at 8.5 percent in California. This tax applies in hotels, restaurants and shops. Prices are shown without the tax added, except in the case of tickets for public transport, taxis, telephone calls and gasoline.

BANKS AND EXCHANGE BUREAUX

The banks are generally open 9am–4pm, Mon. to Fri., 9am–1pm Sat., staying open until 5pm one day a week. It is difficult to get foreign currency exchanged in banks other than the Bank of America ◆ 374. Exchange bureaux perform this service (notably American Foreign Exchange Brokers ◆ 369). If you have travelers' checks, remember that dollar travelers' checks can be used directly as ordinary currency.

POSTAL SERVICES

American mail boxes carry the inscription "US Mail". To send a letter within the US the rate is 32 cents for the first ounce, and 23 cents an ounce thereafter, with postcards costing 20 cents. Letters and postcards going abroad cost 50 cents for the first half-ounce, and 45 cents per half-ounce thereafter. Most photocopying shops also offer fax facilities. There is a post office open daily 10am–5.30pm (Sun. 11am–5pm) in Union Square, in the basement at Macy's.

TIPS

In the US tips are virtually obligatory. Service is not included in prices, and a tip is expected; you may even be asked for one straight out in bars, restaurants, taxis and hairdressers. Fifteen percent is about right. For hotel staff (elevator operators, valet car parking, porters) give 50 cents or a dollar. No tips should be given in movie theaters, cafeterias, fast-food restaurants or gas stations.

CASH

The most commonly used bills are $1, $5, $10 and $20; less common are $2, $50 and $100 bills. There are coins for 1 cent, 5 cents, 10 cents, 25 cents; 50 cents and $1 coins are rarer.

THE COST OF A PHONE CALL (AT&T TARIFFS)

SAN FRANCISCO — *Price in dollars (first minute/following minutes)*

	8am	5pm	11pm	
	0.25/0.25	0.15/0.15	0.13/0.13	→ NEW YORK
	1.94 / 1.09	1.46 / 0.82	1.16 / 0.65	→ LONDON
	1.94 / 1.09	1.46 / 0.82	1.16 / 0.65	→ PARIS
	1.94 / 1.09	1.46 / 0.82	1.16 / 0.65	→ ROME

Local calls : 0.25 $ / min in a phone booth

PHONE BOOTHS

Call boxes contain telephone directories. They work with 5, 10 and 25 cent pieces, but no change is given for coins of less than 10 cents. If the number of coins you have put in is insufficient, an operator will tell you how much more to add. Some public call boxes accept credit cards (Mastercard, Visa); this makes calling abroad easier, but more expensive.

TELEPHONE CALLS

Local calls cost 25 cents per minute. Dial 411 for directory assistance. Toll-free numbers (N.B. international calls cannot be toll free) are those preceded by (1) 800. Telephone numbers have seven digits. An additional three digits preceding the number is an area code. To call a local number just dial the seven digits. To call a different area code, dial 1 + area code + number. San Francisco, the peninsula, and Marin County are in area code 415. East Bay numbers are in area code 510. Calls abroad can be dialled from phone booths. For the operator, dial 0. To call San Francisco from the UK, dial 001 + 415 + number. To dial the UK from San Francisco, dial 01144 + number, but omit the first zero of the area code.

AUTOMATIC TELLERS

It is possible to draw cash with credit cards (Visa, Mastercard, Diners' Club) from ATM (Automatic Teller Machine) dispensers ♦ *368*. These machines can be found just about everywhere in San Francisco. There is a 2% surcharge with the use of an AMEX card.

PRICES

COFFEE: $1

WHISKEY: $4–$8

HAMBURGER: $6

MUSEUM ENTRY FEES: $3–6

CONCERT TICKETS: $7–20

MOVIE THEATER: $7.50

LUXURY RESTAURANT: $35–100

INEXPENSIVE HOTELS: $60–75

The climate in San Francisco is temperate all year round. Do not expect very hot weather; it will be cool, whatever the time of year. The sun is rarely visible in the morning or at the end of the day, because of mist. After building up behind the coastal mountain ranges, the famous San Francisco fog rolls out spectacularly across the bay, a sight that is particularly impressive from Golden Gate Bridge – or from a boat on the water.

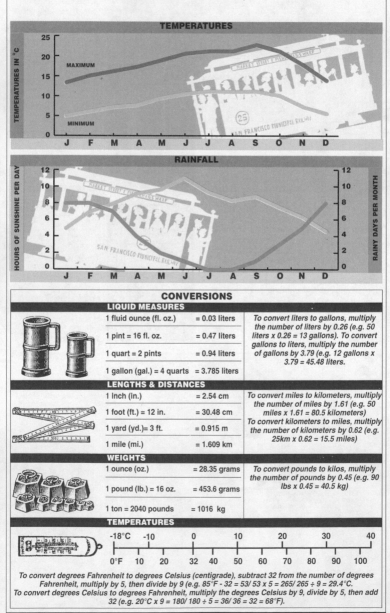

TEMPERATURES

TEMPERATURES IN °C

MAXIMUM

MINIMUM

J F M A M J J A S O N D

RAINFALL

HOURS OF SUNSHINE PER DAY

RAINY DAYS PER MONTH

J F M A M J J A S O N D

CONVERSIONS

LIQUID MEASURES

1 fluid ounce (fl. oz.)	= 0.03 liters
1 pint = 16 fl. oz.	= 0.47 liters
1 quart = 2 pints	= 0.94 liters
1 gallon (gal.) = 4 quarts	= 3.785 liters

To convert liters to gallons, multiply the number of liters by 0.26 (e.g. 50 liters x 0.26 = 13 gallons). To convert gallons to liters, multiply the number of gallons by 3.79 (e.g. 12 gallons x 3.79 = 45.48 liters.

LENGTHS & DISTANCES

1 Inch (in.)	= 2.54 cm
1 foot (ft.) = 12 in.	= 30.48 cm
1 yard (yd.)= 3 ft.	= 0.915 m
1 mile (mi.)	= 1.609 km

To convert miles to kilometers, multiply the number of miles by 1.61 (e.g. 50 miles x 1.61 = 80.5 kilometers) To convert kilometers to miles, multiply the number of kilometers by 0.62 (e.g. 25km x 0.62 = 15.5 miles)

WEIGHTS

1 ounce (oz.)	= 28.35 grams
1 pound (lb.) = 16 oz.	= 453.6 grams
1 ton = 2040 pounds	= 1016 kg

To convert pounds to kilos, multiply the number of pounds by 0.45 (e.g. 90 lbs x 0.45 = 40.5 kg)

TEMPERATURES

-18°C -10   0   10   20   30   40
0°F 10 20 32 40 50 60 70 80 90 100

*To convert degrees Fahrenheit to degrees Celsius (centigrade), subtract 32 from the number of degrees Fahrenheit, multiply by 5, then divide by 9 (e.g. 85°F - 32 = 53/ 53 x 5 = 265/ 265 ÷ 9 = 29.4°C.
To convert degrees Celsius to degrees Fahrenheit, multiply the degrees Celsius by 9, divide by 5, then add 32 (e.g. 20°C x 9 = 180/ 180 ÷ 5 = 36/ 36 = 32 = 68°F).*

HOLIDAYS AND FESTIVALS

	J	F	M	A	M	J	J	A	S	O	N	D
CHINESE NEW YEAR. TEL. 982 3000	●											
THE "BAM" (BAY AREA MUSIC AWARDS) ROCK MUSIC FESTIVAL. TEL. 388 4000		●										
ST PATRICK'S DAY. TEL. 661 2700			●									
CHERRY BLOSSOM FESTIVAL. TEL. 563 2313			●	●								
YACHTING SEASON : OPENING DAY TEL. 563 6363				●								
SAN FRANCISCO GIANTS BASEBALL SEASON TEL. 467 8000				●	●	●	●	●	●	●		
SAN FRANCISCO INTERNATIONAL FILM FESTIVAL TEL. 931 3456				●								
CINCO DE MAYO. MEXICAN FESTIVAL. TEL 826 1401					●							
SAN FRANCISCO EXAMINER BAY TO BREAKERS MARATHON. TEL. 777 7770					●							
MEMORIAL DAY WEEKEND. MEMORIAL DAY REGATTA TEL. 563 6363					●							
CABLE CAR BELL-RINGING COMPETITION TEL. 923 6162						●						
HAIGHT-ASHBURY STREET FAIR TEL. 661 8025						●						
LESBIAN-GAY PRIDE DAY PARADE TEL. 864 3733						●						
SAN FRANCISCO CLASSIC WINDSURFING REGATTA TEL. 563 6363							●					
BLUES AND ART ON POLK STREET TEL. 346 4561							●					
JAZZ AND ALL THAT ART ON FILLMORE TEL. 346 4561							●					
PACIFIC INTERCLUB YACHTING ASSOCIATION REGATTA TEL. 563 6363							●					
WINDSURFING REGATTAS TEL. 563 6363							●	●				
SAN FRANCISCO FORTY-NINERS FOOTBALL SEASON TEL. (408) 562 4949								●	●	●	●	●
SAN FRANCISCO BLUES FESTIVAL TEL. 826 6837									●			
SAN FRANCISCO SHAKESPEARE FESTIVAL TEL. 666 2221									●	●		
LABOR DAY REGATTA: "NOOD". TEL 563 6363									●			
BLESSING OF THE FISHING FLEET TEL. 434 1492										●		
CASTRO STREET FAIR TEL. 467 3354										●		
EXOTIC EROTIC HALLOWE'EN BALL TEL. 864 1500										●		
ST. FRANCIS INTERNATIONAL MASTERS REGATTA SAILBOAT RACE. TEL. 563 6363										●		
SAN FRANCISCO JAZZ FESTIVAL. TEL. 864 5449											●	
GRAND NATIONAL RODEO, HORSE AND STOCK SHOW TEL. 469 6065											●	
DIA DE LOS MUERTOS (FESTIVAL OF THE DEAD) TEL. 826 8009											●	

For a more precise calendar of dates and details of the venues for cultural events, refer to the San Francisco Visitor Information Center, tel. 391 2000

New Year's Day (Jan. 1), Martin Luther King Jr Day (third Mon. in Jan.), Presidents' Day (third Mon. in Feb.), Memorial Day (last Mon. in May), Independence Day (July 4), Labor Day (first Mon. in Sept.), Columbus Day (second Mon. in Oct.), Veterans' Day (Nov. 11), Election Day (Tues. following the first Mon. in Nov., every four years), Thanksgiving Day (last Thurs. in Nov.), Christmas Day (Dec. 25)

TIME CHANGES
The US covers six time zones, east to west (including Alaska and Hawaii). There is an eight-hour time difference between London and San Francisco (at 10am in San Francisco, it is 6pm in London); and a three-hour difference between New York and San Francisco (at 10am in San Francisco, it is 1pm in New York). San Francisco changes over to Daylight Savings Time on the first Sunday in April, and to Winter Time on the last Sunday in October.

◆ SAN FRANCISCO IN A DAY

49-MILE SCENIC DRIVE

This is an easy itinerary by car: follow the blue, white and orange sign with a seagull motif and the words "49-Mile Scenic Drive". Maps of this tour are available at the Visitor Information Center.

Aerial view from Sunset district to downtown.

Aerial view of the Cliff House, Seal Rocks and the Golden Gate.

9AM. One day of frenetic touring under your own steam could, quite literally, bring you to your knees; it is better to take guided tours whenever possible. If your time is limited and you have no car, go to Union Square first ▲ *218*. In front of the *St Francis Hotel*, you will find buses for the Grayline City Deluxe Tour (first bus leaves 9am). Tours also start from Pier 39 and 4b. Reservations: tel: 558 9400. This offers a 3½-hour circuit ($27 adults, $13.50 children aged 5–11) with a commentary in several languages. The tour takes in Civic Center ▲ *224*, Mission Dolores ▲ *295*, Twin Peaks ▲ *304*, Golden Gate Park ▲ *254*, Presidio ▲ *240*, Golden Gate Bridge ▲ *242* and Fisherman's Wharf ▲ *180*. To visit Alcatraz ▲ *184* (Isla de los Alcatraces, or Pelican Island), America's most famous prison from 1933 to 1963, allow an extra $12. If you prefer to walk, choose Roger's Walking Tours at Transbay Terminal (information tel: 743 9611). A guide will show you round the city's key sights (Cable Car Barn ▲ *68*, Chinatown ▲ *152*, Golden Gate Bridge ▲ *242*).

Lunch at the *Fairmont Hotel*. If you have a car, take the 49-Mile Scenic Drive around the city. The itinerary begins at Civic Center in front of City Hall, but you can also pick it up at any point on its course. In a single morning, starting from Civic Center ▲ *224*, you can cover Japantown ▲ *232*, Chinatown ▲ *152*, North Beach ▲ *162*, Fisherman's Wharf ▲ *172* and the coast down to Golden Gate Bridge ▲ *242*. If you go by car, the $3 toll is payable on the return journey (from Sausalito to San Francisco).

1PM. Have lunch at Cliff House ▲ *252* (very touristy) or at one of the many fine Asian restaurants in the area.

3PM. Cross Golden Gate Park ▲ *254*. Within the park, you can visit (in the same building) either the M. H. de Young Museum ▲ *266* or the Asian Art Museum ▲ *270*.

Then, for a magnificent view of the city, ascend Twin Peaks ▲ *304*, south of the park. If you are lucky enough to find that the bay is not obscured by mist, you will see the entire city laid out before you: Market Street cutting diagonally through the Financial District ▲ *206* with its skyscrapers, Chinatown, Union Square, and Golden Gate Bridge emerging from the mist to the westward. From here go to the Mission Dolores ▲ *294* and return to Ferry Building ▲ *208* for a glimpse of the Golden Gate ferry at the quayside.

8PM. Spend the evening by the bay at *Hornblower Dining Yachts*, Pier 33, Embarcadero, tel: 394 8900. You may wish to carry on from here and check out San Francisco's nightlife, in which case try *Three Babes and a Bus*,

tel: 552 2582. This organization supplies a bus that will take you round the city's main clubs for a comprehensive price of $30, including transportation and all entry fees (drinks not included).

> ### FINANCIAL DISTRICT
> The main thoroughfare here is Montgomery Street, by the port, where Sam Brannan ● *48* spread news of the gold strike and where San Francisco's first houses were built out of timbers taken from abandoned ships in the harbor. The banks and other financial institutions arrived later.

For years the "Balclutha" plied between Europe and California by way of the Horn.

The Japanese Tea Garden, built in 1894.

DAY ONE

By Union Square, on Powell and Market Streets, take the cable car (line 3) to Fisherman's Wharf ▲ *180*. Visit the National Maritime Museum ▲ *172*, built in 1939, which offers a good introduction to the importance of ships and navigation in the history of San Francisco. Embark for Alcatraz (Pier 41, tel: 546 2628). Allow about three hours for the crossing and tour. When you get back, visit Pier 39, which was built as a collection of shops and restaurants. Keep an eye open for sea lions offshore.

1PM. Lunch at *Dante's Seafood Grill* tel: 421 5778, Pier 39, one of the best seafood restaurants in San Francisco, with a spectacular view of the bay.

2PM. Walk round the Cannery and Ghirardelli Square ▲ *178* at 900 North Point Street. Heading toward the Marina ▲ *235*, where you will see beautiful waterside houses, visit Fort Mason ▲ *234*. Take bus no. 28 to the Presidio and the Palace of Fine Arts ▲ *238* – a must – and the Exploratorium Museum of Science and Technology ▲ *239*. Take bus no. 28 or 29 to the Golden Gate Bridge.

8PM. A Golden Gate Transit bus will take you back to Market Street. Have dinner at the *Postrio* restaurant, 545 Post Street, tel: 776 7825.

DAY TWO

At North Beach have breakfast at the *Caffè Roma* ◆ *374*, 526 Columbus Avenue, (Vallejo Street). At Washington Square take bus no. 39 along Union Street to Montgomery Street, and continue on foot to the Filbert Steps (beautiful houses). Next visit Coit Tower ▲ *170* on Telegraph Hill. Go down Lombard St (between Leavenworth and Hyde Streets), a picturesque road with famous zigzags. Now take the Powell-Hyde line cable car to the Cable Car Barn ▲ *193* and watch the driver swivel his machine round on the turning plate.

1PM. Eat in Chinatown ▲ *152* at the *Empress of China* ◆ *368*, 838 Grant Street (Clary Street).

2PM. Take bus no. 41 in the direction of Union Street, or no. 30 on Stockton Street, then bus no. 22 up Fillmore to Alamo Square ▲ *230*. The Victorian houses here, built between 1890 and 1900, are splendid; notably nos. 722–4 Fillmore Street, 850 and 908 Steiner Street, 1429 Hayes Street and 1062 Fulton Street. Next, make your way to Golden Gate Park ▲ *254* (bus no. 5 or 21). Visit the California Academy of Sciences with its zoological museum, aquarium and planetarium. Do not miss the Japanese Tea Garden ▲ *263*. Buses nos. 6, 7 and 71 (Haight Street– Market Street) will take you back to Union Square.

8PM. Dinner at *Victor's, Westin St Francis Hotel* ▲ *379*, 335 Powell Street.

FISHERMAN'S WHARF

Those who like old boats can take a trip to Hyde Street Pier ◆ *369*, where there are at least three ancient merchant ships: the *Eureka*, the *Thayer* and the *Balclutha*, built at the end of the 19th century.

Mission Dolores, next to the museum, built 1776.

The Haas-Lilienthal House.

City Hall, completed in 1916.

Mission Dolores on Dolores Street (16th Street) is the Franciscan mission built along the old Camino Real ▲ 293. In the old cemetery adjoining, mossy headstones mark the graves of people who died during the Gold Rush ● 48, as well as of some five thousand Indians who fell victim to epidemics. Take bus no. 49 from here to Civic Center.

10AM. Walk round City Hall ▲ 227, the Opera House ▲ 229 and the San Francisco Public Library ▲ 108. The library contains nearly two million volumes. Visit the Modern Art Museum (SFMOMA), 151 3rd Street, (Mission-Howard). Opening times are Tues., Wed., Fri. and Sun. 11am–6pm, and Thurs. 11am–9pm. Closed Mon.

1PM. Beside Civic Center, lunch at the fashionable *Stars* restaurant, Redwood Alley, Van Ness Avenue, tel: 861 7827. The cooking here is American, and the menu changes daily.

2PM. There are over thirteen thousand Victorian houses in the Western Addition,

Haight-Ashbury, Eureka Valley, Noe Valley, Bernal Heights, Potrero Hill, Mission District and Duboce Triangle areas. Built between 1879 and 1906 of sequoia wood, which was once abundant here, many were destroyed by the 1906 earthquake. These houses are one of the Bay Area's major attractions and a tour of them ▲ 92 can take up to half a day. At 2007 Franklin Street visit the Haas-Lilienthal house ◆ 370. This type of construction, with its towers and elaborate ornamentation, was all the rage during the 1890's. There are others like it on Alamo Square. To get to the Alamo Square area take the no. 21 bus. Bus no. 41 or 45 will

take you on to Pierce Street; then move on to Cow Hollow ▲ 204. Take trolleybus 22 to Jackson Street (Pacific Heights). Walking from Jackson through to Bush Street, note the 1870's Italian style of nos. 2011–15 and 2139–43 Pine St; 30–32 Orben Place (named after the architect who renovated some of these houses during the 1970's) and 1814–22 Bush Street. Go back to Union Square on bus no. 3.

8PM. Spend a quiet evening at the *Redwood Room* piano bar, ◆ 379, 459 Geary Street , tel: 775 4700, in the *Clift Hotel*.

10PM. Spend the night in the Financial District's

Mandarin Oriental Hotel, ◆ 375, 222 Sansome Street, tel: 885 0999, built in the shadow of the fifty-two-story Bank of America by a rich Taiwanese family. The view from the rooms on the fortieth floor of this luxury hotel is remarkable, especially in the evening when the city's lights are glimmering, or early in the morning when the fog lifts.

Chinatown street signs.

Sausalito: houses built on pilings.

DAY TWO

The "Wok Wiz Chinatown Tour" provides a culinary and historical walk around Chinatown. The walk (to reserve, tel: 981 5588) lasts from 10am to 1.30pm and ends in a traditional teahouse. A guide will show you round the Chinese markets and shops, with their snakes pickled in jars and alternative medicinal remedies.

2PM. Visit the Chinese Historical Society Museum ▲ *158* at 650 Commercial Street (Montgomery Street), which traces the history of the Chinese community in the US. Then explore the side streets, with their picturesque, brightly colored architecture, especially Spofford, Ross and Waverly Streets, famed for their ready-made clothing workshops.

3.30PM. On the way back down to Union Square, drop in on some of the art galleries ◆ *376*, such as Harcourts Modern and Contemporary Art, 461 Bush Street, Denenberg Fine Arts, 257 Grant, Rena Bransten, 77 Geary Street, Haines Gallery, Steven Wirtz Gallery, Fraenkel Gallery, 49 Geary Street, Paule Anglim Gallery, 14 Geary Street, Modernism, 685 Market Street, Erika Meyerovich, 251 Post Street, and Jack Hanley Gallery, 41 Grant Avenue. At Union Square, take the cable car 68 (Powell–Hyde line), which crosses Russian Hill ▲ *196* to Fisherman's Wharf ▲ *180*.

8PM. For a fantastic view of Golden Gate Bridge, go for a vegetarian dinner at *Green's*, Building A, Fort Mason, Tel: 771 6222.

10PM. Spend the night at the 19th-century *San Remo Hotel* beside Fisherman's Wharf, 2237 Mason Street (Chestnut Street).

DAY THREE

Take the ferry (Golden Gate Transit, tel: 332 6600, or the Red and White Fleet Ferry, tel: 546 2628), across to Sausalito (about thirty minutes). Embark either from the San Francisco Ferry Building (Waterfront) or from Piers 41 or 43 1/2 (Fisherman's Wharf). If you prefer to go across town, take bus no. 50 along Geary Street, or no. 30 along Sansome Street, which crosses the Golden Gate Bridge ▲ *242* to Sausalito. Once you are there, bus no. 63 (Golden Gate Transit) will take you to Muir Woods National Monument ▲ *30*, the only park on the bay where redwoods can still be seen. If you are a good walker, try the 4-mile trail through the woods to Stinson Beach, where you can bathe if the weather is good enough. Allow approximately three hours to reach the beach; a shuttle bus is available there to take you back to the Muir Woods car park. If you have a car, take Freeway 101, then Shoreline Highway left after Sausalito, towards Muir Beach and Stinson Beach. Muir Woods Road leads to the Muir Woods National Monument.

2PM. Back in Sausalito, have lunch on the waterfront at *Horizons*, 558 Bridgeway, tel: (415) 332 0791, which offers an exceptional view of San Francisco.

4PM. Return downtown (bus no. 30) as far as Telegraph Hill, or take bus no. 39 to the Coit Tower ▲ *170*. From here there's a superb view of Nob Hill ▲ *190*, Russian Hill ▲ *196*, Golden Gate Bridge ▲ *242* and the bay, especially at sunset. Try to see the mural paintings in Coit Tower ▲ *298*.

8PM. Stay in Little Italy ▲ *162* for dinner at the *Bocce Caffè*, 478 Green Street, tel: 981 2044.

10PM. Check out the clubs along Fisherman's Wharf. *Lou's Pier Club* for rock, blues and soul music: 300 Jefferson Street (Jones Street) tel: 7710377. The *Buena Vista Café* serves one of the best Irish coffees in San Francisco, 2765 Hyde Street (Beach Street), tel: 474 5044.

In Japantown (between California–Geary and Octavia–Fillmore Streets), look over the kimonos and porcelain on sale. Also do not miss the Japanese Culture and Trade Center on the Post and Webster Street intersection, which among other things runs courses in Japanese cooking and ikebana (flower arranging).

In California, nearly 300,000 acres of land are planted with vineyards.

Seven distinct species of vine are used for the various California wines.

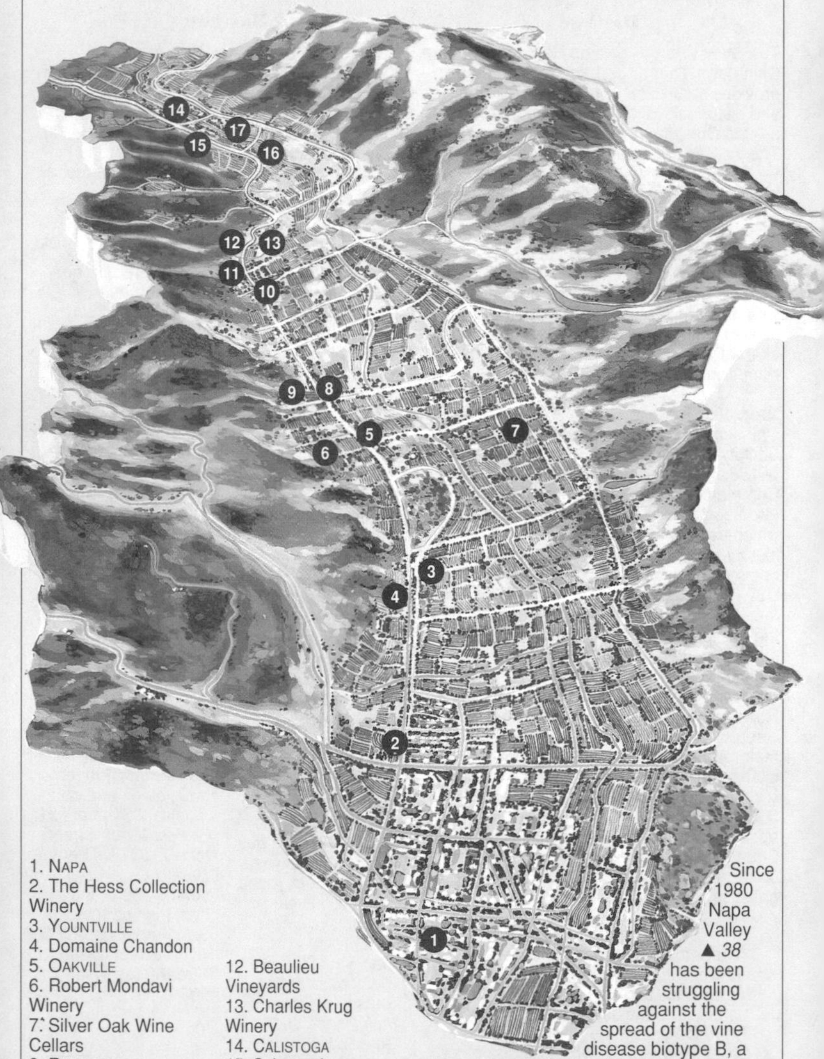

1. NAPA
2. The Hess Collection Winery
3. YOUNTVILLE
4. Domaine Chandon
5. OAKVILLE
6. Robert Mondavi Winery
7. Silver Oak Wine Cellars
8. RUTHERFORD
9. Inglenook Winery
10. SAINT HELENA
11. Beringer Vineyards
12. Beaulieu Vineyards
13. Charles Krug Winery
14. CALISTOGA
15. Schramsberg
16. Sterling Winery vineyards
17. Close Pegase

Since 1980 Napa Valley ▲ *38* has been struggling against the spread of the vine disease biotype B, a variant of the phylloxera that devastated European vineyards at the end of the 19th century, and which at that time spared American winegrowers.

The name "Napa" derives from an Indian word meaning "abundance".

California boasts nearly two hundred different wines.

The Napa Valley wine route runs from Napa to Calistoga, some 27 miles. The trip takes about an hour by car; coming from downtown San Francisco, take the Oakland Bay Bridge and Freeway I-80 as far as Vallejo, where Route 29 leads off to the town of Napa. The valley is home to about two hundred wineries, over a hundred of which have been founded since 1976. The vineyards cover an area of 30,300 acres and produce a wide variety of wines, usually from grapes of European origin, such as Chardonnay (white), Cabernet Sauvignon (red), Pinot Noir (red), Sauvignon (white) and Merlot (red). The wine is marketed under the name of the vine and the vineyard. There can be no doubt that Napa Valley today is a valuable center for research into viticulture; in recognition of this fact a number of great winemakers from France have opened wineries in California since the 1970's.

HISTORY OF NAPA VALLEY

California wine-making dates from the 18th century, when Franciscan monks planted vines around San Diego. By 1830 Communion wine was being made at Los Angeles. The first wine in Napa Valley was produced in 1853 by George Yount on the site of the town that after 1867 was to bear his name, Yountville. Serious winemaking did not begin, however, until the arrival of the Hungarian Agoston Haraszthy, who established himself between Sonoma and Napa in 1857 and planted quality vine stocks from Europe. Today Haraszthy is acclaimed as the founding father of local viticulture; he brought with him from Europe not only an extensive knowledge of wine-making, but also about two hundred varieties of vine, which he planted on 240 acres near Buena Vista. The University of California was also involved in the adaptation of vine varieties to the state's many microclimates, and as a result the industry prospered considerably between 1900 and 1919. After the Prohibition years reorganization was slow, because Americans still tended to prefer sweet drinks to dry wine. By the close of the 1970's, however, the great California wines, produced in the same way as their counterparts in Europe, began to acquire a solid reputation and to be exported to Europe. Local consumption in the United States and Canada has risen dramatically since the 1980's.

Napa Valley cellars are open between 10am and 5pm, by appointment. For a complete list of wineries, try the Visitors' Centre on Hallidie Plaza (Union Street). You can also obtain information on guided tours of vineyards from the Napa Valley Vintners' Association, tel: (707) 942 9775, or Napa Valley Grape Growers Association tel: (707) 944 8311.

Napa Valley is California's principal wine-producing area.

The greatest wineries rival the châteaux of Bordeaux.

NAPA

DOMAINE CARNEROS
(SW of the town), 1240 Duhig Road, Napa, tel: (707) 257 0101. Built in 1987, the house is a copy of the Château de la Marquetterie in Champagne, France, and is owned by the Taittinger family. Contact Catheryn August Shaw for details of opening times.

CARNEROS CREEK WINERY
1285 Dealy (Napa) Tel. (707) 253 9463. Old Sonoma Road, just before Domaine Carneros, coming out of Napa. If you enjoy wines made from the the Chardonnay and

Pinot Noir varieties of grape, do not miss Carneros Creek. This winery is a relatively small producer but it also makes Cabernet Sauvignon and Merlot wines.

THE HESS COLLECTION WINERY
4411 Redwood Road, tel: (707) 255 1144. For Cabernet Sauvignon and Chardonnay, take a slight detour before returning to Yountville on Route 29. The Hess Collection Winery on Redwood Road also has a contemporary art museum. No guide is provided for visiting the vineyards.

YOUNTVILLE
DOMAINE CHANDON
1 California Drive (Route 29), close to the California Veterans' Home, Yountville, tel: (707) 9442280. Moët & Chandon, the well-known French champagne firm, has been established here for twenty years now. The sparkling wines are made by the champagne method. Try the Reserve, Chandon Club Privé aged for at least six years, or the "blanc de noir" made with red grapes. The restaurant is pleasant, and the surrounding gardens are particularly attractive.

RUTHERFORD
INGLENOOK WINERY
1991 St Helena Highway, Rutherford, tel: (707) 967 3362. A fine building dating from 1880. The winery produces Chardonnay, Sauvignon Blanc, Riesling, Merlot, Zinfandel (red) and Pinot Noir varieties. A collection of photographs and contemporary documents gives an idea of what Inglenook and most of the rest of the valley looked like in the late 19th century. Tasting free, except in the case of the winery's Special Reserve.

WINE TRAIN
If you do not feel like covering the wine route by car, there is a luxury Pullman locomotive that does the circuit in three hours, three times daily from Napa (1275 McKinstry Street, tel: (800) 427 4124 or (707) 253 2111. Price: $60 with lunch included). The train provides a wine-tasting and restaurant service.

OAKVILLE

Oakville, like Rutherford, has a microclimate that is similar to that of Bordeaux, France.

ROBERT MONDAVI WINERY
7801 St Helena Highway, Oakville, tel: (707) 259 9463. Various guided tours are provided here. "At the close of the 19th century, vines were imported here from Burgundy and Bordeaux," the guide will inform you, as he begins his account of the early days of Napa Valley's most celebrated winery. The grapes are first fermented in stainless steel vats with the temperature carefully regulated. Some wines are aged in oak barrels that have been imported from France. Among the most famous products of the Robert Mondavi vineyard are their Cabernet Sauvignon and Pinot Noir wines. The association of Robert Mondavi with Philippe de

Rothschild (famed as producer of the great Médoc "premier grand cru", Mouton-Rothschild) has led to the world-renowned "Opus One", one of the best (and most expensive) wines produced in the state of California. The greatest French chefs are invited to give cookery courses at the school sponsored by Mondavi since 1976. The Robert Mondavi Winery was built in 1986, but its architecture evokes the Spanish colonial era (Mission style). Contemporary art exhibitions are also held here.

SILVER OAK WINE CELLARS
915 Oakville Cross Road, tel: (707) 944 8808. This small property produces Cabernet Sauvignon only. The grapes are grown in three separate vineyards, one of which is in Napa Valley.

DOMAINE CARNEROS
CATHERYN AUGUST SHAW
Retail Superstore
CA 94581 ◆ 707.257.0101
◆ FAX: 707.257.1920

California produced 374 million gallons of wine in 1991.

At Saint Helena, the Stratford Winery makes an excellent Chardonnay.

SAINT HELENA

BERINGER VINEYARDS
2000 Main Street, Saint Helena, tel: (707) 963 4812. One of the oldest established vineyards in California (founded 1879). The Rhine House, an Art Nouveau building, was completed in 1883. Original, old-style winemaking methods are taught here; the winery's reserves of Chardonnay and Cabernet are renowned, as are the sweeter wines made late in the season. There is also a professional cookery school and a program of seminars. Guided tours of the cellars.

BEAULIEU VINEYARDS.
1960, Highway 29, Saint Helena, tel: (707) 967 3529. Open daily 10am–5pm. A French couple, Monsieur and Madame Latour, started this estate in 1900. They were soon renowned throughout California for the quality of their wines and also for Madame Latour's charity work. Their wines (Pinot noir and Cabernet Sauvignon) are reckoned among the best in the United States.

CHARLES KRUG WINERY.
2800 Main Street, Highway 29, Saint Helena, tel: (707) 963 5057. The building here was constructed in 1862. Its owner was the second winemaker to come to Napa Valley. The Mondavi family – Robert Mondavi left their business to found his own firm in Oakville ◆350 in 1966 – purchased it in 1943 and has since produced Cabernet, Pinot Noir and Chardonnay wines. Tasting (payment is requested) of C.K. Mondavi wines.

CALISTOGA

Calistoga is a hybrid name, made up by joining California and Saratoga; the town was founded by Sam Brannan ▲ 48.

SCHRAMSBERG WINERY.
(4 miles south of Calistoga, west of Highway 128), 1400 Schramsberg Road, Calistoga, tel: (707) 942 4558. This vineyard was planted by Jacob Schram in 1862 and became famous thanks to a short story by Robert Louis Stevenson, "The Silverado Squatters" (in *The Road to Silverado*). The estate was nearly in ruins when Mr and Mrs Davies took over its restoration, and today it is one of the most celebrated producers of sparkling wines in California. The champagne made here is of very high quality (it was served at the White House in 1972), and there are excellent sparkling wines, notably a "blanc de blanc" and a rosé called Cuvée de Pinot; the best-known is the "blanc de noir".

STERLING VINEYARDS
1111 Dunaweal Lane, Calistoga, tel: (707) 942 3344. The architecture of the buildings is reminiscent of Greek monasteries.The estate itself is perched on the summit of a hill, which is reached by means of a funicular (the price of the trip includes the wine-tasting as well). You are conducted around the vineyards and then to the cellars, which are surrounded by well-tended lawns.The Cabernet Sauvignon is quite straightforward to start with, and can be followed by the Chardonnay. Sterling is perhaps most famous for its Sauvignon Blanc.

CLOS PEGASE
1060 Dunaweal Lane, Calistoga, tel: (707) 942 4981. Built in 1986 after an architectural contest arranged by the owner and the San Francisco Museum of Modern Art ▲ 230, the property is post-modern in style. The site is beautiful, and there are guided tours of the property, in addition to an important collection of sculptures in the grounds. In the cellars try the Chardonnay, the Cabernet and the Merlot.

SILVERADO TRAIL
This is a picturesque trail, running parallel to Route 29, which passes through a number of vineyards.

BALLOON TRIPS
The adventurous may prefer to take a balloon trip over the California vineyards at daybreak (price: from $165 per person inclusive of champagne breakfast). The balloons take off from Yountville; afterwards, there is a champagne lunch at the Domaine Chandon. Reservations: PO Box 2860, Yountville California, 94599 tel: (707) 994 0228 or (800) 253 2224.

The south of San Francisco has many unique sights and interesting walking tours. From extravagant houses to museums, Stanford University and Silicon Valley, there is plenty of choice.

SAN MATEO

FILOLI ESTATE ★
On Canada Road, near Woodside, tel: (415) 364 2880. This fine, English-style brick building now belongs to the state of California. It was built by the mega-rich William Bourne at the turn of the century. Its name, Filoli, is an abbreviation of Bourne's motto: "Fight, Love, Live A Good Life". Now a museum, the Filoli Estate is surrounded by magnificent gardens which are open to the public.

PALO ALTO

STANFORD UNIVERSITY
The campus here, with its large buildings in assorted styles and its wide green spaces, is a haven of peace. The Stanford family, which gave its name to this prestigious university, has its mausoleum here.

STANFORD UNIVERSITY MUSEUM OF ART
Museum Way, tel: (415) 723 4177. The oldest museum in the American West: the principal interest is the collection of sculptures, including notably Rodin's Gates of Hell.

LOS ALTOS

LOS ALTOS FOOTHILL COLLEGE
Not far from Stanford,

on Highway 280, there is a museum of electronics that describes the rise of Silicon Valley ● *76*, from the small firm started by Hewlett and Packard to the giant manufacturers of microprocessors.

SANTA CLARA

MISSION SANTA CLARA DE ASIS
Reconstructed on the campus of the university, which is the oldest in California (1851), this mission gives the visitor some insight into what life was probably like for the first of California's settlers.

SAN JOSÉ
A blend of old Victorian houses and avant-garde architecture, this town has been growing fast in recent years on account of its proximity to Silicon Valley ● *76*. It currently has a population of about one million.

WINCHESTER MYSTERY HOUSE
525 South Winchester Boulevard. tel: (408) 247 2101. With its 160 rooms, 2,000 doors and 10,000 windows, this extravagant house was built by Sarah Winchester, the widow of the rifle manufacturer. She firmly believed she would die the moment the house was completed, with the result that she had it constantly built and rebuilt over a period of thirty-eight years.

ROSICRUCIAN EGYPTIAN MUSEUM
Park Avenue. Naglee, tel: (408) 947 3635. An astonishing collection of mummies and other Egyptian antiquities are displayed here.

MUSEUM OF ART
110 South Market Street, tel: (408) 294 2787. An interesting museum installed in a former post office.

SAN JOSE HISTORICAL MUSEUM
635 Phelan Avenue. Tel. (408) 287 2290 Shows open-air reconstructions of Indian life and early colonial buildings.

VALLEY-SPEAK
Like all valleys, this one has created its own local slang, reflecting its new high-tech identity and "Silicon Culture".
● *Fortune* – Bible of the US financial world. It publishes a list of the nation's top five hundred companies, a list that Apple joined in record time after its creation.
● *Chip* – Silicon chip, the driving force behind computer technology.
● *Mip* – Millions of instructions per second, the unit for measuring the power of chips. To keep pace with their growth, the valley now works in teraMips (1 teraMip = a thousand billion mips).
● *Electronic highways* – Pathways that exchange and guide the data propelled in every direction by chips in volumes of teraMips. Electronic highways are to telephone communications what books were to stone tablets.
● *680X0, JPEG, RISC, HIGH SIERRA, XANADU* – These are the names of some of the many formats and programs that stud the speech of Silicon Valley residents.
● *Garage* – A familiar word, but one with mythical significance in the Valley. According to legend, it was in a garage that the student geniuses Jobs and Wozniak invented the first microprocessor ● *76*.

THEMATIC ITINERARIES

◆ Shopping in San Francisco

San Francisco has always been a mercantile city. It has remained a wonderful place to shop, because it is easy to get about without a car, either on foot or by public transport. "Let's go shopping!" say Americans, when the urge to consume grips them. Here in San Francisco the customer is king, and his realm encompasses both the stores of Union Square and the shops on Fillmore and Union Streets. Prices are highly competitive for many products, notably sportswear and electronic gadgets, but beware of tourist areas such as Fisherman's Wharf and Chinatown.

UNION SQUARE

Union Square is really a shopper's dream; all the streets around it have remarkable stores, particularly Maiden Lane ▲ 218.

DEPARTMENT STORES
Nieman Marcus on the intersection of Stockton and Geary Streets; *Saks Fifth Avenue* (384 Post Street), *Macy's* (Stockton and O'Farrell Streets), *Nordstrom*, occupying the top three floors of the San Francisco Shopping Centre and *Emporium* (835 Market Street) are San Francisco's main department stores ◆ 220.

THE SF SHOPPING CENTRE (Market and 5th Streets) which opened in October 1988, offers over a hundred shops on its nine floors.

READY-TO-WEAR
There are three ready-to-wear lines based in San Francisco: *Esprit* (South of Market), *The Gap* and *Banana Republic*. All are world-famous for their reasonably priced sports and leisure wear (open seven days a week).

◆ THE GAP has twelve outlets (main tel. 952 4400), two of which are downtown at 890 Market Street and 100 Post Street.

◆ BANANA REPUBLIC has three shops: one is at 256 Grant Avenue. Main tel. 777 0250. Products are slightly more up-market than those at The Gap and Esprit.

◆ CAMERA BOUTIQUE for cameras, video equipment and film, rentals and repairs.

342 Kearny Street Tel. 982 4946. (closed Sundays).

◆ THE NORTH FACE, 180 Post Street, has high quality equipment and accessories for sport, outdoor activities and camping: tents, sleeping bags, and so on. This shop, which is open seven days a week, has maintained its excellent reputation for over twenty years.

◆ GUMPS, 135 Post Street (tel. 982 1616) is known for its jade jewelry and other luxury items, including home

accessories and oriental products (closed Sundays).

◆ HOUSE OF BLUE JEANS, at 1029 Market Street, Civic Center. Tel. 255 0575. A major Levi's outlet.

OPENING HOURS
In general, shops open from 10am to 6pm Monday to Saturday, and 12 noon to 5pm on Sundays. The exception is Chinatown, where the shops are open every day from 10am to 10pm, and Ghirardelli Square and Pier 39, where they are open from 10am to 9pm Monday to Saturday (later in summer). The SF Shopping Centre opens 9.30am to 8pm Monday to Saturday. *Emporium*, *Macy's* and *Nordstrom* are open to 9pm and on Sundays from 12 noon to 6pm.

FLEA MARKET
567 Sutter Street (one block from Union Square). There are bargains galore to be had at the San Francisco flea market.

CHINATOWN

Grant Avenue is lined with shops selling Asian products, as well as every kind of gadget and kitsch object.

◆ COACH STORE ★.
190 Post Street. Tel. 392 1772. For quality leatherwork (more or less expensive). All items sold here are guaranteed for life.

FISHERMAN'S WHARF

◆ PATAGONIA ★.
A first-class sporting goods and clothes shop located at 770 North Point.

◆ KRAZY KAPS ★.
For stetsons and cowboy hats in general, this is the place to go. *Krazy Kaps* (Pier 39) is unique of its kind, offering hats of every type from velvet caps to "Forty-Niner" visors ● *82* (for men and women).

◆ THE CANNERY,
2801 Leavenworth. This incorporates three floors of shops, restaurants and souvenir stalls. There are also several art galleries, such as Leavenworth Jefferson.

◆ GHIRARDELLI SQUARE.
A diminutive mall filled with clothes stores, bookstalls and tourist souvenirs, and offering Central and Latin American craftwork at the Folk Art International Gallery.

HAIGHT-ASHBURY

ART GALLERIES
Paintings, collages and jewelry are sold at *O'Desso*, 384 Hayes Street.

SECOND-HAND RECORDS
At *Recycled Records*, 1377 Haight Street; *Rough Trade*, 1329 Haight Street; and *Reckless Records*, 1401 Haight Street. All three shops are open seven days a week.

SECOND-HAND CLOTHES
For original 1960's and 1970's clothes try *Buffalo Exchange*, 555 Haight Street, and *Aardvark's Odd Ark*, 1501 Haight Street. Also try *Wasteland ▲ 284*, 1660 Haight Street.

NORTH BEACH

◆ QUANTITY POSTCARDS
Situated at 1441 Grant Avenue (Green Street), this shop offers all kinds of postcards, old and new; open every day.

SOUTH OF MARKET

◆ ESPRIT
At 499 Illinois Street (16th Street). Sells clothes for all ages, but particularly for teenagers: usually offers excellent value for money.

PACIFIC HEIGHTS

On Fillmore Street there are plenty of luxury clothes stores, but prices are high by comparison with Europe.

SIZE EQUIVALENTS	
UK	US
MEN'S SHOES	
8	8
9	8½
10	9½
11	10½
12	11½
WOMEN'S SHOES	
4	6
5½	6½
6	7
6½	7½
7	8
MENSWEAR	
36	36
38	38
40	40
42	42
44	44
WOMEN'S CLOTHING	
6	4
8	6
10	8
12	10
14	12

San Francisco is the unrivaled cultural focus of Northern California. Most of the city's theaters, concert halls and art galleries are concentrated in Civic Center and Union Square, while museums, libraries and cinemas have overflowed all over town.

CIVIC CENTER
◆ REGENCY, 1 Van Ness Avenue/Sutter Street, Tel. 885 6773.
FISHERMAN'S WHARF
◆ CINEPLEX ODEON Powell/Bay Streets, Tel. 403 8186.

MUSICAL PRODUCTIONS
◆ CURRAN THEATER 445 Geary Street (Mason Street). Tel. 474 3800.
◆ GOLDEN GATE THEATER 1 Taylor Street (Market Street/ Golden Gate Avenue) Tel. 474 3800.
◆ THE ORPHEUM 1192 Market Street (8th St) Tel. 474 3800.
◆ PRESIDIO PERFORMING ARTS CENTRE 99 Morga Ave. (Presidio) Tel. 351 1945

MUSEUMS
The *Culture Pass* ($12.50) allows entry to the five museums of the Golden Gate Park. The pass is sold at the Visitor Information Center (Hallidie Plaza).

MOVIE THEATERS
◆ CLAY, Fillmore/ Clay Streets, Tel. 352 0810.
CASTRO
◆ CASTRO Castro/Market Streets, Tel. 621 6120.

◆ ROXIE 3117 16th Street, Tel. 863 1087.
JAPANTOWN
◆ AMC Kabuki, 8 Post/Fillmore Streets, Tel. 931 9800. In the Japantown center.

THEATERS
Many theaters are concentrated east of Union Square:
◆ AMERICAN CONSERVATORY THEATER (ACT), 30 Grant Avenue. Tel. 834 3200. Classical and contemporary plays. Recently reopened.
◆ GEARY THEATER 415 Geary Street, Tel. 749 2228. This theater, which was damaged by the 1989 earthquake, reopened at the end of 1995.
◆ MARINE'S MEMORIAL THEATER 609 Sutter Street (Mason Street). Tel. 771 6900. Extensive repertoire.
◆ THEATER ON THE SQUARE Kensington

Park Hotel, 450 Post Street (Powell Street). Tel. 433 9500. Comedies and musical comedies.
◆ STAGE DOOR THEATER 420 Mason Street (Geary Street). Tel. 749 2228. Classical and contemporary plays. Away from the Union Square area:
◆ CLIMATE 252 8th Street (Howard Street), Tel. 978 2345. Experimental, avant-garde theater.
◆ THEATER ARTAUD 450 Florida Street, Tel. 621 7797. Experimental theater.
◆ MAGIC THEATER Ft Mason Center, Bldg D. Works by contemporary playwrights.

CLASSICAL MUSIC
◆ The San Francisco Symphony Orchestra gives its concerts at the Davies Symphony Hall, 201 Van Ness Ave (Grove Street). Tel. 864 6000.
◆ HERBST THEATER 401 Van Ness Ave. Tel. 621 6600. Concert hall used for music, lectures and dance.

OPERA
◆ WAR MEMORIAL OPERA HOUSE 301 Van Ness Avenue (Grove Street), Tel. 861 4008. Performances of the San Francisco Ballet are held here. The opera season lasts from September to December.

CONCERT HALLS
For classical music and pop concerts, as well as dance programs:
◆ CIVIC AUDITORIUM 99 Grove Street (beside City Hall), Tel. 974 4060.

RADIO			
AM:	**FM:**		
◆ SPORT: KCBS **740** KGO **810**	◆ CLASSICAL MUSIC: KDFC **102.1**	◆ JAZZ: KCS **91.1** KKSE **103.7** KPOQ **89.5**	◆ TOP 40: KITS **105.3** KMEL **106.1**
◆ JAZZ, POP, ROCK: (No commercials) KQED **88.5** KPFA **94.1** KNOB **1510** (jazz)	◆ COUNTRY MUSIC: KSAN **94.9** ◆ ALTERNATIVE ROCK: KUSF **90.3** ◆ DANCE MUSIC: KBLX **102.9**	◆ ROCK: KOIT **96.5** KRQR **97.3** KFOG **104.5**	◆ NEWS: **88.5** KQED (no commercials) ◆ CHURCH SERVICES: **106.5** KEAR

ADVERTISING PUBLICATIONS
The newspaper racks of San Francisco are stocked with free weekly publications (issued on Wednesdays), such as the *San Francisco Weekly*, which offer cultural programs and restaurant addresses that may interest visitors.

ART GALLERIES
SOUTH OF MARKET
◆ ANSEL ADAMS CENTER 250 4th Street, Tel. 495 7000. Includes photography galleries, one devoted to work by Adams. Open 11am–5pm, Tues. to Sun.
◆ CROWN POINT PRESS 20 Hawthorne Street (2nd and 3rd Sts), Tel. 974 6273.
UNION SQUARE
◆ MEYEROVICH, 251 Post St, Suite 405 Tel. 421 7171
◆ DENENBERG FINE ARTS GALLERY 257 Grant Avenue, Tel. 788 8411.
◆ FRAENKEL 49 Geary Street, Tel. 981 2661.
◆ HAINES GALLERY, 49 Geary Street, Tel. 397 8114 .
◆ JACK HANLEY GALLERY 41 Grant Ave, Tel. 291 8911.
◆ RENA BRANSTEIN 77 Geary Street, Tel. 982 3292.
◆ PAULE ANGLIM GALLERY 14 Geary Street, Tel. 433 2710.
◆ HARCOURTS MODERN AND CONTEMPORARY ART 706 Mission, Tel. 227 0400.
◆ MODERNISM, 685 Market St, Suite 290, Tel. 541 0461.

TEAM SPORTS
◆ CANDLESTICK PARK South of the city (Freeway 101). For American football (the San Francisco Forty-Niners, Tel. 462 2249) and baseball (the San Francisco Giants, tel.467 8000) ▲ *82.*
◆ ALAMEDA COUNTY COLISEUM Oakland, access via BART Metro ◆ *332* (Coliseum stop). Home of the Oakland A's. Tel. (510) 569 BASS. If you prefer basketball, the Golden State Warriors play here. Tel. 510 569 2121.

BOOKSTORES
NORTH BEACH
◆ CITY LIGHTS BOOKSTORE 261 Columbus Avenue, Tel. 362 8193. Open daily 10am–midnight. Specialist bookstore (poetry, art, etc).
◆ EAST WIND BOOKS 1435 Stockton Street, Tel. 772 5877. Open Mon.–Sat., 10am–6pm, Sun. 12–5pm. Asiatic bookstore.
◆ SIERRA CLUB BOOKSTORE 730 Polk Street (Civic Center), Tel. 923 5600. Environmental bookshop. Open 10am–5pm except Sun.
◆ THOMAS BROS MAPS & BOOKS. 550 Jackson Street. Tel. 981 7520. Books, guidebooks and maps. Open 9.30am–5.30pm.

Closed Sat. and Sun.
UNION SQUARE
◆ MCDONALD'S BOOKSHOP, 48 Turk Street, Tel. 673 2235. Open Mon.–Wed., 10am-6pm Thur.-Sat. 10.30am–6.45pm. Second-hand books.
NOB HILL
◆ EUROPEAN BOOK COMPANY 925 Larkin Street (Post Street), Tel. 474 0626. Open Mon.–Fri., 9.30am–6pm, Sat. 9.30am–5pm. International press, general books.
MISSION
◆ ADOBE 3166 16th Street (Guerrero Street). Tel. 864 3936. Rare and secondhand books.
HAIGHT–ASHBURY
◆ THE BOOKSMITH 1644 Haight Street, Tel. 863 8688. General bookstore.

TICKETS
◆ TIC BAY AREA Stockton Street (Union Square) No telephone, personal callers only. Open Tue.–Sat. 12am–7.30pm. Half-price tickets for same-day performances, in which case only travelers' checks and cash are accepted.
◆ BASS/TICKETMASTER Seats available for purchase by telephone (762 2277) with credit card (this will incur a small booking charge).
◆ TOWER RECORDS Bay Street and Columbus Avenue intersection, Tel. 885 0500.
◆ TOWER CLASSICAL Opposite Tower Records. Tel. 441 4880
◆ WHEREHOUSE RECORDS 2083 Union Street (Webster Street), Tel. 346 0944.
◆ ENTERTAINMENT TICKETFINDER Tel. 756 1414 or (800) 523 1515.
◆ CITY BOX OFFICE (Sherman Clay & Co.) 153 Kearny Street, Tel. 392 4400.

TELEVISION STATIONS
ABC (American Broadcasting Company) Channel 7, KGO
CBS (Columbia Broadcasting System) Channel 5, KPIX
KTVU–FOX Channel 2, running for the past two years with an intellectual audience.
NBC (National Broadcasting Company) Channel 4
PBS (Public Broadcasting System), Channel 9, KQED
CABLE CHANNELS: CNN (Cable News Network) for news; HBO (Home Box Office) for films. Most hotels in San Francisco have televisions. Some subscribe to private video networks on the "pay per view system", whereby the viewer pays on a film-by-film basis.

357

The word "jazz" first emerged in 1913 to designate a brand new kind of music. At that time there was a profusion of bars in the Barbary Coast area where people could go to dance, and the variety of music was astonishing. During the 1920's San Francisco saw the arrival of many black groups from the south, at which time it became, with New Orleans, one of the pivots of the jazz scene. The jazz scene today, which incorporates the latest electronic innovations in sound and video images, is enjoying a new lease of life with the proliferation of dinner-jazz evenings and clubs.

OAKLAND ▲ 308

◆ KEYSTONE KORNER YOSHI'S ★. The most active jazz club in the region has recently moved to Jack London Square. Dizzy Gillespie was a regular visitor to this East Bay establishment adjoining a Japanese restaurant. Yoshi's recently improved its acoustics and now attracts some of America's finest musicians. Open until 10pm Wed.–Thurs. and until 11pm Fri.–Sat. Jam sessions every Mon. There are concerts, usually at 8pm and 10pm, each evening.

EMERYVILLE

Away from the center is another club that is well worth the trip. Take Freeway 80 toward Oakland and turn off at Emeryville.
◆ KIMBALL'S EAST & KIMBALL'S CARNIVAL ★. 5800 Shellmound, Emeryville. The latest in-club: four-hundred-seat premises inside a shopping center. Open daily. Concerts

JAZZ AND ALL THAT ART
Bands play on Fillmore Street at the start of July. Ever since Charlie Mingus came to the Monterey Festival south of San Francisco during the 1950's, the second city of California has been a jazz Mecca. The festival takes place in September.
SAN FRANCISCO JAZZ FESTIVAL
This festival takes place over two weeks in October and November.

Wed.–Sun. 9pm–2am. *Kimball's Carnival*, downstairs, hosts evenings of salsa and latin music, Wed.–Sun. (8pm–2am). Tel. (510) 653 5300

NOB HILL
◆ NEW ORLEANS ROOM At the Fairmont Hotel. An intimate club specializing in jazz standards from the 1920's, '30's and '40's. Live music Tues. to Sat. until 1am.

NORTH BEACH
◆ JAZZ AT PEARL'S An Italian restaurant with a thriving jazz club; nightly sessions.

CASTRO
◆ CAFÉ DU NORD. Jazz and blues every evening; cabaret on

Sundays. Billiard room. Authentic 1950's atmosphere.

SOUTH OF MARKET
◆ UP & DOWN CLUB. 1151 Folsom Street. Tel. 626 2388. On the ground floor is a bar and restaurant. The jazz club is on the first floor. It stays open until 2am. Disco Fri. to Sun. and Tues. Jazz and blues on Wed. and Thurs.
◆ JAZZ ON THE BAY The Ramp, 885 China Basin (17th Street). Tel. 415 621 2378. Built as a bridge between a yacht club and the docks, this club has a terrace and offers live music Thurs. to Sun. Well worth a visit. Restaurant open Mon.–Fri. Only

brunch and BBQ on Sat. and Sun.

UNION SQUARE
◆ REDWOOD ROOM A quiet piano bar with soothing décor, situated in the Clift Hotel. Jacket and tie essential. Open from 6pm Fri. and Sat.

ADDRESSES
CAFÉ DU NORD
2170 Market Street,
Tel. (415) 861 5016
JAZZ AT PEARL'S
256 Columbus Ave,
Tel. (415) 291 8255
KIMBALL'S EAST
5800 Shellmound Street, Emeryville,
Tel. (510) 658 2555
NEW ORLEANS ROOM
950 Mason Street
(California Street),
Tel. (415) 772 5259
REDWOOD ROOM
495 Geary Street
(Taylor Street),
Tel. (415) 775 4700
YOSHI'S
6030 Claremont Street
(*Berkeley Line*,
BART), Oakland,
Tel. (510) 652 9200
MONTEREY FESTIVAL
Tel. (408) 373 3366
JAZZ & ALL THAT ART
Tel. (415) 346 4446
SAN FRANCISCO
FESTIVAL
Tel. 864 5449

Since the beginning of the 20th century, San Francisco's nightlife has been among the most intense in America, true to the traditions of the Gold Rush. Today there are over two thousand bars, nightclubs and cabarets in the city. The liveliest districts are South of Market and North Beach; the latest fashionable venue is Valencia Street, west of the Mission district, between 16th and 24th Streets. Bars usually offer live music and charge a cover price of $2 to $8.

THE CASTRO

Gays represent nearly ten percent of San Francisco's population, and the gay district of the Castro has plenty of nightclubs and bars to choose from.

◆ MIDNIGHT SUN
One of the oldest gay bars, specializing in films and original video-clips.

◆ JOSIE'S CABARET AND JUICE JOINT
A vegetarian restaurant by day, after 9pm this establishment is an excellent introduction to authentic San Francisco "weirdness". Theme nights (8pm) and gay shows (10pm) Wednesdays and Saturdays.

CIVIC CENTER

◆ GREAT AMERICAN MUSIC HALL
A former cabaret featuring local performers: comics, dancers, and well-known rock, jazz and blues artists. Shows begin at 8pm; food available until 10.30pm.

NORTH BEACH

On Columbus and Broadway, and lower down on Grant Avenue, are several cafés-concert, including:

◆ FINOCCHIO'S ▲ 168
A transvestite club featuring three shows per night (8.30pm, 10pm, 11.30pm) on Tues., Thurs., Fri., Sat., Sun. Clients can dance here; come dressed in leather if you can.

SOUTH OF MARKET

Most clubs in this district are around Folsom Street, between 13th and 4th Streets.

◆ SOUND FACTORY
A twin of the club of the same name in

New York City, it boasts three dance floors equipped with state-of-the-art sound and lighting.

◆ D V 8
A two-level disco with dance space totalling over 2 acres. Pop, rock or high-tech music.

◆ SLIM'S
Excellent rock groups perform in this well-run, pleasant club.

◆ DNA LOUNGE
Noisy disco featuring almost nightly rock concerts (9pm) followed by dancing until 4am.

◆ PARADISE LOUNGE
Disco with billiard hall; nightly rock concerts.

ALCOHOL

The legal age for buying alcoholic drinks or entering nightclubs is twenty-one. Always carry ID, as it may be requested at any time in liquor stores, bars and restaurants in San Francisco. The sale of alcohol in nightclubs is permitted until 2am only. Most bars feature a "happy hour" (5pm–7pm as a rule) when drinks may be purchased for half price.

ADDRESSES

SOUND FACTORY
525 Harrison Street,
Tel. 543 1300

DNA LOUNGE
375 11th Street
(Harrison Street),
Tel. 626 1409

DV8
540 Howard Street,
Tel. 777 1419

FINOCCHIO'S
506 Broadway,
Tel. 982 9388

GREAT AMERICAN MUSIC HALL
859 O'Farrell Street
(Polk Street),
Tel. 885 0750

JOSIE'S CABARET
3583 16th Street
(Market Street),
Tel. 861 7933

MIDNIGHT SUN
4067 18th Street,
Tel. 861 4186

PARADISE LOUNGE
1501 Folsom Street
(12th Street),
Tel. 861 6906

SLIM'S
333 11th Street
(Harrison Street),
Tel. 621 3330

It Came from Beneath the Sea,
dir. Robert Gordon (1955).

Escape from Alcatraz,
dir. Don Siegel (1979).

Beginning with movies shot in Hollywood, and moving on to real-life locations, the cinema has always been drawn to San Francisco's spectacular setting and atmosphere. Favorite locations include the skyscrapers (the killer in *Dirty Harry* operates from the top of one); the bay (particularly Alcatraz); and the Golden Gate Bridge (one shot of this, and we know instantly where the action is taking place). Directors have exploited every aspect of San Francisco.

CITY OF DANGER

The 1940's saw the demise of the gangster movie and the rise of the *film noir*, in which the hero was invariably a private detective. In 1941 John Huston made *The Maltese Falcon*, based on the book by Dashiell Hammett ● *132*. This, Huston's first movie, was a huge success that eclipsed two earlier versions of the story. The director set out not so much to show the city as it was (most of the filming was done in the studio), but to convey the idea of a corrupt town through the use of indoor locations such as the detective's office and the villains' private villas. San Francisco scarcely features, except in the aerial scene of Golden Gate Bridge ▲ *242* at the start of the movie, the scene of the death of Archer, the detective's associate, in Bush Street, and one or two night scenes. The spectator's idea of the city is formed by the actors' behavior; notably that of Sam Spade (Humphrey Bogart), who turns in the guilty Brigid, a woman he loves only slightly less than he loves his home town.

THE LABYRINTH

San Francisco was perceived as the ideal location for several movies in the "urban labyrinth" style, in which the rôle of the *femme fatale* is associated with the character of the city itself. In *Lady from Shanghai* (Orson Welles, 1946) the action turns into a nightmare, concluding in the hall of mirrors at "Playland at the Beach".

MYSTERY TOWN

Four movies by Alfred Hitchcock use San Francisco as a backdrop. The final scene of *The Birds* (1963) features the anguish of the girl escaping from Bodega Bay to safety in San Francisco, while Golden Gate Bridge in the distance is obscured by a cloud of vampire birds. In *Vertigo* (1958), which was filmed entirely in San Francisco (Paramount Studios), Hitchcock includes all the city's best-known sites: notably the Palace of Fine Arts on Baker and Beach streets ▲ *238*, the Palace of the Legion of Honor in Lincoln Park ▲ *248*, and Fort Point ▲ *241* (for the scene where the heroine throws herself into the bay). Finally, the first meeting between James Stewart and the mysterious Madeleine (Kim Novak) occurs at *Ernie's*, 847 Montgomery Street, Tel. 397 5969, which is still an excellent French restaurant.

"THE STREETS OF SAN FRANCISCO"

This 119-episode television series, starring Michael Douglas and Karl Malden, shows that times have changed. Both TV and cinema tend nowadays to use real-life settings as opposed to the studio. The plots of this series supply what amounts to a virtual guided tour of San Francisco. Standard cop and detective movies that

A View to a Kill, dir. John Glen (1985).

495

Magnum Force, dir. Ted Post (1974), the second of the Dirty Harry movies.

Humphrey Bogart in *The Maltese Falcon*, dir. John Huston (1941)

use San Francisco as a background location invariably feature car chases and elaborate stunts. *Bullitt* (1968), directed by Peter Yates, starred Steve McQueen as the honest cop at the wheel of his Ford Mustang; with *Bullitt*, *film noir* psychological tension was definitively ousted by straight stunt work as a source of drama.

THE CITY FROM ABOVE

The action movie had been born. Next, Clint Eastwood starred as *Dirty Harry* (1971), who pursues a psychopath preying on the city from the top of a skyscraper. In this movie directed by Don Siegel (the first of a series of five), the despair and violence of the characters stems directly from the city itself.

San Francisco is beautifully filmed from above, from a distance, and in every possible light. Ordered to "clean up" the city, Harry Callahan is permanently on the point of giving up completely. In *Escape from Alcatraz* (1979), also by Don Siegel, the documentary style serves a semi-fictional purpose; Frank Morris, the Clint Eastwood character, and his accomplices really did succced in escaping from Alcatraz in 1962, just a year before the famous penitentiary closed.

Steve McQueen in *Bullitt*, dir. Peter Yates (1968)

Task is Cautious
A PEACE TALK FLURRY

San Francisco
Chronicle LARGEST
DAILY

DISASTER CITY

In the James Bond movie *A View to a Kill* (1985), the inevitable megalomaniac plans to witness the destruction of Silicon Valley ● *76* from his dirigible hot-air balloon. The means of destruction is significant: the villain triggers an earthquake, and in the bizarre finale dies by falling out of his balloon above Golden Gate Bridge. When this movie came out, a number of people moved away from San Francisco.

THE CITY AS SYMBOL

The emblem of San Francisco will always be the Golden Gate Bridge, as in the poster for Hitchcock's *The Birds* (1963). The city itself harbors the bitterness and violence of *Dirty Harry*; the gloomy ambiguities of *Vertigo* and its threat to the "American Dream"; the extraterrestrials of *Invasion of the Body Snatchers* (Kaufmann, 1978); the giant octopus of *It Came from Beneath the Sea* (Robert Gordon, 1955); and the earthquakes of *San Francisco* (W. van Dyke, 1936) and *A View to a Kill*. So many visions of death are set in San Francisco, which somehow always emerges unscathed.

◆ DASHIELL HAMMETT'S SAN FRANCISCO

Monroe Street was renamed Dashiell Hammett Street in 1988.

END
DASHIELL HAMMETT
MONROE

When Dashiell Hammett died in New York on January 10, 1961, his name passed into legend. His courage at the time of the McCarthy witchhunts ten years earlier, which had earned him six months in prison, was much praised, and he was credited with inventing the detective thriller when the magazine *Black Mask* published his first Continental Op adventure in 1923. Seven years later came the birth of Hammett's character Sam Spade, the archetypal private eye, described by Ellery Queen as "the wild man from San Francisco who always calls a spade a spade".

Continental Op and Sam Spade, detectives, were modeled on Dashiell Hammett's real-life experiences as a Pinkerton agent. But they also owe plenty to San Francisco, where most of their adventures are set. Though Hammett himself preferred New York and Hollywood, his characters (who were his doubles) were fiercely attached to the "Frisco" of Prohibition, speakeasies, dockland drug-peddling, fight nights and racetracks. When, in *Red Harvest* (1929), Continental Op arrives in Personville, Montana, the first thing he says is that he is from San Francisco; and when the case is solved he quits the scene announcing that he is going back there.

THE STREETS OF SAN FRANCISCO, 1920's STYLE

Sam Spade lives on Post Street, which allows his creator to describe particular places there, such as a garage for automobile repairs, a bookstore, a drugstore and the *Fern Café*: all places Hammett knew well. Hammett also made reference to other streets around the Civic Center, such as Eddy Street (the Hyde Street intersection), where the corpse of Bob Teale is discovered in a story that foreshadows *The Maltese Falcon* (1930). The Geary Theater (where Shakespeare was performed in 1929), and various hotels and restaurants (*John's Grill* is one of several that remain from Hammett's time) all epitomize the 1920's setting of his books. Unremarkable locations such as post offices also have their part to play: for instance the one that has an exit on Mission Street offers the best route through to the *Remedial*, a pawnshop of high standing with Hammett's characters.

WHEELS AND TRANSPORTATION

As practical men with a horror of walking anywhere when they can ride, Spade and the Op are authorities on how to get around San Francisco. For taxis, Sam usually calls Greystone 4500, though he is just as likely to go down to the Union Square rank. Information about trams is also abundant (the Hyde Street stop is close to Spade's place), along with mentions of buses (the Van Ness Avenue halt), train stations (Pickwick on Fifth Street and the Third and Townsend Street Station), garages (Post Street and South of Golden Gate Avenue) and ferries (the Oakland and Couffignal Island crossings).

PROMISING NEIGHBORHOODS

During Prohibition anyone with the means could go up to the North Beach speakeasies to relax: *Ryck's*, *Healy's* and *Pigatti's* were famous dives. They could also dine and dance in one of the restaurants on George Street, or at Julius' Castle on Telegraph Hill. Chinatown, naturally, was part of the Hammett scene. At the end of one inquiry the hero-narrator decides never again to eat in a Chinese restaurant, in fact to avoid the area altogether. Golden Gate Bridge and the adjoining park are also part of Hammett's world.

'FRISCO

Dashiell Hammett always loved San Francisco, though he would seldom admit it; and he shared his affection for the city with his readers. His descriptions of real and invented places there helped to build the myth of 'Frisco as a mysterious, dangerous city.'

USEFUL ADDRESSES

- ⚘ View
- Ⓒ City center
- ⌸• Isolated
- ⊕ Luxury restaurant
- ◑ Typical restaurant
- ○ Budget restaurant
- 🏛 Luxury hotel
- ⌂ Typical hotel
- ⌂ Budget hotel
- Ⓟ Car park
- 🚗 Supervised garage
- ☐ Television
- ⌂ Quiet
- ⌇ Swimming pool
- ☐ Credit cards
- 🕯 Reduction for children
- ✕ No animals
- ♫ Music
- 🎺 Live band

♦ < $20
♦♦ $20 to $50
♦♦♦ > $50

	PAGE	PRICE	VIEW	DÉCOR AND SURROUNDINGS	EUROPEAN CUISINE	AMERICAN CUISINE	LATIN-AMERICAN CUISINE	ASIAN CUISINE	SEAFOOD AND FISH	VALET PARKING	MUSIC
CHINATOWN											
EMPRESS OF CHINA	368	♦	●	●				●			●
HOUSE OF NANKING	368	♦						●			
NORTHERN WATERFRONT											
ALIOTO'S	369	♦♦	●		●				●	●	
DANTE'S SEAFOOD GRILL	369	♦	●			●			●	●	
HORNBLOWER DINING YACHTS	369	♦♦♦	●			●					●
LOU'S PIER 47 CLUB	369	♦				●			●		●
SCOMA'S	369	♦♦	●			●			●	●	
FORT MASON – MARINA – PRESIDIO											
GREEN'S	370	♦♦	●	●							
IZZI'S STEAK AND CHOPS	370	♦♦				●					
JOHNNY ROCKETS	370	♦		●		●					
MAI'S VIETNAMESE REST.	370	♦						●			
MEL'S DRIVE IN	370	♦									
ROSEMARINO	371	♦		●	●						
NOB HILL											
ACQUARELLO	371	♦♦			●					●	
ART INSTITUTE CAFÉ	371	♦	●	●							
FORNOU'S OVEN	371	♦♦		●	●					●	
HARD ROCK CAFÉ	371	♦		●		●					●
LA FOLIE	371	♦♦♦			●	●				●	
SWAN OYSTER DEPOT	371	♦							●		
NORTH BEACH											
BIX	373	♦♦		●		●					●
BOCCE CAFFÉ	373	♦			●						
BRANDY HO'S	373	♦						●			
CAFFÉ SPORT	373	♦♦		●							●
CYPRESS CLUB	373	♦♦		●						●	
ENRICO'S	373	♦♦									
ESSEX SUPPER CLUB	373	♦♦♦			●					●	
FOG CITY DINER ★	373	♦		●		●					
HARBOR VIEW VILLAGE	373	♦♦						●			
IL FORNAIO	373	♦♦			●						
JAZZ AT PEARL'S	373	♦			●						●
JULIUS CASTLE	373	♦♦	●								
LITTLE JOE'S	373	♦			●						
TOMMASO'S ★	373	♦			●						
FINANCIAL DISTRICT											
AQUA	375	♦♦♦		●						●	
BENTLEY'S	375	♦♦	●							●	●
THE CARNELIAN ROOM	375	♦♦♦	●		●					●	
PLOUF	375	♦♦								●	
SAZ	375	♦♦			●						
TADICH GRILL	375	♦♦			●	●				●	
TOMMY TOY'S	375	♦♦		●					●		
YANK SING	375	♦♦						●			
UNION SQUARE											
AIOLI	377	♦♦		●	●	●					
CAFÉ CLAUDE	377	♦♦		●							
FLEUR DE LYS	377	♦♦♦		●	●	●				●	
JOHN'S GRILL	377	♦♦		●							

	PAGE	PRICE	VIEW	DÉCOR AND SURROUNDINGS	EUROPEAN CUISINE	AMERICAN CUISINE	LATIN-AMERICAN CUISINE	ASIAN CUISINE	SEAFOOD AND FISH	VALET PARKING	MUSIC
KULETO'S ★	377	♦♦									
MASA'S	377	♦♦♦		●	●						
POSTRIO	377	♦♦♦			●	●				●	
SEARS FINE FOOD	377	♦		●		●				●	
ST FRANCIS CAFÉ	378	♦	●			●				●	
CIVIC CENTER – JAPANTOWN											
CAL. CULINARY ACADEMY	381	♦♦		●		●					
COCONUT GROVE	381	♦♦♦		●	●	●					●
ISOBUNE (RESTAURANT MALL)	381	♦♦		●				●			
MAX'S OPERA CAFÉ	381	♦		●							
MISS PEARL'S JAM HOUSE	381	♦		●		●					
SPUNTINO	381	♦			●						
STARS	381	♦♦♦		●		●				●	
STARS CAFÉ	381	♦♦				●					
THEP PHANOM ★	381	♦♦						●			
ZUNI'S CAFÉ	381	♦♦									
GOLDEN GATE PARK – HAIGHT ASHBURY											
CHA CHA CHA	382	♦		●			●				
THE PORK STORE CAFÉ ★	382	♦				●					
RICHMOND											
ANGKOR WAT	383	♦						●			
NEW GOLDEN TURTLE	383	♦♦						●			
SOUTH OF MARKET											
BRAIN WASH ★	384	♦		●							
CAFFE CENTRO	384	♦	●	●							
CAFÉ MARS	384	♦									
THE CARIBBEAN ZONE	384	♦		●							
DUBLINER	384	♦				●					
ELEVEN	384	♦		●							●
HAMBURGER MARY'S	384	♦				●					
JULIE'S SUPPER CLUB	385	♦♦		●		●					
LULU	385	♦		●							
THE RAMP	385	♦♦									●
WU KONG	385	♦♦						●			
MISSION											
AUNT MARY'S RESTAURANT	386	♦♦		●			●				
CAFÉ MACONDO	386	♦									●
FLYING SAUCER	386	♦♦		●	●	●					
ESPERPENTO	386	♦♦			●		●				
KATZ BAGELS	386	♦				●					
LA RONDELLA	386	♦					●				
LA TACQUERIA SAN JOSE	387	♦					●				
PASTAIO LUISA'S	387	♦									
TI COUZ	387	♦			●						
CASTRO											
HOT'N'HUNKY	387	♦									
PATIO CAFÉ	387	♦♦				●					
AROUND SAN FRANCISCO											
CHEZ PANISSE	388	♦♦♦			●	●				●	
FRENCH LAUNDRY	388	♦♦♦		●	●	●					
TRAVIGNE	388	♦♦		●	●						
V. SATTUI WINERY	388	♦			●						

◆ Choosing a Hotel

♦ < $ 50
♦♦ $ 50 to $ 120
♦♦♦ $ 120 to $ 200
♦♦♦♦ > $ 200

	PAGE	PRICE	VIEW	QUIET	ARCHITECTURE, DÉCOR	SERVICE AND RECEPTION	GARAGE PARKING	RESTAURANT	POOL, SPORTS FACILITIES	SEMINARS/CONFERENCE	NO. OF ROOMS
CHINATOWN											
ASTORIA HOTEL	368	♦									30
GRANT PLAZA	368	♦♦					●				72
HOLIDAY INN FIN. DISTRICT	369	♦♦♦	●				●	●	●	●	566
FORT MASON – MARINA – PRESIDIO											
THE MANSIONS	371	♦♦♦♦			●	●		●		●	21
SAN FRANCISCO YOUTH HOSTEL	371	♦	●	●		●					21
THE SHERMAN HOUSE	371	♦♦♦♦			●	●	●	●		●	14
NOB HILL											
BEDFORD	371	♦♦♦	●	●		●	●	●		●	144
BERESFORD ARMS	371	♦♦♦			●	●					102
COMMODORE INTERNATIONAL	371	♦♦									113
THE FAIRMONT	372	♦♦♦♦	●		●		●	●		●	336
THE HUNTINGTON HOTEL ★	372	♦♦♦♦	●		●	●	●	●		●	402
MARK HOPKINS INTERCONT'L	372	♦♦♦♦	●		●	●	●	●		●	596
RITZ CARLTON	372	♦♦♦♦	●		●	●	●	●	●	●	140
STOUFFER STANFORD COURT	372	♦♦♦♦	●		●	●	●	●		●	390
NORTH BEACH											
HOTEL BOHEMIA	374	♦♦					●		●		15
SAN REMO HOTEL	374	♦♦			●	●					62
THE WASHINGTON SQUARE INN	374	♦♦♦		●		●	●				15
FINANCIAL DISTRICT											
MANDARIN ORIENTAL ★	375	♦♦♦♦				●	●			●	158
UNION SQUARE											
THE ANDREWS	378	♦♦				●	●	●			48
ANSONIA HOTEL	378	♦						●			150
BERESFORD	378	♦♦				●		●			114
BRADY ACRES	378	♦♦				●	●				25
CARTWRIGHT HOTEL	378	♦♦				●	●			●	114
THE DONATELLO	378	♦♦				●	●	●		●	110
THE GAYLORD	378	♦♦									330
GOLDEN GATE HOTEL ★	378	♦♦			●	●	●				23
KING GEORGE HOTEL	378	♦♦		●				●		●	140
MONTICELLO INN ★	378	♦♦				●		●			140
PACIFIC BAY INN	378	♦				●					91
PAN PACIFIC HOTEL	378	♦♦♦♦				●	●			●	84
SHANNON COURT	378	♦♦				●	●	●		●	173
SHEEHAN	378	♦♦♦				●	●		●	●	68
STRATFORD HOTEL	379	♦♦♦				●					105
HOTEL TRITON	379	♦♦♦			●	●	●	●		●	95
VILLA FLORENCE	379	♦♦♦				●		●			177
WESTIN ST FRANCIS HOTEL	379	♦♦♦♦	●			●	●	●	●	●	1200
WHITE SWAN INN	379	♦♦♦				●	●				26
CIVIC CENTER – JAPANTOWN											
THE ALBION HOUSE INN	382	♦♦♦			●			●		●	48
THE ARCHBISHOP'S MANSION ★	382	♦♦♦			●	●	●			●	9
THE CHATEAU TIVOLI	382	♦♦♦			●					●	15
INN AT THE OPERA	382	♦♦♦			●	●	●	●		●	7
THE NEW ABIGAIL HOTEL	382	♦♦	●		●			●			66
THE PHOENIX INN	382	♦♦	●				●	●	●		44
THE QUEEN ANNE	382	♦♦♦				●	●			●	49
GOLDEN GATE PARK – HAIGHT ASHBURY											
METRO	383	♦♦		●							23
RED VICTORIAN B&B INN	383	♦♦									18
THE SPENCER HOUSE	383	♦♦♦	●	●	●	●				●	6
VICTORIAN INN ON THE PARK	383	♦♦♦	●	●	●	●					12
SOUTH OF MARKET											
HARBOR COURT HOTEL	385	♦♦♦	●			●	●	●	●		131
SHERATON PALACE	385	♦♦♦♦			●	●	●	●	●	●	550

LIFE AND HISTORY OF SAN FRANCISCO		
ALCATRAZ	◆ 369	Pier 41 / **NORTHERN WATERFRONT**
CABLE CAR MUSEUM	◆ 371	Washington St. / **NOB HILL**
CITY HALL	◆ 380	Van Ness Ave / **CIVIC CENTER**
CLIFF HOUSE	◆ 383	1066–1090, Point Lobos Ave / **RICHMOND**
COIT TOWER	◆ 372	Telegraph Hill / **NORTH BEACH**
HAAS LILIENTHAL HOUSE	◆ 370	2007, Franklin St. / **PACIFIC HEIGHTS**
MISSION DOLORES	◆ 386	Dolores St. / **MISSION–CASTRO**
MUSEUM OF THE CITY OF SAN FRANCISCO	◆ 369	Leavenworth St. / **NORTHERN WATERFRONT**
NEPTUNE SOCIETY COLUMBARIUM	◆ 383	Loraine Court / **RICHMOND**
OCTAGON HOUSE	◆ 370	2645, Gough St. / **PACIFIC HEIGHTS**
PRESIDIO ARMY MUSEUM	◆ 370	Lincoln Blvd and Funston Ave / **PRESIDIO**
SAN FRANCISCO HISTORY ROOM	◆ 380	San Francisco Public Library / **CIVIC CENTER**
HISTORY OF CALIFORNIA		
FORT POINT NATIONAL HISTORIC SITE	◆ 370	Lincoln Blvd and Long Ave / **PRESIDIO**
MUSEUM OF MONEY OF THE AMERICAN WEST	◆ 374	Bank of California, 400, California St. / **FINANCIAL DISTRICT**
SOCIETY OF CALIFORNIA PIONEERS	◆ 380	456, McAllister St. / **CIVIC CENTER**
WELLS FARGO HISTORY MUSEUM	◆ 374	420, Montgomery St. / **FINANCIAL DISTRICT**
PACIFIC BASIC		
CHINESE CULTURE CENTER	◆ 368	750, Kearny St. (Holiday Inn, 4th Floor) / **CHINATOWN**
CHINESE HISTORICAL SOCIETY OF AMERICA	◆ 368	650, Commercial St. / **CHINATOWN**
PACIFIC HERITAGE MUSEUM	◆ 374	608, Commercial St. / **FINANCIAL DISTRICT**
UNIVERSITY ART MUSEUM. PACIFIC FILM ARCHIVE	◆ 388	2626, Bancroft Way, Berkeley / **AROUND THE BAY**
ETHNIC COMMUNITIES & CULTURE		
THE JEWISH MUSEUM OF SAN FRANCISCO	◆ 384	121, Steuart St. / **SOUTH OF MARKET**
JUDAH L. MAGNES MUSEUM	◆ 387	2911, Russel, Berkeley / **AROUND THE BAY**
THE MEXICAN MUSEUM	◆ 370	Fort Mason Center, Marina Blvd / **FORT MASON**
MUSEO ITALO AMERICANO	◆ 370	Fort Mason Center, Marina Blvd / **FORT MASON**
SAN FRANCISCO CRAFT AND FOLK ART MUSEUM	◆ 370	Fort Mason Center, Marina Blvd / **FORT MASON**
THE ARTS		
ASIAN ART MUSEUM	◆ 382	**GOLDEN GATE PARK**
CALIFORNIA PALACE OF THE LEGION OF HONOR	◆ 383	Lincoln Park / **RICHMOND**
CARTOON ART MUSEUM	◆ 384	814 Mission / **SOUTH OF MARKET**
M.H DE YOUNG MEMORIAL MUSEUM	◆ 382	**GOLDEN GATE PARK**
NORTH BEACH MUSEUM	◆ 372	Eureka Federal Savings, 1435 Stockton St. / **NORTH BEACH**
SAN FRANCISCO MUSEUM OF MODERN ART	◆ 384	151, 3rd St / **SOUTH OF MARKET**
DISCOVERY		
BAY AREA DISCOVERY MUSEUM	◆ 386	557, East Fort Baker, Sausalito / **AROUND THE BAY**
BAY MODEL VISITORS CENTER	◆ 387	2100, Bridgeway, Sausalito / **AROUND THE BAY**
AQUARIUM, HALLS OF NATURAL HISTORY	◆ 382	California Academy of Sciences / **GOLDEN GATE PARK**
PLANETARIUM	◆ 382	California Academy of Sciences / **GOLDEN GATE PARK**
EXPLORATORIUM	◆ 370	Palace of Fine Arts, 3601, Lyon St. / **FORT MASON**
OAKLAND MUSEUM	◆ 388	Oak and 10th Sts., Oakland / **AROUND THE BAY**
NATURE		
CONSERVATORY OF FLOWERS	◆ 382	**GOLDEN GATE PARK**
JAPANESE TEA GARDEN	◆ 382	**GOLDEN GATE PARK**
MUIR WOODS	◆ 388	Mt Tamalpais Panoramic Highway / **AROUND THE BAY**
SHIPS AND THE SEA		
NATIONAL LIBERTY SHIP MEMORIAL – S.S JEREMIAH O'BRIEN	◆ 370	Pier 2 East, Fort Mason Center / **FORT MASON**
NATIONAL MARITIME MUSEUM	◆ 369	Maritime National Historical Park, Beach St. / **NORTHERN WATERFRONT**
SAN FRANCISCO MARITIME NATIONAL HISTORICAL PARK – HYDE STREET PIER	◆ 369	Beginning of Hyde St. / **NORTHERN WATERFRONT**
USS PAMPANITO	◆ 369	Pier 45 / **NORTHERN WATERFRONT**
TREASURE ISLAND MUSEUM	◆ 388	Building 1, Treasure Island / **AROUND THE BAY**

*Numbers refer to pages in the addresses section,
names in bold print refer to the itineraries section.*

GENERAL INFORMATION

SAN FRANCISCO VISITOR INFORMATION CENTER
Hallidie Plaza (Union Square), 900 Market Street
Tel. 391 2000 or 974 6900
Open Mon. to Fri. 9am–5.30pm, Sat. 9am–3pm, Sun. 10am–2pm.
Cultural programs: Tel. 391 2003

SAN FRANCISCO CONVENTION AND VISITORS BUREAU
201 3rd Street (SoMa)
Tel. 974 6900
Open Mon–Fri. 9am–5pm.

VISITORS INFORMATION CENTER OF THE REDWOOD EMPIRE
785 Market Street (Union Square)
Tel. 543 8334
Open Thur. to Sat. 10am–6pm.
Organizes tours of the city and publishes a free brochure, "The Redwood Empire Visitors Guide".

PRACTICAL INFORMATION

ELECTRICAL APPLIANCES
Plugs 110–115 V
Transformers or adaptors are required for all European electrical appliances.

EMERGENCIES
POLICE, AMBULANCE, FIRE SERVICE
Tel. 911 (toll free)

PHARMACIES
WALGREEN'S (MARINA), Divisadero Street (Lombard Street)
Tel. 931 6417.
Open 24 hours.

or 135 Powell Street
Tel. 391 4466
Open Mon. to Sat. 8am–midnight, Sun. 9am–8pm.
MERRYL'S DRUG CENTER, 498 Castro Street
Tel. 861 3136
Open 24 hours.

LOST AND FOUND
POLICE
Tel. 553 0123
PUBLIC TRANSPORT
Tel. 923 6168

LOSS OR THEFT OF MONEY
CREDIT CARDS:
AMERICAN EXPRESS
Tel. (800) 233 5432
VISA Tel. (800) 847 2911
MASTERCARD
Tel. (800) 826 2181
TRAVELERS' CHECKS:
AMERICAN EXPRESS
Tel. (800) 221 7282
VISA Tel. (800) 227 6811
MASTERCARD
Tel. (800) 223 7373

US POST OFFICE
AIRPORT BRANCH (UNION SQUARE); Basement of Macy's
Tel. 956 3570
Open 10am–5pm.

GENERAL OPENING HOURS
STORES:
Open Mon. to Sat. 10am–6pm and often Sundays.
RESTAURANTS:
Open 11.30am–3pm and 5.30–11pm.
BARS AND DISCOTHEQUES:
Open until 2am.

AUTOMATIC TICKET MACHINES (ATM)
CIRRUS NETWORK
Tel. (800) 424 7787
PLUS NETWORK
Tel. (800) 843 7587

AMERICAN EXPRESS
2500 Mason Street (Fisherman's Wharf)
Tel. 788 3025
455 Market Street (Financial District)
Tel. 512 8250

HOTEL

RESERVATIONS
San Francisco Reservations
Tel. (415) 227 1500 or (800) 677 1550

BED AND BREAKFAST
Tel. 921 7150
BEST WESTERN
Tel. (800) 528 1234
DAYS INN
Tel. (800) 325 2525
HOLIDAY INN
Tel. (800) 465 4329
MIYAKO INN
Tel. 921 4000
QUALITY INNS
Tel. (800) 228 5151
RAMADA
Tel. (800) 228 2828
TRAVEL LODGE
Tel. (800) 255 3050
AMERICAN YOUTH HOSTELS
Tel. 788 5604
SAN FRANCISCO INTERNATIONAL HOSTELS
Tel. 771 7277

◆

CHINATOWN

PRACTICAL INFORMATION

PARKING LOTS
PORTSMOUTH SQUARE GARAGE, 733 Kearny Street (Clay Street)
Tel. 982 6353

POST OFFICE
CHINATOWN STATION, 867 Stockton St (Clay St)
Tel. 956 3566
Open Mon. to Fri. 9am–5.30pm, Sat. 9am–4.30pm.

CULTURE

CHINESE CULTURE CENTER
75 Kearny Street (Holiday Inn Hotel, 3rd floor) Tel. 986 1822
Open Tue. to Sat. 10am– 4pm, Sun. noon–4pm
Exhibitions of Chinese art. Admission free.

CHINESE HISTORICAL SOCIETY OF AMERICA
650 Commercial Street

(Montgomery Street)
Tel. 391 1188
Open Wed., Sun. 10am–4pm.
Museum of the history of the Chinese community in San Francisco. Admission free.

RESTAURANTS

EMPRESS OF CHINA
838 Grant Street (Clay Street)
Tel. 434 1345
Magnificent décor (Han Dynasty art objects).
$10–15

HOUSE OF NANKING
919 Kearny Street (Jackson Street and Columbus Avenue)
Tel. 421 1429
Open Mon. to Tue. 11am–10pm.
Small neighborhood restaurant, very popular. No credit cards.
$10
○ ☉

HOTELS

ASTORIA HOTEL
510 Bush Street
Tel. (415) 434 8889
$49–86

GRANT PLAZA
465 Grant Avenue (Pine Street)
Tel. 434 3883
or (800) 472 6899
Fax 434 3886.

1 SCOMA'S   2 LOU'S PIER 47 CLUB   3 BUENA VISTA CAFÉ   4 ALIOTO'S   5 QUIET STORM

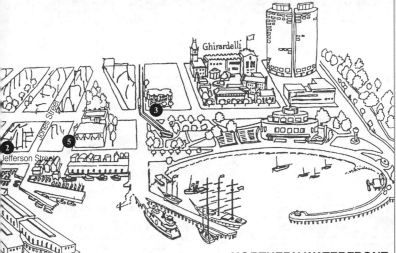

NORTHERN WATERFRONT

Open 24 hours.
Modern hotel with friendly service.
$41–$75

HOLIDAY INN FINANCIAL DISTRICT
750 Kearny Street (Washington Street)
Tel. 433 6600
Fax 765 7891
Standard hotel, with views of the bay and the city. Rooftop pool.
$170–$190

NORTHERN WATERFRONT

PRACTICAL INFORMATION

PARKING LOTS
GHIRARDELLI SQUARE GARAGE, 900 North Point Street, 665 Beach Street (Hyde St)
Tel. 929 1665

EXCHANGE BUREAU
THOMAS COOK CURRENCY
75 Geary Street.
Tel. 362 3452

Pier 39
Tel. 362 6271
Open daily 10am–6pm; 9am–7pm in summer.

CULTURE

THE MUSEUM OF THE CITY OF SAN FRANCISCO
The Cannery, 3rd floor, 2801 Leavenworth St
Tel. 928 0289
Open Wed. to Sun. 10am–4pm.
History of the city. Admission free.

SAN FRANCISCO MARITIME NATIONAL HISTORIC PARK
Hyde Street Pier,
Tel. 556 3002
Open daily 10am–5pm.
Tours of old ships. Admission free.

NATIONAL MARITIME MUSEUM
Beach Street (Polk Street)
Tel. 556 3002
Open daily 10am–5pm.
Museum of maritime life. Admission free.

USS PAMPANITO
Pier 45
Tel. 441 5819
Open 9am–8pm daily, June-Oct.
Tour of submarines: $5 admission.

ALCATRAZ
Red and White Fleet,

Pier 41 (Powell Street)
Daily 9.30am–2.30pm (half-hourly). March to Sep, daily 9am–4pm.
Guided tour of the ex-penitentiary: book in advance.

RESTAURANTS

ALIOTO'S
8 Fisherman's Wharf (Powell Street)
Tel. 673 0183
Open 11am–11pm.
Seafood restaurant, friendly service, fine view, Italian cuisine.
$30

DANTE'S SEAFOOD GRILL
Pier 39
Tel. 421 5778
One of the city's finest seafood restaurants: superb view of the bay.
$20

HORNBLOWER DINING YACHTS
Pier 33, Embarcadero
Tel. 394 8900
Mon. to Sat., leaving 7pm, returning 10.30pm. Weekend brunches 10.30am–2.30pm.
Cruise around the bay, dinner (full menu) and dancing aboard. Reservation essential.
Dinner $62–75, Brunch $36–$41

LOU'S PIER 47 CLUB
300 Jefferson Street (Jones Street)
Tel. 771 0377
Open Mon. to Wed. 4pm–1am. Thur. to Sun. 12 noon–1am.
Restaurant and concert room (rock, blues, soul music).
$15

SCOMA'S
Pier 47 (Jefferson Street)
Tel. 771 4383
11.30am–10.30pm.
Seafood restaurant fronting the bay. Hot reputation, good value.
From $25

NIGHTLIFE

BUENA VISTA CAFÉ
2765 Hyde Street (Beach Street)
Tel. 474 5044
Excellent Irish coffee.

QUIET STORM
The Cannery, 2801 Leavenworth (Beach Street)
Tel. 771 2929
Jazz club.

SHOPPING

KRAZY KAPS
Pier 39
Sells every kind of hat under the sun, including baseball caps in the colors of the San Francisco 49ers team.

GHIRARDELLI SQUARE
900, North Point Street
Shopping center.

PATAGONIA
770 North Point Street
Tel. 771 2050
Excellent for sporting equipment and leisure wear.

FORT MASON–MARINA–PRESIDIO

PRACTICAL INFORMATION

POST OFFICE
MARINA STATION, 2055 Lombard Street
(Fillmore Street)
Tel. 284 0755
Open Mon. to Fri.
8.30am–5.30pm, Sat.
9am–4pm.
PRESIDIO STATION,
950 Lincoln Boulevard
(Presidio Boulevard)
Tel. 563 4975
Open Mon. to Fri.
8.30am–5pm.

PARKING LOTS
CALIFORNIA PARKING
1910 Union Street.,
Tel. 771 2851

CULTURE

THE EXPLORATORIUM
(Palace of Fine Arts)
3601 Lyon Street
(Marina Boulevard)
Tel. 561 0360
Open Tue. to Sun.
10am–6pm.
World-famous science museum. Make an

appointment in advance to visit the tactile dome. Fee for admission.

FORT POINT NATIONAL HISTORIC SITE
Lincoln Boulevard and Long Avenue, Presidio
Tel. 921 8193
Open daily 10am–5pm.
19th century fort under the Golden Gate bridge.
Admission free.

HAAS LILIENTHAL HOUSE
2007 Franklin Street
(Jackson Street),
Pacific Heights
Tel. 441 3004
Open Wed. and Sun.
12 noon–3pm.
Tour of a Victorian house.
Admission fee $5

THE MEXICAN MUSEUM
Building D, Fort Mason Center, Marina Boulevard (Buchanan Street)
Tel. 441 0404
Open Wed. to Sun.
12 noon–5pm.
Small museum of Mexican art, ancient and modern.
Fee for admission.

MUSEO ITALO-AMERICANO
Building C, Fort Mason Center, Marina Boulevard
Tel. 673 2200
Open Wed. to Sun.
12 noon–5pm.
Small museum dedicated to the Italian-American community.
Fee for admission.

NATIONAL LIBERTY SHIP MEMORIAL (SS JEREMIAH O'BRIEN)
Pier 2 East, Fort Mason Center
Tel. 441 3101
Open 9am–3pm.
Closed Sat. and Sun.
Tour of a World War Two Liberty ship. Fee for admission.

OCTAGON HOUSE
2645 Gough Street
(Union Street), Pacific Heights
Tel. 441 7512
Open 2nd & 4th Thur. and 2nd Sun each month, 12 noon–3pm.
Colonial era architecture.

PRESIDIO ARMY MUSEUM
Lincoln Boulevard and Funston Avenue, Presidio
Tel. 561 4331
Open Tue. to Sun.
10am–4pm. Closed on Independence Day, Thanksgiving, Christmas and New Year's Day.
Occupies a former hospital, one of the oldest buildings in the Presidio. This museum traces the military history of San Francisco. Admission free.

SAN FRANCISCO CRAFT AND FOLK ART MUSEUM
Landmark Building A, Fort Mason Center
Tel. 775 0990
Open Mon. to Fri. and Sun. 11am–5pm, Sat.
10am–5pm. Free Sat.
10am–12 noon.
Small craft museum; fee for admission.

MOVIE THEATERS
CINEMA 21
Corner of Chestnut and Steiner streets, Pacific Heights
Tel. 921 6720
CLAY
Corner of Fillmore and Clay streets, Pacific Heights
Tel. 346 1123
PRESIDIO
Corner of Chestnut and Scott streets, Marina
Tel. 922 1318
U.A. METRO
Corner of of Union and Webster streets, Marina
Tel. 931 1685

THEATER
LIFE ON THE WATER
Building B, Fort Mason
Tel. 824 9394
Avant-garde and experimental theater

RESTAURANTS

GREEN'S
Building A, Fort Mason
Tel. 771 6222
Open 11.30am–2.15pm.
Closed Sun. and Mon.
In a former warehouse; this was one of the first vegetarian restaurants to open in San Francisco. Terrific view of the Bay and Golden

Gate Bridge. Relaxed, friendly service.
Fixed price dinner $35, Fri. and Sat.
$30
◑ ☐••

IZZI'S STEAK AND CHOPS
3345 Steiner Street
(Chestnut and Lombard streets), Marina
Tel. 563 0487
Open 5.30–11pm.
Closed Sun.
A traditional steakhouse with a regular clientèle. Copious, reasonably priced food.
$30
◑

JOHNNY ROCKETS
2203 Chestnut Street
(Pierce Street), Marina.
Tel. 931 6258
Open 10am–12 midnight. Closed Fri., Sat.
1950's ambience with neon lighting, jukebox, ice cream and first-class hamburgers.
$5–10
○

MAI'S VIETNAMESE RESTAURANT
316 Clement Street,
Richemont
Tel. 221 3046
Open 11am–10pm, closed Fri. to Sun.
Small Vietnamese restaurant with, during summer, a few terrace tables. Excellent traditional cuisine, more-or-less like that of the New Golden Turtle (Richmond). Very reasonable prices.
$20
○

MEL'S DRIVE-IN
2165 Lombard Street
(Fillmore and Steiner streets), Marina
Tel. 921 3039
Open 6am–1am. Closed Fri. and Sat.
Typical drive-in. Great for children though the food's nothing to write home about.
$12
○

PASAND MADRAS CUISINE
1875 Union Street
(Laguna Street), Pacific Heights
Tel. 922 4498
Indian restaurant.

ROSEMARINO
3665 Sacramento
Street (Spruce Street),
Presidio
Tel. 931 7710
Open 11.30am–2pm,
5.30–10pm.
Closed Sat. to Mon.
*An intimate little
restaurant in an inner
courtyard. Terrace, with
a pretty wrought-iron
porch roof.*
$10–16
◑ ▯ ▱••

HOTELS

THE MANSIONS
2220 Sacramento Street
(Laguna/Buchanan
streets), Pacific Heights
Tel. 929 9444
Fax. 567 9391
Open 24 hours.
*Two Victorian
houses. In the evening,
ghost-and-magic
show: rowdy but fun.
Breakfast included,
no TV in bedrooms.*
$129–$350
⌂ ◑ ♨ ▯•• 🚗

SAN FRANCISCO
INTERNATIONAL
AYH HOSTEL
(YOUTH HOSTEL)
Building 240, Fort
Mason, Marina
Boulevard
(Buchanan Street)
Tel. 771 7277
Fax. 771 1468
Open 7am–2pm and
3pm–1am.
*Green, peaceful
surroundings, with a
fine view across the bay.
No age limits.
Non-smokers
preferred. Free car
parking. Rooms with
kitchenette.*
$13
⌂ ○ Ⓟ

THE SHERMAN
HOUSE
2160 Green Street
(Fillmore and Webster
streets),
Pacific Heights
Tel. 563 3600
Fax 563 1882
Open 24 hours.
*Magnificent Victorian
house. First-rate
service; hotel
transportation in
vintage cars is
provided to hotel
guests.*
$295–$825
🏨 ⑪ ♨ ▯•• ⤳
🚗

NIGHTLIFE

JACK'S BAR
1601 Fillmore Street,
Tel. 567 3227
*Blues concerts, nightly
9pm–1.30am;
weekends 3.30–8pm
and 9pm–1.30am.*

JULIE RING'S HEART
AND SOUL
1695 Polk Street
Tel. 673 7100
Open 5pm–2am.
*Hip, chic soirées.
Californian cuisine at a
reasonable price. Jazz
concerts every evening.
Dinner $20.
Shows Mon. to Thur.
$4, Sat. to Sun. $10.*

SHOPPING

WRITER'S BOOKSTORE
2848 Webster (Union)
Tel: 921 2620
*Unusual variety of
discounted new and
used books.*

STONESTOWN
GALLERIA
Corner of 19th Ave and
Winston Drive.
*Stylish goods for the
home, exotic food. Free
parking.*

NOB HILL

PRACTICAL
INFORMATION

PARK AND LOCK
PARKING LOT
400 Taylor Street

CULTURE

CABLE CAR MUSEUM
Washington Street
(Mason Street)
Tel. 474 1887
Open daily 10am–6pm.
*Tour of the cable car
terminal; admission
free.*

MOVIE THEATERS
ALHAMBRA
Corner of Polk and
Union streets
Tel. 775 2137

LUMIERE 3
Corner of California
and Polk streets
Tel. 885 3200

RESTAURANTS

ACQUARELLO
1722 Sacramento
Street (Van Ness
Avenue)
Tel. 567 5432
Open 5.30–10.30pm.
Closed Sun.
*This small restaurant
offers friendly
service and excellent
traditional Italian
cooking. Valet parking
is available.*
$40
⑪

ART INSTITUTE CAFÉ
Chestnut Street
(Jones Street)
Tel. 771 7020
Open 9am–5pm,
Sept. to May. Closed
Sat. and Sun.
*On a large terrace near
the galleries with a
superb view of San
Francisco. The café
mounts exhibitions of
students' artwork. This
is a pleasant place to
eat lunch in summer on
account of its garden.*
$15
○ ▱••

FORNOU'S OVEN
(Stanford Court Hotel)
905 California Street
(Powell Street)
Tel. 989 3500
Open 6.30am–2.30pm,
5.30–10pm.
*Rustic, country inn
décor. French food,
good cellar, valet
parking.*
$35
⑪ Ⓒ

HARD ROCK CAFÉ
1699 Van Ness
Avenue (Sacramento
Street)
Tel. 885 1699
Open 11.30am–11pm.
*Bar-restaurant.
The menu is
international, including
sandwiches and
inexpensive buffet
food. Music.*
$20
○

LA FOLIE
2316 Polk Street
(Union and Green
streets)
Tel. 776 5577

Open 5.30–10.30pm.
Closed Fri. to Sun.
and Independence
Day (July 4).
*This restaurant has a
French chef and is
renowned for its
nouvelle cuisine.
Pleasant atmosphere.
Valet parking.*
$40
⑪

SWAN OYSTER
DEPOT
1517 Polk Street
(California Street)
Tel. 673 1101
Open 8am–5.30pm.
Closed Sun.,
Christmas, New Year
and Thanksgiving.
*Simple décor and
excellent seafood.*
$18
○

HOTELS

BEDFORD
761 Post Street
(Jones Street)
Tel. 673 6040
or (800) 227 5642
Fax 563 6739
Open 24 hours.
*Pleasant, comfortable
rooms, many offering a
fine view of the city.
Transportation to
Financial District on
weekdays. Good
value. Breakfast not
included in prices.*
$149–$200
🏨 ⌂ Ⓒ ⤳ 🚗

BERESFORD ARMS
701 Post Street
(Jones Street)
Tel. 673 2600
or (800) 533 6533
Fax 929 1535
Open 24 hours.
*Elegant lobby, spacious
rooms, some with
adjoining kitchenette.
Free tea and coffee is
provided in the lobby.
Very comfortable. Good
value.*
$99–$150
⌂ Ⓒ 🚗

COMMODORE
INTERNATIONAL
825 Sutter Street
(Jones Street)
Tel. 923 6800
or (800) 338 6848
Open 24 hours.
*Large rooms, closets,
bathrooms. Good
value. Coffee shop.*
$79–$119
⌂ Ⓒ

NORTH BEACH

THE FAIRMONT HOTEL
950 Mason Street
(California Street)
Tel. 772 5000
or (800) 527 4727
Fax 772 5013
or (800) 527 4727
Open 24 hours.
*Favored by groups.
Comfortable rooms (the
ones in the tower have
especially good views).*
$150–$400

THE HUNTINGTON HOTEL
1075 California Street
(Taylor and Mason
streets)
Tel. 474 5400
or (800) 227 4683
Fax 474 6227
Open 24 hours.
*Small luxury hotel,
friendly service. The
rooms are beautifully
decorated. The hotel
also offers panoramic
views over the city and
the bay.*
$195–$695

MARK HOPKINS INTERCONTINENTAL
1 Nob Hill Street
(California Street)
Tel. 392 3434
or (800) 327 0200
Fax 421 3302
Open 24 hours. *Faded
grandeur, with luxurious,
if characterless, rooms.
The hotel bar, The Top
of the Mark, on the top
floor, has a 360° view.*
$180–$360

RITZ CARLTON
600 Stockton Street
(California Street)
Tel. 296 7464
or (800) 241 3333
Fax 291 0288
*Not far from Nob Hill.
A number of services
are provided here,
among them free
access to the hotel
spa (pool, sauna,
jacuzzi). Free transport
provided to Union
Square and Financial
District.* $240–$325

STOUFFER STANFORD COURT HOTEL
905 California Street
(Powell Street)
Tel. 989 3500
or (800) 227 4736
Open 24 hours.
*Avoid the 'standard'
category rooms. Free
coffee and newspaper.
Free transport in luxury
automobiles.*
$165–$295

NIGHTLIFE

NEW ORLEANS ROOM
950 Mason Street (Clay
Street)
Concerts Tue. to Sat.
until 1am.
*Intimate jazz club inside
the Fairmont Hotel.
Jazz classics from
between the wars.*

SHOPPING

EUROPEAN BOOK COMPANY
925 Larkin Street
(Post Street)
Tel. 474 0626
Open Mon. to Fri.
9.30am–6pm,
Sat. 9.30am–5pm.
*International press
available here and
a wide variety of
books.*

NORTH BEACH

PRACTICAL INFORMATION

PARKING LOTS
VALLEJO STREET
GARAGE
766 Vallejo Street
(Stockton and Powell
streets)
Tel. 761 0270

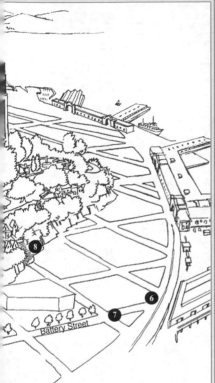

MOSCONE CENTER GARAGE
255 3rd Street
Tel. 777 2782

POST OFFICE
North Beach Station,
1640 Stockton Street
Tel. 956 3581
Open Mon., Wed. and
Fri. 9am–5.30pm, Tue.
and Thur. 8am–6pm,
Sat. 9am–1pm.

CULTURE

COIT TOWER
Telegraph Hill

THE NORTH BEACH MUSEUM
Eureka Federal
Savings, 1435 Stockton
Street (Vallejo Street)
Tel. 626 7070
Open Mon. to Fri.
9am–4pm.
Free admission.

MOVIE THEATERS
CINEPLEX ODEON
CINEMA NORTH POINT
Corner of Powell

and Bay streets
Tel. 403 8187
GATEWAY
215 Jackson Street
(Battery Street)
Tel. 420 3353

RESTAURANTS

BIX
56 Gold Street
(Sansome Street)
Tel. 433 6300
Open 11.30am–
2.30pm, 5.30–11pm.
Closed Fri. to Sun.
*This elegant restaurant
has a décor reminiscent
of the best 1930's jazz
bars. Relaxed
atmosphere; patrons
tend to be young, chic,
hip. Jazz concerts.*
$25
◐

BOCCE CAFFÉ
478 Green Street
(Stockton Street)
Tel. 981 2044
*Italian restaurant with
terrace; excellent value.*
$6–$10

BRANDY HO'S
452 Broadway Street
(Kearny Street)
Tel. 362 6268
Open 11am–10pm.
*You can't miss the red
portico decorated with
peppers. Pleasant
surroundings, a blend of
Chinese architecture
and high-tech. Good,
spicy Chinese cooking.*
$8–$12
○ ▣

CAFFÉ SPORT
574 Green Street
(Columbus Avenue.)
Tel. 981 1251
Open 12 noon–2pm,
5–10.30pm.
*Décor cluttered with
accessories (fishing
nets, mosaic-covered
tables and chairs,
dangling hams), which
is fun, but the service,
the long wait for food
and the prices are less
so. Reservations
essential, no credit
cards.*
$25
◐

CYPRESS CLUB
500 Jackson Street
(Montgomery Street)
Tel. 296 8555
Open 11.30am–2.30pm,
5.30–11pm. Closed
Sat., Sun.
*A new restaurant,
1940's décor. Reserve.
Valet parking.*
$23–$29
◍ ▣

ENRICO'S SIDEWALK CAFÉ
504 Broadway St.
Tel. 982 6223
Open 12 noon–2am.
*Jazz every evening.
Good atmosphere, but
not cheap. An ideal spot
to unwind and enjoy the
San Francisco lifestyle.*

ESSEX SUPPER CLUB
847 Montgomery Street
(Pacific Avenue)
Tel. 397 5959
Open 11.30am–2.30pm,
5–11pm. Closed
Jan. 1–10
*High-class restaurant
founded in 1934; a
scene from Hitchcock's
"Vertigo" was shot here.
Discreet service,
excellent cuisine. Smart
clothes (tie) and
reservation essential.
From $50*
◍ ▣

FOG CITY DINER
1300, Battery Street
(Lombard Street)
Tel. 982 2000
Open 11.30am–11pm.
Closed Fri., Sat.
*With its chrome façade,
this place looks like a
1950's soda fountain
but the clientèle and the
cooking are are
sophisticated.
Reservation essential.*
$7–$17
◐

HARBOR VIEW VILLAGE
Embarcadero Center 4
(Front Street)
Tel. 781 8833
Open 11am–2.30pm,
5.30–9.30pm. Sat.
10.30am–1pm,
5.30–10pm, Sun.
10am–1pm, 5.30–10pm.
*Chic Chinese
restaurant, ideal for
business lunches. A
fast-food service around
the back is cheaper.*
$25
◐ ▣

IL FORNAIO
Levi's Plaza, 1265
Battery St (Greenwich
St). Tel. 986 0100
Mon. to Thur. 7am–
10.30pm, Fri. to Sun.
10am–midnight.
*Big Italian restaurant,
relaxing décor. Lively
by day, often packed
in the evening. Good
food at moderate
prices. Good breakfasts.
Also a bakery.*
$27
◐

JAZZ AT PEARL'S
256 Columbus Avenue
(Broadway Street)
Tel. 291 8255.
Closed Sun.
*Italian restaurant with
jazz concert nightly.*

JULIUS CASTLE
1541 Montgomery St
(Greenwich St)
Tel. 362 3042
Open 5–10pm.
*At the top of Telegraph
Hill, in a château-style
house. Lovely bay view.
Traditional restaurant,
uninspired cooking.*
$40
◐ ▭••

LITTLE JOE'S
523 Broadway Street
(Columbus Avenue)
Tel. 433 4343

Open 11am–10.30pm. Fri., Sat. 11am–11pm, Sun. 12 noon–10pm.
In the sex-shop district; a small Italian restaurant popular with locals. Good, honest cooking at reasonable prices. Expect a queue.
$8–$15

TOMMASO'S
1042 Kearny Street (Broadway)
Tel. 398 9696
Open 5–10.30pm. Closed Mondays.
A San Francisco institution since 1935. Small, dark, lively restaurant serving customers elbow to elbow with pizzas (wood oven) and traditional Neapolitan dishes.
$20
○

HOTELS

HOTEL BOHEMIA
444 Columbus Avenue (Green and Vallejo sts)
Tel. 433 9111
Fax. 362 6292
Open 7.30am–midnight.
Décor in the style of the 50's and 60's, the 'beat' period of Jack Kerouac.
$115
⌂ © ⌿

SAN REMO HOTEL
2237 Mason Street (Chestnut Street)
Tel. 776 8688
or (800) 352 Remo
Open 24 hours.
Between Fisherman's Wharf and North Beach, an odd Victorian building renovated and decorated with a few antiques. Small but unusual rooms. Good value. Baths and toilets shared (except in the case of one room which has its own bathroom: $85). No televisions.
$45–$85
⌂ ○ ⌂ 🚖

THE WASHINGTON SQUARE INN
1660 Stockton St (Filbert and Union sts)
Tel. 981 4220
or (800) 388 0220
Fax. 397 7242
Open 24 hours.
On the edge of the park, a friendly, cozy inn. The smallness of some of the rooms is more

than compensated for by the extras: bathrobe, free breakfast and newspaper, snacks in the afternoon, hors d'oeuvres in the evening. Non-smokers only. Television free on request.
$95–$185
⌂ © 🚖

NIGHTLIFE

CAFFÉ ROMA
414 Columbus Avenue (Vallejo Street.)
Tel. 296 7662
Open Mon. to Thur. 7–11pm, Fri. and Sat. 7pm–1am, Sun. 7pm–midnight.
This pleasant café-bar-restaurant was formerly a bakery.
$6–$13

CAFFÉ TRIESTE
609 Vallejo Street (Grant Avenue)
Tel. 392 6739
Open Mon. to Thur. 7am–11.30pm; Fri., Sat. 7am–midnight.
A classic of the 1960's. Beatnik hangout, once frequented by Jack Kerouac and Allen Ginsberg.

FINOCCHIO'S
506 Broadway (Kearny Street)
Tel. 982 9388.
Transvestite club: three shows a night, 8.30, 10, 11.30pm Tue., and from Thur. to Sun.

MARIO'S BOHEMIAN CIGAR STORE
566 Columbus Avenue (Union Street)
Tel. 362 0536
Open Mon. 10am–midnight, Tue. to Sun. 10am–midnight.
Closed two weeks at Christmas.
Café-restaurant full of character. Delicious home-made pastries and cappuccino. Lively; often full of regulars.

SAN FRANCISCO BREWING COMPANY
155 Columbus Avenue (Pacific Avenue)
Tel. 434 3344
Open all year round. Sun. to Wed. 11.30am–1pm, Thur. to Sat. 11.30am–2am.
Early 20th-century brewery, astonishing

copper fermentation vats. Beers of all kinds, including the one made by the house. Convivial, lively atmosphere.

SAVOY TIVOLI
1434 Grant Avenue. (Green and Union stts)
Tel. 362 7023
Open 3pm–2am. Closed Mon., two weeks at Christmas and Easter.
One of the few terrace bars in San Francisco; a place to see and be seen. Kitsch décor, relaxed service. Clients mostly young people.

TOSCA CAFÉ
242 Columbus Ave.
Tel. 391 1244
Open 5pm–2am.
European ambience attracts local artists, and manages to be both bohemian and chic. No service charge. Try the cappuccino with cognac and chocolate!

VESUVIO
255 Columbus Avenue (Broadway Avenue)
Tel. 362 3370
Open 6am–2am.
Close by the City Lights Bookstore. A pleasant café with an intimate atmosphere, often patronized by local artists and writers.

SHOPPING

CITY LIGHTS BOOKSTORE
261 Columbus Avenue (Broadway Street)
Tel. 362 8193
Open daily 10am–midnight.
Specializing in art and poetry publications.

EAST WIND BOOKS
1435 Stockton Street (Vallejo Street)
Tel. 772 5888
Open Mon. to Sat. 10am–6pm,
Sun. 12 noon–5pm.
Bookstore specializing in Asian subjects.

QUANTITY POSTCARDS
1441 Grant Avenue (Green Street)
Tel. 986 8866
Open Mon. to Fri. 11am–11pm,
Sat., Sun. 11am–1pm.
A vast and diverse selection of postcards.

◆

FINANCIAL DISTRICT

PRACTICAL INFORMATION

CURRENCY EXCHANGE
BANK OF AMERICA,
345 Montgomery Street
Tel. 622 2451
Open Mon. to Fri. 9am–6pm,
Closed Sat., Sun.

POST OFFICE
SUTTER STATION
150 Sutter
Tel. 284 0755
Open Mon. to Fri. 8.30am–5.30pm.
Sat. 8.30am–12 noon.

CULTURE

MUSEUM OF MONEY OF THE AMERICAN WEST
Bank of California,
400 California Street (Sansome Street)
Tel. 765 0400
Open Mon. to Thur. 10am–4pm, Fri. 10am–5pm.
Admission free.

PACIFIC HERITAGE MUSEUM
608 Commercial Street (Montgomery Street)
Tel. 399 1124
Open Mon. to Fri. 12 noon–4pm.
Museum commemorating exchanges between the countries of the Pacific Basin. Admission free.

WELLS FARGO HISTORY MUSEUM (WELLS FARGO BANK)
420 Montgomery Street (California Street)
Tel. 396 2619
Open Mon. to Fri. 9am–5pm.
The history of the West from the founding of Wells Fargo to the beginning of the 20th century. Admission free.

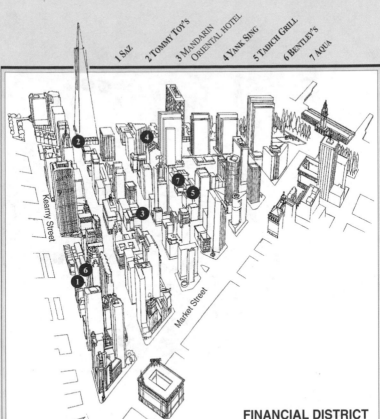

1 SAZ 2 TOMMY TOY'S 3 MANDARIN ORIENTAL HOTEL 4 YANK SING 5 TADICH GRILL 6 BENTLEY'S 7 AQUA

Kearny Street

Market Street

FINANCIAL DISTRICT

MOVIE THEATERS
U.A. THE MOVIES
280 Metro Center
Tel. 994 1065.

RESTAURANTS

AQUA
252 California Street
Tel. 956 9662
Superb seafood dishes, elegant décor. Large mirrors on the walls. Reservation advisable.
$65.

BENTLEY'S
185 Sutter Street
(Kearny Street)
Tel. 989 6895
Open 11am–10pm.
Closed Sun., Christmas and Thanksgiving.
Seafood specialties. Piano bar.
$28
◗ 🄲 ⊨

THE CARNELIAN ROOM
555 California Street
(Montgomery Street)
Tel. 433 7500
Open 6–10.30pm.
Luxury restaurant. Choose the 3-course

menu (about $45) *or have a drink at the bar and admire the view.*
$80

PLOUF
40 Belden Place
Tel. 986 6491
Open Mon. to Fri.
11.30am–2.30pm,
5.30–10pm.
Sat. 5.30–10pm.
Superb seafood and fish. Try the mussels.
$20

SAZ
161 Sutter Street
(Kearny Street)
Tel. 362 0404
Open 11.30am–9pm
Situated on the first floor. Elegant décor. Superb Mediterranean cooking.
$20
◗ 🄲

TADICH GRILL
240 California Street
(Battery Street)
Tel. 391 2373
Open 11am–9.30pm.
Closed Sun.
This is the city's oldest restaurant (1849).

Smart dress and reservations essential.
$20
◗ 🄲

TOMMY TOY'S
655 Montgomery Street
(Clay Street)
Tel. 397 4888
Open 11.30am–2.30pm,
6–9.30pm.
High-class restaurant; a footman shows you through to a dining room full of works of art. Sophisticated Chinese cuisine.
$38–48
🝮 🄲

YANK SING
427 Battery Street
(Clay Street)
Tel. 362 1640
Open Mon. to Fri.
11am–3pm, Sat.
10am–4pm.
Excellent dim-sum. Waitresses wheel in trolleys loaded with dishes of steamed food, from which you make a selection of the dishes you want to eat.
$20
◗ 🄲

HOTELS

MANDARIN ORIENTAL HOTEL
222 Sansome Street
(California and Pine streets)
Tel. 885 0999
or (800) 622 0404
Fax 433 0289
Open 24 hours.
This splendid hotel offers a breathtaking view of the bay; rooms are elegant as well as spacious.
$285–$1200
🏛 🝮 ⌂ 🄲 ⎠ 🚗

375

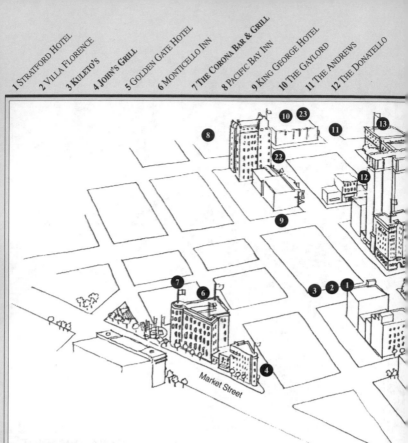

UNION SQUARE

UNION SQUARE

PRACTICAL INFORMATION

PARKING LOTS
SUTTER AND STOCKTON GARAGE
330 Sutter Street
or 444 Stockton Street
Tel. 982 7275
UNION SQUARE GARAGE
333 Post St, entrances on Geary, Powell and Stockton sts
Tel. 397 0631
ELLIS-O'FARRELL GARAGE
123 O'Farrell St, Powell and Stockton sts
Tel. 986 4800

CURRENCY EXCHANGE
BANK OF AMERICA
Powell and Market sts

Tel. 622 4498
Open Mon. to Thur, 9am–4pm, Fri. 9am–7pm, Sat. 9am–2pm.
AMERICAN FOREIGN EXCHANGE
260 O'Farrell Street
Tel. 391 9913
Open Mon. to Fri. 9am–6pm, Sat. 9am–3pm.
AMERICAN EXPRESS
231 Post Street
Tel. 981 5533
AMPARO'S FOREIGN EXCHANGE
233 Sansome Street
Tel. 362 0426
FOREIGN EXCHANGE LTD
415 Stockton Street
Tel. 677 5100
Open Mon. to Fri. 8am–5.30pm, Sat. 9am–1pm.
PACIFIC FOREIGN EXCHANGE, INC.
527 Sutter Street
Tel. 391 2548
Open Mon. to Fri. 9am–6pm, Sat. 10am–3pm, Sun. 10am–3pm.
Closed October through April.

POST OFFICES
MACY'S (BASEMENT)
121 Stockton Street
(O'Farrell Street)
Tel. 956 3570
Open Mon. to Sat. 9.30am–5.30pm, Sun. 11am–5pm.
EMPORIUM STATION
835 Market Street
(5th Street)
Tel. 543 2606
Open Mon. to Fri. 9.30am–5.30pm.
SUTTER STATION
150 Sutter Street
(Kearny Street)
Tel. 284 0755
Open Mon. to Fri. 8.30am–5pm.

CULTURE

THEATERS
AMERICAN CONSERVATORY THEATER (ACT)
30 Grant Avenue
(Mason and Taylor Street)
Tel. 749 2228
Classical and contemporary plays.
CURRAN THEATER
445 Geary Street
(Mason Street)

Tel. 478 3800
Major musicals.
GOLDEN GATE THEATER
1 Taylor Street
(Market Street)
Tel. 474 3800
Major musicals.
MARINES MEMORIAL THEATER
609 Sutter Street
(Mason Street)
Tel. 771 6900
Eclectic repertoire.
THEATER ON THE SQUARE
Kensington Park Hotel,
450 Post Street
(Powell Street)
Tel. 433 9500
Comedies and musical comedies.

ART GALLERIES
CALDWELL-SNYDER ART GALLERIES
357 Geary Street
Tel. 296 7896.
FRAENKEL
49 Geary Street,
Tel. 981 2661.
GALLERY PAULE ANGLIM
14 Geary Street
Tel. 433 2710

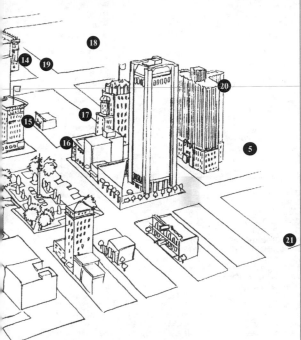

Superb brasserie-style restaurant; long bar adorned with garlands of garlic and other spices (design by Pat Kuleto, who also did the décor for the Postrio). Excellent Italian cooking, very reasonable prices: highly recommended.
$30
◑ ☒

MASA'S
648 Bush Street
(Powell Street)
Tel. 989 7154
Open 6pm–9.30pm.
Closed Sun., Mon. and ten days during summer.
Named for its former chef, this restaurant is still one of the best in town. Sophisticated surroundings and impeccable service. Suit and tie obligatory, reserve in advance. Valet parking.
$100
⓪ ☒

POSTRIO
545 Post Street
(Taylor Street)
Tel. 776 7825
Open 7am–10am, 11.30am–2pm, 5.30pm–10pm.
Opened in 1989 by a famous chef, Wolfgang Puck, this is a chic, fashionable restaurant, usually packed. Refined cooking. Reserve in advance. Valet parking.
From $50
⓪ ☒

PUCINI PINATI
88 Cyril Magnin St
(Ellis St)
Tel. 392 5500
Open 11.30am–11pm.
Closed Sun.
Pleasant, but not authentic, Mexican restaurant. Bright and friendly décor. Fairly expensive.
$27
◑ ☒

SEARS FINE FOOD
439 Powell Street
(Post and Sutter streets)
Tel. 986 1160

HAINES GALLERY
49 Geary Street
Tel. 397 8114
HARCOURTS MODERN AND CONTEMPORARY ART
706 Mission Street
Tel. 227 0400
RENA BRANSTEN
77 Geary Street
Tel. 982 3292

RESTAURANTS

AIOLI
469 Bush Street
(Kearny Street)
Tel. 249 0900
Open daily
6.30–10.30am,
11am–3pm,
5.30–10pm.
Relaxed atmosphere. Refined entrées but main dishes less good. This restaurant in the Hotel Triton is close by the Café de la Presse.
$23
◑ ☒

CAFÉ BASTILLE
22 Belden Place
(Bush-Kearny/ Montgomery)
Tel. 986 5673
This restaurant offers a very Parisian atmosphere.
$20

CAFÉ CLAUDE
7 Claude Lane
(Bush and Kearny sts)
Tel. 392 3505
Open 8am–9pm.
Closed Fri. to Sun.
Flamboyant Parisian bistro. Drinks and a meal if you want one.
$20
◑ ☒

FLEUR DE LYS
777 Sutter St
(Taylor and Jones sts)
Tel. 673 7779
Open Mon. to Thur.
6–9pm, Fri. Sat.
5.30–10.30pm.
Closed Sun. and some public holidays.
The best French restaurant in town. Slightly intimidating entrance; this is a place for the wealthy élite. Luxurious dining room, heavy draperies and crystal chandeliers. Suit and tie essential, as is a reservation. Valet parking.
$80
⓪ ☒

JOHN'S GRILL
63 Ellis Street
(Stockton Street)
Tel. 986 0069
Open 11am–10pm.
Favorite restaurant of Dashiell Hammett's well-known character Sam Spade. Retains the turn-of-the-century atmosphere for which it is famous. The food is rather overpriced.
$25
◑ ☒

KULETO'S
221 Powell Street
(Geary and O'Farrell streets)
Tel. 397 7720
Open 11am–10pm.

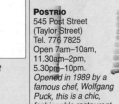

U.S. MAIL

Open 7am–2.30pm.
Closed Mon., Tue.
A veritable institution: American breakfast, old-fashioned décor, heavy food in large quantities.
$13
○ ⓒ

ST FRANCIS CAFÉ
Westin St Francis Hotel, Union Square
Tel. 956 7777
Open 6.30–11.30am, 5–10pm.
Elegant décor, with superb top floor view over the city. Franco-Californian cooking.
$18

HOTELS

THE ANDREWS
624 Post Street (Jones and Taylor streets)
Tel. 563 6877
Fax. 928 6919
Open 24 hours.
Small, comfortable hotel. Breakfast included, self-service on each floor. Wine gratis in the evenings.
$86–$119.

ANSONIA HOTEL
711 Post Street or 630 Geary Street (Leavenworth Street).
Tel. 673 2670
or (800) 221 6470
Fax 673 9217
Residential hotel frequented by students. Half-board, with breakfast and dinner, is a bargain

here. Weekend discounts and reductions for students.
$46–$69
⌂ ○ ⓒ

BERESFORD
635 Sutter Street (Mason Street)
Tel. 673 9900
or (800) 533 6533
Fax 474 0449
Small, dark rooms, cramped bathrooms. A convenient, if somewhat charmless, hotel. Bar and restaurant.
$99
⌂ ○ ⓒ 🚗

BRADY ACRES
649 Jones Street (Post Street and Geary Boulevard)
Tel. 929 8033
or (800) 6BRADY6
Fax 441 8030
Reception open 10am–4pm daily.
An attractive, four-story white building where you can rent small studios with bath or shower, kitchenette, shelves, telephone (local calls free). Television or tape machine. Prices reasonable: a good place if you are contemplating a long stay in San Francisco. Visa and Mastercard only.
$50–$85
⌂ ⓒ 🚗

CARTWRIGHT HOTEL
524 Sutter Street (Powell Street)
Tel. 421 2865
or (800) 227 3844
Fax 421 2865
Charming hotel; friendly reception, comfortable rooms well equipped with bathrobes, vases of fresh flowers, matching flowered curtains and bed covers. Tea and cakes free of charge to guests.
$139–$249
🏨 ⓒ 🚗

THE DONATELLO
225 Powell Street (Geary Boulevard)
Tel. 397 7700
or (800) 553 4411
Fax 397 1006
Beside Kuleto's restaurant; comfortable but charmless hotel.

Bright, clean rooms.
$155–$175
🏨 ○ ⓒ 🚗

THE GAYLORD
620 Jones Street (Post Street and Geary Boulevard)
Tel. 673 8445
or (800) 336 8445
Reception open daily 10am–4pm.
A friendly residential hotel in a quiet street. Rental (one week minimum) of large, bright, extremely comfortable studios with bath and kitchenette. Television on request. Excellent address. Travelers checks and cash only.
$250–$450 per week
⌂

GOLDEN GATE HOTEL
775 Bush Street (Powell and Mason streets)
Tel. 392 3702
or (800) 835 1118
Fax 392 6202
Half-way between Nob Hill and Union Square, this is a ravishing Victorian bed and breakfast run by a charming couple. Pretty, carefully decorated rooms, shared bathroom. An excellent address. Breakfast included.
$65–$99
⌂ ⓒ 🚗

KING GEORGE HOTEL
334 Mason Street (Geary Boulevard)
Tel. 781 5050
or (800) 288 6005
Fax 391 6976
Attractive 19-floor building dating from 1914 (Victorian style). Pleasant staff, elegant, comfortable rooms. Snacks in the hotel salon, the Bread and Tea Room.
$115–$125
🏨 ⓒ 🚗

MONTICELLO INN
127 Ellis Street (Powell Street)
Tel. 392 8800
or (800) 669 7777
Comfortable, impersonal hotel. Colonial décor. Small rooms. Free wine in the evening. Free

limo transport to Financial District. Breakfast included.
$109–$179
🏨 ◑ ⓒ 🚗

PACIFIC BAY INN
520 Jones Street (O'Farrell Street)
Tel. 673 0234
Fax 673 4781
Modern, entirely renovated hotel. Friendly service. Small, bright rooms, anemic gray tones, wall-mounted televisions. Nevertheless, an excellent view of San Francisco and good value for money. Four nights minimum stay (in theory).
$325 per week
⌂ ⓒ 🔆 🚗

THE PAN PACIFIC HOTEL
500 Post Street (Mason Street)
Tel. 771 8600
or (800) 533 6465
Fax 398 0267
Tinted glass elevators and an elegant marble foyer with bedrooms distributed around it. Friendly staff, restful rooms. On request, physical exercise and muscle-toning equipment supplied to rooms.
$235–$1700
🏨 ◑ ⓒ 🚗

SHANNON COURT
550 Geary Street (Jones and Taylor streets)
Tel. 775 5000
or (800) 228 8830
Fax 928 6813
The pearl gray lobby of this renovated 1929 building is somewhat unusual. Large rooms (de luxe category). Breakfast included.
$93–$300
🏨 ◑ ⓒ 🚗

SHEEHAN
620 Sutter Street (Mason Street)
Tel. 775 6500
or (800) 848 1529
Fax 775 3271
Friendly reception. Quiet, bright rooms, but rather on the small side. Free access to the covered Olympic-size swimming pool in the basement and to the hotel health club.

Breakfast included.
$45–$100

STRATFORD HOTEL
242 Powell Street
(Geary Street)
Tel. 788 3304
*Low-price address
(for students). Simple
bedrooms, with or
without showers.
Unbeatable prices (but
only travelers' checks
and cash accepted).
$30–$39*

HOTEL TRITON
342 Grant Avenue
(Bush and Sutter
streets)
Tel. 394 0500
or (800) 433 661
Fax (415) 394 0555
*Situated on the edge
of Chinatown. No
detail has been
forgotten in the effort
to make this hotel a
temple of design.
Extremely kitsch,
funny, fashionable and
sophisticated, all at
the same time. Don't
miss it. A gymnasium
is available to the
residents.
$135–$185*

VILLA FLORENCE
501 Post Street
(Mason Street)
Tel. 441 7100
or (800) 227 3184
*Small luxury hotel,
italianate lobby,
friendly, helpful
reception. Spacious,
comfortable rooms,
free limo transport to
Financial District.
Breakfast included.
$115–$250*

WESTIN ST FRANCIS HOTEL
Union Square,
335 Powell Street
Tel. (800) 521 5203
or 397 7000
*Luxury hotel with
1200 rooms, of
which 83 are suites.
$195–$345.
Suites from $270.*

WHITE SWAN INN
845 Bush Street
(Mason and Taylor
streets)
Tel. 775 1755 or
(800) 999 9570
Fax 775 7517

*Open 24 hours
A charming inn
offering pretty rooms.
Attentive, friendly
staff. Large breakfast
and snacks included.
Nearby is the
Petite Auberge (which
is under the same
management). This
establishment offers
the same services
with smaller, cheaper
rooms.
$145–$250*

NIGHTLIFE

COMPASS ROSE
Westin St Francis
Hotel, Union Square
Tel. 774 0167
*Open Mon. to Thur.
11.30am–midnight,
Fri., Sat. 11.30am–1am.
This lounge bar
situated in one of
the oldest hotels in
town has long been
a fashionable
haunt.*

PUNCH LINE COMEDY CLUB
444 Battery Street
Tel. 397 7573
*Shows Sun. to Thur.
9pm, Fri. Sat. 9pm
and 11pm.
This lively venue
stages improvization
shows. It is a
breeding ground for a
number of comedians
who have since
risen to fame.*

REDWOOD ROOM
Four Seasons Clift
Hotel
459 Geary Street
(Taylor Street)
Tel. 775 4700
*Open 11am–2.30pm
and (Sun. to Thurs.)
4pm–midnight, Fri.,
Sat. 4pm–2am.
Piano bar, named
after the old sequoia
wood panels (installed
in 1933) on its walls.
Intimate, refined
atmosphere.*

SHOPPING

BANANA REPUBLIC
256 Grant Avenue
*Ready-to-wear
clothing, a little more
chic than The Gap.*

CAMERA BOUTIQUE.
342 Kearny Street
Tel. 982 4946
Closed Sun.
*Cameras, video
equipment, films,
rentals, repairs.*

COACH STORE
190 Post Street
Tel. 392 1772
*Quality leatherware.
Expensive, but lifetime
guarantees.*

THE GAP
100 Post Street
*Ready-to-wear
clothing.*

GUMP'S
135 Post Street
Closed Sun.
Tel. 982 1616
*Known primarily for
its jade objects, but
also for luxury
articles, household
accessories, and
oriental products.*

DEPARTMENT STORES
NIEMAN MARCUS
I. MAGNIN & CO
Stockton and Geary
streets
SAKS FIFTH
384 Post Street
*These are three
major luxury
department stores
in the city.*
MACY'S
Stockton and
O'Farrell streets
EMPORIUM
835 Market Street
SAN FRANCISCO
SHOPPING CENTRE
Corner of Market
Street and
5th Street
*More than one
hundred stores on
nine levels, including
Nordstrom.*

HOUSE OF BLUE JEANS
1029 Market Street
Tel. 255 7699
Ready-to-wear.

McDONALD'S BOOKSHOP
48 Turk Street
(Mason Street)
Tel. 673 2235
Open Mon. to Wed.
10am–6pm, Thur. to
Sat. 10.30am–6.45pm.
*This is San
Francisco's largest
second-hand
bookstore.*

INTERNATIONAL CAMERA & ELECTRONICS
206 Powell Street
Tel. 421 9124
*Low-priced electronic
equipment and
cameras.*

THE NORTH FACE
180 Post Street
Tel. 433 3223
Open daily.
*Quality goods, with
a reputation of more
than twenty years
now. Specializing in
sports clothing and
accessories, and
everything for camping
and outdoor activities.*

MARKETS

FLEA MARKET
567 Sutter Street
(Union Square).
Antique market.

HEART OF THE CITY
United Nations Plaza,
1182 Market Street
Tel. 558 9455
Open Sun. and Wed.,
7am–5pm.
*Fresh produce (milk,
dried fruit, olives, etc.)*

1 STARS
2 INN AT THE OPERA
3 THE ARCHBISHOP'S MANSION
4 ISOBUNE (RESTAURANT MALL)
5 THE PHENIX INN
6 MISS PEARL'S JAM HOUSE
7 MAX'S OPERA CAFÉ
8 SPUNTINO
9 STARS CAFÉ
10 CALIFORNIA CULINARY ACADEMY
11 THE NEW ABIGAIL HOTEL
11 COCONUT GROVE

Fillmore Street

Golden Gate Avenue

Hayes Street

Market Street

CIVIC CENTER – JAPANTOWN

PRACTICAL INFORMATION

PARKING LOTS
The major parking lot in this area is:
CIVIC CENTER PLAZA GARAGE
Taylor and O'Farrell sts
Tel. 863 1537

POST OFFICES
FOX PLAZA STATION
1390 Market Street
Tel. 252 9325
Open Mon. to Fri.
8.30am–4.30pm.
1550 STEINER STREET
Japantown
Tel. 563 5955
Open Mon. to Fri.
9am– 5.30pm,
Sat 9am–3pm.
GROUND FLOOR OF FEDERAL BUILDING
450 Golden Gate Avenue
Tel. 621 7505
Open Mon. to Fri.
8.30am–5pm.

CULTURE

CITY HALL
Van Ness Avenue
Civic Center
Tel. 771 8853

DAVIES SYMPHONY HALL
Concerts by the San Francisco Symphony Orchestra, Sept. to June.
Tel. 864 6000

GREAT AMERICAN MUSIC HALL
859 O'Farrell Street (Larkin and Polk sts)
Tel. 885 0750
Open Fri. to Sat.
and other evenings during the week according to program schedule. Collect tickets Mon. to Sat.
10am–6pm.
This theater has contrived to maintain its turn-of-the-century music hall charm, with rococo décor, balconies and small tables. Soul music, rhythm and blues, jazz and Latin music are now fixtures on the program. Quality performers. Dinner available.
♪ ⌐

WAR MEMORIAL AND PERFORMING ART
401 Van Ness Avenue (Grove Street)
Tel. 621 6600
Performances of the San Francico Ballet, opera season programs, Sept.–Dec.

THE ORPHEUM
1192 Market Street (8th Street), Civic Center
Tel. 474 3800
Musical comedies.

CIVIC CENTER

RESTAURANTS

CALIFORNIA CULINARY ACADEMY
625 Polk Street (Turk Street), Civic Center
Tel. 771 3500
Open 11.30am–1.45pm and 6–8pm. Closed Sat. and Sun.
In a celebrated cooking school, a restaurant run entirely by the students.
$30
◑

COCONUT GROVE
1415 Van Ness Street
Tel. 776 1616
Open Mon. to Fri. 11am–10.30pm, Sat. Sun. 5pm–2am. Shows 7pm and 10.30pm.
Neo-continental cuisine; décor in a 40's theme. Big band, pop and jazz concerts. Reservation advisable.
$25–$45 after 6.30pm.
⬤ ♫

ISOBUNE (IN THE RESTAURANT MALL)
1737 Post Street (Webster Street)
Tel. 563 1030
Open 11.30am–10pm.
Traditional sushi bar; the sushis float past you on mini-canals.
$20
◑

MAX'S OPERA CAFÉ
601 Van Ness Avenue (Golden Gate Avenue), Civic Center
Tel. 771 7300
Open Mon 11.30am–10pm, Tue. to Wed. 11.30–12 midnight, Fri., Sat 11.30am–1am.
Drugstore restaurant, with shows and a patio. No reservations.
$10
○

MISS PEARL'S JAM HOUSE
601 Eddy St (Larkin St), Civic Center
Tel. 775 5267
Wed. Thur. 6–10pm, Fri. Sat. 5–9.30pm, Sun. 11am–2.30pm (poolside brunch!), and 5–9.30pm.
Loud tropical décor; work of local painters on show; fashionable clientèle. Parking lot.
$12
○

SPUNTINO
524 Van Ness Ave (McAllister), Civic Center
Tel. 861 7772
Open 7am–8pm, Sun. 10am–7pm
Closed Christmas and Thanksgiving.
Near the opera, trattoria with modern décor for young people who like pasta and pizza. Good for a quick meal.
$16
○

STARS
150 Redwood Alley (Polk Street), Civic Center
Tel. 861 7827
Open 11.30am–2pm, 6–10pm.
Closed for lunch Sat., Sun.
One of the best-known restaurants. Superb brasserie, California cooking, wealthy customers. Valet parking.
$50
⬤

STARS CAFÉ
500 Van Ness Avenue, Civic Center
Tel. 861 4344
Open 11.30am–11pm
Next door to Stars, this more reasonably priced annex serves excellent food in a less formal atmosphere (but still quite pricey).
$35
◑

THEP PHANOM
400 Waller Street (Fillmore Street), Japantown
Tel. 431 2526
Open 5.30–10.30pm.
Excellent Thai restaurant. Soft lighting, quiet ambience, maybe one of the best restaurants in town.
$20
◑ ▭··

ZUNI'S CAFÉ
1658 Market Street (Gough Street), Civic Center
Tel. 552 2522
Open 7.30am–midnight. Closed Mon., Christmas and Thanksgiving.
On the edge of South of Market, this sophisticated and trendy restaurant

---

SAN FRANCISCO HISTORY ROOM
6th floor of the San Francisco Public Library (Larkin and McAllister streets)
Tel. 557 4567
Open Tue., Fri. noon–6pm; Wed. 1pm–6pm, Thur., Sat. 10am–6pm. Closed Sun. and Mon.
Room containing the city's historical archives, a collection of pamphlets, books, photographs and other historic items. Admission free.

SOCIETY OF CALIFORNIA PIONEERS
2nd floor, 1 Hawthorne Street
Tel. 957 1849
Open Mon. to Fri. 10am–4pm.

19th-century art; also a gallery for children specializing in California history. Free admission.

MOVIE THEATERS
AMC KABUKI 8
Corner of Fillmore and Post streets, Japantown
Tel. 931 9800
OPERA PLAZA
601 Van Ness Avenue (Turk Street), Civic Center
Tel. 771 0102
REGENCY I
Corner of Van Ness Avenue and Sutter Street, Japantown
Tel. 885 6773
UA GALAXY
Corner of Van Ness Avenue and Sutter Street, Japantown
Tel. 474 8700

with its two-story glass façade is well known in the area for its excellent food.
$35
◐

HOTELS

THE ALBION HOUSE INN
135 Gough Street (Oak at Page Street), Japantown
Tel. 621 0896
Open 24 hours.
Situated on the first floor of a shopping mall, this bed and breakfast is rather reminiscent of an old family boarding house. Rustic décor. Breakfast included.
$95–$135
Suite $195
⌂ ○ ⌂ C

THE ARCHBISHOP'S MANSION
1000 Fulton Street (Steiner Street)
Tel. 563 7872
or (800) 6 ALBION
Open 24 hours a day.
1904 mansion near Alamo Square. Beautifully decorated; every suite is named after a different opera. Breakfast served in the rooms; wine served gratis in the evenings. Television in bedrooms. Free parking. Excellent address.
$129–385
⌂ P

THE CHATEAU TIVOLI
1057 Steiner Street (Alamo Square)
Tel. 776 5462
or (800) 229 1647
Fax: 776 0505
Handsome 1892 Victorian mansion designed by William Armitage. The seven rooms (no smoking) are richly decorated with antique bibelots, many of which are for sale. The suites are expensive but very comfortable. Breakfast included.
$80–$200
⌂ ⌂ ☼

INN AT THE OPERA
333 Fulton Street (Franklin Street), Civic Center

Tel. 863 8400
Fax. 861 0821
Open 24 hours.
Luxurious hotel close to the opera. Small but extremely elegant and comfortable rooms (mini-bar, bathrooms equipped with hairdryers and bath robes). Breakfast included in the price.
$140–265
⌂ ◐ 🚗

THE NEW ABIGAIL HOTEL
246 McAllister Street (Larkin and Hyde streets) Civic Center
Tel. 861 9728
or (800) 243 6510
Fax: 861 5848
Open 24 hours.
A charming hotel which has recently been completely renovated. Small rooms, decorated in a 19th century style.
$84
⌂ ○ ⌂ C ☼

PHŒNIX INN
601 Eddy Street (Larkin Street), Civic Center
Tel. 776 1380
or (800) 248 9466
Fax: 885 3109
Open 24 hours.
Fashionable hotel with character and excellent quality for the price. Free parking. Breakfast included.
$99–$139
⌂ ◐ ⌂ C ☼ 🏊 P

THE QUEEN ANNE
1590 Sutter Street (Octavia Street)
Tel. 441 2828
or (800) 227 3970
Fax: 775 5212
Open 24 hours.
1890's mansion; attractive rooms (some have small sitting room areas with fireplaces). The luxury rooms are spacious. Breakfast and newspaper included; sherry and biscuits served in the afternoon.
$109–$160
⌂ ⌂ □ 🚗

SHOPPING

JAPAN CENTER
Post and Buchanan streets
Tel. 922 6776

A comprehensive range of boutiques, book stores, galleries and restaurants.

MARKUS BOOKS
1712 Fillmore Street, Japantown
Tel. 346 4222
Open Mon. to Sat. 10am–7pm.
African bookstore.

◆

GOLDEN GATE PARK • HAIGHT–ASHBURY

CULTURE

ASIAN ART MUSEUM (THE AVERY BRUNDAGE COLLECTION)
Golden Gate Park
Tel. 379 8801
Open Wed. to Sun., 10am–4.45pm.
One of the most beautiful private collections of Asian art. Fee for admission.

CALIFORNIA ACADEMY OF SCIENCES
STEINHART AQUARIUM
HALLS OF NATURAL HISTORY
Golden Gate Park
Tel. 750 7145
Open 10am–5pm.
Admission fee.

CONSERVATORY OF FLOWERS
Golden Gate Park
Tel. 752 8080
Enormous Victorian greenhouse.

JAPANESE TEA GARDEN
Golden Gate Park
Open daily 9am–6.30pm; during summer 8am–6pm.
Admission fee.

M. H. DE YOUNG MEMORIAL MUSEUM
Golden Gate Park
Tel. 863 3330
Open Thur. to Sun., 10am–4.45pm.
American art

(17th- century to contemporary). Fee for admission.

MORRISON PLANETARIUM
Golden Gate Park
Tel. 750 7138
Open daily.
One-hour displays. Fee for admission.

MOVIE THEATERS
BRIDGE
3010 Geary Street (Masonic Avenue), Western Addition
Tel. 751 3212
RED VIC MOVIE HOUSE
1727 Haight Street
Tel. 668 3994

RESTAURANTS

CHA CHA CHA
1801 Haight Street (Shrader Street), Haight-Ashbury
Tel. 386 5758
Open Mon.–Sat. 11.30am–3pm, 5–11.30pm.
Closed Sun.
Colorful and chaotic décor. Sandwiches, assorted tapas. A very popular address, often packed.
$15

THE PORK STORE CAFÉ
1451 Haight Street (Ashbury Street), Haight-Ashbury
Tel. 864 6981
Open 7am–3.30pm.
Sat., Sun. 7am–4pm
Only the sign remains of the original old butcher shop. Well known in the locality for its excellent and copious breakfasts. Highly popular.
$7–10
◐

HOTELS

THE METRO
319 Divisadero Street (Oak and Page streets), Haight-Ashbury

Tel. 861 5364
Fax. 863 1970
Open 7am–midnight.
*Modest hotel. The
rooms with double
beds are extremely
small and also rather
dark; queensize
bedrooms open onto
a patio (garden view)
and are more
expensive but nicer.*
$50–94
⌂ ⬮ ⤨ ◻ ℙ

**THE RED
VICTORIAN BED
& BREAKFAST INN**
1665 Haight Street
(Cole and Clayton
streets),
Haight-Ashbury
Tel. 864 1978
Fax. (415) 863 3293
Open 8am–10pm.
*Situated in the
neo-Beatnik quarter
of San Francisco,
this somewhat
unusual building
combines bed
and breakfast
(non-smoking), art
gallery, meditation
room, café and
boutique. Friendly
atmosphere. No
television available
in the rooms.
Breakfast included.
$76–200*
⌂ ○

**THE SPENCER
HOUSE**
1080 Haight Street
(Baker Street),
Haight-Ashbury
Tel. 626 9205
Fax. 626 9230
Open 24 hours.
*This delightful 1887
Victorian house;
rather difficult to
find as there is no
sign on the exterior.
The rooms are
luxuriously decorated
with antique furniture,
and are extremely
comfortable. No
children. No credit
cards. Excellent
value. Breakfast
included.
$105–165*
⌂ ⤨ ℙ

**VICTORIAN INN
ON THE PARK**
301 Lyon Street
(Fell Street)
Tel. 931 1830 or
(800) 435 1967
Fax. 931 1830
Open 24 hours.
*This 1897 building,
classified as an
historical monument,
looks out over part
of the Golden Gate
Park. Cozy rooms.
Breakfast in the
price of the room.
$99–164*
⌂ ⌂ ⤨ ⼞ ⇜

SHOPPING

**AARDVARK'S
ODD ARK**
1501 Haight Street
Haight-Ashbury
Tel. 621 3141
*Second-hand
clothing.*

THE BOOKSMITH
1644 Haight Street,
Haight-Ashbury
Tel. 863 8688
*Open Mon. to Sat.
10am–6pm.
Stocks a general range
of books.*

**RECYCLED
RECORDS**
1377 Haight Street,
Haight-Ashbury
Tel. 626 4075
Second-hand records.

RECKLESS RECORDS
1401 Haight Street,
Haight-Ashbury
Tel. 431 3434
*New and used
records.*

**ROUGH TRADE
RECORDS**
1529 Haight Street,
Haight-Ashbury
Tel. 621 4395
Second-hand records.

THE WASTELAND
1660 Haight Street,
Haight-Ashbury
Second-hand store.

◆

RICHMOND

PRACTICAL
INFORMATION

POST OFFICES
GEARY STATION
5654 Geary Boulevard
(21st Avenue)
Tel. 752 0231
Open Mon., Wed.,
Fri., 9am–5.30pm,
Tue., Thur. 9am–6pm,
Sat. 9am–4.30pm.

CULTURE

**CALIFORNIA
PALACE OF
THE LEGION OF
HONOR**
Lincoln Park
Tel. 863 3330
This has recently
reopened after
renovation.

CLIFF HOUSE
1066–1090 Point
Lobos Avenue
(Ocean Beach)
Tel. 386 1170
(museum)
Tel. 386 3330
(restaurant and bar)
*This house offers a
beautiful view of
Seal Rock and the
Pacific Ocean.*

**NEPTUNE SOCIETY
COLUMBARIUM**
Loraine Court
(Arguello and
Stanyan streets)
Tel. 221 1838
Open 10am–1pm.
Closed Mon.
*This building contains
over 10,000 urns of
earthquake victims.
Entrance free.*

MOVIE THEATERS
BALBOA
Corner of 38th
Avenue and Balboa
Street
UA ALEXANDRIA
Corner of Geary
Boulevard and 18th
Avenue
Tel. 752 5100

RESTAURANTS

ANGKOR WAT
4217 Geary
Boulevard (6th Avenue)
Tel. 221 7887
Open daily
11am–2.30pm,
5–10pm.
*Good, traditional
Cambodian restaurant.
Fri., Sat. special
performances by the
Royal Cambodian
Ballet. Attractive setting;
reasonable prices.
Dinner only.
$20*
○

NEW GOLDEN TURTLE
308 5th Avenue
(Geary Boulevard)
Tel. 221 5285
Open 11am–11pm,
Mon. 5–11pm
*In a new Asiatic
neighborhood; good
address to try
Vietnamese cooking.
From $20*
◑

◆

**SOUTH OF
MARKET**

PRACTICAL
INFORMATION

POST OFFICES
RINCON FIANANCE
180 Steuart Street

(Howard Street)
Tel. 284 0755
Open Mon. to Fri.
7am–6pm, Sat.
9am–2pm.
STATION E
460 Brannan Street
(4th Street)
Tel. 543 7729
Open Mon. to Fri.,
8.30am–5pm.

CULTURE

CARTOON ART MUSEUM
814 Mission Street,
(4th and 5th streets)
Tel. 546 3922
Open Wed. to Fri.
11am–5pm.
Sat. 10am–5pm.
Sun. 1–5pm.
*Museum dedicated to
the history of cartoons.*
$4 admission.

THE JEWISH MUSEUM OF SAN FRANCISCO
121 Steuart Street
(Howard and Mission
streets)
Tel. 543 8880
Open Mon. to Wed.
12 noon–6pm, Thur.
12 noon–8pm, Closed
Sat., Sun.
*This museum is
dedicated to the
history of the*

Jewish community.
$3 admission.

ART GALLERIES
ANSEL ADAMS CENTER
250 4th Street
Tel. 495 7000
Open Tue. to Sun.,
11am–5pm.
*Five art galleries
(one displaying photos
by Ansel Adams) and
a bookshop.*
$4 admission

SAN FRANCISCO MUSEUM OF MODERN ART
151 3rd Street (Mission
and Howard streets)
Tel. 357 4000
Open Tue.–Sun.
11am–6pm, Thur.
11am–9pm
*This is the new address
of the SFMOMA.*

RESTAURANTS

BRAIN WASH
1122 Folsom Street
(7th Street)
Tel. 861 FOOD
Fax. 861 WASH
Open 7am–9pm.
*1950's washateria and
snack bar. Eccentric:
not to be missed.*
$10
○

CAFFÉ CENTRO
102 South Park
Tel. 882 1500
Open 7.30am–6.30pm.
*Perfect for a light lunch
(sandwiches and
desserts) or a snack.
Situated in a good
location on a charming
little park. Good value
for money.*
$12
○ ⌂

CAFÉ MARS
798 Brannan Street
Tel. 621 6277
Mon.–Sat. 4pm–2am,
closed Sun.
*Good food at a
reasonable price.
Hip clientèle typical of
the SoMa district.*
$15

THE CARIBBEAN ZONE
55 Nahoma Street
(1st and 2nd streets)
Tel. 541 9465
11.30am–2.30pm,
5–10pm. Closed Sun.
*Decoration has been
designed to look
like an airplane
fuselage with
televisions in the
portholes showing a
Rio landing (tropical
plants, cardboard*

*rocks). Passable
food, but the décor
is a little off-putting.*
$20
○

DUBLINER
1539 Folsom Street
(11th Street)
Tel. 621 4752.
Open 11.30am–
midnight.
*Very lively in the
evening.*
From $12
◑

ELEVEN
374 11th Street
Tel. 431 3337
5.30pm–2am.
Closed Sun.
*Italian cuisine. One
of SoMa's most
popular restaurants:
reservation is advised.*
$20
♫

HAMBURGER MARY'S
1582 Folsom Street
(12th Street)
Tel. 626 5767
Open 10–2am.
Closed over Christmas
and Thanksgiving.
*A wooden shack full of
agreeable bric-à-brac.
The hamburgers are*

17 TROCADERO TRANSFER   18 CAFFÉ CENTRO   19 SHERATON PALACE   20 THE CARIBBEAN ZONE   21 DV8   22 WU KONG   23 CHALKERS BILLIARDS CLUB   24 HARBOR COURT HOTEL

SOUTH OF MARKET

excellent and the prices are low. A friendly place with a generally young crowd and a boisterous atmosphere.
$15
○

JULIE'S SUPPER CLUB
1123 Folsom Street (7th Street)
Tel. 861 0707
Open Tue., Wed. 5.30–11pm, Sat. 5.30pm–midnight.
In front of the Brain Wash, this kitsch 1950's bar has a pink-quilted bar, multicolored barstools and snaps of movie stars on the walls. Simple, copious food.
$25
◑

LuLu
816 Folsom Street
Tel. 495 5775
Open Mon. to Thur. 5.30–10.30pm, Sat. Sun. until 11.30pm.
Well-lit and airy, with the feel of an Italian piazza. French and Italian cuisine. Popular, so reservation advised.
$35

THE RAMP
885 China Basin (17th Street)
Tel. (415) 621 2378
Open daily.
Jazz, flamenco and Brazilian concerts Thur. to Sun. Brunch and barbeque Sat. Sun. Restaurant bar on the Bay between a yacht club and some old cargo vessels.

WU KONG
Rincon Center
101 Spear St (Mission St). Tel. 957 9300
Open 11am–2.30pm, 5.30–9.30pm.
In a modern shopping arcade. Essentially Chinese clientèle in the large, attractive dining area. Authentic cooking.
$25
◑

HOTELS

HARBOR COURT HOTEL
165 Steuart Street (Market Street)
Tel. 882 1300
or (800) 346 0555
Fax. 882 1313
Open 24 hours.
At the water's edge. Relaxed reception;

the rooms are small but charming and offer a spectacular view of the bay. Tea and wine are offered free along with access to the sporting facilities of the YMCA (sports center, pool, aerobic exercise rooms, basketball court). Free transport to the Financial District.
$105–165
⌂ ◑ ⊂ ⌣ 🚗

SHERATON PALACE
2 New Montgomery Street (Mission and Market Street)
Tel. 392 8600
or (800) 325 3535
Fax. 543 0671
Located not far from Moscone Center, this is the oldest luxury hotel in San Francisco and is dated 1875. It has elegant, very comfortable, spacious and tasteful rooms. Facilities include an indoor pool, health club and the famous Garden Court restaurant.
$195–$295.
Suites $650
⌂ ⓘ ⊂ ⌣ 🚗

NIGHTLIFE

CHALKERS BILLIARDS CLUB
101 Spear Street (Mission Street)
Rincon Center
Tel. 512 0450
Open Mon. to Fri. 11.30am–2am, Sat. 2pm–2am, Sun. 2pm–midnight.
Enjoy food and cocktails around handsome cherrywood billiard tables. A chic spot.

CW (COVERED WAGON) SALOON
917 Folsom Street
Tel. 974 1585
This rock and funk venue holds concerts every evening. Disc jockey plays reggae on Tue. evenings.

DNA LOUNGE
375 11th Street
(Harrison Street)
Tel. 626 1409
Open 9.30pm–4am.
*Old warehouse made
over into a huge disco
for the SoMa set.
Regularly holds good
rock concerts.*
$8

DV8
Howard Street
(1st and 2nd Street)
Tel. 777 2217
Open Tue. to Sat.
10pm–4am.
*One of the biggest
disco-nightclubs in the
whole area, in a
charmless cement
block. New wave
psychedelic décor (pop
art, mirrors and marbled
columns). Attracts a
young clientèle.*
$5 or $10

HOLY COW
1535 Folsom Street
(10th and 12th streets)
Tel. 621 6087
Thur. to Sat.
6pm–2am.
*Long queues and a
huge cardboard cow
stand in front of this
disco, which attracts a
young clientèle. Free,
but selective admission.*

TEN 15
1015 Folson Street
Tel. 431 1200
Open 10am–4am.
*Popular disco with three
separate rooms, each
one featuring a different
type of music.*
$7

PARADISE LOUNGE
1501 Folsom Street
(11th Street)
Tel. 861 6906

*Disco with billiard
room. Features rock
concerts nightly.*

SLIM'S
333 11th Street
(Folsom and
Harrison streets)
Tel. 522 0333
Open 8pm–2am.
*Rhythm and blues,
country and jazz
venue in an old
warehouse.*
$6

SOUND FACTORY
525 Harrison Street
Tel. 543 1300
*Three rooms
equipped with state-of-
the-art sound and light.
Pop and industrial
music.*

THE STUD
399 9th Street
(Harrison Street)
Tel. 863 6623
Open Mon. to Fri.
5pm–2am, Sat., Sun.
5pm–3am.
Gay bar and disco.
$3

TWENTY TANK
316 11th Street
Tel. 255 9455
Open 11.30am–2am.
Jazz on Tue. to Thur.
and every other Wed.
(free admission).
*The best pub in
town: light meals, fine
beers.*

UP & DOWN CLUB
1151 Folsom Street
(7th Street)
Tel. 626 2388
Open 8pm–2am.
*Restaurant-club
featuring jazz
concerts.*
$5

PRACTICAL INFORMATION

PARKING
FIFTH AND MISSION
GARAGE
833 Mission Street
(4th and 5th streets)
Tel. 982 8522

POST OFFICE
BELL BAZAAR
4304 18th Street
Tel. 621 5317
Open Mon.
to Fri.
9am–5pm.
Closed Sat.
and Sun.

CULTURE

MISSION DOLORES
Dolores Street
(16th St)
Tel. 621 8203
Open 9am–4pm.
*Founded in 1776
and now the only
surviving old mission.
Church, gardens a
nd historic cemetery.
Admission $2*

MOVIE THEATERS
ROXIE
3117 16th Street
Tel. 863 1087
STRAND
1127 Market Street
Tel. 431 1259

THEATERS
THE MARSH
1062 Valencia
Street
Tel. 641 0235
*Performances
here range from
contemporary
theater to
cabaret.*
THEATER ARTAUD
450 Florida Street
(17th and
Mariposa streets)
Tel. 647 2200
*Specializes in
experimental and
improvisational
works.*

RESTAURANTS

AUNT MARY'S RESTAURANT
3159 16th Street
Tel. 626 5523
Open Sun. to Thur.
7am–10pm, Wed. to
Sat. 7am–midnight.
Closed Mon.
*American/Mexican
cuisine; picturesque
décor. Excellent
breakfast.*

CAFÉ MACONDO
3159 16th Street
Tel. 863 6517
Sat. to Mon. 9am–
10pm, Thur. to
Fri. 11am–10pm.

*Cafés are an
institution in San
Francisco: somewhere
to read the newspaper
while enjoying a pastry.*

FLYING SAUCER
1000 Guerrero Street
Tel. 641 9955
*Charming abstract
décor; New American
cuisine. Very popular, so
reservation essential.*
$45

ESPERPENTO
3295 22nd Street
Valencia
Tel. (415) 282 8867
Open Mon. to Sat.
11am–3pm, 5pm–2am.
*Spanish restaurant
known for its paella and
delicious tapas.*

KATZ BAGELS
3147 16th Street
Open 6am–5pm,
Sat. Sun. 6am–4pm.
*Wide selection of
bagels.*

LA RONDELLA
901 Valencia Street
Tel. 647 7474
*Classic local Mexican
restaurant. Christmas
decorations all year
around. Passable food,
good margaritas.*
$10

LA TACQUERIA SAN JOSE
2830 Mission Street
(25th and 26th streets)
Tel. 282 0203
Mon. to Thur.
8am– 1am, Fri. to
Sun. 8am–4am.
*Very good fast food,
serving superb burritos.
Authentic and very
popular eatery where
English is rarely heard.
Cheap. No credit cards.
$6*

PASTAIO LUISA'S
3182 16th Street
Tel. (415) 255 2440
Open daily 11am–2pm,
4pm–midnight.
*Luisa has had
fifteen years of
success with her
Castro restaurant,
with its friendly, family
atmosphere.*

TI COUZ
3108 16th Street
Tel. 252 7373
Open Mon. to Fri.
11am–11pm, Sat.
10am–11pm,
Sun. 10am–10pm.
*Probably every port in
the world has its
crêperie. Good, cheap
authentic-tasting food.*

NIGHTLIFE

BLONDIES
540 Valencia Street
Tel. 864 2419
Open to 2am. Blues
and jazz concerts
Sat. Sun.
*Local bar with billiard
tables, juke box.*
♫ ☛

CAESAR'S LATIN PALACE
2140 Mission Street
(Army Street)
Tel. 648 6611
Open Thur. and Sun.
8pm–2am,
Fri. 9pm–5am,
Sat. 9pm–6am.
Closed Mon. to Wed.
*A lively Latino bar in
the local Hispanic
neighborhood.
Musical groups and
dance lessons offered
Fri., Sat. and Sun.
afternoons (salsa,
mambo).*
♫ ☛

ELBO ROOM
647 Valencia
(17th Street)
Tel. 552 7788

*Colorful café-concert in
a young and bohemian
neighborhood.
Billiards.*
♫ ☛

JOSIE'S CABARET
3583 16th Street
(Market Street)
Tel. 861 7933
Open from 9pm.
*Theme nights with
open debates are
frequent. A good
introduction to the
weird side of the San
Francisco nightlife
scene.*

RADIO VALENCIA
1199 Valencia Street
Tel. 826 1199
Open 11am–midnight
*Colorful café, decent
light meals, music by
the proprietor himself
(an ex-DJ). Jazz and
blues concerts Fri.–Sun.
A minimum charge is
set.*

SHOPPING

ADOBE BOOKSHOP
3166 16th Street
(Guerrero Street)
Tel. 864 3936
*Rare and second-hand
books.*

ESPRIT
499 Illinois Street
Potrero
Tel. 648 6900
Clothing for teenagers,
low-cost items for all
ages (end-of-season
stock, for example).

CASTRO

CULTURE

MOVIE THEATERS
CASTRO THEATER
429 Castro Street
(Market Street)
Tel. 621 6120
ST FRANCIS
At the corner of Market
and 15th streets
Tel. 362 4822
STRAND
1127 Market Street
Tel. 431 1259

RESTAURANTS

HOT 'N' HUNKY
4039 18th Street
Tel. 621 6365
Open 11am–midnight
Fri., Sat. 11am–1am.
*Order a delicious
hamburger at the bar in
this friendly restaurant.
Walk out across the
street to picnic in
Dolores Park and enjoy
an unbeatable view
across the Bay.*

PATIO CAFÉ
531 Castro Street
(18th and 19th streets)
Tel. 621 4640
Open 8am–10.30pm.
*A pretty bar-restaurant
with an exotic garden.*

HOTELS

TWIN PEAKS HOTEL
2160 Market Street
Tel. 621 9467
Fax. 863 1545
*Good address in the
Castro; sixty rooms.
$35–55*

NIGHTLIFE

CAFÉ DU NORD
2170 Market Street
Tel. 861 5016
Open nightly.
*Often packed, this hip
bar puts on theme
evenings. Plenty of jazz.*
♫ ☛

MIDNIGHT SUN
4067 18th Street
Tel. 861 4186
*One of the oldest gay
bars in the town.
Original movies and
video clips.*

AROUND THE BAY

CULTURE

BAY AREA DISCOVERY MUSEUM
557 East Fort Baker,
Sausalito
Tel. (415) 487 4398
Open 10am–5pm.
Closed Mon., Tue.
*Especially designed
for large families with
many activities for
children. Two film
projections each
evening. Fee for
admission.*

BAY MODEL VISITORS CENTER
2100 Bridgeway
Sausalito
Tel. (415) 332 3871
Open in winter Tue.
to Sat. 9am–4pm;
summer, Tue. to Fri.
9am–4pm, Sat. and
Sun. 10am–6pm.
*A simulation of the
effects of the different
currents of the bay.
Admission free.*

JUDAH L. MAGNES MUSEUM
2911 Russell St
Berkeley
Tel. (510) 549 6950
Open Sun. to Thur.
10am–4pm.
*Museum honoring
the history of the Jewish
community, with a
collection including
10,000 objets d'art.
Free admission.*

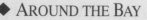

MUIR WOODS
Mount Tamalpais
Panoramic Highway
(20 miles north of San
Francisco)
Tel. 388 2595
Open daily 8am
until dusk.
*Sequoia woods.
Park with asphalt paths
by which you can reach
Stinson Beach.*

OAKLAND MUSEUM
Corner of Oak and 10th
streets, Oakland
Tel. (510) 238 3401
or (510) 834 2413
Open 10am–5pm.
Sun. 12 noon–5pm.
Closed Mon., Tue.,
and certain holidays.
*Three floors; natural
sciences, history and
art. Admission free.*

SILVERADO MUSEUM
1490 Library Lane
PO Box 409
St Helena
CA 94574
Tel. (707) 963 3757
Open daily
12 noon–4pm, except
Mon. and public
holidays.
*A museum dedicated to
the works of Robert
Louis Stevenson, built
in 1979 nearby the
St Helena library.*

**TREASURE ISLAND
MUSEUM**
Building 1,
Treasure Island
Tel. (415) 395 5067
Open 10am–3pm.
*History of the US Navy.
Admission free.*

**UNIVERSITY ART
MUSEUM (PACIFIC
FILM ARCHIVE)**
2626 Bancroft Way,
Berkeley
Tel. (510) 642 1412
Open Wed. to Sun.
11am–5pm,

Thur. 11am–9pm
*Western and Asiatic
art museum.
Admission fee.*

**WINE & VISITORS'
CENTRE**
5000 Roberts Lake Rd
Rohnert Park
CA 94928
Tel. (707) 586 3795
Open daily 10am–5pm.

RESTAURANTS

CHEZ PANISSE
1517 Shattuck Avenue,
Berkeley
Tel. (510) 548 5525.
Meals served at 6pm,
6.30pm, 8.30pm,
9.15pm. Closed Sun.
*Excellent restaurant
near the Berkeley
university campus.
The chef, Alice Waters,
was the first to introduce
"nouvelle cuisine" to
California. Valet parking.
$45–75*

**FENG NIAN CHINESE
RESTAURANT**
2650 Bridgeway,
Sausalito
Tel. 1 415 331 5300
Open Mon., Wed., Thur.
11.30am–9pm;
Sun. 12.30pm–9.30pm.
*One of the top Bay Area
spots for Chinese food.
More than 90 different
items on the menu.
Vegetarian meals
available.
$15*

FRENCH LAUNDRY
6640 Washington Street
Yountville
Napa Valley
Tel. (707) 944 2380
*This restaurant, in
an authentic stone
building, offers a fusion
of French and California
cuisine. Three Michelin
stars. Reservation
advisable.*

HORIZONS
558
Bridgeway
Tel. 1 415
331 3232
*Wonderful
view of
San
Francisco. Food nothing
special.
$8*

LARK CREEK INN
234 Magnolia Avenue,
Larkspur, Marin County.
Tel. 1 425 924 7766

Open Mon. to Fri.
11.30am–2.30pm;
Sun. and Thur.
5.30–10pm;
Fri., Sun. 5.30–11pm;
Sunday brunch
11.30am–2.30pm.
*The house dates from
1889; the restaurant is
certainly worth the trip
to Larkspur. Top-quality
Californian cooking.
Menus vary depending
on the season; fish is a
constant. Extensive
choice of Californian
wines at moderate
prices.
$20*

**LARRY BLAKE'S
R&B CAFÉ**
2367 Telegraph Avenue,
Berkeley
Tel. 1 510 848 0886
Open Mon. to Sat.
11am–2am,
Sun. 11am–10pm.
*A restaurant, bar and
club (concerts nightly
Mon. to Sat.) on three
floors. Very good
American cooking.
$15*

PELICAN INN
Muir Beach,
Highway 1,
Marin County.
Tel. (415) 383 6000
Pretty English-style pub.

SCOMA'S
588 Bridgeway,
Sausalito
Tel. 1 415 332 9551
Open from April to Oct.,
Mon. to Sat.
11.30am–10.30pm,
Sun. 11.30am–9.30pm.
Open from Nov. to
March, Mon., Fri., Sat.
11.30am–10.30pm,
Tues., Thur.
5.30pm–10.30pm,
Sun. 11.30am–9.30pm.
*Seafood and Italian
cooking.
$25*

**SPENCER'S FISH
GROTTO**
1919 4th Street,
Berkeley
Tel. 1 510 845 7771
*Family-style American
restaurant. Fish is the
house specialty.
$25*

TRAVIGNE
1050 Charter Oak
St Helena, Napa Valley
CA 94574
Tel. (707) 963 4444
Fax. (707) 963 1233

*Superb traditional
Italian cuisine,
courteous service,
lovely décor.
Reservation advisable,
especially for dinner
on the patio. A list of
young, but carefully
selected wines.*

**V. SATTUI
WINERY**
At the crossing of
Highway 29 and
White Lane
(less than
2 miles south of
St Helena)
Tel. (707) 963 7774
*Earns its reputation
primarily as a
cheese producer
("one of the world's
best", according to
the LA Times).
Offers two hundred
makes of cheese, a
selection of meats,
dried fruit, pastries,
wine . . . dining tables
available outside.*

HOTELS

**ACCOMMODATION
REFERRAL
RESERVATION**
Tel. (707) 942 5900
*Make a reservation
by telephone, to
select a room from
more than 150 bed
and breakfasts in
the Napa Valley
region.*

NIGHTLIFE

KIMBALL'S EAST
5800 Shellmound
Street, Emeryville
Tel. 1 510 658 2555
*Very fashionable jazz
club in a shopping
center. The room
seats 400. Local groups
play on Sundays
11am–2pm.*

YOSHI'S
6030 Claremont Street
Metro BART
(Berkeley Line),
Oakland
Tel. 1 510 652 9200
Open Wed. to Sat.,
Wed. and Thur. until
10pm,
Fri. and Sat. until 11pm.
*Very lively jazz club
which attracts top
talent. Jam sessions
every Monday.*

ESSENTIAL ◆ READING ◆

◆ Borley (D.) and Jansen (J.): *San Francisco, the Rough Guide*, Harrap Columbus, London, 1991.
◆ Hittel (T.H.): *History of California*, Pacific Publishing House and N.J. Stone and Co., San Francisco, 1885–97.
◆ Mayer (R.), ed: *San Francisco, A Chronological and Documentary History*, Oceana Publications, New York, 1974.

◆ GENERAL ◆

◆ *San Francisco Stories, Great Writers on the City*, ChronicleBooks, San Francisco, 1990.
◆ *San Francisco*, Sunset Books, San Francisco, 1986.
◆ Caen (H.): *Only in San Francisco*, Doubleday, Garden City, New York, 1960.
◆ Caen (H.) and Kingman (D.): *One Man's San Francisco*, Doubleday, Garden City, New York, 1967.
◆ Cameron (R): *Above San Francisco*, Cameron, San Francisco, 1975.
◆ Delehanly (R.): *San Francisco, The Ultimate Guide*, Chronicle Books, San Francisco, 1989.
◆ Dikson (S.): *Tales of San Francisco*, Stanford University, 1971.
◆ Dillon (R.): *Embarcadero, Tales of Sea Adventure and the San Francisco Waterfront from 1849 to 1904*, Coward-McCann, New York, 1959.
◆ Federal Writers Project: *San Francisco, the Bay and its Cities*, San Francisco, 1940.
◆ Gilliam (H.): *San Francisco Bay*, Doubleday, New York, 1957.
◆ Johnson (C.) and Reinhardt (R.): *San Francisco as It Is, as It Was*, Doubleday, Garden City, New York, 1979.
◆ Kemble (J.H.): *San Francisco Bay: A Pictorial Maritime History*, San Francisco, 1957.
◆ Moorhouse (G.): *San Francisco*, Time-Life Books, Amsterdam, 1979.
◆ O'Brien (R.): *This is San Francisco*, 1948.
◆ Palmer (P. & M.): *Cable Cars of San Francisco*, Howell-North Books, Berkeley, 1959.
◆ Pettitt (G.A.): *Berkeley: The Town and Gown of It*, Howell-North Books, Berkeley CA, 1973.
◆ Scott (M.): *The San Francisco Bay Area: A Metropolis in Perspective*, University of California, Berkeley and Los Angeles, 1959.

◆ HISTORY ◆

◆ Ashbury (H.): *The Barbary Coast*, Comstock Ed., Sausalito CA, 1973.
◆ Bancroft (H.H.): *History of the Pacific States of North America*, A.L. Bancroft and Co., San Francisco, 1882–90.
◆ Beebe (L.) and Clegg (C.): *San Francisco's Golden Era: A Picture Story of San Francisco before the Fire*, Howell-North Books, Berkeley, 1960.
◆ Bonnett (W.): *A Pacific Legacy*, Chronicle Books, San Francisco, 1991.
◆ Bronson (W.), *The Earth Shook, the Sky Burned*, Doubleday, Garden City, New York, 1959.
◆ *California History*, San Francisco, n°3, 1982.
◆ Chandler (A.): *Old Tales of San Francisco*, Kendall/Hunt Co., San Francisco, 1977.
◆ Cole (T.): *A Short History of San Francisco*, San Francisco, 1947.
◆ Gentry (C.): *The Madams of San Francisco*, Comstock Ed., Sausalito CA, 1964.
◆ Gordon (T.) and Witts (M.M.): *Earthquake: The Destruction of San Francisco*, Arrow, London, 1981.
◆ Hansen (G.) and Condon (E.): *Denial of Disaster*, Cameron and Company, San Francisco, 1989.
◆ Lewis (O.): *San Francisco: Mission to Metropolis*, Howell-North Books, Berkeley, 1966.
◆ Lotchin (R.W.): *San Francisco, 1846–1856*, Oxford, New York, 1974.
◆ Muscante (D.): *Old San Francisco, Biography of a City*, Putman, New York, 1975.
◆ Potter (E.G.) and Gray (M.T.): *The Lure of San Francisco*, P. Elder & Co, San Francisco, 1915.
◆ Salzman (E.) and Brown (A.L.): *The Cartoon History of California Politics*, California Journal Press, Sacramento, 1978.
◆ Soule (F.), Gihon (J.H.) and Nisbet (J.): *The Annals of San Francisco*, 1854.

◆ ART ◆

◆ Albright (T.): *Art in the San Francisco Area 1945–1980*, University of California Press, London, 1985.
◆ Alinder (M.S.), Heyman (T.T.) and Rosenblum (N.): *Seeing Straight*, The Oakland Museum, 1992.
◆ Dreschler (T.W.): *San Francisco Murals, a Community Creates Its Muse, 1914–1990*, Pogo Press, St Paul, Minnesota, 1991.
◆ du Pont (D.C.): *San Francisco Museum of Modern Art, The Painting and Sculpture Collection*, Phaidon, Oxford, 1985.
◆ Oakland Museum: *The Art of California, Selected Works from the Collection of the Oakland Museum*. The Oakland Museum and Chronicle Books, 1984.

◆ ARCHITECTURE ◆

◆ Aidala (T.): *The Great Houses of San Francisco*, Thames and Hudson, London, 1974.
◆ Bernhardi (R.C.): *Great Buildings of San Francisco*, Dover Publications, New York, 1980.
◆ Corbett (M.R.): *Splendid Survivors, San Francisco's Downtown Architectural Heritage*, California Living Books, San Francisco, 1979.
◆ Delehanty (R.) and Sexton (R.): *In the Victorian Style*, Chronicle Books, San Francisco, 1991.
◆ Gebhard (D.) and others : *A Guide to Architecture in San Francisco and Northern California*, Peregrine Smith Books, Santa Barbara and Salt Lake City, 1976, 1985.
◆ Mitchell (Eugene): *American Victoriana*, Chronicle Books, San Francisco, 1979.
◆ Olmsted (R.) and Watkins (J.H.): *Here Today, San Francisco's Architectural Heritage*, Chronicle Books, San Francisco, 1968.
◆ Pomada (E.) and others: *Painted Ladies, San Francisco's Resplendent Victorians*, E.P. Dutton, New York, 1978.
◆ Woodbridge (Sally B.): *California Architecture*, Chronicle Books, San Francisco, 1988.

◆ LOCAL COLOR ◆

◆ Altrocchi (J.C.): *The Spectacular San Francisco*, 1949.
◆ Burchell (R.A.): *The San Francisco Irish, 1848–1880*, Manchester University Press, Manchester, 1979.
◆ Dumas (A.): *A Gil Blas in California* (trans. M.E. Wilbur), Hammond, Hammond and Co., London, 1947.
◆ Fong-Torres (S.): *San Francisco Chinatown*, China Books, USA, 1991.
◆ Margolin (Malcolm): *The Ohlone Way, Indian ILfe in the San Francisco Monterey Bay Area*, Heyday Books, Berkeley, 1978.
◆ Salter (C.L.): *San Francisco's Chinatown: How Chinese a Town?* R. and E. Research Association, San Francisco, 1978.
◆ Stevenson (R.L.): *The Silverado Squatters, Sketches from a Californian Mountain*, London, 1883.

◆ LITERATURE ◆

◆ Dana (R.H.): *Two Years Before the Mast*, London, 1841.
◆ Ginsberg (A.): *Howl and Other Poems*, City Lights Books, San Francisco, 1959.
◆ Hammett (D.): *The Maltese Falcon*, London and New York, 1930.
◆ Harte (B.): *The Luck of Roaring Camp and Other Tales*, Boston, 1870 .
◆ Kerouac (J.): *On the Road*, London and New York, 1958.
◆ Norris (F.): *The Octopus, A Story of California*, Doubleday, New York, 1901.
◆ Wolfe (T.): *The Electric Kool-aid Acid Test*, Farra, Strauss and Giroux, New York, 1968.

◆ LIST OF ILLUSTRATIONS

When a city name is not given the reference is to San Francisco. Exceptions are: the Bibliothèque nationale, in Paris and the Patrick Bertrand collection in Nuits-St-George.

We would like to thank the following people for their assistance:
Dr Albert Shumate, Mr Oscar Lemer, Mr Marvin Nathan, Mr J.P. Delman, Mr John Garzoli, San Francisco Maritime Museum, San Francisco Museum of Modern Art, San Francisco Museum of Fine Art, Asian Art of San Francisco, Oakland Art Museum, The San Francisco Public Library Room, Bancroft Library U.C. Berkeley, The Museum of the City of San Francisco, Visitors and Convention Bureau, Maxwell Gallery, Montgomery Gallery, Andrew McKinney, Lisa Baldauf, Jennifer Kerr, Gladys and Richard Hansen.

We have not been able to trace the heirs or publishers of certain documents. An account is being held open for them at our offices.

Acknowledgments
Grateful acknowledgement is made to the following for permission to reprint previously published material:

◆ THE HELEN BRANN AGENCY, INC. Excerpt from "The Gathering of a Californian" by Richard Brautigan from *Revenge of the Lawn: Stories 1962–1970* (Pocket Books 1972), © 1963 by Richard Brautigan. Reprinted with permission of The Helen Brann Agency, Inc.
(UK: reprinted by permission of Murray Pollinger Literary Agency, on behalf of the Helen Brann Agency.)

◆ FARRAR, STRAUS & GIROUX, INC. Excerpt from "Black Shiny FBI Shoes" from *The Electric Kool-Aid Acid Test* by Tom Wolfe © 1968 by Tom Wolfe. Reprinted by permission of Farrar, Straus & Giroux, Inc.
(UK: reprinted by permission of Peters, Fraser & Dunlop Ltd.)

◆ THE FRIENDS OF THE BANCROFT LIBRARY. Excerpt from *Kipling in California* edited by T. Pinney (The Friends of the Bancroft Library, University of California, 1989). Reprinted by permission of The Friends of the Bancroft Library.

◆ HARPERCOLLINS PUBLISHERS, INC. Excerpt from "Sunflower Sutra" from *Collected Poems 1947–1980* by Allen Ginsberg, © 1955 by Allen Ginsberg. Reprinted by permission of HarperCollins Publishers, Inc.
(UK: reprinted by permission of Penguin Books Ltd.)

◆ DAVID HIGHAM ASSOCIATES. Excerpt from April, 7, 1950, Letter from Dylan Thomas to Caitlin from *The Collected Letters of Dylan Thomas* edited by Paul Ferris (J.M. Dent & Sons Ltd., London 1985). Reprinted by permission of David Higham Associates.
(UK: reprinted by permission of David Higham Associates.)

◆ WILLIAM HEINEMANN LTD: Excerpt from *The Old and New Pacific Capitals*, by Robert Louis Stevenson (William Heinemann Ltd, London 1922). Reprinted courtesy of William Heinemann Ltd.

◆ WILLIAM MORROW & CO., INC. Excerpt from *Off the Road* by Carolyn Cassady, © 1990 by Carolyn Cassady. Reprinted by permission of William Morrow & Co., Inc.
(UK: reprinted by permission of Black Spring Press Ltd, London.)

UK only:
Jack Kerouac, *Lonesome Traveler*, André Deutsch 1960. Reprinted by permission of André Deutsch Ltd.

Blaise Cendrars, *Sutter's Gold*. Reprinted by permission of William Heinemann Ltd.

INDEX

◆ INDEX

Page numbers in bold refer to the practical information section.

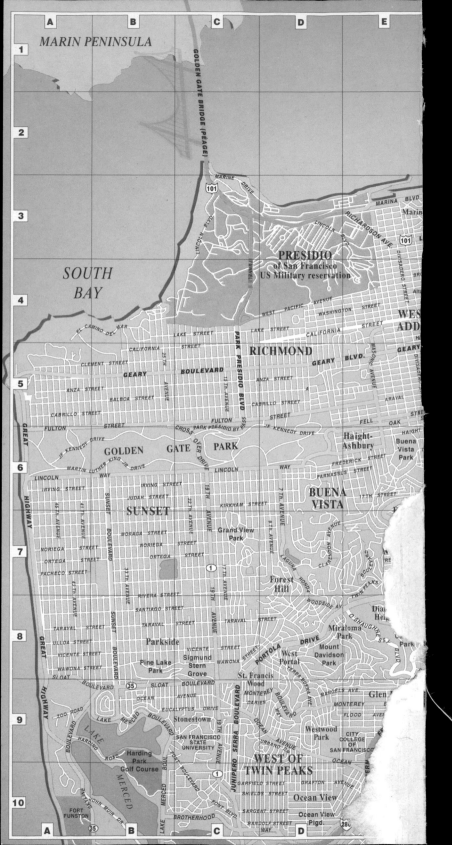